S0-AHX-065

ST. MAR

THE MORTAL
PRESIDENCY

THE MORTAL
PRESIDENCY

Illness and Anguish in the White House

ROBERT E. GILBERT

FORDHAM UNIVERSITY PRESS
New York • 1998

Copyright © 1998 by Fordham University Press
All rights reserved
LC 97–50051
ISBN 0–8232–1836–8 (hardcover)
ISBN 0–8232–1837–6 (paperback)

Second Edition

Library of Congress Cataloging-in-Publication Data

Gilbert, Robert E.
    The mortal presidency : illness and anguish in the White House /
Robert E. Gilbert.—2nd ed.
        p.   cm.
    Includes bibliographical references and index.
    ISBN 0–8232–1836–8 (alk. paper).—ISBN 0–8232–1837–6 (pbk. :
alk. paper)
    1. Presidents—United States—Health.   I. Title.
E176.1.G55   1998
973'.099—dc21   97–50051
                                                                   CIP

Designed by Barbara DuPree Knowles

Printed in the United States of America

To the Memory of my Mother

Contents

Acknowledgments

In preparing both the first and second editions of this interdisciplinary study, the advice and assistance of individuals of widely varying backgrounds was essential. I take pleasure in acknowledging, therefore, the contributions made to this project at its various stages by Betty Glad (University of South Carolina), Fred I. Greenstein (Princeton University), Dennis R. Goldenson (Carnegie-Mellon University), George McKenna (City University of New York), Steven A. Peterson (Alfred University), Barbara Dowd Pearce (University of Massachusetts, Lowell), Stanley R. Renchon (City University of New York), Robert Swansbrough (University of Tennessee, Chattanooga), Kenneth W. Thompson (University of Virginia), and the late Thomas C. Wiegele (Northern Illinois University). Also, a number of colleagues at Northeastern University contributed in important ways, especially Helen Lambert (Biology), Irene A. Nichols (Education), and Robert L. Cord, Michael S. Dukakis, W. D. Kay, David A. Rochefort, and Michael C. Tolley (Political Science).

Thanks must go as well to Drs. Benjamin Aaron, Joseph Giordano, S. David Rockoff, and Samuel Spagnolo (George Washington University Medical Center), Dr. Eric Louie (Loyola University Medical Center), Drs. Kevan Hartshorn and Jerrold Levine (Boston University Medical School), and the late Dr. Tema Carter, a rehabilitation specialist in Brookline, Massachusetts.

Also, I am indebted for their help and guidance to the late Dr. Janet Travell, White House Physician to President Kennedy, Dr. James M. Young, White House Physician to Presidents Kennedy and Johnson, Dr. Daniel Ruge, White House Physician to President Reagan, Dr. Lawrence Mohr, White House Physician to Presidents Reagan and Bush, and Dr. E. Connie Mariano, White House Physician to President Clinton.

I would like to thank my research assistants at Northeastern University for their help over the years this project has been in progress, the staff of the Forbes Library (who assisted me with my Coolidge research), and the staffs of the Franklin D. Roosevelt, Dwight D. Eisenhower, John F. Kennedy, and Lyndon B. Johnson Libraries for the invaluable assistance they provided, expecially James Leyerzapf, Maura Porter, Ron Whealan, and Mary Knill. Special thanks go to John Coolidge, the late President's son, for his unique insights and frankness. Also I acknowledge with gratitude two Research and Scholarship Development Grants from Northeastern University that allowed me to spend several weeks at both the Dwight D. Eisenhower and Lyndon B. Johnson Libraries exploring documents pertinent to the medical histories of these two presidents.

To those individuals at Basic Books who provided guidance and support in the publication of the first edition of this book, especially Phoebe Hoss, the late Martin Kessler, Akiko Takano, Randall Pink, and Michael Wilde, I express my appreciation. To Frances Ricker, Adelle Robinson, and Christine Sheris, I offer a word of thanks for their expert typing of various portions of the first edition.

In facilitating the publication of the second edition of this work, I am grateful to Mary Beatrice Schulte and Loomis Mayer of Fordham University Press and to Marion K. Pinsdorf of Fordham University.

I would like to thank, too, the Working Group on Presidential Disability, co-chaired by Dr. James F. Toole of the Bowman-Gray School of Medicine and Arthur S. Link of Wake Forest University. Interacting with Group members at three multi-day meetings over two years sharpened my awareness and deepened my understanding of issues relating to presidential disability.

Finally, I am grateful to those family members and friends who encouraged me along the way. Their support meant a great deal, especially at those low moments that are inevitable.

Boston, Massachusetts   ROBERT E. GILBERT

Introduction
A President Falls,
Another Collapses

t was late winter in Florida. The President of the United States had arrived at Hobe Sound shortly after midnight on March 14, 1997, looking forward to a golfing excursion later that day. Golf pro Greg Norman, at whose estate William Jefferson Clinton was staying, gave his guest a tour of his home and then, at 1:20 A.M., the President started to depart for his guest cottage. As he walked down a flight of stairs, President Clinton's heel caught on a step, and he stumbled badly. As he fell, his leg snapped so loudly that it was actually heard by his host. Norman caught the President in mid-fall and eased him to the ground, where he sat in great pain. The physician on duty, Dr. William Lang, immediately evaluated the President, treated his injured leg with ice and immobilization, and summoned an ambulance.

Dr. E. Connie Mariano, Senior White House Physician, received the news at her hotel that the President had been injured and she rushed to St. Mary's Hospital in West Palm Beach, arriving there about twenty minutes before he did. At St. Mary's, the President was examined by Dr. Joel Cohen, an orthopedic surgeon. An MRI (Magnetic Resonance Imaging) test showed that while Clinton's bone was not damaged, 90 percent of his right thigh muscle was shredded. Interestingly, during the time when the MRI test was being conducted on the President, a military aide sat just outside the door, holding the codes for unleashing nuclear missiles as well as the presidential succession agreement that had been drawn up between the President and Vice President. In the meantime, both Vice President Gore and his Chief of Staff had been notified of the President's accident.[1]

Dr. Cohen recommended surgery and although Dr. Mariano concurred, she preferred to have the procedure performed in Washington. She had discussed with one of the President's closest aides, Bruce Lindsay, various scenarios under which the Twenty-fifth Amendment should be invoked and Vice President Gore made Acting President of the United States. After consulting with Dr. Cohen about the type of anesthesia that leg surgery of this sort would require, she was informed that the procedure is normally performed under epidural (not general) anesthesia. Since the President would be conscious throughout the surgery, Dr. Mariano informed Lindsay that, in her view, the Twenty-fifth Amendment would not apply in this instance.

The President's leg was put in another splint, and he was given a shot of Ketorolac (an injectible anti-inflammatory drug similar to motrin) to ease his pain. At 8 A.M., after periods of fitful sleep, President Clinton was placed in a Secret Service van and taken to the airport. He was carried up the stairs of Air Force One by Secret Service agents while Dr. Lang held his leg in place. The President reportedly had little pain at the time.

As the plane made its way back to Washington, Dr. Mariano instructed Clinton's staff that only family members should see him in the hospital and that he should be spared phone calls and nonessential business. Upon arrival at Andrews Air Force Base, the presidential party left immediately for Bethesda Naval Hospital where the President signed a consent form for surgery. He was given an electrocardiogram and underwent blood work and at 1:40 P.M. he was given an epidural injection which made him numb from the waist down but which did not affect his reasoning abilities in any way. Around the same time, an IV was put in his arm for fluids. Surgery commenced at 2:30 P.M. and lasted for two hours and four minutes. The President was awake throughout.

A five-inch longitudinal incision was made by Dr. David Adkison in the President's leg about four inches above the right knee. His muscle—the quadriceps tendon—which had been torn diagonally was sutured together, and the sutures were extended past his tendon into his knee cap. Three holes were drilled in his knee cap and the sutures were attached through them to his knee. When he heard the unpleasant drilling noise, Clinton asked what it was and seemed nonplussed at the answer.

The President was wheeled back to his suite at 5:10 P.M. with the epidural still in place. Dr. Mariano had told him earlier that if at any time he received any medication that would affect his central nervous system, invocation of the Twenty-fifth Amendment would have to be considered. The President responded by instructing his medical team not to give him anything that would make him feel "dopey." Within two hours, Clinton was well enough to speak to the press by speaker phone. On the following day, he taped a speech to the Gridiron Dinner, although his leg pain had begun to increase and an extra dose of Ketorolac had had to be administered to him.

At 11 A.M. on March 16, with no temperature and no sign of infection in his incision, the President was discharged from the hospital. Seated in a wheelchair, he returned to the White House in a van borrowed from Jim Brady, press secretary to Ronald Reagan who was seriously wounded in the 1981 assassination attempt against that President. At the White House, rugs had been taped down in the living quarters and bars installed in the shower (which will remain in place for future Presidents). In order to reduce the swelling, the President's knee was iced down two or three times a day. Also, he began aggressive physical therapy twenty-four hours after his release from the hospital, at first from bed to chair and then on parallel bars and crutches. Not surprisingly, he experienced some pain as he moved his leg, but the President proved to be a very good patient and faithfully followed the regimen laid out for him by his doctors.

On March 19, President Clinton left for a meeting with Russian President Boris Yeltsin in Helsinki. He used a wheelchair there at Dr. Mariano's insistence because crutches tended to tire him out. In Helsinki, he was on blood-thinning medication so that blood clots to the leg would not develop, his leg was elevated, and he continued to get physical therapy which caused him some discomfort. During the week following his return from Finland, the President began working again in the Oval Office. Although pleased that his recovery was proceeding on schedule, he experienced some frustration at being so limited in his activities. He had, after all, been a very mobile Chief Executive and now felt somewhat dejected at his newly restricted lot in life. His travel schedule had to be modified, with trips to Mexico and the rest of Latin America postponed until later in the year. Reportedly, aides worried about the unaccustomed image of a normally robust President being lifted in and out of vehicles, and one of them remarked that "we don't want things looking too FDRish around here."[2]

As time passed, however, the President progressed rapidly. He bicycled for 45 minutes every day, guarded against a weight increase by eating smaller portions of food and more fruit, and swam in the White House pool two or three times a week. Finally, on his birthday in August, which he celebrated while vacationing on Martha's Vineyard, Clinton began once again to jog. In September, Dr. Mariano indicated that the President was a full month ahead of schedule in his recovery.

It is interesting to note that although White House officials discussed conditions under which the Twenty-fifth Amendment would be invoked during President Clinton's surgery and subsequent convalescence, it was, in fact, not invoked. Nor was it invoked during the Bush Administration immediately preceding, even though the matter was discussed at that time as well and even though those circumstances were even more ominous and unsettling.

In early May 1991, while jogging at Camp David, President Bush suddenly felt unusually fatigued and became short of breath. Accompanied by Secret Service agents, he went immediately to the presidential retreat's infirmary, where Dr. Michael Nash, the physician on duty, found that Bush's heartbeat was irregular. The President left almost immediately by helicopter for Bethesda Naval Hospital for further tests and treatment.

Although the story immediately dominated the news media, medical reports issued by the White House press secretary, Marlin Fitzwater, were uniformly positive. The President had not suffered a heart attack, he had not lost consciousness, he had had no chest pains, he was "entirely stable," and there was no cause for alarm. The President, Fitzwater reported, had even taken his briefcase to the hospital so that he could continue to work.[3]

The President's irregular heartbeat—diagnosed as atrial fibrillation—continued into the following day, but doctors indicated that the cardiac irregularity represented nothing very unusual or dangerous. One cardiologist suggested, however, that "the sudden appearance of atrial fibrillation in a 66-year-old man . . . has to be taken seriously."[4] The condition might be an indication of an underlying heart problem, possibly a heart attack, or, more likely, a narrowing of the heart's arteries or a damaged heart valve.

Atrial fibrillation is a condition that is not uncommon throughout the United States. It can be caused by stress, exercise, or even excessive caffeine and results in an unusually rapid heartbeat—up to 150 beats per minute rather than the normal rate of between 60 and 100 beats. The condition in itself normally is not life-threatening; but if it continues for a long period, it can lead to the formation of blood clots which may become dislodged and strike the brain.[5]

The news of the President's cardiac condition came as a surprise to a nation that thought of its President as active, vibrant, and robust. Although Bush was the fourth oldest man ever inaugurated as President, he seemed to radiate good health.* In fact, after a five-hour physical examination in late March 1991, he had received glowing reports from his doctors. His cholesterol levels were described as being within the desirable range, his

---

*Former President Bush has had and has now a number of medical problems. As a teenager, he suffered from hepatitis. He has hay fever, allergies, and mild arthritis of the hips and knees. He has had irritable bowel syndrome; and in 1986, a small noncancerous polyp was removed from his colon. He has a slightly enlarged prostate and had a small skin cancer removed from his face during his vice presidency. In 1989, a small, benign cyst was removed from one of his fingers; and in 1990, he was diagnosed as having a mild case of glaucoma.[6]

blood pressure was normal, and his blood chemistry tests were said to be satisfactory.

For a man about to turn sixty-seven, the President's medical history gave no real hint of impending heart trouble. Many years before, while he was in his early thirties, Bush had collapsed in a London hotel room, suffering from a bleeding ulcer. He was told by his doctor at the time that he tried to do too much and worried too much and that if he didn't mend his ways, he "wouldn't be around in ten years, maybe five." Bush later wrote that his doctor's blunt words forced him to accept the fact that he couldn't do everything, and that his energy should be directed toward those things that could be accomplished rather than those that could not.[7] Later, he also found that exercise was helpful in reducing stress and shortly after the age of fifty, began jogging on a regular basis.[8]

Nevertheless, a number of the President's friends indicated that he still internalized a good deal of tension.[9] Prior to developing atrial fibrillation, Bush appeared fatigued to some associates and upset over news stories that in 1980 he had helped stop U.S. hostages from being released by Iran in order to damage President Carter's re-election campaign. Also, the pressures of the successful Gulf War undoubtedly had taken their toll on the commander in chief, and he was particularly stung by criticism that he had badly mishandled the plight of the Kurdish refugees in Iraq. In other words, Bush had been under greater than usual stress for several months before he was stricken, and his irregular heartbeat may well have reflected this fact.

At Bethesda Naval Hospital, the President underwent an electrocardiogram and ultrasound tests which revealed no structural problems in his heart. By Monday, his heartbeat had returned to normal after digoxin, and then procainamide, were administered to him. Had these medications failed to slow down the President's heart, doctors were considering the use of electrical shocks to achieve this result. Bush would have had to undergo a general anesthetic for a limited period of time, and the shocks would have been used to stop his heart for a moment so that its normal rhythm would resume. According to White House Physician Lawrence Mohr, although this is considered a low-risk procedure, the Twenty-fifth Amendment would have been invoked and Vice President Dan Quayle would have become acting president for a short time.[10]

This thought and, in fact, the entire subject of Quayle's standing just a heartbeat away from the presidency caused considerable distress throughout the country. At the time, Quayle's favorablility rating stood at an abysmal 19 percent, and his competence to handle the office of the presidency was widely questioned, even by Republican party leaders. When Bush returned to the White House on 6 May, he tried to bolster his vice president's position by saying that Quayle "has my full support, always has, and he's doing a first class job."[11] The President's words did not reassure the nation, however; nor did they quiet talk that Quayle's place on the 1992 Republican ticket might be in jeopardy.

Shortly after the President's discharge from the hospital, doctors announced that his heart condition had been due to thyroid dysfunction, and surprisingly diagnosed him as having Graves' disease, the same ailment from which his wife, Barbara, suffers. Since the disease is not thought to be contagious, the chances that both husband and wife would have it were estimated at 1 in 10,000.[12]

Graves' disease is of unknown origin. Researchers suspect, however, that it may be caused by bacteria and/or stress. Whatever its cause, Graves' disease forces the thyroid gland to become overactive, which, in turn, intensifies the body's metabolism. If untreated, the condition can lead to fever, rapid pulse, breathing difficulties, exhaustion, and even heart failure.[13]

Bush began receiving large doses of radioactive iodine—so large, in fact, that doctors advised him to avoid close contact with family members for several days, in order to avoid exposing them to the radioactivity. The iodine rectifies the thyroid dysfunction, normally within two to six weeks, and the atrial fibrillation tends to disappear. Although the treatment occasionally results in too severe a slowdown in thyroid function, hormone tablets taken on a daily basis usually provide an effective remedy.[14]

Within a short period of time, Bush seemed to return to good health. Eight months later, however, the President's physical condition suddenly and dramatically became the center of news attention once again after he was stricken in Tokyo at a state dinner being given in his honor by Prime Minister Kiishi Miyazawa.

President Bush's visit to Japan was the culmination of a 12-day, 26,000-mile journey through the western Pacific to advance the cause of American business and improve the nation's balance of trade. To some of the reporters who were traveling with the President, Bush had occasionally seemed fatigued and out of sorts.[15] On 8 January, he played a vigorous game of tennis with the American ambassador, the Japanese emperor, and the crown prince and lost badly. By evening, the President did not feel well and summoned his personal physician, Dr. Burton Lee, who diagnosed enteritis (intestinal flu). Since Bush wanted very much to attend the prime minister's state dinner that evening, he ignored his doctor's advice to remain in his quarters, and traveled instead to Miyazawa's official residence. Secret Service agents reportedly were warned, however, that the President might not "make it through the meal."[16] Then, while standing in a receiving line, Bush became quite ill. He excused himself, rushed to a men's room, and vomited. He believed that "that had taken care of" his stomach problems, but soon learned that it "was just the beginning."[17]

At 8:20 P.M., as he finished the first course of his meal, the President suddenly became very pale and then fainted. His head dropped to his chest, his body rolled to his left, and he vomited onto his own clothing and that of Prime Minister Miyazawa. The First Lady rushed forward with a napkin which she held to her husband's mouth, and a Secret Service agent leaped onto and over the table to take hold of the President and ease him gently onto the floor. The Japanese prime minister held the President's head in his arms, and aides removed his jacket as the audience stared in shock. Secretary of Commerce Robert Mosbacher, seated near the President, later described the scene as "scary."[18]

Within a short time, Bush regained consciousness and, after an interval of several minutes during which he was examined by Dr. Lee, rose to his feet and smiled reassuringly at the relieved and applauding crowd. Immediately, however, he departed from the prime minister's official residence, wearing an overcoat that had been provided by a Secret Service agent to cover his soiled clothing, and returned by limousine to Akasaka Palace, where he was staying during his visit. He was examined there by Dr. Lee and by Dr. Allen Roberts and given an antinausea medication (Tigan).[19] Although he had a reasonably good night's sleep, he was still somewhat shaky the next morning, and most of the next day's engagements were canceled.

In Washington, the President's press secretary indicated that the White House physician did not believe that any "special monitoring" was necessary, since "all aspects of the examination indicate that it is a common case of the flu."[20] Nevertheless, an electrocardiogram was administered to the President in order to monitor his heartbeat. It revealed no abnormalities and no return of the irregular heartbeat that had afflicted him eight months earlier.[21]

Gastroenteritis is a common ailment whose sufferers sometimes become severely dehydrated and, after suddenly changing their position (for example, rising to their feet from a sitting position), occasionally faint. Doctors indicate, however, that it is uncommon for sufferers to faint while seated at a table. Dr. Gerald Mandell of the University of Virginia explained that "the fainting at the table puts it in the unusual category because it doesn't happen very often"[22]

The film footage of the President's collapse also fell into the unusual category. Shown over and over again in the United States, the scenes of the President slumping into the arms of the Japanese prime minister struck some as being all too symbolic of the central problem the President had gone to Japan to resolve—an ailing American economy slumping into the "arms" of Japan.

Inevitably, the President's collapse, coming within weeks of the New Hampshire presidential primary, sent political shock waves through the country. One of his aides understated the case when he pointed out that "collapsing and falling under the table in full view is never a political plus for a president."[23] In addition to Bush's political embarrassment, there were medical concerns as well. Dr. David Benditt, a Minnesota cardiologist, has indicated that patients who are dehydrated, fatigued, or under stress, or who have engaged in physical exercise, may be more susceptible to short-term fainting spells.[24] But several life-threatening medical conditions can also provoke this physical reaction. Specifically, a heart attack, a stroke, and/or gastrointestinal bleeding could have been responsible for the President's symptoms.[25] This fact not only caused concern but also resurrected once again the "Quayle issue."

According to the President's chief of staff, Samuel Skinner, no thought was given at any time to a transfer of power to the vice president.[26] Quayle had been informed of Bush's sudden illness at 6:20 the following morning. He later remarked that while he was confident of his ability to become President if necessary, that thought "didn't even cross my mind."[27] The thought of Quayle's ascendancy certainly did cross the minds of other people, however, and provoked another flurry of uneasiness.

President Bush appeared to recover quickly from his embarrassing indisposition and tried hard to downplay the episode. He told reporters, "I don't think there is any political downside," and joked that even "Democrats get the flu."[28] Bush's campaign strategists had to hope, however, that no further health scare would cast a cloud over his campaign for re-election.

President Bush's medical problems in both 1991 and 1992—and President Clinton's in 1997—call renewed attention to the subjects of presidential health, presidential disability, and presidential mortality. The presidency is a tension-filled position, and tension, as I shall discuss in some detail, is intimately related to both illness and death.

In contrast to the many authors who have written about the constitutional and extraconstitutional duties of the American presidency, I focus here on the physical and psychological dangers of the office rather than on its powers and responsibilities. My goal is not only to uncover a sobering historical record but also to establish a framework that will explain and refine it. Furthermore, in case studies, I illustrate more specifically the subject of presidential ill health and analyze the impact of ill health on the presidencies of six twentieth-century chief executives—Calvin Coolidge, Franklin Roosevelt, Dwight Eisenhower, John Kennedy, Lyndon Johnson, and Ronald Reagan.

Coolidge died at the age of sixty, just a few years after leaving the White House, where he suffered from debilitating psychological and physical illness. Roosevelt died in office of natural causes at the age of sixty-three, after years of disability and disease. Eisenhower actually exceeded his life expectancy, but endured a life of illness and pain, accentuated during the period of his presidency. Kennedy was assassinated at the age of forty-six, after suffering painful and debilitating illnesses for much of his life. In 1961, he became the youngest man ever elected to the presidency; in 1963, he became the youngest president ever to die in office. Johnson died at the age of sixty-four, four years after leaving the White House and after an adult lifetime filled with painful and dangerous afflictions. And although Reagan, who also exceeded his life expectancy, was sometimes described as having lived a charmed life as the nation's chief executive, his presidency brought him face to face with painful and life-threatening medical crises.

In addition to providing a medical profile for each of these presidents, I shall examine in detail the political effects of their illnesses and medical emergencies and wherever appropriate, construct a psychological "profile" in an effort to provide a broad context for each president's reactions to his disabilities and pain.

Finally, in the concluding chapter, I will explore a number of general implications of presidential illness. Presidential disability comes in a variety of forms, almost all of which were unrecognized and unaddressed by the Framers of the Constitution. Even the Twenty-fifth Amendment, added to the Constitution in 1967, fails to resolve all aspects of the problem. Further work is needed in this important area of public policy. Also, in light of the historical record, new attention must be focused on the vice presidency and efforts made to "upgrade" both the office and the process by which individuals are chosen to fill it. Moreover, consideration should be given to reducing some "presidential pressures" by downsizing his/her responsibilities as chief administrator of the United States. In short, the fact that so many of our presidents have been, to some degree and in some form, disabled must be addressed in terms of both public policy and political practice. I hope that my concluding chapter will at least point out helpful directions in which to move.

THE MORTAL
PRESIDENCY

Chapter ONE
Presidential Pathology
and Mortality

istorians and political scientists often describe the presi-
dency of the United States as a stressful, burdensome,
debilitating position. Dorothy James refers to the office
as "literally a killing job whose pressures continue to
mount."[1] Milton Plesur argues that "no responsible union would ever
approve the President's hours for a 'hard hat.'"[2] Richard Pious points
out that "always there is the burden of office which takes its toll on the
health and well-being of the incumbent."[3] And Thomas Cronin begins
and ends his 1980 volume on the presidency by quoting John Steinbeck:
"We give the President more work than a man can do, more responsibility than a man should take, more pressure than a man can bear."[4]

Since 1789, forty-one men have occupied the office of President.
Taken as a group, presidents of the United States have tended to die
prematurely, either while in office or shortly after retirement from the
White House. The position, then, surely would seem injurious to the
health of those who hold it.

It is, first of all, disturbing to note that four presidents have died in
office at the hands of assassins: Lincoln was assassinated at the age of
fifty-six, Garfield at forty-nine, McKinley at fifty-eight, and Kennedy at
forty-six. While assassinated presidents have not been included in all
mortality computations of this study, since their deaths were due to
wholly unnatural causes, it still remains true that murder comes rather
too often to American presidents. Also, physical attacks on presidents
are both common and frequent. During this century, almost half of all
presidents have been physically assaulted.[5] Unfortunately, every Presi-

This chapter is derived from two of my earlier publications on this subject: "Death and the
American President," *Il Politico* 42 (4 [1977]): 719–41; and "Personality, Stress and Achieve-
ment: Keys to Presidential Longevity," *Presidential Studies Quarterly* 15 (1 [Winter 1985]):
33–50, published by the Center for the Study of the Presidency.

dent stands in clear and present danger of injury and death from physical assaults by potential assassins. In 1981, President Reagan became the first incumbent President in American history to survive being shot by an assailant. All others have died, either immediately or soon thereafter.

The history of the American presidency has been filled with so much violence, in fact, that Stephen Sondheim's musical production that opened Off-Broadway in early 1991 was entitled *Assassins*. The focal points of the play were the men who assassinated presidents Lincoln, Garfield, McKinley, and Kennedy and the men and women who tried unsuccessfully to kill presidents Roosevelt, Nixon, Ford, and Reagan. That a musical intended ultimately for Broadway would center on the actual and planned murders of American presidents is a sad—indeed, a shocking—commentary on American political life.

Even excluding the four assassinated presidents and excluding, of course, President Clinton and the living former presidents (Bush, Reagan, Carter, and Ford), the remaining thirty-two presidents together paint a striking picture of premature death. The factors responsible for this sobering reality are worthy of detailed scrutiny.

Table 1 presents a historical view of life expectancies for white men in the United States born between 1730 and 1956. Because the federal government did not begin computing life tables until the start of the twentieth century, the data found in table 1 are composites of life tables for the United States and for the state of Massachusetts, which did compute life tables fairly regularly in the pre-1900 period. It is worth noting that as an urbanized, densely populated state, Massachusetts almost certainly would not have boasted the most favorable mortality levels in early American history.[6] White men born outside of that and other urbanized states, therefore, might have been expected to live even longer than the data in table 1 suggest.

While the data in table 1 pertain to the average white male, a number of subgroups of the white male population have had higher life expectancies. For example, children of wealthy parents have been less likely to succumb to infant mortality, and mortality levels for the college-educated and for lawyers have been below the average.[7]

Since a large majority of presidents (34 out of 41) have been college graduates, and since most (26 out of 41) have been lawyers,* their life

---

*All presidents have been college graduates except Washington, Jackson, Van Buren, Fillmore, Lincoln, Cleveland, and Truman. All have been lawyers except Washington, William Henry Harrison, Taylor, Andrew Johnson, Grant, Theodore Roosevelt, Harding, Hoover, Truman, Eisenhower, Kennedy, Lyndon Johnson, Carter, Reagan, and Bush.

Table 1 Life Expectancy for White Males

Year	At Birth	At 20 Years	At 40 Years	At 60 Years
1730	30.7	28.3	22.5	14.0
1740	31.34	29.25	22.96	14.8
1750	31.96	30.22	23.4	14.0
1760	32.58	31.19	23.84	14.0
1770	33.20	32.16	24.28	14.0
1780	33.82	33.11	24.72	14.0
1789	34.5	34.2	25.2	14.8
1800	35.18	35.27	25.68	14.8
1810	35.8	36.24	26.12	14.8
1820	36.42	37.21	26.56	14.8
1830	37.04	38.18	27.0	14.8
1840	37.66	39.15	27.44	14.8
1850	38.3	40.1	27.9	15.6
1855	38.7	39.8	27.0	14.4
1860	39.35	40.32	27.39	15.0
1870	40.67	41.32	28.17	15.6
1878–82	41.74	42.2	28.86	15.6
1880	44.06	43.09	29.5	15.6
1884–90	40.39	41.09	27.8	14.7
1890	42.5	40.6	27.4	14.7
1893–97	44.09	41.2	27.4	14.38
1900–02	48.23	42.19	27.7	14.3
1901–10	49.32	42.3	27.5	14.1
1909–11	50.23	42.7	27.4	14.0
1919–21	56.34	45.6	29.8	15.2
1920–29	57.85	45.8	29.3	14.7
1929–31	59.1	46.02	29.2	14.7
1930–39	60.6	46.8	29.6	14.9
1939–41	62.8	47.76	30.0	15.0
1942	63.6	48.02	30.3	15.1
1943	63.3	47.5	29.9	15.3
1945	64.4	48.6	30.6	15.4
1949–51	66.3	49.5	31.1	15.8
1955	67.3	50.1	31.7	16.0
1956	67.3	50.1	31.6	15.9

SOURCES: United States Department of Commerce, *Historical Statistics of the United States,* 1949, p. 45; U.S. Bureau of the Census, *The Statistical History of the United States* (New York: Horizon Press, 1965), p. 24; U.S. Bureau of the Census, *Statistical Abstraction of the United States,* 1941–70, Washington, D.C., Life-expectancy projections for the years 1730–80 have been computed from data for the years 1789–1850.

expectancies should be higher than the life expectancy figures cited in table 1. In addition, upon attaining the office of President, the best of medical care has been available to these men; and even after retirement from the White House, former presidents have access to medical attention that is normally beyond the reach of the average white male citizen. One would think, therefore, that presidents and former presidents would have a greater-than-ordinary prospect of a long life. Unfortunately for them, however, this is not the case.

Table 2 cites each deceased president, his age at death and his life expectancy (based on the data contained in table 1). For those presidents who died between the ages of forty and sixty, the data found in column 4 of table 1 were used to compute life-expectancy projections. For those presidents who died after the age of sixty, the data found in column 5 of table 1 were applied. The differential column of table 2 indicating the actual longevity of each president (age at death in relation to life expectancy) dramatically discloses the large number of presidents who died prematurely.

Table 2 reveals that of the thirty-six deceased presidents, twenty-five died prematurely. Excluding the four assassinated presidents, twenty-one out of thirty-two deceased chief executives failed to reach their individual life expectancy. The trend toward premature death has been even more starkly dramatized during the past 150 years (1841–1991). Of the twenty-eight deceased presidents who served during this period, twenty-three died prematurely. Excluding the four assassinated chief executives, nineteen of the remaining twenty-four presidents died premature deaths.

Table 2 Presidential Mortality

President	Age at Death	Life Expectancy	Differential
Washington (1732–99)	67.8	74.0	− 6.2
Adams (1736–1826)	90.7	74.4	+ 16.3
Jefferson (1743–1826)	83.3	74.3	+ 9.0
Madison (1751–1836)	85.3	74.0	+ 11.3
Monroe (1758–1831)	73.2	74.0	− 0.8
J. Q. Adams (1767–1848)	80.6	74.0	+ 6.6
Jackson (1767–1845)	78.3	74.0	+ 4.3
Van Buren (1782–1862)	79.7	74.2	+ 5.5
W. H. Harrison (1773–1841)†	68.2	74.0	− 5.8

Table 2 *(continued)*

President	Age at Death	Life Expectancy	Differential
Tyler (1790–1862)	71.8	74.8	− 3.0
Polk (1795–1849)	53.6	65.4	− 11.8
Taylor (1784–1850)†	65.7	74.4	− 8.7
Fillmore (1800–1874)	74.2	74.8	− .6
Pierce (1804–69)	64.9	74.8	− 9.9
Buchanan (1791–1868)	77.1	74.8	+ 2.3
Lincoln (1809–65)★	56.2	66.1	− 9.9
A. Johnson (1808–75)	66.6	74.8	− 8.2
Grant (1822–85)	63.3	74.8	− 11.5
Hayes (1822–93)	70.3	74.8	− 4.5
Garfield (1831–81)★	49.8	67.0	− 17.2
Arthur (1830–86)	56.1	67.0	− 10.9
Cleveland (1837–1908)	71.3	74.8	− 3.5
B. Harrison (1833–1901)	67.6	74.8	− 7.2
McKinley (1843–1901)★	58.8	67.4	− 8.7
T. Roosevelt (1858–1919)	60.2	75.0	− 14.5
Taft (1857–1930)	72.5	74.4	− 1.9
Wilson (1856–1924)	67.1	74.4	− 7.3
Harding (1865–1923)†	57.8	67.8	− 10.0
Coolidge (1872–1933)	60.5	75.6	− 15.1
Hoover (1874–1964)	90.2	75.6	+ 14.6
F. D. Roosevelt (1882–1945)†	63.2	75.6	− 12.4
Truman (1884–1972)	88.7	74.7	+ 14.0
Eisenhower (1890–1969)	78.4	74.7	+ 3.7
Kennedy (1917–63)★	46.5	65.6	− 19.1
L. B. Johnson (1908–73)	64.4	74.1	− 9.6
Nixon (1913–94)	81.3	74.0	+ 7.3
Arithmetic mean (all Presidents)			− 3.4
Arithmetic mean (nonassassinated Presidents)			− 2.1
Median (all Presidents)			− 6.0
Median (nonassassinated Presidents)			− 4.0

★Assassinated President.
†Non-assassinated President who died in office.
‡In tables 2 and 3 and in the footnote on page 14, both the arithmetic mean and the median averages are included to describe presidential mortality and the proclivity of presidents to premature death. While the arithmetic mean is the more commonly used statistic, it may be subject to misinterpretation due to a few extreme cases, especially when the total number of cases is small. Therefore, the more conservative medians (the value attained by half of the group in question) are also included for all comparisons.

Throughout the entire history of the presidency, the longest-lived presidents are, somewhat surprisingly, the first ten (Washington through Tyler): as a group, they lived 3.7 years beyond their life expectancy. Six of the chief executives within this comparatively hardy group lived beyond their life expectancy, and only four died prematurely.

The shortest-lived presidents are the ten men, excluding the assassinated Lincoln and Garfield, who followed the first ten. These chief executives (Polk through Cleveland) fell 6.7 years short of their collective life expectancy. Among this group of presidents, nine died premature, but natural, deaths, and only one (Buchanan) reached or exceeded his individual life expectancy.

The final group of deceased presidents (Benjamin Harrison through Richard Nixon, excluding the assassinated McKinley and Kennedy) failed to reach their collective life expectancy by 3.2 years. Individually, eight of these presidents died premature deaths, and only four reached or exceeded their life expectancy.

One might suspect that the substantial differences in mortality among these three groups of presidents could be attributed to changes that have taken place within the office itself and to the increase or decrease of pressures that result from such changes. During the twentieth century, the presidency has become increasingly institutionalized and it is tempting to conclude that the burdens of the office have been lessened by the addition of layers of assistants onto the executive branch. As already noted, the most recent group of deceased presidents, excluding the assassinated McKinley and Kennedy, enjoyed somewhat longer lives than the group of presidents who served immediately before them. They were not, however, as long-lived as either the first ten presidents or the general white male population. Also, a close analysis would indicate that the institutionalization of the presidency cannot be credited with any increase in the life span of our more recent presidents.

It must be noted immediately that the relatively favorable mortality level of the more recently deceased presidents is due essentially to Presidents Hoover and Truman, who reached the ripe old age of ninety and eighty-eight, respectively—14.6 and 14.0 years beyond their individual life expectancies. If these two chief executives are removed from consideration, the mortality level of our more recent group of deceased presidents is as poor as that of their immediate predecessors.

Also, considerable misunderstanding surrounds the concept of the institutionalization of the presidency. Undoubtedly the office has been in-stitutionalized to some degree, particularly since the administration of Franklin D. Roosevelt. But no matter how institutionalized the presidential office has become, the occupant of that office simply cannot escape its duties or its tensions. Even during vacation periods, when most of us can leave our work far behind us, presidents find that their breaks from the Washington scene are, in the strictest sense of the term, working vacations. For example, one of President Kennedy's aides gives us a revealing glimpse into that President's "restful" visits to Hyannisport and Palm Beach.

Wherever he went, Kennedy was linked by telephone to the White House switch-board, guarded by the Secret Service, and discreetly followed by one of an alternat-ing team of Army warrant officers carrying in a slender black case the secret codes by which the Presidential order for nuclear retaliation would be given. Wherever he went, he received the same daily CIA briefing from a military or other aide and read most of the same daily newspapers, which were flown in to him if necessary. Wherever he went, he took with him the bulky black alligator briefcase he had carried since his first days in the House—the same bag he often took over to the Mansion in the evening—bulging with whatever he and his staff felt he needed to read by way of mail, magazines, briefing memos and assorted dispatches and docu-ments. During absences of forty-eight hours or more, additional materials were flown to him regularly. Wherever he went, he kept in constant touch with Wash-ington, signed bills and executive orders, and conferred on or contemplated current crises.[8]

Not only are the burdens of the presidency inescapable, those burdens are, in some respects, even heavier today than in the past because the mental stresses of the office have grown in recent decades. This can be attributed to the advent of the nuclear age and to the complexity of international politics, both of which present new burdens for contempo-rary occupants of the White House. Lyndon B. Johnson has confided:

I heard Richard Nixon conclude his oath of office with the words 'so help me God.' To me they were welcome words. I remember two thoughts running through my mind: first, that I would not have to face the decision any more of taking any step, in the Middle East or elsewhere, that might lead to world conflagration—the nightmare of my having to be the man who pressed the button to start World War III was passing.[9]

Johnson, of course, occupied the White House during very difficult times, with a divisive war, urban riots, and other crises demanding his attention. When he spoke on television late in his term about his efforts to end the war in Vietnam, one of his former aides was struck by the deterioration in his appearance:

I had not seen LBJ on television for quite a while and I was shocked. My mind went back over the changes in his appearance and manner during his five years in the White House. There were the days immediately after the assassination, the rangy, rugged figure, every antenna alert, . . . looking around him with those hard, piercing eyes, always as if he were sniffing out friend and foe, always as if he were remembering that a smile or a handshake might be needed here or there. . . . Now in March of 1968, an old weary battered man was on the television screen. The face was deeply lined and sagging; the drawl occasionally cracked and wavered. His manner gave no intimation of FDR, and little of the LBJ of 1964. Rather, it suggested a lecturish, querulous schoolmaster.[10]

Johnson left the presidency as a sad and troubled figure and died prematurely just four years later. It should be noted, however, that the presidents who served after him are, with the exception of Richard Nixon, still living. In fact, despite his agony as the "Watergate President," Nixon survived to the age of eighty-one. Gerald Ford, Jimmy Carter, Ronald Reagan, and George Bush have, at this writing, reached the ages of eighty-four, seventy-three, eighty-six, and seventy-three, respectively.[11] This means, of course, that two of these presidents (Ford and Reagan) have already well-exceeded their life expectancy and two (Carter and Bush) are close to reaching theirs. But only time will tell what the overall longevity record will be for contemporary presidents. Also, it is not clear whether the recent *apparent* improvement in presidential longevity is due to an unusually hardy group of presidents or to the advanced state of medical treatment available in the modern period.

What *is* clear, however, is that the burdens of the presidency have not diminished. In addition to the new tensions visited on presidents by the nuclear age, terrorism, and other complexities of international politics, even the proliferating personnel of the executive branch can be a problem in itself for the person who is chief executive since it is *he* who must provide them with direction and supervision. As Ronald Reagan learned to his great dismay in 1986, this is no easy task. The labyrinth of the executive branch is large and sprawling. Put succinctly: it is supervised "more or less closely with more or less success by successive Presidents."[12] Presidents who are careless or unsuccessful in supervising their subordinates may find themselves imperiled by them.

One astute observer points out that "institutionalization brings attendant problems of supervision and a general slowdown in execution and development of policy. It also reinforces the isolation of [the President's] office."[13] Somewhat ironically, as the executive branch has grown in size, the presidency is still, and perhaps increasingly, a lonely office. The loneliness of the office is not a consequence of the physical isolation sought by some presidents—most recently by Richard Nixon, who craved "long periods alone . . . for reading, writing and just plain thinking."[14] Rather, the type of loneliness inherent in the presidential office is reflected in the words sometimes quoted by John F. Kennedy:

> *Bullfight critics ranked in rows*
> *crowd the enormous Plaza full*
> *But only one is there who knows*
> *And he's the man who fights the bull.*[15]

The President, in other words, stands on a very conspicuous stage. No other person shares the ultimate responsibilities of his office—or his blame or shame if those responsibilities are not carried out effectively.

A former president of the American Psychiatric Association, Dr. Francis Braceland, has stated that "the executive's most common enemy is loneliness."[16] The chief executive of the United States must confront this enemy every day of his presidency. Franklin D. Roosevelt once remarked to a prominent Republican leader, "Someday you may well be sitting here where I am now. . . . You'll learn what a lonely job this is, and you'll discover the need for somebody like Harry Hopkins who asks for nothing except to serve you."[17]

A more recent President wrote, "[I]t has been said that the Presidency is the loneliest office in the world. I did not find it so . . . but if I was seldom lonely, I was often alone." He explained further that "no one can experience with the President of the United states the glory and agony of his office . . . no one can share the burdens of his decisions or the scope of his duties. His experience is unique among his fellow Americans."[18] The very uniqueness of the President within the American political structure compounds the pressures of the office he occupies, pressures that seem to be contributing factors in the shortening of his life.

It is important to note that while American presidents have tended to die prematurely, it is difficult in many instances to ascertain the immediate cause of death. Because of the rudimentary state of American medicine in the nineteenth century, it is simply not possible to pinpoint the principal cause of death of most of our presidents. This fact underlies the recent flurry of interest in the untimely demise of Zachary Taylor, our twelfth President and the second to die in office. We have never known—and still do not even today—the exact cause of his death. At least now, however, we do know that Taylor was not assassinated by arsenic poisoning, as some suspected.[19]

During the twentieth century, the principal cause of presidential death can more easily and accurately be identified. Of the seven presidents who died premature but natural deaths in the twentieth century, cardiovascular disease was responsible for the death of six of them (Johnson, Coolidge, Harding, Wilson, and the two Roosevelts).

Among the factors that contribute to cardiovascular disease, individual personality factors and the human nervous system must be regarded as important. Medical researchers have found that persons who can be characterized as having "excessive drive, aggressiveness and ambition, frequently in association with a relatively greater preoccupation with competitive creativity, vocational deadlines and similar pressures," tend to be significantly more subject to heart disease than individuals with personality traits running counter to these.[20] Additionally, the personality needs of the former group bring them into closer and more frequent contact with stressful situations, thereby heightening their tendency toward cardiovascular illness.

Rufus P. Browning and Herbert Jacob point out that "men who are strongly power-motivated are likely to be attracted only to certain offices or roles within the [political] system"[21] In the United States, political figures with personality needs that compel them to be "at the top" understandably are drawn to the presidency. Since the presidency is a place of great emotional stress, those who occupy the office confront various forms of pressure and tension.

If pressure is one of the key factors in unfavorable presidential mortality levels, a comparison between the most successful and least successful presidents should be revealing. In the mid-1990's, William Ridings and

Stuart McIver conducted a broad-ranged evaluation of American presidents, combining specific qualitative ratings and overall evaluations. In contrast to the 1996 Schlesinger poll of presidents which relied on the judgments of only thirty-two individuals, the "jury" here consisted of more than seven hundred scholars from throughout the United States and Canada. After a process combining all available responses into a possible overall score of almost seventy-two thousand points, presidents (not including Clinton or Bush) were then ranked in order of points received, with Lincoln placing first with almost sixty thousand points and Harding placing last with just under nine thousand. Since the Ridings-McIver poll is so broad in scope and reflects the judgments of so many experts, it is useful to our purposes here.

Table 3 lists the twelve presidents—excluding the assassinated Lincoln—who scored highest (more than thirty-eight thousand points) in the Ridings-McIver surveys and the twelve—excluding the assassinated Garfield—who received the lowest number of points (fewer than twenty-four thousand), as well as the mortality record of each man (age at death in relation to life expectancy).

Table 3 Comparative Presidential Evaluations and Mortality

Most Successful	Mortality Level	Least Successful	Mortality Level
F. D. Roosevelt	−12.4	Taylor	−8.7
Washington	−6.2	B. Harrison	−7.2
Jefferson	−9.0	Nixon	+7.3
T. Roosevelt	−14.5	Coolidge	−15.1
Wilson	−7.3	Tyler	−3.0
Truman	+14.0	W. Harrison	−5.8
Jackson	+4.3	Fillmore	−.6
Eisenhower	+3.7	Pierce	−9.9
Madison	+11.3	Grant	−11.5
Polk	−11.8	A. Johnson	−8.2
L. Johnson	−9.6	Buchanan	+2.3
Monroe	−.8	Harding	−10.0
Arithmetic mean	−1.7	Arithmetic mean	−5.9
Median	−3.5	Median	−7.7

SOURCE: "1990's Presidential Poll by William J. Ridings, Jr. and Stuart McIver," *Presidential Studies Quarterly*, Spring, 1995, pp. 375–77.

As table 3 reveals, although both groups of presidents tended to die prematurely, the presidents who accomplished the most fared better in terms of both reputation and longevity of life than did their less successful counterparts. I can offer only a hypothesis for the greater longevity of life of the more successful presidents, but it is a hypothesis that will find support later in this study. Effectiveness, as measured by concrete accomplishments, may ease some of the emotional stresses of the office and give to its occupant some sense of comfort and satisfaction. Thus, the successful presidents had occasional respites from some of the debilitating stresses of the presidency even though they could not escape them completely. On the other hand, their unsuccessful counterparts, recognizing their weakness and ineffectiveness and continually facing their inability to cope with the demands of office, may well have been subjected to greater mental anguish during their tenure in office than anyone may have imagined.

Mental stress seemed a close companion to Warren Harding, commonly regarded as one of the two least successful presidents in American history. Harding clearly recognized his shortcomings and tried to compensate for them through hard work. According to one scholar:

Whatever his intellectual limitations, Harding was a hard-working President. After his first several months on the job, he rarely retired before midnight and was at his desk at 8 A.M. . . . He claimed that he had to work hard in order to compensate for his limited capabilities, and he hoped that diligence would counterbalance his weaknesses.[24]

Despite Harding's labors, his administration was marred by scandal and by inept and fumbling leadership. The President was not only well aware of these facts but apparently was tormented by them. Two episodes in his administration are revealing. A friend who once visited Harding in the White House was told by the faltering President:

Jud, you have a college education, haven't you? I don't know what to do or where to turn on this taxation matter. Somewhere there must be a book that tells all about it, where I could go to straighten it out in my mind. But I don't know where the book is, and maybe I couldn't read it if I found it! There must be a man in the country somewhere who could weigh both sides and know the truth. I don't know who he is, and I don't know how to get him. My God, this is a hell of a place for a man like me to be.[25]

The second episode occurred shortly before Harding's sudden death of a stroke in August 1923. During his trip to Alaska in June of that year, the President's ship was involved in a collision with another ship, and out of concern that it might sink, all persons were instructed to go up on deck. When Harding did not appear, one of his aides, going below to fetch him, found the President

Lying on his bed, his face hidden in his hands. Without uncovering his face, the President asked what had happened, and the aide told him there had been a slight collision. Even though everyone had been ordered on deck, it was not serious. Harding lay there, motionless. "I hope the boat sinks," he said softly, his face still hidden.[26]

Harding's self-perceived incompetence, his inability to supervise the behavior of his subordinates, and the resulting wrongdoing undoubtedly tormented the president and damaged his health. In early 1922, he was stricken with what was diagnosed as influenza but might well have been an unrecognized or misdiagnosed heart attack.[27] It has been reported that Harding suffered from shortness of breath whenever he lay flat and had to be propped up on pillows in order to sleep. Also, as Harding delivered his last public address before his death, Herbert Hoover noticed that he "faltered, dropped his notes, and grasped the desk."[28] One commentator concluded that "it is difficult to deny that the burdens of guilt, and a sense of personal inadequacy and failure may have precipitated his final illness."[29] Warren Harding died after little more than two years in office. He was only fifty-seven, ten years short of his life expectancy.

The same pattern of self-perceived inadequacy can be seen in the presidency of one of America's soldier presidents, Zachary Taylor. President Taylor suffered adversely from a lack of political experience while he was in the White House. One of his biographers writes that "the pressures on him were tremendous. Superior experience in partisan politics might have supplied immunity, which his army background failed to provide. His friends noticed a deterioration in Taylor's appearance."[30] Also, some of his contemporaries thought that he was dejected, haggard, and despondent; their judgments were substantiated by the President himself, who confided to a visitor that "he longed to return . . . to his quiet home—being sorely tired of . . . harassing responsibilities of . . . high office."[31] Another biographer discussed some of Taylor's disappointments and frustrations as the nation's chief executive:

President Taylor was cruelly disappointed by the widespread criticism of his trusted advisors, and regarded it, as indeed it was frequently intended, as criticism of himself. . . . Mindful that he had not sought the office, and conscious of his own integrity and desire to promote the welfare of the whole nation, he saw no justification for the attacks; indeed he was deeply wounded by them.[32]

Zachary Taylor occupied the presidential office for sixteen unhappy months and then succumbed somewhat suddenly to an unknown ailment. On the day he was stricken, the President was emotionally distressed and severely fatigued.[33] After he became ill, his doctors felt that he was suffering from intestinal difficulties, brought on, perhaps, by his consumption of raw fruit and vegetables and chilled liquids.[34] However, since Taylor complained of dizziness and headache shortly before being stricken,[35] the root cause of death may well have been cardiovascular. In any event, Zachary Taylor passed away at the age of sixty-five, almost nine years short of his life expectancy.

The frustrations, aggravations, and disappointments of the presidency, unrelieved by any major sense of accomplishment, must be particularly debilitating. The importance of this point has been underlined by a group of medical researchers who concluded that physiological illness is linked both to stress and to such moderating factors as the range of decision-making freedom and the degree of situational control available to the individual facing the stressful work environment.[36] In other words, an individual's attitude toward his work, and his ability to cope with the stressful demands that arise from it, have important psychological and physiological consequences. Constraints on decision making, then, rather than decision making per se, may well be the critical element.[37] The higher mortality of our weaker presidents points to these same conclusions. While a majority of presidents within each group have died prematurely, the longevity record of the less successful presidents has been particularly poor. Of the twelve least successful presidents, ten died prematurely; of the twelve most successful ones, eight fell short of life expectancy.

Another factor to be considered in a study of presidential mortality is the effect produced by length of tenure in the presidential office. Among deceased but non-assassinated presidents, fifteen served more than one term as the nation's chief executive, and seventeen served one term or less.★ Within each group of presidents, a substantial proportion (9/15 or 60 percent, of the first group; and 12/17, or 71 percent, of the second) failed to reach their individual life expectancies. However, a comparison of the actual mortality levels of the two groups of presidents, with the recently deceased Richard Nixon now included, does not indicate that the longest-serving presidents are the shortest-lived.† Such factors as war, internal disorder, scandal, and economic crisis merit future scrutiny.

I have compared the mortality record of successful presidents and unsuccessful presidents, of presidents who served more than one term in the White House with presidents who served for a shorter period of time. After studying both of these variables, it would appear that degree of effectiveness is more closely related to presidential mortality than length of tenure in office, although the number of cases in each subgrouping is necessarily small. It must be recognized, however, that even the successful presidents were short-lived when compared with white males in the general population and even more short-lived when compared with white males of their own educational and prior occupational groups.

The poor longevity record of American presidents stands in sharp contrast with the longevity record of male members of the other two branches of the national government. A 1970 study revealed, "Members of the United States Congress . . . are longer-lived than men in the general population."[38] Insofar as the judicial branch is concerned, Supreme Court justices fare noticeably better than the general white male population in terms of longevity of life.[39] Significantly, the advantages in life span enjoyed by congressmen, senators, and Supreme Court justices over white men in the general population have grown steadily greater over the years. [40] The low mortality levels of these officials is attributed generally to their favorable socioeconomic status and their high educa-

★Those non-assassinated presidents who served more than one term were Washington, Jefferson, Madison, Monroe, Jackson, Grant, Cleveland, Theodore Roosevelt, Coolidge, Wilson, Franklin D. Roosevelt, Truman, Eisenhower, Lyndon Johnson, and Nixon; those serving one term or less were John Adams, John Q. Adams, Van Buren, William Henry Harrison, Tyler, Polk, Taylor, Fillmore, Pierce, Buchanan, Andrew Johnson, Hayes, Arthur, Benjamin Harrison, Taft, Harding, and Hoover.
†The arithmetic mean and the median differentials in mortality (age at death in relation to life expectancy) are as follows: for presidents who served one term or less, − 2.2 years (mean) and − 4.5 years (median); for presidents who served more than one term, − 2.1 years (mean) and − 3.5 years (median).

tional attainments. However, as we have seen, similar factors have not kept American presidents from premature death.

It is, of course, difficult, if not impossible, to isolate definitively the factors responsible for the unfavorable mortality record of presidents in comparison with the record set by members of Congress and the Supreme Court. We may, however, hypothesize as to the reasons for the differential. The most obvious reason, perhaps, is that the presidency is characterized by a type and degree of pressure that does not devolve on the other two branches of government. While legislators and judges make important decisions, those decisions are collective, and individual members of Congress and the Court typically do not become the focal point for the controversy such collective decisions may provoke. In other words, members of Congress and the Court can often "hide" behind the collectivity to which they belong. Presidents, however, find that their great visibility in American society makes "hiding" behind the institution of the presidency rather difficult. The pressures of that office, therefore, tend to be thoroughly inescapable. A second reason is that members of Congress and the Court are able to somewhat "forget about" their legislative or judicial responsibilities when they leave Washington or when their respective bodies are not in session. Presidents, of course, are not so fortunate, and find that the pressures of their office are unrelenting, following them wherever they go every day of their tenure.

As already noted, medical researchers have determined that strong linkages exist between stress and cardiovascular illness.[41] In recent years, a new field of medical research—psychoneuroimmunology—has produced research findings that throw a new and dramatic light on the interrelationship between stress and illness. Scientists at Georgetown University write that "a direct link between abnormal immune responses, the growth of malignant tumors, and various forms of emotional disturbance and stress exists."[42] Researchers at Boston University report that "persons who cope poorly with stress appear to suffer deficits in cell-mediated immunity against certain diseases.[43] Dr. Elizabeth Whalen points out that "physiological changes which accompany stress may damage our immunological apparatus to the extent that we are left vulnerable."[44] The important factor in this equation seems to be that anxiety causes the release of hormones that destroy infection-fighting cells, lowering, in turn, the body's ability to fight disease.[45] These hormones also damage the body's thymus gland, which helps produce infection-fighting cells, thereby further reducing an individual's resistance to illness.[46]

It is likely, therefore, that diseases that have not formerly been linked to stress (for example, cancer) should be. In support of this point, researchers at Carleton University in Canada have concluded that "stress plays a role in the development of carcinoma [tumors]."[47] Similarly, research findings at Case Western Reserve University indicated that "physical stress increases the incidence and severity of tumor development."[48] Dr. Hans Selye, president of the International Institute of Stress, writes that if an individual is predisposed to cancer, "a severe distress can trigger the disease."[49]

While it is not unusual to see a causal relationship between stress and cardiovascular illness, medical science now seems to be establishing firm linkages between stress and noncardiovascular disease. More broadly, researchers are concluding that "virtually every ill that can befall the body—from the common cold to cancer and heart disease—can be influenced, positively or negatively, by a person's mental state."[50] Research developments such as these are important to a study of presidential mortality because they raise the possibility, if not the likelihood, that personality attributes and the tensions of the presidential office may well have been related to the premature deaths of even those presidents who did not die of cardiovascular illness. For example, in the nineteenth century, cancer was determined to be the cause of death of at least one president. Ulysses S. Grant, generally rated as one of the least effective presidents in American history, died of cancer of the throat in 1885 at the age of sixty-three, more than eleven years short of his life expectancy.[51] Significantly, several researchers believe that President Grant's frustrations and disappointments as President contributed to his development of cancer.[52]

The application of political, psychological, and medical factors to the subjects of presidential pathology and presidential mortality leads to several conclusions. First, presidents are short-lived in comparison both with the general white male population and with white male members of their own socioeconomic groups. Second, presidents are even more disadvantaged in terms of longevity of life when compared with white male members of Congress and the Supreme Court, even though the educational attainments, prior occupational experience, and, in many instances, the socioeconomic background of these three groups are similar. Third, there are medical indications that cardiovascular disease occurs more frequently in persons of a certain personality type; and that stress, and the failure to cope effectively with it, are contributing factors. Fourth, recent research findings raise the strong possibility that tension may well reduce immunity to most, if not all, diseases; and that it likely is linked to any number of illnesses, both life-threatening and otherwise.

Those who reach the office of President find themselves subjected to a constant stream of stressful situations that may well compound their susceptibility to cardiovascular disease and also increase the likelihood of their contracting various noncardiovascular illnesses as well. Woodrow Wilson once remarked, "I work hard, of course, . . . but it is not that that tells on a fellow. It's the anxiety attending the handling of . . . affairs in which you seem to be touching quicksilver."[53] Wilson, of course, was seriously stricken during his second term in the White House and spent his last eighteen months in office essentially as an incapacitated invalid, frustrated and tormented by his unsuccessful attempts to secure senatorial consent to ratification of the Treaty of Versailles. It was, after all, in the midst of his strenuous speaking tour on behalf of that treaty that he suffered the debilitating stroke that virtually brought his presidency to an end. Wilson retired from the White House in 1921 and died three years later at the age of sixty-seven, more than seven years short of his life expectancy.

The personality traits that draw individuals to the presidency, and the great stress they encounter there, are vital factors in any examination of presidential pathology and presidential mortality. Inability to cope with the tensions of power and responsibility is another important factor. Regardless of the contributing causes, however, the fact remains that the often-stated belief that the presidency is a punishing and even a killing job is dramatically substantiated by the medical histories of many of our presidents and also in the frequency of premature visits to presidents and former presidents by the proverbial angel of death.

Chapter TWO
The Trauma of Death:
Calvin Coolidge

ven though Calvin Coolidge, our thirtieth President, is held in high esteem by former President Ronald Reagan, he is commonly rated by historians and political scientists as one of the least successful presidents in American history. Not only has Coolidge regularly emerged near the bottom of the list of presidents in various polls conducted among historians and political scientists over the years,[1] but the relevant literature also gives low marks to Coolidge's conduct of the presidential office: "Coolidge voluntarily abdicated the leadership which the Constitution intended that the chief executive should exercise";[2] "lacked both imagination and idealism" and was "a below average president";[3] was a "figure-head"[4] president whose performance was "lackadaisical";[5] was a president whose "inviolate schedule was breakfast at eight, to work at nine, lunch at twelve-thirty, back at his desk at three and at four, he called it a day."[6]

Coolidge had, however, not reached the White House on the basis of weak and desultory performance. Indeed, the faltering leadership style which he showed as President was strikingly different from that which he had exhibited previously, in more than a quarter of a century in public service. Moreover, when upon President Warren G. Harding's sudden death in 1923, Vice President Coolidge succeeded to the presidency, he took control of the Republican Party in a way that won widespread praise and that reflected his history as an astute Massachusetts political leader. This dramatic cleavage in Coolidge's political style dates from the summer of 1924, when he was preparing to run for President in his own right. It

This material is derived heavily from my earlier article, "Psychological Pain in the White House: The Case of Calvin Coolidge," *Political Psychology* (March 1988): 75–100.

was eleven months after his succession to the presidency, and he had just been nominated by the Republican convention—a nomination he very much wanted—when his younger son, sixteen-year-old Calvin, Jr., died of blood poisoning. This was the last in a series of deaths that had deeply affected Coolidge from his childhood on. As I shall attempt to show in this chapter, I believe that those deaths and Coolidge's upbringing combined to produce in him a profound psychological vulnerability that made it impossible for him to transcend his grief after his son's death and, thus, destroyed his presidency.

The Early Years

Calvin Coolidge was born in Plymouth Notch, Vermont, on 4 July 1872, the son of John and Victoria Coolidge. John Coolidge, twenty-seven at the time of his son's birth, was intelligent, prosperous, interested in politics, and involved in local political life. Victoria, a year younger than her husband, was a caring but sickly woman who would die before she reached forty.

Soon after Calvin's birth, John Coolidge was elected to the Vermont legislature and spent part of each year in Montpelier, separated from his family. The frequent letters he wrote home, however, reveal warmth and affection for his wife, son, and eventual daughter. Typically he began each letter with the salutation "Dear Vic and Baby" or "Dear Vic and Calvin," often urged them "to take good care" of themselves, and told them that he longed to see them. Sometimes he complained that his wife was not writing him in Montpelier often enough. For example, on 19 November 1876, he wrote, "As I have not received any answers to my letters, I will write again and see if I will not have better success." The next day he wrote again, "I will keep writing to you if you do not answer me. . . . Wish I was at home so I could see you and the children."[7]

As the years went by, Calvin's father showed real interest in and concern for his young son. On 11 October 1874, for example, he wrote his wife and asked, "How does Calvin do? Is he a good boy? Tell him to send word what he wants me to bring him." He concluded the letter by admitting, "I am anxious to see you and Calvin."[8]

Young Calvin's parents put great stress on developing in him the traits of reliability and responsibility. Under their guidance and by their example, Calvin became a serious, conscientious, and industrious boy. Although neither a natural leader nor a standout as scholar or athlete, he was reliable and hard-working. His father wrote, "If I left any work for my son to do while I was away, I was always sure of finding it done when I came back."[9] One of his teachers agreed, commenting, "If I said, do that, he did it, not half did it. With Cal, law and order began with strict obedience to parents, no questions asked."[10]

Calvin's boyhood school records reveal his conscientiousness. From April 1878 to April 1886, he attended 868 days of school, received consistently good deportment ratings, and was late for class only fifteen times. In a class of about thirty, Calvin ranked among the top 20 percent.[11]

Calvin was a shy, quiet child who did not join in the roughhousing of his peers. He was discouraged from dancing and had it made clear to him that he could make few mistakes.[12] His behavior was such that only rarely did he need or encounter punishment. But those rare occasions when he was disciplined—normally by his paternal grandmother, whom he later described as "a true daughter of the Puritans"[13]—were unpleasant. Donald McCoy tells us that he would be "shut up in a dark, cobwebby attic," and adds, "It was little wonder, as a result of his upbringing, that he was shy."[14]

Calvin Coolidge grew up in generally comfortable surroundings. While his parents were not rich, they were prosperous enough to be able to provide him with the material things he needed. The money he earned during his schooldays was put in a bank account for him. His father reported that "he did not have to work his way through school as some boys do."[15] Still, although better off financially than many of his peers, Calvin was raised much like the other boys of the community:

He filled the kitchen woodbox, drove the cows to pasture and went after them at night, fed the pigs and chickens, rode the horses to cultivate corn and potatoes, dropped potatoes, picked them up in the fall and when old enough probably drove the mowing machine and horse-rake and helped in heavier tasks on the farm.[16]

While Calvin's childhood was similar in these respects to that of many other Vermont boys, it was also marked by unusual dislocation and travail. Not only was his father away from home during part of his earliest years, but his mother was sickly, probably suffering from tuberculosis, and died when he was only twelve. Calvin may have blamed himself for her death,[17] possibly because his birth and childhood exacerbated her frailty. Of her death, he later wrote:

*When she knew that her end was near she called us children to her bedside, where
we knelt down to receive her final parting blessing. In an hour she was gone. It was
her thirty-ninth birthday . . . we laid her away in the blustering snows of March. The
greatest grief that can come to a boy came to me. Life was never to seem the same
again.* [18]

As President, Coolidge often mentioned his mother to Colonel Edmund W. Starling, his closest Secret Service agent, speaking "of his deep
affection" for her, "of her fair-haired beauty, of her love of flowers, of her
understanding of him, and of the help she gave him in the problems he
faced from day to day." [19] Starling reported that Coolidge "communed
with her, talked with her, and took every problem to her." The President
once told him, "I wish I could really speak to her. . . . I wish that often." [20]

A few years after his mother's untimely death, Calvin's sister Abigail
(Abbie), who was two years his junior and with whom he was very close,
died of apparent appendicitis at the age of fourteen. When his sister's
condition turned critical, Calvin left school and returned to his home; he
stayed "beside her until she passed to join our mother." [21] After returning
to classes, however, at Black River Academy in Ludlow, Vermont, where
he had enrolled in 1886 and where his sister had joined him two years
later, the future President wrote to his father and admitted, "It is lone-
some here without Abbie." [22] Shortly after the second anniversary of his
sister's death, Calvin, always the dutiful son, tried to raise his ailing father's
spirits by telling him that "we must think of Abbie as we would of a happy
day, counting it as a pleasure to have had it but not a sorrow because it
could not last forever." [23]

The letters written by young Calvin to his father after he went away
to school at Black River Academy, and even while he was at Amherst
College, reveal both his close relationship with those back home and his
loneliness. He often asked his father to send him money or stamps and
occasionally told his father and the stepmother whom his father had
married in 1891, that he missed them. On 7 October 1891, he wrote,
"Remember, I am always looking for a letter from home, so let me hear
as often as you can." After returning to school in 1892 from a Christmas
vacation, he wrote, "Each time I get home, I hate to go away worse than
before." [24]

Despite the loneliness and the two great losses of his adolescence,
Calvin Coolidge went on to graduate from Amherst College in 1895 and
then move to Northampton, Massachusetts, where he studied law at the
law firm of Hammond and Field. He was admitted to the Bar in June 1897

and opened a law office in Northampton several months later. Although he soon began his political career, his most important decision at the time was to marry Grace Goodhue, the daughter of a Vermont steamboat inspector, in 1905. The marriage produced a son (John) in 1906 and another son (Calvin) two years later.

The Massachusetts Politician

Calvin Coolidge carried the lessons of his early years well into adulthood and successfully exercised the Puritan virtues of thrift, hard work, and civic responsibility in his early life of public service. Before entering national politics, Coolidge held several political positions on the state and local levels. He served as a city councilman (1898–1900), city solicitor (1900–1902), a clerk of courts (1903), state representative (1906–8), mayor of Northampton (1910–12), state senator (1912–16), president of the State Senate (1914–16), lieutenant governor (1916–19), and governor of Massachusetts (1919–21). In his early days as chief executive of the United States, Coolidge revealed patterns of executive behavior he had developed earlier, in particular as chief executive of his adopted state.

When, in November 1918, Calvin Coolidge was elected governor of Massachusetts, he was regarded as a moderately liberal Republican since as chairman of the state party's Resolutions Committee in 1917, he had drafted a generally liberal platform for the Republican party. That document included such progressive proposals as a shortened workweek for laborers, workmen's compensation, urban sanitation, the protection of children, and various public health measures.[25] Coolidge's inaugural address as governor reinforced his image as a progressive. Perhaps the most representative line in that address, one directed toward the legislature, was: "Let there be a purpose in all your legislation: to recognize the right of man to be well-born, well-nurtured, well-educated, well-employed and well-paid."[26]

During his tenure as governor, Coolidge was true to the planks of the platform he had drafted in 1917 and to the language and promise of his inaugural address, even though the Republican party had become steadily more conservative after the election of Woodrow Wilson to the presidency in 1912. Working closely and well with both parties in the state legislature, Coolidge fashioned a progressive agenda and secured much of its passage. It was during his administration, for example, that the workweek for women and children was reduced from fifty-two to forty-eight hours, that maximum weekly payments under the Workman's Compensation Law were increased, and that the Women's Suffrage Amendment was approved.[27] At his urging, the legislature also enacted laws that gave greater protection than before to tenants by prohibiting annual rent increases exceeding 25 percent, allowed courts to delay eviction proceedings for as long as six months, and imposed penalties on landlords for failing to provide tenants with promised utilities.[28] Coolidge also took aim at rent profiteers through a special message to the legislature urging that tenants be protected from eviction without adequate notice—a protection he soon signed into law.[29]

In his administration, in an effort to enhance the environment, outdoor advertising was made subject to state regulation, and the reforestation of 100,000 acres of Massachusetts wasteland was authorized. To aid middle- and lower-class litigants, legislation was passed to make it easier to file small-claims cases in the courts;[30] to aid the unemployed, Coolidge requested a statewide public-works program;[31] to curb the spread of disease, he urged that provision be made for further research in preventive medicine;[32] to benefit returning servicemen, a bonus of one hundred dollars was granted to each veteran at his urging, and a state employment commission for veterans established.[33]

On the purely executive front, Governor Coolidge took action that won him considerable public praise. He consolidated more than one hundred state departments into twenty in an effort to enhance efficiency and effectiveness.[34] Also, he appointed a commission to study the possible establishment of a pension system for public employees. Other commissions were established to recommend a system of maternity benefits for female workers and to study the problems of housing in the Commonwealth. In a prescient move, the governor set up the Office of Fuel Administration to increase the supply of fuel available to citizens and businesses of the state. McCoy points out that Coolidge "badgered officials of Massachusetts, other New England states and the federal government to facilitate the supply of coal."[35]

Perhaps most surprising in light of his subsequent pro-business reputation, Governor Coolidge showed an active interest in raising the salaries of factory workers and public employees. With respect to teachers, he complained publicly that "the compensation of many teachers . . . is far less than the pay of unskilled labor. . . . We compensate liberally the manufacturer and the merchant; but we fail to appreciate those who guard the minds of our youth. . . . The Government must adequately reward the teachers in its schools."[36] In response to his urging, pay raises were voted for teachers and other public employees, although a pay-raise bill for members of the state legislature incurred a stinging rebuke from the governor.

In labor-management disputes which flared up during his tenure, Coolidge took an activist and even-handed role. For example, during a textile strike in Lowell, Massachusetts, the governor was asked by the American Woolen Company to send in the militia to break up the strike. Instead, Coolidge dispatched to Lowell a *Boston Herald* reporter with self-admitted pro-worker sympathies to investigate conditions and to make a report on his findings. After hearing those findings, Coolidge told the managers of the corporation that he would *not* send in the militia and urged its president to settle the strike as quickly as possible.[37]

Three months later, Coolidge helped settle a strike by New England Telephone workers by urging restraint and reason on both sides and by asking the federal government for authority to take over telephone lines in the event of a protracted strike. Faced with the governor's resolve, the parties to the dispute reached a quick resolution.

During the summer of 1919, Coolidge intervened in a strike by employees of the Boston Elevated Street Railway and worked out an agreement that sent the dispute to arbitration and brought the strikers back to work. The outcome of the agreement was that the workers received a sizable pay increase.[38]

It was a labor dispute that brought Calvin Coolidge national publicity and widespread applause. In September 1919, the Boston police went out on strike. After several days of hesitation, the governor called out the entire state militia for service in Boston, demanded that all loyal policemen obey him, and ordered the police commissioner of Boston to carry out his responsibilities "under my command and in obedience to such orders as I shall issue from time to time."[39]

When the police commissioner fired striking policemen and announced that none would be rehired, Coolidge supported him in full. It was, however, the governor's response to the labor leader Samuel Gompers's strong request for police reinstatement that won Coolidge national acclaim. Refusing to reinstate the striking policemen, Coolidge proclaimed the words long associated with his name: "There is no right to strike against the public safety by anybody, anywhere, anytime."[40] With these words, Coolidge moved onto the national political scene, as newspapers across the country trumpeted his name and a landslide re-election victory now loomed on the horizon. As he himself wrote, "No doubt it was the police strike of Boston that brought me into national prominence.

That furnished the occasion and I took advantage of the opportunity."[41]

It seems clear that in his two years as governor of Massachusetts, Calvin Coolidge was active, hardworking, and progressive. In both his executive and legislative activities, he established a record of accomplishment, balance, and political astuteness that set him apart from many of his contemporaries, both within and outside the Republican party. It was that record, and the skill with which he compiled it, that led two of his principal biographers to rate his gubernatorial administration in strongly positive terms. Claude Fuess writes that Coolidge, true to his upbringing, avoided ostentation in office, gave evidence of "thoroughgoing simplicity," and "was a good Governor, worthy of the best traditions of the Commonwealth."[42] And McCoy concludes that "Coolidge had acquitted himself well as Governor. He had, in fact, been an effective, responsible, and conscientious executive, one well above the average of post-war governors in the various states."[43] The capacity of hard work and the trait of conscientiousness fostered in him as a child were clearly active during his years as chief executive of Massachusetts.

The Vice Presidency

During the summer of 1920, Senator Warren G. Harding of Ohio, a dark horse candidate, became the Republican nominee for president of the United States on the ninth ballot at the Republican national convention in Chicago. Calvin Coolidge was chosen for second place on the Republican ticket as an act of revolt against party leaders in the Senate by angry convention delegates. Also, as governor of Massachusetts, he provided geographical balance to the ticket and had become something of a celebrity during the Boston police strike.

Ironically, Coolidge had had some—albeit not much—support for first place on the ticket, but his interest in fighting for the nomination waned due, at least in part, to the death of his stepmother in May 1920.[44] Since Carrie Brown had become his stepmother in 1891, their relationship had grown very close. He later wrote: "I was greatly pleased to find in her all the motherly devotion that she could have given if I had been her own son. For thirty years she watched over me and loved me, welcoming me when I went home, writing me often when I was away, and encouraging me in all my efforts."[45] Indeed, Calvin's letters home reveal both concern and affection for her. At various times, he thanked her for her kindness to him, urged that she ought to have a nurse to care for her, suggested that his father stay with her as much as possible since "she is more important than the farm," and expressed concern over her physical condition as she approached the end of her life.[46]

With her death coming just before the 1920 Republican convention, Coolidge undoubtedly found it difficult, in the midst of his mourning, to concentrate on winning the presidential nomination of his party. Also, his stepmother was no longer there to encourage him in his efforts, which, by his own words, was one of the important roles she had played in his life. Therefore, he ended his exploratory moves for first place on the 1920 Republican ticket.

His nomination for vice president came as something of a surprise to Coolidge and his wife. When he received the telephone call telling him that he had been nominated as Harding's running mate, his wife asked, "You're not going to take it, are you?" He replied, "I suppose I'll have to."[47]

The Harding-Coolidge ticket swept to victory, capturing 60 percent of the popular vote and the electoral votes of thirty-eight states. The size of the victory did not, however, portend a happy presidency for Warren Harding. Betrayed by his friends and castigated by his enemies, Harding felt overwhelmed by the burdens of office. Surrounded by growing scandals, the tormented president left Washington in June 1923 for a cross-country speaking tour which was to culminate in vacation visits to Alaska and then San Francisco. On 2 August, President Harding died suddenly in his San Francisco hotel room. After midnight on 3 August, the oath of office was administered to Calvin Coolidge by his father, a notary public, in the very room of their Vermont home where his sister and stepmother had both died and where his mother had spent years as an invalid.[48] During the trip back to Washington later that morning, the new President stopped to visit the grave of his mother. He later wrote, "It had been a comfort to me during my boyhood when I was troubled to be near her last resting place, even in the dead of night. Some way, that morning, she seemed very near to me."[49]

No one knew exactly what to expect of the new President. As vice president, Coolidge had been largely invisible. Assistant Navy Secretary Theodore Roosevelt, Jr., wrote, "I do not know his policies. Though I sat more than two months in the Cabinet with him, I never heard him express his opinion on major questions."[50] This, of course, was not too surprising. As every student of American politics knows, the vice presidency is not an office of power; and Coolidge's years as vice president

were typically uneventful. Two features of his vice presidency are, however, worthy of note.

First, Coolidge apparently worked hard at being vice president. He was
at his desk from 9:00 A.M. until 5:00 P.M. every day, even when the Senate
was not in session. This practice was so unusual for vice presidents at the
time that one Washington official remarked:

> That's a new one on me. . . . I've seen Vice Presidents who were busy attending
> luncheons and dinner parties. But those other Vice Presidents never had much else
> to do. They never received any mail to talk about. Presidents seemed to forget them
> completely. No one ever thought of consulting them. As the weeks sped on, they
> became more and more forgotten. I think it must be different this time. It is
> different.[51]

Second and perhaps most striking, Coolidge viewed his role as presiding officer of the Senate as giving him the right to decide not only who
was to have the floor at a specific time but also what legislation was to be
considered by the Senate.[52] This latter view was a sharp departure from
custom and seems to indicate a strong, if not expansive, political personality. Coolidge, after all, was the man who wrote his father in 1915 that
"men do what I tell them to do."[53]

The White House Years

Calvin Coolidge's ascension to the presidential office was impressively
smooth. He moved swiftly and sure-footedly to consolidate his hold over
the reins of government and to establish rapport with both the liberal and
the conservative factions of the Republican party.[54] In an effort to present
an image of stability to the nation, the new chief executive determined
at once that all of President Harding's cabinet officers should remain at
least until the present term of office came to an end, and held his first
regular cabinet meeting just eleven days after his accession to the White
House.[55]

Coolidge was sensitive to the political realities that confronted him as
a new President, and demonstrated both strong political acumen[56] and a
well-developed publicity sense.[57] He promised to meet with the press
twice a week, telling journalists, "I rather look forward with pleasure to
having you come in twice a week, in order that I may talk to you, give
you a little of the idea I may have of what the government is trying to do,

and satisfy you, insofar as I can, on the questions that you ask."[58] The *Boston Globe* commented on 2 September 1923, that "the veterans, and there are correspondents here who have seen Presidents come and go for a quarter of a century, declare that thus far President Coolidge is more communicative than any man, with the possible exception of Theodore Roosevelt, who ever sat in the White House."[59] In his vigorous cultivation of the press, Coolidge went so far, in March 1924, as to ask reporters to make suggestions to him on possible appointees for the position of secretary of the navy.[60]

Almost immediately after he became President, Coolidge invited two key congressional leaders to meet with him at the White House. During that meeting, he asked the two men to recommend to him a personal secretary who understood "the political work of the President's Office and who knew Congress and its members."[61] Another function for such a secretary was to help the new President secure the 1924 Republican presidential nomination.

During his first months in office, Coolidge worked assiduously but not always successfully at cultivating Congress. One of his earliest steps was to pardon people who had been convicted of violating the Sedition Act during the Wilson administration. He issued this pardon over the objections of officers of the American Legion[62] as well as of the attorney general because he felt that the congressmen and senators who favored the pardon could be important legislative allies.[63]

In September 1923, he announced that a prominent administration critic, Senator Robert LaFollette, would always be welcome at the White House, and said that he hoped that he could rely on the progressive Wisconsin senator to support his programs.[64] Two months later, Coolidge wrote a letter to each Republican senator asking for suggestions for appointments to administrative offices.[65] The President breakfasted with members of Congress to sound them out and to show good will and, in March 1924, launched a series of White House dinners for congressional leaders as a way of developing greater rapport with them and eliciting their help in the enactment of his programs. Even though unsuccessful in his support for the 1923–24 Mellon tax bill, Coolidge took an active and firm interest in trying to secure congressional approval of it.[66]

In addition to these legislative activities, President Coolidge also showed initiative and flexibility in the realm of international relations. Soon after becoming President, he healed a three-year breach in U.S.-Mexican relations by recognizing the government of Mexico and by requesting funds to settle claims springing from the 1914 American occupation of Vera Cruz. Also, he announced that his administration would welcome an international meeting on matters of international law, particularly on the rights of neutrals and on rules for submarine warfare. When parts of Japan suffered a severe earthquake and typhoon, Coolidge dispatched the Pacific fleet with aid so quickly that the American ships arrived on the scene even before their Japanese counterparts. The new President's personal expression of sympathy was the first the Japanese emperor received from any foreign head of state.[67]

On 6 December 1923, President Coolidge delivered in person his first annual message to Congress. This was the first presidential address in history to be broadcast on radio; and "Silent Cal"—the nickname given him because of the "taciturnity in his conversations with visitors, in his press interviews and even with persons whom he met in lighter social contacts"[68]—proved to be an effective radio performer.[69] In that address, he presented Congress with a long list of legislative requests and set forth in unmistakable terms his own position on a wide variety of subjects. Coolidge urged the establishment of a permanent court of international justice, the abolition of certain kinds of taxes, the expansion of the civil service system, the abolition of the right to issue tax-exempt securities, the resumption of the opening of intercoastal waterways, and the enactment of oil-slick laws. He also urged that Congress appropriate funds for medical courses at Howard University, set up reformatories for women and for young men serving their first prison sentence, provide for the recodification of navigation laws, expand health care for veterans, and establish a separate cabinet-level department of education and welfare.[70] In all, Coolidge made almost thirty identifiable requests to Congress in his first annual message.

Moreover, Coolidge made his first requests to the legislature in forceful, direct, and unequivocal language. Examples abound: "I favor the establishment of [a permanent court of international justice] and I commend [this proposal] to the favorable consideration of the Senate, with the proposed reservations clearly indicating our refusal to adhere to the League of Nations"; "I do not favor the cancellation of the foreign debt"; "I recommend that Congress appoint a small joint committee to consider offers, conduct negotiations, and report definite recommendations [on Muscle Shoals★]"; "I recommend that the field force for prohibition enforcement be brought within the classified service."[71]

★The Muscle Shoals controversy involved a federal project initiated by the administration of Woodrow Wilson on the Tennessee River to produce hydroelectric power and to manufacture defense-related nitrates. Coolidge apparently wanted private enterprise to replace the government in running the project.

In both language and substance, Coolidge's first message to Congress conveyed the image of a President who would be comfortable in his role as chief executive and would not shirk his responsibilities as legislative leader—an image not at all in harmony with the one of Coolidge common today. Indeed, it is precisely Coolidge's passive, noninterventionist image that President Reagan holds in such esteem. Nonetheless, Coolidge's first message to Congress was that of a strong, even activist chief executive urging an extensive and detailed agenda on the legislative branch. Even the liberal Senator William E. Borah of Idaho, who had consulted with Coolidge frequently during the fall of 1923,[72] was pleased with his first message, commending him for his "program and courage."[73]

Two days after his address to Congress, Coolidge announced his candidacy for the Republican presidential nomination. One reason for his early announcement was to dissuade other Republican hopefuls from entering the race. The new President clearly wanted the nomination of his party for a term in his own right. One of his first acts as President had been, after all, to appoint to his staff as personal secretary a political operative from Virginia, E. Bascom Slemp, whose primary responsibility was to work toward Coolidge's nomination and election in 1924.

The Coolidge drive for nomination proceeded without serious obstacle, as the President bolstered his political advantage by adroit use of the patronage power.[74] Several potential rivals felt that the President had the nomination all but won, and decided to avoid entering the fray. One of the other hopefuls, the former Illinois governor Frank Lowden, remarked that Coolidge was revealing himself to be "an accomplished politician and able."[75]

As during his gubernatorial years, Coolidge showed himself to be a hard-working executive. The *Boston Traveler* reported that during his first year as President, he was "almost constantly at his desk."[76] A typical day of his calendar bears out this report. He arose at 6:30 A.M., reviewed the morning papers at 6:40, and met with staff members before breakfast at 7:00. After breakfasting with Mrs. Coolidge, his day from 9:00 A.M. until after 1:00 P.M. was punctuated with some sixteen appointments (with twenty-four individuals) and time for correspondence. Returning from lunch at 2:00 P.M., Coolidge had additional appointments and official obligations, which carried him through to 6:00 P.M. After dinner he had a 30-minute meeting with Senator Henry Cabot Lodge, bringing to an end a long official day.[77]

Coolidge's long hours of work during his early months in the White House reflect not only the demanding nature of the presidency but also his real enjoyment of the office. A close associate reported that "the President would almost tiptoe around, touching things and half smiling to himself." He acted "as if he were a small boy whose daydreams of being king had suddenly been made real by the stroke of a magic wand."[78]

In early summer 1924, the Republicans nominated Calvin Coolidge for President. He received 1,065 delegate votes against 34 for Robert LaFollette and 10 for Sen. Hiram Johnson of California. Barely, however, had Coolidge had time to enjoy his victory when tragedy struck—a tragedy that would seriously undermine his presidency.

It began innocently enough—with a game of tennis. One day President Coolidge's sixteen-year-old son and namesake, Calvin, Jr., played tennis on the South Grounds of the White House. Reportedly, he wore sneakers but no socks. Soon afterward, he developed a blister on one of his toes which became infected. A doctor examined the boy and termed his condition serious. The President was thoroughly distracted by his son's illness, "going about as if in a dream."[79] According to Kansas journalist William Allen White:

The President moved a dozen times a day back and forth from his desk to the boy's sickbed. One day, remembering little Calvin's love of animals, he coaxed and caught a small brown rabbit among the plants in the White House garden, picked it up gently and came trotting through the White House to the sick room. In return, across the pained young face came a smile and they took the bunny away and the President went back to his work.[80]

On 3 July, the President's son was moved to the Walter Reed Hospital. McCoy reports that "the President went helplessly about official business, joining Grace Coolidge whenever possible at their son's bedside."[81] The Coolidges' family physician, Dr. Edward Brown, reported how he had, one evening after the President had left his son's hospital room accompanied by his elder son, John, looked out the hospital window—and "there below in the street, standing quite still with John's hand in his, was Mr. Coolidge looking up fixedly at the boy's room—a forelorn and touching picture."[82]

On 4 July, his own birthday, the President wrote his father a sad letter:

Calvin is very sick so this is not a happy day for me. He blistered his toe and infection got into his blood. The toe looks all right but the poison spread all over his system . . . We think his symptoms are a little better now at 1 P.M. but he had a bad night.

Of course he has all that medical science can give but he may have a long sickness with ulcers, then again he may be better in a few days.[83]

Three days later, Calvin Jr. died. His body was taken to the White House where it lay in state. The President was overcome with grief. Dr. Joel Boone, a presidential physician, writes that hours after the boy's wake had ended, President Coolidge came downstairs from the White House living quarters dressed in a bathrobe and walked up to his son's casket. For long moments he stood there, gazing at his son's face and stroking his hair. Several hours later, when young Calvin's casket was removed from the White House, Coolidge's surviving son reveals that the President broke down and sobbed, "they're taking our boy away." Afterwards, a friend who visited him in the Oval Office reported that the distraught Chief Executive wept openly, the tears running down his face, while he kept repeating, "I just can't believe it has happened. I just can't believe it has happened."[84] When, on 9 July, he received the undertaker's bill for young Calvin's burial, the usually prompt-paying President ignored it for three months, a sign perhaps that he could not yet accept the fact of the boy's death.[85]

Indeed, Coolidge seems to have lost real interest in politics and the presidency after his son died. As he said later, "when he [Calvin, Jr.] went, the power and glory of the Presidency went with him."[86] In the fall of 1924, just before the election, Coolidge told his father that he would never again be a candidate for public office.[87] Grace Coolidge went so far as to say that the President "lost his zest for living" as a result of his son's death.[88]

Although Coolidge won a sweeping victory in 1924, after a campaign in which he did strikingly little on his own behalf,[89] his friends thought he was a changed man who could neither forget nor escape from grief.[90] To the press, Coolidge remarked, "I expect we shall observe Christmas at the White House about the same as usual. My boy John is coming home from college. . . . I expect the observance of the holidays will be about the same as usual. The only difference, which will be apparent to all of you, is that three of us will be present, rather than four, as in the past."[91] To one of his associates, Coolidge remarked, "[W]hen I look out that window, I always see my boy playing tennis on that court out there."[92] One visitor to the White House was "astonished to hear him [the President] say, as if his visitor might not have heard the news: 'How are your boys? One of my boys has gone.' "[93]

It is obvious that his dead son was much on the President's mind. On 22 December 1924, he wrote his father, saying, "I wish you a Merry Christmas. If only Calvin were with us we should be very happy." On the following day, he wrote again to his father, "Now John is home I miss Calvin more." Two months later, on 26 February 1925, he told his father, "You and John and I are all that is left"; and soon afterward, he wrote more than once that it was time to begin sending flowers to little Calvin's grave.[94]

Shortly before Christmas 1925, a year and a half after the boy's death, the President wrote his father a strangely brooding letter: "It is getting to be Christmas time again. I always think of mother and Abbie and grandmother and now of Calvin. Perhaps you will see them all before I do, but in a little while we shall all be together for Christmas."[95]

Perhaps Coolidge's state of mind following his son's death can best be seen in an episode recounted by his Secret service bodyguard, Colonel Starling:

Very early one morning when I came to the White House I saw a small boy standing at the fence, his face pressed against the iron railings. I asked him what he was doing up so early. He looked up at me, his eyes large and round and sad. "I thought I might see the President," he said. "I heard that he gets up early and takes a walk. I wanted to tell him how sorry I am that his little boy died." "Come with me, I'll take you to the President," I said. He took my hand and we walked into the grounds. In a few minutes the President came out and I presented the boy to him. The youngster was overwhelmed with awe and could not deliver his message, so I did it for him. The President had a difficult time controlling his emotions. When the lad had gone and we were walking through Lafayette Park, he said to me: "Colonel, whenever a boy wants to see me, always bring him in. Never turn one away or make him wait."[96]

Grace Coolidge's response to her son's death was somewhat different. Although deeply stricken, the First Lady nevertheless seemed more positive and less morbid in her grief, as several of her letters bear witness. In a letter dated 3 August 1924 to one of her closest friends, Mrs. R. B. Hills, she spoke of her son's funeral: "As we stood beside the grave, the sun was shining, throwing long, slanting shadows and the birds were singing their sleepy songs. Truly it seemed to me God's acre . . . I came away with a 'peace which passeth understanding,' comforted and full of courage."[97] To Judge Richard Irwin on 13 August 1924, she wrote, "[T]here's an awful ache way down deep inside but my boy is safe and happy and nothing can hurt him now." On 9 December 1924, she again wrote to Mrs. Hills of her dead boy: "[A]lways he seems to be just ahead of me and I can see his smile." In still another letter to Mrs. Hills, this one dated 3 January 1925, she said that "we couldn't see our Calvin but we could think of him and how happy his first Christmas in heaven must be."[98]

In personal terms, his son's death was extremely unfortunate for Coolidge, the loss of a child being for most parents the most difficult of all losses. According to the grief specialist Marian G. Secundy, "strong emotions are often displayed overtly for a longer period of time," and "overt psychiatric problems may result more frequently."[99] In a political sense, however, the President's loss was the nation's—and was, moreover, compounded by having occurred so early in his presidency. Coolidge lost much of his interest in politics and much of his political self-confidence just at the moment he most needed these qualities. The change in his behavior as President is clear.

Both as governor of Massachusetts and during his first year as President of the United States, Coolidge was an active "chief legislator." He tried hard to cultivate important legislative leaders and commonly presented a detailed list of legislative requests for enactment. Then, after his son's death in July 1924, Coolidge lost interest in working with Congress; and despite the fact that his own party controlled both houses, his relationship with the legislature became steadily more strained. He played no role in trying to influence the organization of Congress in 1925 and made no attempt to moderate the Republican leadership's plan to punish Senator LaFollette and his progressive followers for forming a third party in the 1924 election.[100] The progressive wing of the Republican party never forgave Coolidge for this inaction.

The practice of consultation he had followed during his first year in the White House was largely abandoned in subsequent years. Robert Murray, reviewing his almost six years in office, tells us that Coolidge's "contact with congressional leaders was infrequent and perfunctory."[101] He generally ignored individual members of key committees and made no attempt to influence their votes on pending legislation. The interchange he did have with members of Congress tended to be social and devoid of substance. His aloofness extended even to those senators and representatives who were leading the fight for administration measures. He shunned strategy sessions with these allies and refrained from trying to assist them in their labors. Wilfred E. Binkley points out that in this regard Coolidge's record is even worse than that of Warren Harding, commonly regarded, with Ulysses S. Grant, as one of the two poorest American Presidents.[102]

The same disengagement can be seen in Coolidge's post-1924 messages to Congress. He did not even deliver those messages in person but, rather, had them read to both houses by clerks.[103] Also, their language was quite unlike that of his first message, described earlier. The language of his messages in 1925, 1926, 1927, and 1928 was vague, noncommittal, and deferential, indicating an unsure and timid chief executive. A few examples testify to their flavor: "It is for Congress to decide whether they judge it best to make such a [tax] reduction or leave the surplus for the present year to be applied to retirement of the war debt" (1926); "if a sound solution of a permanent nature can be found for this [agricultural production and marketing] problem, the Congress ought not to hesitate to adopt it" (1926); "it is believed that a thorough investigation and reconsideration of this proposed policy [on fuel administration] by the Congress will demonstrate that this recommendation [for appointment of a Board of Mediation and Conciliation] is sound and should be adopted" (1927); "I recommend that a survey be made by the proper committees of Congress dealing with this subject [establishing a Department of Veterans' Affairs], in order to determine whether legislation to secure this consolidation is desirable" (1928).[104]

Few presidents have enjoyed so little success with Congress. Simply put, Coolidge was a failure as chief legislator of the United States even though his party controlled both houses. Sidney Warren has accurately summarized Coolidge's record with the legislative branch: "Although he [Coolidge] was highly popular with the American people, the Republican Congress to an unusually large degree passed laws that he opposed, overrode laws that he vetoed and failed to enact legislation that he advocated."[105]

Two episodes illustrate the change in Coolidge's leadership style as expressed by his increasing delegation of authority to members of the cabinet. In the first, when during a crisis in relations with China the acting secretary of state came to the White House to consult with the President, Coolidge told him, "I don't know anything about this. You do . . . and you're in charge. You settle the problem and I'll back you up."[106] On the second occasion, the secretary of labor, James J. Davis, tried to learn through a subordinate whether the President approved of some action he had taken in the Labor Department. When the relevant papers were offered to the President, he refused to read them, saying, "You tell ol' man Davis I hired him as Secretary of Labor and if he can't do the job I'll get a new Secretary of Labor."[107]

Undoubtedly the best description of Coolidge's relationship with his cabinet can be gleaned from his own words. At a meeting with the press on 15 April 1927, Coolidge remarked, "There isn't any division in the Cabinet over the policy that is pursued in China. I don't think that would be possible in my Cabinet. The way I transact the Cabinet business is to leave to the head of each Department the conduct of his own business."[108]

Coolidge felt that he had men around him "of sufficient ability so that they can solve all the problems that arise under their jurisdiction."[109] This attitude was in striking contrast to his past history. Even as a member of the Massachusetts House of Representatives, Coolidge had won attention for always being present at committee meetings and at sessions of the House: "He never missed the opening prayer and he never seemed in a hurry to get away during the daily sessions. He always voted and thoroughly investigated every matter before both of his Committees."[110] As governor of Massachusetts, he had performed effectively and established himself as a moderately progressive Republican leader.

It had been obvious since the beginning of his political career that, unlike William Howard Taft and other strict constructionist presidents, Coolidge did not have a theoretically negative or restrictive attitude toward the scope of executive power. That he was unwilling to restrict presidential powers to the language of the Constitution is evident in this passage from his autobiography:

The Constitution specifically vests him [the President] with the executive power. Some Presidents have seemed to interpret that as an authorization to take any action which the Constitution, or perhaps the law, does not specifically prohibit. Others have considered that their powers extended only to such acts as were specifically authorized by the Constitution and statutes. This has always seemed to me a hypothetical question which it would be idle to attempt to determine in advance. It would appear to be the better practice to wait to decide each question on its merits as it arises.[111]

Nonetheless, despite this elastic view of presidential power, Coolidge's administration began to crumble after the summer of 1924. The President withdrew almost completely from interaction with Congress and showed little inclination even to participate in the activities of the departments of his own government. His workdays began to shrink in length, and his naps grew considerably longer and more frequent. Sadly, his shrewdness turned to lack of interest, his involvement to indifference; and his well-developed leadership skills were abandoned.

It is clear from his behavior and also from his autobiography, published in 1929, that Coolidge's grief went beyond what most parents feel at a child's death. He saw his son's death as intertwined with, inseparable from, his presidency. He saw himself as guilty in several ways. In the first place, he blamed himself and his own political ambitions for creating the environment in which his son died: "We do not know what would have happened to him under other circumstances, but if I had not been President, he would not have raised a blister on his toe, which resulted in blood poisoning, playing lawn tennis on the South Grounds."[112] It appears also from the autobiography that Coolidge suffered another kind of guilt feeling which commonly afflicts those who have lost someone close to them. In this, according to the mental health specialist Erich Lindemann, the "bereaved searches the time before the death for evidence of failure to do right by the lost one. He accuses himself of negligence and exaggerates minor omissions."[113] Thus, Coolidge may well have looked back to the busy months before young Calvin died—months when, suddenly thrust into the presidency, he was relishing establishing his own administration and launching a campaign for the 1924 nomination and election battles—as a time when he was neglectful of his son.

Two additional and very striking themes emerge from Coolidge's autobiographical work. The first was that even though he was the President, with all the power of that office, he was powerless to help his own son: "In his suffering, he was asking me to make him well. I could not."[114] The President made the same remark in a conversation with William Allen White: "[W]hen he was suffering he begged me to help him. I could not."[115]

Second, Coolidge interpreted his son's death as a sign that he was being punished for being President: "I do not know why such a price was enacted for occupying the White House."[116] Perhaps, however, he did know, at least subconsciously. He had delighted intensely in the trappings of office—being the center of attention, having more clothes than other presidents, being surrounded by Secret Service men, and even in being able to insist on riding alone in his automobile while aides were forced to follow behind in other vehicles.[117] The chief White House usher at the time found that Coolidge displayed more "egotism, self-consciousness or whatever you call it" than any of the nine presidents he had served.[118] Subconsciously, the Puritan Coolidge may have viewed his son's death as God's veto of such frivolous behavior but he may have been reluctant, if not unable, to accept it as such.

Psychological Vulnerability

The early losses suffered at key points in Calvin Coolidge's boyhood created in him a vulnerability to loss which he could not transcend as President. Growing up in a household where one parent or the other was absent, his father through election to political office and his mother through sickness and death, and where he was expected to obey his elders without question, the future President developed a tendency to seek and find fault within himself. This is a not uncommon behavior pattern of children raised in a relationship based on authoritative power.[119] As an adult, the supposedly cool Coolidge gave evidence of severe tension and inner anger. The psychoanalyst Karen Horney tells us that inner rage is externalized in three principle ways, the first being irritability and temper tantrums: "Where giving vent to hostility is uninhibited, anger is easily thrust outward. It is turned then against others and appears either as irritability in general or as a specific irritation directed at the very faults in others that a person hates in himself."[120]

While Calvin Coolidge is well known for his long bouts of silence, another and much darker side of the man generally has escaped notice. Coolidge was not only nervous but also intensely irritable, keeping White House personnel "in a state of constant anxiety."[121] His surviving son later recalled that his father was "short-tempered [and] impatient," and that the presidency "got on his nerves."[122] In fact, this President was capable of volcanic eruptions of temper. As a long-time White House employee reported: "Those who saw Coolidge in a rage were simply startled. The older employees about the White House who had known [Theodore Roosevelt] used to think he raved at times, but in his worst temper, he was calm compared with Coolidge. . . . Many times, too, the cause was of but trifling importance."[123]

Thus, the President who projected the image of taciturnity and silence was, in fact, highly irascible and explosive in temperament. Irritability is often a close companion to bereavement,[124] and Coolidge's series of bereavements exacerbated his tendency toward impatience and ill temper. As a boy, growing up in a strictly controlled household, he had had to repress his anger; as a man, he allowed that anger to burst into view with surprising frequency. The outbursts that startled personnel in the White House throughout Coolidge's tenure there almost surely constituted an externalization of inner anger and deep depression, brought about by his tragic losses as both boy and man. In the most recent instance, if he had not been President, he wrote, his son would not have played that fateful game of tennis on the White House grounds and might have lived a long, productive life. Instead, he died at the age of sixteen, a victim, in a sense, of his father's own political ambitions.

A second method of externalizing rage is to focus on bodily disorders. Horney writes that "rage against the self . . . apparently creates physical tensions of considerable severity, which may appear as intestinal maladies, headaches, fatigue and so on."[125]

During Coolidge's years in the White House, he suffered various bouts with physical distress. He had trouble with his stomach and complained frequently of indigestion.[126] In the spring of 1925, he suffered a severe illness which may have been an indication of heart trouble. At a dinner for the cabinet in 1928, he became so ill that he had to leave the dining room.[127] Also in 1928, Grace Coolidge complained that her husband was exhausted and experiencing "quite a lot of trouble with his asthma—or whatever it is."[128] She also reported that he took "various sorts of pills upon slight provocation."[129] So concerned was the President with the possibility of cardiovascular disease that he insisted on having two electrocardiograms taken every day, and often sat at his desk taking his own pulse.[130]

While Coolidge's illnesses have not been reported widely, his presidential fatigue certainly has been. In his pre-1924 political career, he worked long hours at his desk, impressing many observers with his personal diligence. It is reported that as governor he consistently arrived at the office early and was busy throughout the day. Later, as vice president, he was at his desk from 9:00 A.M. until 5:00 P.M. every day, causing one Washington official, as I previously noted, to exclaim that Coolidge was different from other vice presidents in being busy not with social engagements but with matters of substance. Although one of his most famous remarks as a Massachusetts state senator had been "Do the Day's Work," after his son's death in July 1924, Calvin Coolidge ceased to live up to his own admonition, choosing instead to lose himself and to forget his problems in sleep. As President of the United States, he often slept as many as eleven hours a night—and then regularly took a nap each afternoon.[131] The President's proclivity for spending more than twelve of every twenty-four hours asleep became common knowledge. His typical workday of approximately four and a half hours is a far lighter schedule than that of most other presidents—indeed, of most other people.

A third way of externalizing rage "takes the form of an incessant conscious or unconscious fear or expectation that the faults which are intolerable to oneself will infuriate others." Horney suggests that "increased compliance is, in fact, one of the major consequences of this form of externalization."[132] Of course, such compliance was not characteristic of Coolidge's early years in political life or of his first year as President, when he showed initiative, shrewdness, and leadership in both foreign and domestic affairs. But, as I have indicated, after being elected to the office of President in his own right, Coolidge became less forthright, less interested, and more deferential to Congress and even to other executive-branch officials. Indeed, so disengaged did Coolidge become in the diplomatic realm that he has been described as being one of only two presidents in the twentieth century to make no significant contribution to foreign policy.[133] In short, Calvin Coolidge's withdrawal into a compliant self-effacement after his son's untimely death was yet another manifestation of his inner rage.

The American Psychiatric Association has established diagnostic criteria for major depressive episodes: (1) dysphoric mood or loss of interest or pleasure in all or almost all usual activities and pastimes, (2) insomnia or hypersomnia, (3) fatigue, (4) feelings of worthlessness or excessive or inappropriate guilt, (5) recurrent thoughts of death, and (6) indecisiveness.[134] In the period following his son's death, President Coolidge demonstrated patterns of behavior that correspond to each of these criteria.

Coolidge's unrelenting depression and self-directed anger can be explained by Erik H. Erikson's theory of life cycles. Erikson theorized that during the earliest months of life, the child develops its basic sense of trust and mistrust, which remains the source of both primal hope and of doom throughout life.[135] He postulated also that as a child matured, parental overcontrol led to a "lasting sense of doubt and shame."[136] During the last period of childhood, industriousness develops, although in conflict with feelings of unworthiness: Erikson warned that "the danger at this stage lies in the development of a sense of inadequacy."[137] Later, in middle age, the characteristic crisis is that of generativity, defined as "primarily the concern for establishing and guiding the next generation."[138] According to Erikson, "the crisis of middle age occurs when an original man first stops to realize what he has begun to originate in others."[139]

Calvin Coolidge's boyhood experiences established a framework for his later crisis of generativity. Although he was born into a comfortable and caring family, the various events of severe deprivation he suffered in his youth likely engendered in him feelings of mistrust toward his environment. It began shortly after his birth with his father's spending part of each year away from home in the Vermont legislature, leaving young Calvin in the care of his sickly and complaining mother. Then young Calvin found that faithfully doing his duty and successfully carrying out his responsibilities, in accordance with the dictates of his elders, did not always result in personal happiness and self-contentment. Nor could they compensate for the deaths of his beloved mother and sister when he was an adolescent.

For years, Calvin Coolidge continued to persevere, eventually establishing a family and building a successful and productive political career in Massachusetts. Although his devoted stepmother's death in 1920 contributed to his decision to terminate an early move at the White House that year, later—during his first year as President—Coolidge clearly "did the day's work," just as he had as vice president, as governor, and as state legislator. Although not an unabashed activist or extrovert, he demonstrated distinct leadership abilities and considerable political shrewdness in the months following his elevation to the White House. The culmination of his efforts came in his easy nomination victory at the Republican National Convention of 1924. Once again, however, his hard work and conscientious activity did not prevent tragedy from entering his life. This time, his younger son and namesake was taken from him at a key point in his life. His power as President of the United States was not sufficient to allow him to save his child. This was a crisis of generativity which Calvin Coolidge, as President, did not survive.

Blaming his political ambitions and his intense enjoyment of the presidency for his son's death, he withdrew from his executive responsibilities, lost interest in politics, and served out his years in the White House as an essentially broken man. He had worked long, hard, and successfully but had still been forced to pay intolerably for occupying—and for wanting to occupy—the White House. His response to the "punishment" was obvious: political withdrawal and immobilization.

Of Mahatma Gandhi, Erikson has said:

That . . . he emerged as the father of his country only lends greater importance to the fact that the middle span of life is under the dominance of the universal human need and strength which I have come to subsume under the term generativity. I have said that in this stage a man and a woman must have defined for themselves what and whom they have come to care for, what they care to do well, and how they plan to take care of what they have started and created.[140]

Calvin Coolidge also became father of his country in middle age. As a result of his belief that he had "failed" as father to his son at the ultimate crisis, Coolidge's sense of himself as father to his country suffered and died. He spoke too truly when he recognized that with his son's death there vanished also the power and glory of the presidency.

Chapter THREE
Functioning in Chains:
Franklin D. Roosevelt

ranklin D. Roosevelt served as President of the United States for a longer time than any other man in American history. Despite the image of energy and strength he projected, Roosevelt was afflicted by both disability and serious illness while in the White House. He had never recovered fully from his 1921 bout with polio, a fact concealed from the public for many years lest it might be detrimental to his political career. The methods of concealment, involving both image control and media management, produced a veil of secrecy that was not penetrated until long after his death. Also, after several years in office, Roosevelt began to suffer from cardiovascular disease which eventually ended his life. Contrary to the widespread belief at the time, his death was in no way sudden or unanticipated.

Although, to his critics, Roosevelt's physical deterioration had a negative influence on his performance as President during the crucial years of the Depression and the Second World War, particularly at the Yalta Conference in early 1945, it is now possible to judge more fully the accuracy of this notion.

The Early Years

Franklin Delano Roosevelt's medical problems began on the day of his birth, 30 January 1882. An excessive amount of pain-killing chloroform was given to his mother, and the child entered the world "in a deathlike respiratory standstill, the skin blue, the body limp," requiring mouth to

Much of this chapter was published in my article "Disability and Illness in the White House: The Case of Franklin D. Roosevelt," *Politics and the Life Sciences* (August 1988): 33–50.

mouth resuscitation to bring him around.[1] Franklin's mother later said that the nurse attending the birth never expected the baby to survive and was surprised that he did.[2] Although the dangerous level of chloroform was not fatal to the child, it proved damaging to his mucous membranes and likely brought on, just a few days after his birth,[3] the first of the colds that would afflict him frequently during the rest of his life.

As a young man, Franklin was afflicted with a wide variety of ailments. In 1912, he was stricken with typhoid fever; in 1913, severe stomach distress; in 1915, appendicitis and lumbago; in 1916 and 1917, serious throat infections; in 1918, double pneumonia and severe influenza.[4] A year later, at the age of thirty-seven, he had his tonsils removed. Throughout these years, sinusitis was the constant companion from which he could not escape.

Roosevelt's frequent episodes of ill health did not prevent him from engaging in a vigorous life of public service. Within five years of his marriage to his distant cousin Eleanor—a marriage that would produce a daughter and five sons, one of whom would die in infancy—he ran for the New York State Senate and captured a traditionally Republican seat for the Democrats. He was re-elected in 1912 but not long after was appointed Assistant Secretary of the Navy by President Woodrow Wilson. While holding that position in Washington, Roosevelt entered the 1914 New York State Democratic primary for the United States Senate but went down to defeat. In 1920 he was nominated for Vice President of the United States on a ticket headed by Governor James Cox of Ohio. Although he waged a strenuous campaign, the Republican ticket of Harding and Coolidge swept the nation.

In August 1921, while vacationing with his family in Campobello, Maine, the future President was stricken with an illness that would dramatically affect the rest of his life. He had been complaining for several days of "feeling logy and tired,"[5] but was following his usual vigorous regimen. One day, while riding in a boat, he fell overboard, and the water seemed extraordinarily cold. The next day, after intense exercise, he went for a swim in Glen Severn Lake and then in the icy waters of the Bay of Fundy. After returning home, he sat in his bathing suit reading letters, soon began to complain of a severe chill, and went to bed. On awakening the next morning, he felt acute pain in his left leg. His wife later wrote of that day:

He had quite a temperature. . . . I decided that the best thing to do was to get everybody off on a camping trip, though I was sufficiently worried not to consider going myself. . . . The trip lasted three days, and by the time the campers were back it was evident that my husband's legs were getting badly paralyzed.[6]

Roosevelt's son James later wrote that, by the third day of the illness, "the paralysis had spread to practically all of Father's muscles from the chest down."[7] Unfortunately the first two doctors who examined the stricken man misdiagnosed his illness, first as a bad cold, then as a blood clot in the lower spinal cord, and finally as a spinal cord lesion.[8] The physician who offered the latter two erroneous judgments recommended heavy leg massages as the most appropriate remedy, but that remedy may well have worsened the situation.[9] Finally, in the face of Franklin's deepening paralysis and intense pain, another doctor was summoned to the bedside, and he diagnosed the illness as poliomyelitis. Roosevelt was removed secretly from Campobello—he wanted no outsider to know the extent of his illness—and began a long and difficult period of convalescence, with six weeks spent in the hospital and many months of treatment undergone at his home in Hyde Park, New York.

In November, Roosevelt took a turn for the worse. The tendons in his right leg stiffened so severely that both legs had to be placed in plaster casts; and every day for several weeks, wedges had to be forced deeper and deeper into each cast behind the knee so that the legs would become unlocked and unbent.[10] The pain accompanying this treatment was severe.

Also severe was the strain on Roosevelt's family. His camaraderie with his children was necessarily curtailed, and there was acrimonious friction between his wife and his mother over his care.[11] Eleanor later wrote that she tried to maintain both her composure and a semblance of family life during her husband's convalescence, but that one day, while reading to her two youngest sons, she broke down uncontrollably:

I suddenly found myself sobbing as I read. I could not think why I was sobbing, nor could I stop. Elliot [another son] came in from school, dashed in to look at me and fled. Mr. Howe [Louis Howe, a Roosevelt aide] came in and tried to find out what the matter was, but he gave it up as a bad job. The two little boys went off to bed and I sat on the sofa in the sitting room and sobbed and sobbed.[12]

During this dark period, Roosevelt himself experienced moods of fear and despondency.[13] His secretary, Missy LeHand, once said that "there were days . . . when it was noon before he could pull himself out of depression and greet his guests wearing his lighthearted façade."[14] Roosevelt later told Labor Secretary Frances Perkins that in the early days of his illness, when even his arms were affected, his despair had been absolute because he felt that God had abandoned him.[15]

In his outward behavior, however, Roosevelt did not complain or give vent to his frustrations. His wife heard him express discouragement or bitterness on only one occasion when, years after the onset of the disease, he referred to himself as a "helpless individual."[16] To some of his associates, he indicated that he expected to recover fully from his affliction which, among friends, he treated without embarrassment, even allowing them to see him crawling across the floor.[17] In 1924, he talked about playing golf again and, a year later, remarked that he hoped "to be able to walk by this time next year."[18]

To facilitate his recovery, Roosevelt began spending a considerable amount of time at Warm Springs, Georgia, where the pool was rich in minerals and stood at a constant temperature of 88 degrees. During his first six weeks at Warm Springs in October 1924, he regained for the first time some sensation in his toes, the most significant advance he had made against his illness since being stricken.[19] Two years later, he would buy the entire Warm Springs property for use as a hydrotherapeutic center.

In the mid-1920s, Roosevelt also began to re-emerge as a public figure. In 1924, he agreed to put into nomination at the Democratic National Convention the name of New York's Governor Alfred E. Smith. Each day of the convention, prior to the arrival of the other delegates, Roosevelt would be taken by wheelchair to the auditorium entrance closest to the seats of the New York delegation. There his leg braces "would be locked and he would be pulled to a standing position. With James [his son] on one arm and a crutch under the other, he would slowly make his way down the aisle."[20] After giving his eloquent speech on behalf of Smith on the climactic night of the convention, Roosevelt allowed himself to be seen being wheeled from the hall, an event that would not soon be repeated.[21]

Four years later, he again placed Smith's name in nomination. This time, loath to use crutches since they symbolized invalidism, Roosevelt developed a method of movement that made it appear he was walking:

Elliot would stand, holding his right arm flexed at a ninety-degree angle, his forearm rigid as a parallel bar. Roosevelt would stand beside Elliot, tightly gripping his son's arm. In his right hand Roosevelt held a cane. His right arm was straight and held rigid with his index finger pressing firmly straight down along the line of the cane. In this posture he could "walk," although in a curious toddling manner, hitching up first

one leg with the aid of the muscles along the side of his trunk, then placing his weight
upon that leg, then using the muscles along his other side, and hitching the other leg
forward—first one side and then the other, and so on and so on.[22]

It was also in 1928 that Franklin Roosevelt actively—if somewhat ambivalently[23]—resumed his own political career by accepting the Democratic party's nomination for governor of New York. Anxious to counteract public rumors and Republican newspaper intimations that he was physically not up to the demands of high office, Roosevelt forbade newspaper photographers and cameramen to take pictures of him being pushed in his wheelchair or being lifted in or out of automobiles. Remarkably by contemporary media standards, the press complied, enabling the Democratic candidate to portray himself as a recovered polio patient. He told one audience:

Seven years ago in the epidemic in New York, I came down with infantile paralysis,
a perfectly normal attack, and I was completely, for the moment, put out of any
useful activities. By personal good fortune I was able to get the very best of care and
the result of having the best kind of care is that today I am on my feet.[24]

During his gubernatorial campaign, Roosevelt championed the cause of state aid for people crippled by disease. In a speech at Rochester, New York, he pointed out:

More than 100,000 adults and children in this state are crippled from infantile
paralysis and other diseases, most of them so seriously that they are unable to live
normal or useful lives. Unfortunately, most of the crippled in this state are unable to
afford either the cost or the time for treatment. Clearly it is the duty of the state and
local Governments to help provide the definite medical help available. It is just as
much a State duty as the providing of education.[25]

Although 1928 was a Republican year, Roosevelt was elected governor of New York and immediately became a leading and apparently willing contender for the Democratic party's 1932 presidential nomination.[26] Even though governor of a northern state, Roosevelt had considerable southern support, in part because of all the time he had spent in Georgia trying to recover from his physical affliction. On the fourth ballot at their nominating convention, the Democrats nominated Franklin D. Roosevelt for President. In a then-unprecedented move clearly designed to demonstrate his vigor, the candidate became the first in history to travel to his party's convention to accept personally his nomination.

Deeply concerned that the image of a "permanently crippled man"[27] seeking to lead a crippled nation out of the Depression would be damaging to his campaign, Roosevelt's aides made every effort to portray the Democratic nominee as a man who had conquered polio and who could walk. As he traveled across the country, his leg braces, without which he could not stand, had to be put on and locked into place before each campaign appearance and then taken off again immediately thereafter because of the discomfort they caused him. In getting on and off his campaign train, he was often seen "walking" up and down a long, narrow ramp specially constructed with a strong hand railing which he could grip and use to pull himself forward.[28]

The lecterns at which he spoke were normally bolted to the floor so that he could lean on them for support while in a standing position. Once, while speaking in Georgia, the table against which he was leaning slipped away from him, and he fell to the floor. Aides quickly lifted him to his feet, and he resumed his speech without making any public reference to the unpleasant and awkward experience that had just occurred.[29] The press, observing the unwritten rule imposed on them by the Roosevelt camp, made no mention of the incident.

The First Two Terms: 1933–41

Even after his landslide election, Roosevelt continued his efforts to conceal the effects of his illness. His leg braces were painted black so as to be indistinguishable from the black shoes and socks he wore.[30] His wheelchairs were armless so that he could move more rapidly into and out of automobiles or onto other chairs. One of his Secret Service agents described the method he used for moving from wheelchair to car:

[H]e would turn his back to the car and allow an agent to lift him from his wheelchair to a standing posture. He would reach backward and grab the car door with both hands and then he'd actually surge out of your arms first to the jump seat, then to the rear one. He did this with such speed and grace that literally thousands who saw him at ball games, rallies and inaugurations never suspected his condition.[31]

At the White House, no pictures of Roosevelt in his wheelchair were permitted, nor were pictures of the President being heavily assisted up flights of stairs or carried by his bodyguards.[32] If this rule was violated, members of the Secret Service were not averse to seizing the camera of the offending party and exposing the film.[33] Photographs were normally taken from the waist up, and those that did show FDR's leg braces were generally touched up so as to be obscured. Rumor has it that in 1936 an unfriendly newspaper publisher attempted to assemble pictures harmful to Roosevelt and publish them before the November election, but that the President's friends in the White House press corps assisted the Secret Service by preventing the damaging photographs from being taken.[34] In 1937, a popular magazine carried a picture of Roosevelt being pushed in his wheelchair but at such a distance from the camera as to substantially mute the impact.[35]

Of all the many thousands of pictures taken of Roosevelt, only a small handful clearly showed him seated in his wheelchair, even though toward the end of his long presidency he became more candid about his incapacity. The vast majority of photographs gave no hint of his physical limitations and instead showed a smiling, jaunty President, with head thrown back in delight, as he grappled with the problems besetting the nation. He was even photographed while standing at the rear of railway cars, speaking and waving to cheering crowds, and in the presidential box as he threw out the first ball of the Washington baseball season. Roosevelt's physical presence as conveyed by the press and movie newsreels, coupled with his strong, self-assured radio voice,[36] encouraged a stricken nation to believe that all would be well.

So completely and successfully was Roosevelt's image controlled that even the head usher at the White House reports that he was shocked when he saw the President for the first time:

On my second day in the White House, Charles Claunch, the usher on duty, took me on the elevator to the second floor. The door opened, and the Secret Service guard wheeled in the President of the United States. Startled, I looked down at him. It was only then that I realized that Franklin D. Roosevelt was really paralyzed. Immediately I understood why this fact had been kept so secret. Everybody knew that the President had been stricken with infantile paralysis, and his recovery was legend but few people were aware how completely the disease had handicapped him.[37]

The cooperation of news photographers and cameramen was, of course, essential to the managing of Roosevelt's physical image, but the White House took other steps at image control as well. For example, at state dinners, President Roosevelt was wheeled into the dining room and seated first, before other guests began filing into the room. The wheelchair would be removed from the premises before the dining room doors were opened.

More elaborate mechanisms were used at formal receptions. White House gardeners would set up a wall of ferns at one end of the reception room, and a special seat, similar to that of a bicycle, would be placed among and concealed by the ferns. Sitting on the hidden seat, the President would appear all the time to be standing. At some formal ceremonies, aides would close the double doors of the reception room after all the guests had entered. The President would ride or be pushed in his wheelchair to the closed doors and be helped to his feet. Then the doors would be thrown open dramatically, and the President, on the arm of an aide, would swing his legs two or three steps to the podium which he would grasp for support as he spoke.[38] While these entrances were sometimes regarded as presidential theatrics, they were, in fact, skillful attempts to camouflage the President's severe physical affliction. The White House was so effective at managing news about the President's crippled legs that one prominent writer recalled that "during the 1930's when I lived in Europe I repeatedly met men in important positions who had no idea that the President was disabled."[39]

The effects of polio were not Roosevelt's only physical problems during his early years in the White House. He also suffered from severe head colds and persistent sinusitis for which he received daily treatments. Although Dr. Ross McIntire, the White House physician during the Roosevelt years, prescribed these daily sinus treatments, the First Lady later admitted, "I always worried about the constant treatment for I felt that while this might help temporarily, in the long run it might cause irritation."[40]

According to one of his closest associates, President Roosevelt also suffered from "irregular but not infrequent intestinal disturbances" and once had a problem with a wisdom tooth "which spread some infection into his jaw."[41] He also had bronchitis and suffered several bouts with influenza. But with his strong recuperative powers, he always seemed to bounce back quickly from these ailments.

The one illness at this point in his life from which he did not bounce back satisfactorily was, of course, poliomyelitis. That disease sharply limited his mobility, contributed to the kidney problems resulting from years spent in a sitting position,[42] and produced occasional instances of acute embarrassment—for example, when he fell in the 1932 campaign and again in 1936, as he approached the podium to accept his second nomination for the presidency. Although he was reported to be "badly shaken" by the latter incident,[43] he went on to deliver a memorable address, telling his audience, "This generation of Americans has a rendezvous with destiny."[44]

In addition to the overt physical impact of polio, the disease had other, more subtle effects on Roosevelt and his career. First, if Roosevelt had not been stricken in 1921, he might well have run for office again during the high point of the Harding and Coolidge era and suffered a defeat more serious than that of his 1920 vice-presidential bid. Back-to-back electoral routs might well have ended his political career. Columnist Joseph Alsop has suggested that if Roosevelt had never become afflicted with polio, he might have challenged Alfred E. Smith for the New York governorship in 1922; but since Roosevelt's physical condition at the time prevented him from running, "he was the leader of the New York Democrats who pressed Smith to make the fight, and he gained thereby,"[45] eventually being chosen by Smith to be his successor in Albany. Roosevelt's polio attack, then, may have, in slowing down his political career, ultimately advanced it.

Second, Roosevelt may have moved further to the political left as he came to recognize the need for government intervention to help people in great distress.[46] Greater rapport with those in need of help was a likely and understandable consequence of his bout with debilitating disease, as noted by some of the people closest to him. One of his sons later said that he believed that polio had "broadened his father's compassion."[47] His wife, in answer to the question whether she thought that her husband's illness had "affected his mentality," replied, "I am glad that question was asked. The answer is yes. Anyone who has gone through great suffering is bound to have a greater sympathy and understanding of the problems of mankind."[48] And, in one of his most memorable addresses, the President himself underscored this point when he proclaimed: "Governments can err. Presidents do make mistakes, but the immortal Dante tells us that divine justice weighs the sins of the cold-blooded and the sins of the warm-hearted on different scales."[49]

Third, Roosevelt clearly was sensitized by his illness to the importance of adequate health care for the general public. In his first message as governor to the New York State legislature in 1929, he advocated state aid to cripples.[50] And as President, he stated that he regarded "the building of a vigorous and healthy population as one of the most important movements for adequate national defense."[51]

Fourth, Roosevelt's long and difficult bout with polio seems to have strengthened his character by giving him greater self-control and by making him more patient and perhaps less arrogant. Grace Tully, his secretary, described Roosevelt's equinamity as he confronted his physical limitations: "The Boss never indulged in self-pity or otherwise gave outward indication that he felt annoyance at the restrictions caused by his illness."[52] The President himself once remarked that "if you had spent two years in bed trying to wiggle your big toe, after that anything else would seem easy."[53] Labor Secretary Perkins, one of his closest confidantes, believed that in addition to making him more patient, FDR's bout with polio had caused him to lose "the slightly arrogant attitude he had displayed on occasion before he was stricken."[54] Perhaps a 1933 *New York Times* article summarized the situation best when it pointed out that Franklin Roosevelt functioned smoothly because "he has learned to function in chains."[55]

Polio's effects on the development of Roosevelt's character, although not as obvious as the physical effects I have described, may have been the most important in terms of his presidency. Compassion and perseverance were the characteristics that, at least in part, led his administration to be judged one of the most successful in American history. The cartoons and caricatures that portrayed Roosevelt not as a cripple but as an active, vibrant, and sympathetic leader may well have captured the essence of the man and his presidency.

During Roosevelt's second term in the White House, some of his associates saw early signs of physical deterioration. His postmaster general has recounted that he found indications of poor health as early as 1937.[56] According to his secretary, the President suffered a fainting spell at Hyde Park in 1938 but recovered within fifteen minutes and joined his guests at dinner.[57] While some commentators have suggested that it was around this time that Roosevelt began to show the symptoms of small strokes,[58] his physician, his secretary, and his son-in-law, himself a medical doctor, have each denied that the President ever suffered a stroke prior to the two massive cerebral hemorrhages that ended his life.[59]

Questions about Roosevelt's health began to multiply at his press conferences. Whereas nine health-related questions were put to him by reporters during his first term in the White House, fourteen questions on the subject were asked of him during his second term.[60] In 1940, despite the concerns of the press, Franklin Roosevelt shattered precedent by seeking and being elected to a third term as President, even though apparently he had intended to follow the two-term tradition until events in Europe caused him to change his thinking.[61]

The Third Term: 1941–45

During his third term, Roosevelt's physical condition began clearly to deteriorate, and the deterioration did not pertain to his crippled legs. Indeed, he had become more open about that disability: he even allowed himself to be seen in his wheelchair while visiting soldiers who had lost their legs in the war, as he wanted them to see that he was crippled just as they were.[62] More serious than infantile paralysis, the physical problems that began to show themselves at this time were directly life threatening.

Roosevelt had been President of the United States longer than any other man in history. He had faced a domestic crisis of severe proportions and then saw his nation go to war against the Axis powers. It is not surprising that the stress which Roosevelt encountered and its unusual duration began to undermine his health, whatever the respites his successes as President may have provided.

The respites, however, were only temporary, since no president can escape completely from the heavy responsibilities of the office. Even while on vacation, presidents find that the White House and its cares follow them wherever they go. Franklin Roosevelt's secretary underscored this point when she wrote that the President had no opportunity for rest and relaxation from his responsibilities since his "so called vacations were punctuated by periods of daily work, dropped on his desk wherever it was by air-borne daily mail pouches and a car filled with radio and telegraph equipment."[63]

Whereas systolic hypertension had been detected in Roosevelt as early as 1937, diastolic hypertension, much more serious, was diagnosed in 1941, the year of formal U.S. entry into the Second World War.[64] Also, electrocardiogram readings in 1941 showed signs of lack of oxygen to the heart; the level of hemoglobin in the blood at this time was considerably below normal, and iron deficiency anemia was detected.[65] Records indicate that five scheduled press conferences were canceled during 1941 because of the President's illnesses.[66]

Roosevelt's physician later wrote that at this time the President's "blood pressure remained on an excellent level . . . and his cardiovascular measurements were within normal standards for a man of his age."[67] Still, Dr. McIntire was a nose-and-throat specialist who, because of the President's sinusitis, was described by one of the President's sons as "just the man for Pa."[68] Perhaps a cardiovascular specialist would have viewed Roosevelt's condition differently and taken effective steps to treat his ailments.

After his return from the Teheran Conference in December 1943, the President's decline accelerated. At that conference he had suffered such an acute abdominal attack that fears were actually expressed that he might have been poisoned.[69] One of his closest aides described him as being "bone tired" and "exhausted" from the trip.[70] Roosevelt went to Hyde Park to recuperate and to celebrate the Christmas holidays with his family and friends. Instead, he came down with a severe case of influenza which proved particularly resistant to treatment. Almost certainly the worst feature of this flu attack was the racking cough the President developed which prevented him from sleeping. Even his perennially optimistic physician admitted that this gave him his "greatest concern."[71] McIntire later explained, "His heart, of course, became a subject of concern because of his continual coughing and in order to lessen the load on it, we decided to institute a gradual reduction in diet that would lower his weight by ten pounds."[72]

The First Lady has reported that throughout the winter of 1943–44, the President ran "a low fever at intervals" and "seemed to feel miserable."[73] He himself pointed out that during the first three months of 1944 he had suffered from bronchial pneumonia.[74] In early February, he had a cyst removed from the back of his head[75]—an operation that was conducted by two doctors at Bethesda Naval Hospital and lasted some thirty minutes. In recognition of the President's heavy smoking habit, a reporter asked him whether the doctors had allowed him to smoke while they were "hacking." Roosevelt replied that they had not, but that he had called for a cigarette right after it was over.[76]

During this period, the President's color was ashen gray, his hands trembled badly, his appetite was poor, and he complained of headaches.[77] For several months he had experienced difficulty in sleeping in a supine position and had had thick boards placed under the head of his bed in order to elevate his upper body so that he could rest more peacefully.[78] Nevertheless, he often seemed tired even shortly after awakening in the morning, and deep circles appeared below his eyes. He also suffered from recurrent upper-tract respiratory infections and from brief periods of abdominal discomfort and distention, accompanied by heavy perspiration.[79]

In late March 1944, after the President's cough had persisted for several months, he was given an extensive physical examination by Dr. Howard Bruenn, a cardiologist called in for consultation. Dr. Bruenn found that in addition to his acute bronchial difficulties, Roosevelt suffered from moderately severe and well-advanced hypertension, obstructive pulmonary disease, and congestive heart failure.[80] Fluid was entering his lungs, and their ability to oxygenate his slowly circulating blood was impaired, causing a bluish tinge in his lips and fingernails.[81]

Bruenn found that the President's heart was grossly enlarged, particularly the left ventricle. The cardiologist heard a "blowing sound," which indicated that the mitral valve was not closing properly, and detected a "blowing systolic murmur," resulting from too much pressure being exerted on the aortic valve.[82] In all, Bruenn was deeply concerned by Roosevelt's physical decline. The report he made to Dr. McIntire was dire in its ultimate judgment: The President might die at any moment. With proper treatment, he might live on for months, maybe even a year or two.[83]

Dr. McIntire had ordered Bruenn to report his findings directly to him and to no one else. As a result, neither Roosevelt nor members of his family were told of the disturbing facts, and the President did not even bother to ask. Perhaps he knew without asking or no longer cared; perhaps he feared that even his doctors did not know the cause of his decline.[84] In any event, he showed no interest at all in discussing his prognosis.[85] Even after Dr. Bruenn became one of Roosevelt's regular attending physicians, he continued to send his reports on the President's condition directly to McIntire, and there are even suggestions that McIntire may have hidden or destroyed them.[86]

It has also been reported that McIntire was so guarded about the President's condition as to be reluctant to provide Bruenn with the results of his previous physical examinations, initially claiming that he was uncertain he could locate them.[87] This made a real problem for the cardiologist in light of Roosevelt's unwillingness to volunteer medical information about himself;[88] and Bruenn properly reminded McIntire that, without the results of previous checkups, he could make no comparative analysis of Roosevelt's condition. McIntire finally sent them to his colleague but ordered their return as soon as the examination was completed.

While secrecy was to be strictly maintained, McIntire did assemble a group of prominent physicians to discuss Bruenn's findings. The group included three physicians from the Bethesda Naval Hospital as well as an Atlanta cardiovascular specialist, an internist, and the director of the Lahey Clinic in Boston. The latter member of the group was particularly interested in the President's gastrointestinal tract but felt at the time that surgery was not indicated.[89] The medical team came to agree, however, that other treatment was necessary. Digitalis began to be given to the President for his symptoms of heart failure, and cigarettes were curtailed immediately. A low-fat, salt-restricted, 2,600-calorie diet was prescribed, and phenobarbital was administered for his high blood pressure.[90] Dr. McIntire, however, still told the press that "the check-up is satisfactory. When we got through, we decided that for a man of sixty-two we have very little to argue about."[91]

It was around the same time that Roosevelt's secretary noticed that he would doze off while reading his mail or even while giving dictation. Even though she detected no "diminution of clarity or sparkle in his words or his thoughts," the condition began to show itself more and more frequently, and she was seriously alarmed.[92] Tully consulted the President's daughter, who had become his constant companion since December 1943 and had recently noticed that, while watching motion pictures, her father's mouth hung open for long periods.[93] Both women spoke with Dr. McIntire and were pleased to learn that, while there was no cause for alarm, a new schedule was being instituted for the President which was designed to conserve his strength and energy. He was to have breakfast in his quarters each morning, spend two hours in the office, preferably with no irritation, then return to his quarters for lunch. After lunch, the President was to lie down for an hour before returning to his desk for two hours of afternoon work—again, preferably with no irritation. This period of work would be followed by an ultraviolet-light treatment, a rubdown, and then another hour of lying-down rest. There would be no working after dinner, and the President was to get ten hours of sleep each night.[94] While McIntire assured the women that Roosevelt was not dangerously ill, the sharply restricted workday of only four hours, along with the prescribed ten hours of sleep and two hours of lying-down rest, strongly suggests otherwise.

By the spring of 1944, the President's voice had grown so weak that he could not always be heard at press conferences.[95] Reporters could not help but notice his lack of animation, his flashes of irritation, and, of course, his gaunt physical appearance. They asked him questions about his health at five press conferences during that spring alone.[96] Journalist Merriman Smith wrote that Roosevelt's press conferences became increasingly less productive, and that he became "listless," "poor of voice," and "increasingly quarrelsome about petty things."[97]

The Fourth Campaign and Inauguration: 1944–45

Despite the President's obvious and dangerous physical decline, he agreed to accept his party's nomination in 1944 for a fourth term. Although several of his associates intended to tell Roosevelt that he was too ill to seek another term, at the last moment they failed to do so.[98] One New York leader urged the First Lady to try to dissuade her husband from running again;[99] but her attitude was that it would have been extremely difficult to have a transition in power at that difficult point in history, and that if the President would follow his doctors' orders, "he could stand going on with his work."[100] The latter assessment was shared by Dr. McIntire, who stated that "every possible checkup proved him organically sound," and that he could "stand up under the strain of four more years."[101] Yet, on the very eve of the convention, one of his sons became alarmed when the President suddenly "began to groan and his face took on an expression of suffering." He told his son that he had "a horrible pain," and that "I don't know if I can make it."[102] The problem appears to have been a severe gallbladder attack.

At the Democratic conclave in July, Roosevelt's health was the major topic of conversation, although "discussed largely in whispers."[103] By that time he had lost not only the prescribed ten pounds but five additional pounds as well, bringing his weight substantially below normal. The weight loss made him look ten years older, caused his clothes to appear too large for his shrunken frame, and conveyed an unmistakable impression of physical deterioration.[104] One visitor at the time described the appearance of the President's face as "almost ravaged."[105] Roosevelt's gauntness was not unusual for persons with severe heart problems. Doctors would term this condition "cardiac cachexia."[106]

Because of the belief of many party leaders that Roosevelt would not survive another term in the White House, great attention began to be focused on the vice-presidential nomination. Many influential Democrats perceived the incumbent vice president, Henry Wallace, as being too left-wing to stand only a heartbeat away from the presidency. Roosevelt's first vice president, John Nance Garner, looked upon the possibility of Wallace's accession to the White House as "repulsive," and Secretary of State Cordell Hull echoed that sentiment.[107] The most likely replacements for Wallace included Supreme Court Justice William O. Douglas, former South Carolina Senator James Byrnes, and Missouri Senator Harry Truman. Despite Eleanor Roosevelt's efforts to keep Wallace on the ticket,[108] the vice president was replaced by Truman, a more moderate Democrat.

The President himself was highly ambivalent about the identity of his vice presidential running mate, plunging convention delegates into a "delicious state of confusion" and disappointing both Wallace and Byrnes by failing to fully back them.[109]

As his final campaign got under way, Roosevelt delivered a speech at the Puget Sound Naval Base in a standing position. Because of his weight loss, his leg braces no longer fit him properly and gave him little support as he spoke; instead, he had to cling to the podium in order to remain on his feet.[110] At the conclusion of his remarks, the President suffered sharp chest pains, apparently an angina attack which indicated coronary deficiency.[111] Roosevelt was then advised by his doctor to refrain from engaging in a strenuous speaking tour and to rely instead on radio speeches.[112] However, the rumors of ill health, fanned by publication of a picture of a haggard and glassy-eyed President delivering his nomination acceptance speech,[113] became so prevalent that the Democrats scheduled campaign appearances in New York, Boston, Chicago, and Washington, D.C. During his New York appearance, the gravely ill chief executive rode in an open car through a driving rain for more than four hours. From time to time, Roosevelt's car would drive into heated garage areas along the parade route where

Secret Service agents quickly lifted [him] from the car and stretched him out full length in blankets laid on the floor. They removed his clothes down to the skin. He was towelled dry and given a rubdown. He was redressed in dry clothes, brandy was poured down his throat and he was lifted back into the car.[114]

One of his aides reported that the President emerged from his drenching visit to New York in "a state of high exhilaration, grateful to the disagreeable elements for giving him such a fine opportunity to prove that he could take it."[115] His campaign speeches proved that he could give it as well, filled as they were with flashes of the style and combativeness that had endeared him to millions. His speech to the Teamsters Union that fall was a political masterpiece. In that address, he dismissed complaints that he was a tired old man, reminded voters again of the Hoover Depression, attacked Old Guard Republicans, and objected to the "libelous statements" being made about "my little dog Fala." Roosevelt told the delighted crowd that Fala's "Scotch soul was furious" about a story concocted by "Republican fiction writers" that he had been rescued from an Aleutian island by the navy at a cost of "two or three or twenty million dollars" and that he had "not been the same dog since."[116]

Although his speeches and campaign appearances rekindled public confidence in Roosevelt's well-being, they undoubtedly inflicted a toll on the seriously ill President. One observer reported that "the strain of campaigning showed on the President's face."[117] Another remarked that he was "shocked" at Roosevelt's physical appearance on election night, that he "looked older than I had ever seen him" and that his "speech was irrelevant much of the time. . . ."[118]

The dying President received more than 53 percent of the popular vote in 1944 and carried thirty-six states. On the night of his victory, he refused to put on his leg braces and instead allowed himself to be wheeled out to speak to his Hyde Park neighbors. A photograph captured the smiling President, seated in his wheelchair and wearing the hat and cape that had become his trademarks, as he responded happily to the cheers of the moment.

Throughout the campaign months, Roosevelt had continued to lose weight and, by December 1944, was some 23 to 30 pounds below his normal weight of 188 to 190. Concerned about this severe weight loss, his doctors temporarily stopped giving him digitalis in the hope that his appetite would improve. When his appetite remained poor, the digitalis treatments were resumed, and the weight loss continued.[119]

The problem was compounded by the fact that Roosevelt had ignored his prescribed rest regimen during part of the campaign and continued to do so in the weeks before the inauguration. McIntire has written that the "President did not seem able to rid himself of a sense of terrible urgency and even [his daughter] could not keep him from working through the entire day and well into the night. . . . Any reminder of his promise to live within his reserves brought the old answer that there was a job to be done."[120] As a result, his condition seems to have worsened.[121] At a cabinet meeting on 19 January 1945, Labor Secretary Perkins thought that he looked to be in poor shape, the worst she had ever seen him.[122] When she spoke with him afterward, the President had to support his head, as though it were too heavy to hold up, with one of his hands. When Perkins tried to discuss her planned resignation from the cabinet, as well as possible replacements, Roosevelt interrupted her impatiently: "No, Frances. You can't go now. You mustn't put this on me now. I just can't be bothered now. I can't think of anyone else and I can't get used to anyone else. Not now! Do stay there and don't say anything. You are all right."[123]

The President had determined that his fourth inaugural would be a subdued affair, without the customary parades, pomp, and circumstance.

While the war effort was cited as the reason for the shortened and simplified ceremony, Roosevelt's poor health was an unspoken but important factor. The President did insist, however, that all thirteen of his grandchildren must attend the ceremony no matter how reduced in splendor it might be. Eleanor believed that his insistence was due to the fact that this would certainly be his last inauguration and perhaps to his "premonition that he would not be with us long."[124]

On Inauguration Day, President Roosevelt delivered his address at the White House instead of the Capitol. He spoke well[125] but, to some onlookers, appeared to be in considerable distress. Vice President Truman saw expressions of pain on the President's face,[126] and Secretary of State Edward R. Stettinius noted that "he seemed to tremble all over. It was not just his hands that shook but his whole body as well."[127] One of Roosevelt's sons has reported that the President looked very ill at his final inauguration: his color was bad, he looked extremely tired, and he was short of breath. When he spoke with his father in private about his physical condition, the President tried to assure him that he was all right, even though a little tired, but then confided that he did not think he could make it through the day's inaugural reception where he would have to shake hands with so many people. He also discussed his will and the plans he had made for his burial.[128] Under ordinary circumstances, these would have been unusual topics for a day set aside to celebrate new beginnings, but Franklin D. Roosevelt, already President for twelve years, was entering the last twelve weeks of his life.

The Yalta Conference: February 1945

It was during Roosevelt's final weeks that he undertook his most difficult diplomatic journey as President. In early February 1945, just a few days after his fourth inauguration, he traveled fourteen thousand miles to Yalta on the Black Sea coast to meet with the Soviet premier, Marshal Josef Stalin, and the British prime minister, Winston Churchill. At this meeting, the "Big Three" were to thrash out the structure of the proposed United Nations and determine the borders of European nations after the Second World War, matters important to the next generation. Roosevelt's performance at the Yalta Conference has been harshly evaluated by critics. One commentator has pointed out:

It is the simple truth that Stalin had out-generaled Roosevelt at every point. Or perhaps it would be nearer the truth to say that Roosevelt had out-generaled himself. Stalin had merely to sit tight, to make known his wishes and Roosevelt laid them in his lap with eager compliance in the notion that he could thus soften Stalin.[129]

Another has said that "again and again the President seems to have fallen into traps set by Stalin—and to some extent even by Churchill—losing points he would never have conceded had he been in good health and with his earlier ability to control situations."[130] Despite such negative judgments, an analysis of Roosevelt's behavior at Yalta will show, I believe, that his illness was not significantly detrimental to it.

There is no doubt that when the President left Washington for the "Big Three" meeting at Yalta, he was tired and ill; and during much of the sea journey, a severe cold confined him to his cabin.[131] Although the State Department had prepared a series of briefing books and position papers which pertained to the main topics to be discussed at Yalta, one participant reported that the President, perhaps because of poor health, did not study these documents as much as he should have, although he was undoubtedly helped to some degree by them.[132]

When Roosevelt arrived at Yalta, after a one-day stopover in Malta for discussions with Churchill, his appearance stunned those who saw him. One aide reported that he "was terribly shocked at the change since our talks in Washington, after the November election. The signs of deterioration seemed to me unmistakable."[133] Another member of the American delegation, who had just seen the President at the inauguration, found that "his condition had deteriorated markedly. . . . He was not only frail and desperately tired, he looked ill. I never saw Roosevelt look as bad as he did then, despite a week's leisurely voyage at sea, where he could rest."[134]

Foreign observers were equally disturbed. Churchill's physician told associates that the President had "all the symptoms of hardening of the arteries of the brain in an advanced stage. So I give him only a few months to live."[135] Even Marshal Stalin was affected by Roosevelt's physical appearance and is reported to have said that, had he known he was so ill, he would have been willing to hold the conference at a more convenient location for the American President.[136]

The pictures taken of Roosevelt by the uniformed service photographers allowed at the Yalta meeting convey some sense of the shock felt by those who saw him there: in them, he looks clearly to be a dying man.

The worst photographs were, however, suppressed by the White House, and only the kindest appeared in print. One of the President's press aides reported that "it was my job to screen those pictures and to release . . . only those least marked by the deadly haggard weariness of the commander. . . . I held back the most shocking pictures."[137]

In an effort to spare the President any additional exertion, all plenary meetings were held at the Livadia Palace, his official residence during the conference.[138] Despite this small accommodation, the President was forced to his limits at Yalta. There were not only daily formal meetings with Stalin and Churchill but occasional informal meetings with one or both leaders and with members of the American diplomatic and military delegations. There were also long dinners where he was on center stage and his strength further taxed. Roosevelt had brought his daughter with him to the conference, and she tried to ensure, but not always successfully, that he would get his proper rest. One of the President's grandsons wrote:

She watched him sometimes tire suddenly and worried, as she wrote John [her husband], about those occasions when 'he gets all wound up, seems to thoroughly enjoy it all, but wants too many people around, and then won't go to bed early enough. The result is that he doesn't sleep well.' She feared that his heart was vulnerable, and must have been distressed to see the gauntness of his face.[139]

Because of his weakened health, Roosevelt has been described as finding it difficult in 1945 to concentrate for long periods on any subject and as being increasingly reluctant to engage in argument.[140] Aides noted his tendency to nod off for brief moments[141] or to fall into a state of "unaccustomed reverie, from which he awoke with a start."[142] Missouri neurologist Bert E. Park describes this phenomenon as the manifestation of secondary metabolic encephalopathy, a condition resulting from lack of oxygen to the brain. Congestive heart failure, pulmonary disease, and hypertension are common causes of the problem, and they are the very ailments from which Roosevelt suffered.[143] Indeed, a sudden sharp rise in blood pressure may induce episodes of encephalopathy, and Roosevelt's blood pressure was subject to particularly striking ebbs and flows. Even Dr. McIntire admitted this latter point when he told the press in 1951 that Roosevelt "had a blood pressure that bounced. He could vary 20 to 30 points easily in two to three hours."[144]

Most patients with metabolic encephalopathy cannot concentrate well and suffer from brief periods of confusion, disorientation, and lethargy.[145] Descriptions of Roosevelt during the latter months of his presidency suggest that he suffered from periods of quiet delirium or stupor, most of which were very brief.[146]

A medical doctor and a handwriting expert, who together examined samples of the President's writing at various stages of his lifetime, found that every sample since 1944 showed "pathological changes which may be accounted for by vascular spasms in an arterio-sclerotic brain."[147] Samples from the days of the Yalta Conference are notable for the variability of the script, not only from one day to the next but even from hour to hour. The two researchers concluded, "What happened to Roosevelt happens rather frequently in arterio-sclerotic brains. There occur vaso-motoric spasms that for some time interfere with the normal oxygen supply. Functionally, the performance becomes erratic, and the general lack of functioning is reduced."[148]

Nonetheless, although the President was clearly impaired at Yalta, and may have been more subdued and less loquacious than in the past, his judgments were sound, and his foreign-policy initiatives were consistent with both long-range and immediate American goals. At Yalta, Roosevelt had two primary objectives. First, he was deeply committed to the establishment of a postwar international organization which he viewed as the only way of preventing the United States from slipping back into the isolationism that had prevailed before the war.[149] And, second, he wanted very much to bring the Soviet Union into the war against Japan. The State Department also urged him to discuss such additional topics as the future of Germany and the status of Poland in the postwar period, and he did so with determination.[150]

With regard to the creation of an international organization, Roosevelt had succeeded in eliciting promises of support from Great Britain and the Soviet Union. At Yalta, however, debate was intense over the structural details of the proposal, and one of the areas of sharpest dispute involved representation for member states in the General Assembly. Simply put, Great Britain wanted votes in the Assembly for each of the six members of the Commonwealth, and the initial Soviet gambit was to demand representation for each one of the sixteen Soviet republics.[151] In a shrewd counterstroke, Roosevelt let it be known that if the Soviet position remained unchanged, he would ask for representation and voting rights for each of the forty-eight American states then in the union.[152]

As the week progressed, Stalin withdrew his demand for sixteen votes and asked instead for "three or at any rate two" additional votes in the Assembly. His concession greatly relieved the other conferees,[153] and they agreed to give votes in the assembly to Byelorussia and the Ukraine.

Roosevelt announced, however, that domestic political considerations might force him to ask for three votes for the United States as well.[154] Stalin acquiesced, saying that "if it is necessary, I am prepared officially to accept this proposal."[155] While Roosevelt later decided not to go forward with his demand for three American votes in the General Assembly, at Yalta he argued for, and won, the principle of voting parity for the United States with the Soviet Union.

Also in dispute at Yalta was the issue involving voting arrangements on the Security Council of the United Nations. Three months before going to Yalta, Roosevelt had been advised by the acting secretary of state to advocate acceptance of a formula giving each member one vote, with procedural matters being decided by the affirmative vote of seven members. Substantive matters would be decided by a vote of seven, including the concurring votes of all permanent members, with any party to a dispute not voting in that case.[156] In other words, the United States supported the concept of a veto power for permanent members of the Security Council as a means for ensuring American sovereignty;[157] and Roosevelt remained true to that position and argued it aggressively at Yalta. Stalin urged, however, that the voting procedure that should be adopted should be based on the unanimity of permanent members, with voting rights in all matters.[158] After intense debate at the conference table, Stalin accepted Roosevelt's position—although at their final meeting, the Soviet leader asked that the communiqué to be issued upon adjournment not mention the fact that the agreed-upon proposal relating to Security Council voting arrangements had been proposed by the American President.[159]

The "Big Three" also agreed to hold a conference on 25 April 1945 in the United States in order to draw up the charter of the proposed United Nations, with the Soviet Union making an important concession by accepting the American formula under which countries would be invited to send delegates. Specifically, those nations that had declared war on the Axis powers by 1 March 1945 would be invited to participate in the conference as original members. The practical result of this agreement was to allow a number of Latin American countries to participate, another victory for the United States.[160]

President Roosevelt's second major goal at Yalta was to bring the Soviets into the war against Japan. Since at the time, the atomic bomb was still an unproven weapon, the United States was preparing plans for two major amphibious assaults on Japan; and the joint chiefs of staff reminded the President, on 23 January 1945, that "Russia's entry at as early a date as possibly consistent with her ability to engage in offensive operations is necessary to provide maximum support possible."[161] It was believed that Soviet entry into the Japanese conflict would reduce American casualties by somewhere between 200,000 and 1,000,000.[162]

At a meeting with the President on 4 February 1945, W. Averell Harriman, then ambassador to the Soviet Union, anticipated the price the Russians would exact for entering the war with Japan: he listed the southern half of Sakhalin and the Kurile Islands, maintenance of the status quo in Outer Mongolia, and control over the railroad running to Dairen. Roosevelt indicated that he wanted to consult with Chinese leader Chiang Kai-shek before entering into any agreement concerning the status quo in Mongolia, but that on all other questions he was "ready to go ahead."[163] The southern part of Sakhalin had been seized by Japan from Russia in 1904 and would now be returned. Roosevelt seems to have believed that Japan had also taken the Kurile Islands away from Russia by force; in fact, possession had been transferred by treaty. The President's error explains—but does not fully justify—his willingness to have them returned to the Soviet Union. Charles E. Bohlen (a member of the State Department delegation to Yalta) suggests that "if the President had done his homework, or if any of us had been more familiar with Far Eastern history, the U.S. might not have given all the Kuriles to Stalin as easily."[164] Apparently the President was not alone in failing to do his homework, but his health would seem to have had little to do with that failure. The American position, which Roosevelt fully supported, was simply that Soviet entry into the war, with the consequent saving of many thousands of American lives, was well worth this modest price.

The arrangements Roosevelt and Stalin worked out essentially reflected the previously agreed upon American position. The Soviet Union would enter the war against Japan within two or three months after Germany had surrendered. In return, the southern part of Sakhalin and the Kurile Islands would be given to the Soviet Union, Port Arthur would be leased to the Soviets for a naval base, and the port of Dairen would be internationalized.[165] On the latter point, Roosevelt had long since believed that the Russians should have access to a warm-water port and, at the Teheran Conference in 1943, had suggested that the Soviet Union might be given the port of Dairen in Manchuria.[166]

Believing Soviet entry into the war against Japan was crucial to ultimate victory,[167] and because of the urgency of the situation, the President simply did not have time to consult his Chinese allies on the matter of Outer Mongolia and agreed that the status quo would be maintained. He did get from Stalin, however, a pledge to withdraw his support from the Communists in China and to back the Nationalist government of Chiang Kai-shek.[168] The American-Soviet agreement also provided for Soviet recognition of China's sovereignty over Manchuria.[169]

For very good reason, the decision was made to hold this agreement temporarily in secret. At the time, Soviet military strength was focused on the defeat of Germany. If the terms of the agreement were announced, it might well have provoked an invasion by Japanese troops across Russia's borders.[170] After Germany surrendered, the Soviet Union would have sufficient time to move its armies from the German front in order to confront the Japanese. Although the secrecy contributed to the displeasure in some quarters over the specifics of the agreement, it was necessitated by the pressures of war.

In the several other matters discussed at Yalta, Roosevelt seems to have done rather well in articulating and implementing the American position. The American draft of the "Declaration of Liberated Europe," which Roosevelt proposed and Stalin tried unsuccessfully to amend, was accepted. The Soviets agreed—despite initial strong objections—to give France a seat on the German Control Commission, after Roosevelt announced that he favored French participation. Stalin promised that Soviet air bases near Budapest and elsewhere would be available to the American air force.[171] Roosevelt and Churchill's position that the question of German reparations should not include a specific amount eventually prevailed, although Stalin had definite feelings to the contrary.[172]

The question of Poland was perhaps the most difficult one to be discussed at Yalta. On no other question was so much time spent, the British record indicating an exchange of nearly eighteen thousand words among the "Big Three."[173] Roosevelt had initially, and perhaps unwisely, stated that he did not believe that American troops would stay in Europe more than two years, and that the United States could not maintain "an appreciable American force in Europe."[174] The Soviet armies were already in place in Eastern Europe and, short of being countered by military force, were not likely to allow themselves to be dislodged.[175] Despite these realities, the Western leaders at Yalta tried to reach an agreement that would lead to a new and broadened Polish government in which Polish exiles in London would participate, to free and secret elections in Poland, and to the establishment of appropriate Polish boundaries. The discussions over Poland were often acrimonious; and on one occasion, Roosevelt's doctor detected in him symptoms of an impending cardiovascular crisis.[176]

Had the agreements hammered out on Poland been observed, they might well have prevented the later breakdown in American-Soviet relations. At the insistence of Roosevelt and Churchill, Stalin agreed that the Polish government then in power would be reorganized so as to include democratic Polish leaders from abroad. This reorganized Polish government would be committed to holding "free and unfettered elections as soon as possible on the basis of universal suffrage and a secret ballot," with all democratic and anti-Nazi parties having the right to participate.[177] Stalin had even gone so far, in response to a query from Roosevelt, as to indicate that elections could be held in Poland "in a month, provided no catastrophes occurred on the front."[178]

With respect to Polish boundaries, there was agreement that the Curzon line should provide the eastern border, with some digressions in favor of Poland. The Curzon Line had been proposed by the Allied Armistice Commission in 1919 as the Polish–Soviet border. At the beginning of the Second World War, the Polish–Soviet border was very similar to that established by the Curzon Line and the Allied leaders argued that it should remain essentially unchanged in the postwar period. Roosevelt had rejected the Soviet proposal that the Niesse River should form Poland's western border,[179] and a consensus could not be reached while the conference was in session. In their final communiqué, the three heads of government recognized that "Poland must receive substantial accessions of territory in the north and west," and that the final delimitation of the western frontier should benefit from the opinion of the new Provisional Government of National Unity.[180] One American participant reports that the American delegation viewed the agreement on Poland as "acceptable."[181] Roosevelt described it to Congress as "frankly a compromise."[182]

At the conclusion of the conference, Roosevelt and his aides were generally satisfied with the outcome,[183] as were the British.[184] The President had presided over the formal sessions with skill, adroitly moving the agenda despite the acrimony that sometimes developed, and occasionally punctuating the proceedings with flashes of humor. When Churchill remarked that he had sent a copy of one of his statements to Wendell Willkie, Roosevelt's 1940 Republican opponent who had recently died, the President quipped, "Was that what killed him?" And when the Soviets asked that Poland's ancient frontiers in East Prussia and on the Oder River be returned to Poland, Roosevelt persuaded Stalin to withdraw the proposal by observing that "this might lead the British to ask for the return of the United States to Great Britain."[185]

The President was generally well informed and alert, even on many technical and legalistic questions. On one occasion, when his aides were trying to work out the intricate wording of the Polish boundary statement, Roosevelt suddenly said, "I've got it"; he proceeded to tell the conference that

the Amendments he was proposing were necessary for American constitutional reasons. He suggested, therefore, that instead of the first words "The three powers," he would like to substitute "The Three Heads of Government consider." In the second sentence he proposed eliminating the words "three powers" and in the last sentence, the word "feel" instead of "agree" should be used. These changes transformed the statement on boundaries from a governmental commitment to an expression of views in which Roosevelt concurred. [186]

Most participants at the conference viewed the President as having performed well. Churchill remarked that "his mind moved quickly and acutely over the great range of problems that the Conference considered."[187] The British foreign secretary, Anthony Eden, was impressed by the fact that the American leader "not only kept up with Churchill in the round of formal and informal conferences but also found time to conduct a whole separate enterprise at Yalta—negotiations with Stalin over the Far East."[188] Secretary of State Stettinius reported, "At Yalta, the President was extremely steady and patient. At no time did he flare up. He was kind and sympathetic but determined. . . . I always found him mentally alert and fully capable of dealing with every situation as it developed."[189] Bohlen agreed that "when important moments arose, he was mentally sharp. Our leader was ill at Yalta . . . but he was effective."[190] Finally, the cardiologist who had diagnosed Roosevelt's serious physical ailments in March 1944, and had accompanied him to Yalta, has written that "his mental clarity was truly remarkable. His memory for past and recent events was unimpaired and his recollection of detail was such as to continually impress me when compared with some of his associates ten and twenty years younger than himself."[191]

En route back to the United States, the exhausted President summoned up enough strength to conduct shipside meetings with King Farouk of Egypt, Ibn Saud of Saudi Arabia, and Emperor Haile Selassie of Ethiopia. It was also during the journey home that Roosevelt's aide and close friend Edwin ("Pa") Watson became sick on board ship and died. This was not the first personal loss the President had suffered over the preceding few years. His mother's death in 1941 was a great sorrow to him.[192] Missy LeHand and Marvin McIntyre, two close associates, had recently died, and now Pa Watson was gone. Uncharacteristically, Roosevelt could not control his grief,[193] and gave vent to it to such an extent as to worry the people closest to him.[194] Indeed, the President was so despondent that it was days before he was able to work on his report to Congress and the American people.[195]

The Aftermath: March–April 1945

On 1 March 1945, Franklin Roosevelt delivered his final address to Congress. His delivery was halting,[196] and he spoke in a seated position, making reference for the first time to his crippled legs: "I hope you will pardon me for the unusual posture of sitting down during the presentation of what I have to say, but I know you will realize it makes it a lot easier for me in not having to carry about ten pounds of steel around the bottom of my legs."[197] He then went on to tell Congress that he had been well the entire time at Yalta, despite rumors to the contrary; and that he had come away from the Crimea "with a firm belief that we have made a good start on the road to a world of peace." Correctly, he reminded Congress and the public that

the question of whether [the trip] was fruitful lies to a great extent in your hands. For unless you here in the halls of Congress—with the support of the American people—concur in the general conclusions reached at Yalta, and give them your active support, the meeting will not have produced lasting results.[198]

In his final address to Congress, however, the President seems to have made two errors in judgment. First, he failed to mention the formula that had been agreed upon for representation in the United Nation's General Assembly. His silence may have been due to the fact that some American officials still hoped to be able to persuade the Soviet Union to withdraw its request for three votes, and Roosevelt may have been playing for time.[199] But when news of the formula leaked into the press a few weeks later, it made it appear that the President had deceitfully held back information from Congress and the public, and excited fears that other "hidden" agreements might have been reached as well. Even one of Roosevelt's sons described this as "a serious miscalculation."[200]

Second, the President had stated that "the Conference concerned itself only with the European war and the political problems of Europe—and not with the Pacific War."[201] Perhaps in a technical sense, this statement was accurate since the agreement concerning Soviet entry into the war was arrived at by Roosevelt and Stalin alone. Even Churchill described it as "an American affair" in which he was "not consulted."[202] Therefore, in a legalistic sense, no plenary session of the conference dealt directly with the Pacific war. Also, as I noted previously, there was need to keep the agreement secret until Soviet troops were in a position to confront the Japanese. Nevertheless, from the perspective of hindsight, Roosevelt might better have simply avoided any allusion to this subject at all, since future revelations created the impression of duplicity.

Within days of his address to Congress, the President began to grow concerned over Soviet violations of the agreements reached at Yalta. Eleanor Roosevelt later reported that Roosevelt had initially felt confident that he could work with Stalin, but not long after returning from Yalta, "he began to feel that the Marshal was not keeping his promises. This was something he [Roosevelt] could not overlook."[203]

The secret messages between Roosevelt and Churchill at the time testify to the growing disillusionment of both men about Stalin's behavior. On 11 March 1945, Roosevelt cabled the British prime minister: "I am fully determined . . . not to let the good decisions we reached at the Crimea to slip through our hands and will certainly do everything I can to hold Stalin to their honest fulfillment." With regard to Poland, the President asserted, "You are quite correct in assuming that neither the Government nor the people of this country will support participation in a fraud or a mere whitewash of the Lublin government [the Communist government of Poland], and the solution must be as we envisaged it at Yalta."[204] Two weeks later, he informed Churchill that he had "been watching with anxiety and concern the development of Soviet attitude since the Crimea conference. I am acutely aware of the dangers inherent in the present course of events."[205]

On 5 April, a week before his death, Roosevelt sent a strong message to Stalin expressing "bitter resentment toward your informers . . . for such vile misrepresentations of my actions or those of my trusted subordinates."[206] And on the following day, he sent Churchill a most provocative message: "We must not permit anybody to entertain a false impression that we are afraid. Our armies will in a very few days be in a position that will permit us to become 'tougher' than heretofore appeared advantageous to the war effort."[207]

Roosevelt spent his final days in growing disillusionment over the breakdown in the spirit of cooperation he thought had been developed at Yalta. Some of the President's aides believed that Stalin had, upon his return to Moscow, confronted strong opposition to some of the Yalta agreements by members of the Politburo who felt that he had been too friendly and accommodating. British Foreign Secretary Eden was convinced that "something had happened in Moscow after the Yalta Conference," and that the Soviet Union was hardening its position as a result.[208]

Shortly before Roosevelt left for a much-needed vacation at Warm Springs on 29 March, he was visited at the White House by the Canadian prime minister, MacKenzie King. King later said, "My old friend looked so badly, so haggard and worn that I almost sobbed. I went up to him and kissed him on both cheeks."[209] The President indicated his anger and disillusionment as he left Washington for Georgia, first ascertaining that the Russians already owed eleven billion dollars and then ordering that Lend Lease (aid to American allies) be shut off as soon as Germany was defeated.[210] What other actions he might have taken against Stalin upon his return from Warm Springs can, of course never be known.

On 12 April 1945, the President saw Dr. Bruenn at 9:20 A.M. and complained to him of a slight headache and some stiffness in his neck. A light massage relieved these symptoms,[211] and the President felt better. In the late morning, he bathed, shaved and dressed, and then began to pose for a portrait. At 1:15 P.M., the President raised his left hand to his forehead and said, "I have a terrific headache." According to most accounts, he then collapsed into unconsciousness and was taken to his bedroom, where he died two hours and twenty minutes later.

One of the President's physicians, however, offers a somewhat different version of events. Dr. James Paullin, who was summoned to Warm Springs from Atlanta after Roosevelt was stricken, arrived there at 3:28 P.M. and found that the "President was in extremis. . . . He was pale, in a cold sweat, ashy gray, breathing with difficulty, numerous rhonchi in his chest. . . . His pupils were dilated. His hands were slightly cyanosed and Commander Bruenn had just started artificial respiration." Paullin went on to say that, according to the notes of Dr. Bruenn, the attending physician at Warm Springs, the President was carried *conscious* into his bedroom at 1:15 P.M. and put to bed after complaining of a severe headache. Bruenn had reached his bedside at 1:30 P.M. and found the President still conscious, "with his hand on the back of his head, complaining of intense pain."[212] His blood pressure was extremely high, and his pupils were contracted. It was at that time, some fifteen minutes after being stricken, that the President lapsed into unconsciousness. He died two hours later, the victim of a massive cerebral hemorrhage.

It is generally accepted that the President's death was precipitated by hypertension and cardiovascular disease. Indeed, the President's arterial deterioration was so pronounced that funeral directors had a hard time preparing his body for lying in state. Since his arteries had become so clogged that embalming fluid could not be injected into them in the normal way, the undertakers had to make individual syringe injections in many parts of his body in order to accomplish their task.[213] Clearly, the President had suffered from arteriosclerosis for some time, and it had affected all of his arteries.[214]

Throughout the over twelve years of the Roosevelt presidency, rumors about his health were common. In the decades since his death, the rumors have perhaps slowed but not stopped. A 1979 publication reported that Dr. Frank Leahy, one of Roosevelt's physicians, had discovered a cancerous tumor that had metastasized in the President's body, had informed the President of this fact, and had advised him not to run for a fourth term.[215] The author of this article pointed out that an examination of photographs of the late President at various points in his adult life revealed a small but slowly growing lesion over his left eyebrow until 1943–44, when it was no longer visible and appeared to have been replaced with a small scar. The possibility was raised that the facial lesion might have been a melanoma which could have spread into the President's gastrointestinal tract. Pictures indicating the disappearance of a lesion from over the President's left eyebrow cast considerable doubt over Dr. McIntire's explicit statement that the President never had any operation other than the removal of a cyst from the back of his head and the extraction of a wisdom tooth.[216]

Also, Hugh L'Etang reports that doctors from Walter Reed Hospital presented a provocative paper concerning malignant melanoma at a medical conference in 1949. All of the slides and specimens included in the presentation were marked with special serial numbers except for one. The unmarked specimen was a section of brain with a large metastatic melanoma in the right hemisphere and simply bore a date: 14 April 1945.[217] This was the day on which Roosevelt's body arrived in Washington from Warm Springs—perhaps only a coincidence, but also perhaps not.

Possibly the entire matter will be clarified if and when a memorandum written by Dr. Leahy concerning the President's health, and long the subject of litigation, is published.[218] That decision, however, now rests with the owner of that memorandum and her heirs.

Franklin D. Roosevelt's presidency was conducted in the face of enormous, but well-concealed, physical difficulties. Crippled by polio; afflicted with sinusitis, frequent colds, and bouts of flu; and later beset by hypertension, pulmonary disease, and congestive heart failure, Roosevelt was a sick man, particularly in his latter years.

The public initially was spared knowledge of Roosevelt's serious infirmity out of concern that a disabled man might not be accepted by an electorate in search of a strong and vigorous leader. Later, the President's serious cardiovascular illness was concealed from the nation, almost certainly in the belief that an impaired commander in chief during wartime would be preferable to a new one, possibly one even chosen from the opposition party. The President himself reflected this view when he explained his decision to run for a fourth term as an effort to maintain "a continuity of command in a time of continuing crisis."[219] Such reasoning, no matter how controversial, cannot be easily dismissed as invalid.

Nonetheless, Roosevelt's various ailments, the most serious of which eventually ended his life in 1945 at the age of sixty-three, did not significantly prevent him from carrying out his presidential responsibilities, even at Yalta just a few short weeks before his death. Not only would Franklin Roosevelt's standing among the great presidents of American history seem to be secure, but that standing is actually enhanced by the fact that he discharged his duties so well even as he coped with serious disability and illness.

Chapter FOUR
Pain and Duty:
Dwight D. Eisenhower

H e is known as a son of the Kansas plains, a West Point graduate, an eminently successful military commander, and a two-term President of the United States. Dwight D. Eisenhower, one of America's army generals who became, in 1953, commander in chief of our armed forces, was a highly popular President whose eight-year administration is receiving increasingly positive evaluation and re-evaluation as the years pass. Of his health, President Eisenhower boasted, at a press conference on 8 February 1956, "Rarely have I known any time in my life when I had to be concerned about my own physical feeling outside of flu or a cold or something like that. I have been one of those fortunate creatures of good health."[1] In fact, however, Eisenhower's life was filled with pain and illness, and his presidency was marked by three heavily publicized medical crises—a heart attack, abdominal surgery, and a stroke—and many largely unpublicized medical problems as well. When he died in March 1969 at the age of seventy-eight, it was after an adult lifetime filled with serious illness, discomfort, and pain. Medical information about the extent and frequency of Eisenhower's illnesses before and during his White House years was actively suppressed and has only recently, more than twenty years after his death, come to light. In this chapter, I shall explore Eisenhower's illnesses, along with the attempts to conceal them, with their effects on his ability to function, and, above all, with the sense of duty that drove Eisenhower to accept challenges that many a man in better health than he would have refused.

The Early Years

It was during his formative years that the future President developed the strong sense of duty that would guide and even dominate his life. Also, although he was active and athletic as a boy and a young man, his early years were marred by several serious and unpleasant bouts with illness. Indeed, in high school he feared the amputation of a leg that had become badly infected,[2] and at West Point he injured his knee so seriously that he thought he might have to give up plans for a military career.[3] In this section and the next, I will try to identify the key influences that shaped Eisenhower's life, some of the experiences that eventually shaped his presidency, and the many indispositions that beset him throughout his early—and later—years.

On 14 October 1890, Dwight David Eisenhower was born to Ida and David Eisenhower in Denison, Texas, where the Eisenhower family lived briefly after David's general store in Abilene, Kansas, had gone bankrupt. David Dwight, whose names his mother soon reversed in order to avoid confusion with his father, was the third of seven sons. One, Paul, died in early childhood of diphtheria. The other six survived and grew to manhood, each building a successful career in his own right—and one eventually becoming an international figure of the first order.

The boys' parents had met at Lane University in Kansas, a school affiliated with the United Brethren Church, and the locale of their meeting is not without significance. Since women of her day rarely attended college, Ida demonstrated spirit, independence, and character when she became a student at Lane.[4] After her marriage to David in 1885, she became a major force in her household and eventually in the lives of her children.

Ida emphasized the virtues of self-reliance, hard work, and doing one's duty as the most important of personal values. Despite her righteousness, she had a happy disposition and a sunny smile. Years later, one of her grandsons could still remember her humming.[5] Deeply religious, her favorite reading material was the Bible. Dwight later remembered that his mother's greatest belief was that of self-discipline which she "preached constantly."[6] Indeed, she had such strong self-discipline and was so righteous in her personal life that she actually studied law at home so that she would be prepared if she ever met up with her husband's business partner who had absconded with their grocery store's money.[7] Her attitude in this instance was said to reflect no anger toward her husband. Dwight once said that each time his father failed "my mother just smiled and worked harder."[8]

The future President's feelings toward his mother were positive and strong. She was the most powerful guiding force in his life, and Dwight paid frequent tribute to her for teaching him and his brothers that hatred was futile, and that "each of us should behave properly not because of the fear of punishment but because it was the right thing to do."[9] He once wrote, "I think my mother is the finest person I've ever known."[10]

Dwight's father, on the other hand, was a bitter and irascible man, a figure more to be feared than loved by his sons.[11] After the family returned to Abilene in 1891, David worked long hours managing the Abilene creamery for generally meager wages and never fully escaped the effects of his early financial failures. A God-fearing man, he joined Ida each evening for family Bible readings and, like her, stressed the virtues of hard work and adherence to duty. Because of his family's tenuous financial situation, Dwight had to work long hours at the creamery as well. His grandson wrote much later that the future President "pulled ice, washed cans in the butter rooms and ran a compressor, which ground ice into powder. . . . Young Eisenhower developed strength, a capacity for hard work, and a determination steeled by a strict and domineering father."[12]

While Edgar Eisenhower, Dwight's older brother, has described his father as the "anchor" of the family,[13] Dwight seems to have had somewhat mixed feelings about his Dad. One commentator reports that Eisenhower "ascribed few of the personal qualities he sought to develop in himself and others to his father";[14] and while he included his father among the "main faces and forces" that shaped his early years,[15] it was clearly his mother who occupied center stage in his emotions.

Young Dwight Eisenhower seems to have had a boyhood of many happy memories. He achieved better-than-average grades in school and loved to study history. In fact, he spent so much time exploring the exploits of heroes of the past that his other subjects tended to suffer. His high school yearbook predicted that one day he would become a professor of history at Yale. Eisenhower was one of only sixty-seven children of the two hundred who entered first grade with him to go on to high school. And of the sixty-seven who entered Abilene High School in his company, he was one of the only thirty-one who graduated.

A popular figure in Abilene, Dwight was known as an energetic and extroverted young man. He enjoyed sports greatly and seemed happiest on the athletic playing field and in outdoors life generally. Known for his fierce temper, Dwight recounted that at the age of ten he became so infuriated when his parents refused to let him go trick-or-treating on Halloween that he pounded his fists into an apple tree until they were bloody.[16] Years later, he would beat his head against a tree trunk out of frustration with his ineptitude at tennis.[17]

As a boy, Ike enjoyed generally good health, even though he contracted measles, mumps, and chickenpox. Sniffles and head colds hit him, however, "with any few degrees change in temperature or a slight shift in the wind."[18] He also had an irregularly developed right kidney as well as a minor malformation in a portion of his spine. Mild clubbing of his fingers and toes, a family characteristic, was also noted in his early years.[19] While in high school, young Dwight fell, injured his knee, and developed a severe streptococcal infection. After two or three days, Ike's fever broke, and he began to recover. He missed so many days of school, however, that he was forced to repeat the entire school year. This unpleasant early experience was the forerunner to Dwight Eisenhower's many subsequent illnesses.

FORTY YEARS OF MILITARY SERVICE

Dwight D. Eisenhower had long wanted to go to West Point and entered in the fall of 1910. He was a respectable but not outstanding student. At the end of his first year, he stood among approximately the top 25 percent of his class. By the time he graduated, he had slipped somewhat in his academic performance but still ranked among the top 40 percent.[20]

Ike's record in academic subjects was far superior to his record in discipline and deportment. His temper as well as his stubborn disposition took their toll in terms of the number of demerits he received from superior officers.[21] He later admitted that he stood 125th out of about 162 cadets in discipline, and attributed his record "in compiling a staggering catalogue of demerits" largely "to a lack of motivation in almost everything other than athletics, except for the single and stark resolve to get a college education."[22]

Clearly, athletics were Dwight Eisenhower's greatest love at West Point, and his interest in playing football was particularly intense. The team trainer described him as "the first cadet on the field for practice and the very last to leave."[23] One commentator has described him as "one of the best quarterbacks West Point ever had."[24]

Whether or not this latter judgment was justified, Eisenhower's football career came to a sudden halt after he suffered a severe knee injury during a game against Tufts. Although he felt little pain at the time, the knee swelled so badly that he required hospitalization. A few days after his release, he re-injured his knee performing mounted gymnastics and badly ruptured both cartilage and tendons. Eisenhower later recounted that "in the hospital, the doctors spent four days straightening my leg, a process so painful that I scarcely slept during the ordeal."[25] Although Eisenhower's damaged knee produced recurrent joint problems for him for many years, it was overshadowed, indeed dwarfed, by other, far more debilitating illnesses, which began to manifest themselves during his subsequent military career and then came into full force during the years of his presidency and thereafter.

After graduating from West Point in 1915, Dwight Eisenhower began a slow ascent through the military hierarchy. In 1917, he was promoted to captain and, by 1918, had attained the temporary rank of lieutenant colonel. During the First World War, however, he saw no combat, a fact that disappointed him greatly;[26] but after the war's end, he did receive a Distinguished Service Medal for successfully developing a tank corps.[27] It was during his early military career, in 1916, that Eisenhower met and married Mamie Doud of Denver, Colorado. A year later, the couple was blessed with the birth of their first son, Doud Dwight. That boy, nicknamed Icky, died of scarlet fever at the age of three, after contracting the disease from a maid who had been hired to help Mamie with the housework. Dwight and Mamie's only other child, John, was born some nineteen months later.

In 1920, Eisenhower was promoted to the rank of major, which he held until 1936. During this period, he studied at the Command and General Staff School at Leavenworth, ranking first out of 275 officers, and went on to study at and graduate from the Army War College, where the army prepared officers for high command. In 1936 Eisenhower was promoted to the rank of lieutenant colonel and, in March 1941, was made a full colonel.[28] In September 1941, with the approach of the Second World War, Eisenhower was promoted to brigadier general and, a year later, to lieutenant general. In 1942, he took over command of the European Theater of Operations, and was promoted to four-star general. In 1944, Dwight D. Eisenhower became general of the army—equal in rank to General Douglas MacArthur and to General George Marshall, under both of whom he had served. From 1945 until 1948, he served as chief of staff (head of the army) and, in 1950, became commander of the forces of the North Atlantic Treaty Organization.

During his military career, he took his responsibilities seriously and worked hard in whatever activity he was assigned, winning a string of plaudits from his commanding officers but bringing himself to the limits of endurance. He once told a relative, "I must admit that sometimes I feel a thousand years old when I struggle to my bed at night."[29] Later, as chief of staff of the army, he worked some fourteen hours a day, often pushing himself to exhaustion.[30] He later wrote, "I was, when working, driven by the need to go at top speed, day after day, starting early and continuing past midnight."[31] His driver, Kay Summersby, remarked that he probably worked harder and longer than anyone under his command, and related that "charwomen reporting for cleaning duties in the early hours became hardened to the shock of seeing the General already hard at work."[32]

Eisenhower also showed great organizational and diplomatic skill in his military activities—skill that served him well in the White House. He gave his greatest attention to the structure of command—establishing clear lines of communication and promoting unity of command.[33] He was committed to an efficient organization and managed to develop an effective Allied military force despite the inevitable rivalries and clashing ambitions. He succeeded here through superior political skills and his ability to convince allied leaders that he was acutely aware of and sensitive to their individual needs back home. His grandson later wrote that he became "known for his affability, his abilities as a negotiator and his talent for reconciling differences among strong personalities."[34] Franklin Roosevelt reportedly explained that, although he considered General Marshall the wisest of American generals, he chose Eisenhower to be the head of the Army because he "was the best politician among the military men. He is a natural leader who can convince men to follow him."[35]

Eisenhower was forced by his position to establish contacts with political leaders of all stripes both at home and abroad. A key member of his White House staff later pointed out that his "career had not been strictly a military career. He'd had quite a lot of contact with men in high political office, and his job particularly in Europe, where he had to deal with Mr. Churchill, Mr. DeGaulle, men of that calibre—it had given him quite an insight into that end of the show."[36]

In Washington, the general acquired useful experience when he testified before committees of Congress and established rapport with key legislators. As one observer pointed out, Eisenhower "learned what a hothouse of weeds Washington is, and became sharply aware of the insensate, insinuating, vagaries of politicians."[37] He himself later wrote that "there's no more active political organization in the country or in the world than the armed services of the United States. I think I am a better politician than most so-called professionals."[38] His military career even helped him deal as President with the military high command: it was impossible "for the Pentagon brass to overawe him; he handled them as no big businessmen or corporation lawyer could."[39]

EARLY ILLNESSES

It was during Eisenhower's military career that his physical ailments and disabilities began to show themselves with both frequency and force. In 1917, he was hospitalized for malaria. Two years later, a severe throat infection required hospitalization, and then he was rehospitalized for removal of his tonsils.[40]

Shortly after his son's death in 1920, he experienced the onset of the painful abdominal discomfort that would trouble him for the rest of his life. After several years of recurring pain, he became convinced that he was suffering from appendicitis and insisted that doctors remove his appendix;[41] but it was found to be free of disease. No other subsequent treatment effectively corrected this problem, and Eisenhower suffered from it greatly for almost fifty years, until his death. In 1923, chest X rays revealed that he had inactive tuberculosis, a condition that, if known earlier, might have prevented him from entering West Point and/or from his military commission.[42]

High blood pressure was noted in Eisenhower in the early 1930s, and intestinal difficulties nagged at him. In his diary, he wrote, "Lots of trouble with my insides lately."[43] In addition, he began to experience back trouble that was diagnosed and treated as lumbago, but that probably was related to his spinal malformation. By 1933, he was viewed as having a cancer phobia or as being neurotic.[44] He was hospitalized in 1934 because of back pain which interfered with the performance of his duties, and diagnosed as having arthritis of the spine and sacroiliac joints.

In 1936, he was hospitalized for a recurrent sore throat and underwent a second tonsillectomy for the removal of remnants of his tonsils. He also suffered at this time from bursitis, and his intestinal difficulties became more acute. Since he was at the time serving with General MacArthur in the Philippines, he thought erroneously that he had contracted tropical dysentery. Instead, his condition was diagnosed as enteritis, close to the ileitis condition diagnosed in 1956 while he was President.

Gastrointestinal specialists would almost certainly agree that the stresses Eisenhower experienced during this phase of his military career aggravated his abdominal difficulties. In 1938, intestinal blockage was so severe that surgery was contemplated, but spontaneous relief led to the operation's cancellation.

In 1940, Eisenhower developed a painful case of shingles. Shortly after, he was treated for neuritis at a London clinic. In late 1942, he came down with a severe and persistent respiratory infection and a case of the flu that might well have been pneumonia. He had not fully recovered when he flew to Casablanca for the conference held there for Allied leaders.

In 1943, the diagnosis of high blood pressure was again confirmed, and he was found to be suffering from fatigue. In 1944, he fell on a beach near Mont-Saint-Michel and painfully injured his good knee. He was in intense pain, and the attending physician prescribed a rubber brace and extended bed rest, orders that the general grudgingly obeyed.[45] Nevertheless, it took Eisenhower several months to recover.

Just prior to D-day in June 1944, the general developed "his usual upper respiratory infections with recurring throat infections, irritating cough and sinusitis."[46] General Bedell Smith felt that Eisenhower was so exhausted and under so much stress that he was close to "having a nervous breakdown."[47] In 1945, he developed bronchitis and was hospitalized at Ashford Hospital in West Virginia. In 1946, Eisenhower experienced an episode of nausea, vomiting, and abdominal pain and swelling and, a year later, suffered a "very puzzling episode" of dizziness, disturbances of equilibrium, and mystagmus, which was diagnosed as Menieres disease, or syndrome.[48]

THE "MYSTERY ILLNESS" OF MARCH 1949

In 1949, Eisenhower suffered one of his most severe and also most puzzling illnesses. At this time, he was president of Columbia University, a frustrating position he had been pressured to accept after writing his memoirs of the Second World War,[49] and commuting back and forth to Washington as a consultant to the secretary of defense.

Dr. Howard Snyder, Eisenhower's long-time personal physician, maintained that this 1949 illness was nothing more than another episode of abdominal blockage or acute gastroenteritis. In a draft chapter of a book manuscript on Eisenhower which he was preparing for publication, Snyder reported that in March 1949 his patient developed "colicky pains throughout his middle abdomen from the late morning hours," but that "his symptoms became exaggerated about noon":

He had no temperature, his pulse was not accelerated. . . . There was tenderness in the lower right quadrant. . . . There was beginning distention of the lower abdomen. He was not nauseated. . . . His heart sounds were regular and strong. . . . I was confronted with suggestions of a partial block in the lower lesser intestinal track.[50]

Although Eisenhower later wrote that Dr. Snyder treated him in this instance "as though I were on the edge of the precipice and teetering a bit,"[51] Snyder himself states that he called in no special consultant, and that Eisenhower improved rapidly after traveling to Key West in late March. He stayed there with Snyder for some fifteen days, and then the two men moved on to Augusta, Georgia, where they were joined by Mamie and "where Ike played 18 holes of golf each day." The Eisenhower party returned to Washington on 11 May and to New York on 13 May. Snyder later admitted that he actively suppressed news of Eisenhower's illness from the press and the public:

Nothing leaked out . . . about the probability of an intestinal obstruction being responsible for the abdominal attack the General had suffered. I feared that if the General got into politics, someone would surely pin upon him the label that he was a chronic invalid and couldn't stand the strain of office.[52]

In subsequent years, the Snyder account of Eisenhower's 1949 illness has been widely accepted.[53] Eisenhower had, after all, suffered from acute abdominal discomfort ever since he was a young man, and Snyder's description of the general's 1949 symptoms conformed to a pattern established over several decades. Recently, however, a medical history of Dwight D. Eisenhower compiled by Dr. Thomas Mattingly, Eisenhower's cardiologist during his White House years and beyond, has been made available for review at the Eisenhower Library in Abilene; and in it Mattingly introduces a new and startling interpretation of the events of 1949. Mattingly reports that in 1982 he was told by a retired army medical officer, Dr. Charles Leedham, that he had treated Dwight Eisenhower in 1949 for a heart attack at Oliver General Hospital in Augusta, Georgia. After investigating the symptoms and circumstances of Eisenhower's 1949 illness, Mattingly concludes that Eisenhower had, in fact, suffered a mild heart attack rather than an abdominal obstruction in 1949, and that Snyder had deliberately misdiagnosed the nature of Ike's collapse in order to avoid damaging his likely future political career. A sixty-two-year-old man who had suffered a heart attack three years earlier would have been seriously handicapped in the presidential campaign of 1952—undoubtedly the reason for Mattingly's belief that Eisenhower "sanctioned and collaborated in the deception."[54]

Mattingly argues that Snyder was untruthful in stating that he had consulted no other physician, since other physicians certainly seem to have been consulted in Washington, Key West, and Augusta. Also, whereas Snyder had indicated that Eisenhower had played golf every day, weather permitting, while in Augusta, Dr. Leedham revealed that Eisenhower had been hospitalized there under his care, and that Dr. Snyder and Eisenhower's military aide had been in "almost constant attendance in the hospital."[55]

Mattingly found lab tests Leedham had ordered at the time on Eisenhower's gastrointestinal and genitourinary system, as well as an electrocardiogram, dated 4 April 1949, taken at the U.S. Naval Hospital in Key West. After reviewing the cardiac readings with other cardiologists, Mattingly concluded that "the single tracing . . . does fall into the category of an abnormal electrocardiogram suspicious of myocardial damage."[56]

At the time of his 1949 illness, Eisenhower abruptly stopped smoking, bringing an end to a habit begun at West Point many years before. He had smoked as many as four packs of cigarettes a day and refused, or been unable, to stop smoking on any previous occasion. He is reported to have told Clare Booth Luce, the author and the wife of the publisher Henry Luce, in 1950 that he had given up smoking because he had had "a little heart trouble."[57] In 1967, Eisenhower ascribed his giving up cigarettes to the fact that he "wanted above everything else to avoid another collapse."[58]

Although Mattingly views Eisenhower's behavior in this instance as supporting the diagnosis of a mild heart attack, he is not able to demonstrate conclusively that his version of 1949 events is accurate. In fact, his statement that the 1949 electrocardiogram reading was "suspicious of myocardial damage" is seriously undermined by a letter Mattingly himself wrote to Dr. Leedham on 15 January 1984. In that letter, Mattingly points out that while Eisenhower's 1949 heart readings were suggestive of cardiac damage, similar readings were seen in both a 1947 and a 1952 electrocardiogram, "thus indicating that these were chronic configurations and not the result of resolving changes of a recent myocardial damage."[59]

Despite the fact that the true nature and extent of Eisenhower's 1949 illness may never be known with certainty, Snyder added considerably to the mystery—and indirectly provided substantiation for Mattingly's diagnosis—in another draft chapter of his book manuscript. Earlier in that volume, he had written that Eisenhower's 1949 ailment had been intestinal in nature. Later, however, he commented that "during the 2 ½ years at Columbia University . . . , the General had suffered no severe abdominal disturbances."[60] Since Eisenhower was president of Columbia at the time of his 1949 collapse, Snyder's words lend credence to Mattingly's argument. To be sure, Dr. Snyder was quite old when he was writing the Eisenhower manuscript, and this apparent contradiction may simply reflect a temporary loss of memory.

Also, the approximately seven weeks it took Eisenhower to recuperate after being stricken in March 1949 seems inordinately long if the ailment were only another episode of his recurring abdominal discomfort, particularly since no surgery was performed on the general at the time. Moreover, two possibly interrelated events, which occurred early in the Eisenhower administration, at least suggest that Mattingly's interpretation of the 1949 illness may well be on the mark, and that Eisenhower's well-publicized heart attack in 1955 may not have been his first. In fact, as I shall discuss, it may not even have been his second.

The First Term: 1953–57

Beginning in 1943, there was considerable speculation throughout the country about Dwight D. Eisenhower's possible presidential candidacy. Both parties wooed the general for several years; but in January 1952, he announced that he was a Republican, and this "reduced by half the partisan pressures."[61] Later in 1952, Eisenhower sought his party's nomination for president as the candidate of moderate Republicans. His principal opponent was Senator Robert A. Taft of Ohio, the favorite of party conservatives. After an intense struggle, Eisenhower won the nomination and then chose California's Senator Richard Nixon as his vice-presidential running mate.

During the fall campaign, Eisenhower celebrated his sixty-second birthday, making him one of the oldest presidential nominees in American history. The campaign he waged, however, belied his age. He traveled more miles than his younger opponent, spoke more extensively, met more often with the press, and never appeared as exhausted as Adlai Stevenson occasionally did.[62] On election day, in a landslide victory, Eisenhower became the first Republican to capture the White House since Herbert Hoover won it in 1928. In January 1953, he became the oldest man to be inaugurated President of the United States since William Henry Harrison's inauguration in 1841 at the age of sixty-eight.

THE "MYSTERY ILLNESS" OF APRIL 1953

On 16 April 1953, President Eisenhower delivered a speech on world peace to the American Society of Newspaper Editors. He had worked hard on the speech and, during the hours before giving it, had become nauseated and experienced stomach pains.[63] In the course of his remarks later that evening, he became pale, began to perspire heavily, and then became so dizzy that he thought he was about to faint. Racked by chills, the President had to hold onto the podium with both hands so as not to collapse.[64] His voice faltered; and as he neared the end of his remarks, he was skipping sentences.[65] Afterward, the White House announced that he had been suffering from food poisoning.[66] An alternative view would be that the President had simply experienced another of his many bouts with abdominal pain and discomfort.

Recently, however, Dr. Thomas Mattingly has offered a new interpretation of Eisenhower's 1953 illness, suggesting that the symptoms experienced by the President were indicative of serious heart problems. Mattingly has written that there is "abundant evidence" for believing that the 1953 illness was a manifestation of coronary heart disease; and he diagnoses Eisenhower's condition that spring evening as "an impending" or "a mild" heart attack. Moreover, he again accuses Snyder of a deceptive diagnosis which was announced to the press.[67]

Just as Snyder would have been reluctant for political reasons to reveal an Eisenhower heart attack in 1949, so, too, would he have been to reveal a heart attack in 1953. An announcement that the President had suffered a heart attack or serious heart difficulties after less than three months in office would have undermined confidence in the likelihood of his surviving even his first term in office and badly damaged his presidency in its infancy.

It is not possible to determine now whether Snyder or Mattingly was correct in diagnosing Eisenhower's 1953 "mystery illness." In 1954, however, when Mattingly was about to complete his assignment as chief of cardiology at Walter Reed Hospital and being considered for possible assignment overseas, the White House intervened. Mattingly was informed that his transfer to Europe was canceled, and that his continued assignment at Walter Reed was desired. Moreover, "he was to be assigned to quarters on the post at WRGH [Walter Reed General Hospital] so as to be more available at all hours."[68] Why the White House would have taken these actions if Eisenhower had had no prior history of cardiac problems is puzzling. Indeed, the reassignment of Mattingly to his chief of cardiology position, and the change in his living arrangements in order to increase his availability at the White House, suggest strongly that Eisenhower had, in fact, experienced serious heart problems prior to his acknowledged heart attack in 1955. It even suggests that the 1955 attack may have been Eisenhower's third.

THE HEART ATTACK OF SEPTEMBER 1955

Whether it first manifested itself in 1955 or earlier, Dwight Eisenhower was a prime candidate for coronary disease. Not only was his family history studded with cardiovascular and vascular illness, but he was hard-driving, tense, and impatient—definite signs of a type-A personality—and his temper had become legendary. His cholesterol levels were normal, but he had abnormally high levels of beta lipoprotein, "the lipid fraction identified as a high risk factor." For many years, he suffered from transient hypertension, a condition that may well have been caused by the small tumor discovered in one of his adrenal glands during his post-mortem in 1969. On top of his heavy smoking habit, he had not, during middle age, followed a sound regimen of physical activity.[69] In addition, one of his doctors went so far as to write of his 1955 attack that "the heart attack was about due anyway."[70]

Eisenhower's first acknowledged heart attack occurred while he was on vacation in Colorado. His schedule there was an abbreviated one, with ample time for relaxation and rest. He would work for a relatively brief period each day and then play golf, go fishing, play bridge, or work on one of his paintings. But the White House and its pressures follow presidents wherever they go. On the day of his heart attack, the President had cooked a hearty breakfast of eggs, sausages, ham, and blackeyed peas for his companions at Aksel Nielsen's ranch in Fraser, Colorado. He had then driven to Denver and worked in his office at the Lowry Air Force Base for several hours; afterward, he adjourned to Cherry Hills Golf Course, where he played a morning round of eighteen holes and an afternoon round of nine holes, separated by a luncheon of hamburger and raw onions which he thought brought on indigestion.

His physician reports that the President was "exuberant" up to the fourteenth hole of the first golf game, but then experienced a string of interruptions that irritated him considerably. Eisenhower later explained that while golfing he had received word of a phone call from Washington and, after returning to the Clubhouse, learned that Secretary of State John Foster Dulles wanted to talk with him. This upset him greatly because he felt it was an unnecessary call.[71] Before he could telephone Dulles, however, he was informed that the secretary of state was en route to an engagement and would call back in an hour. At the appointed time, Eisenhower returned to the clubhouse, only to be told that there was a problem with the phone lines and that he would be notified as soon as the call could go through. After returning to the golf course, the President was informed that the call from Dulles had come through, so he had to rush back to the clubhouse once again to take it. Later that afternoon, Eisenhower was again called to the telephone from the golf course for another conversation with Dulles. After a period of waiting, he learned that Dulles had not requested another conversation, and that the latest interruption had been an error. The President perhaps understated his reaction to all of this when he wrote that "my disposition deteriorated rapidly."[72] Snyder recalled that "at this point his [Eisenhower's] anger became so real that the veins stood out on his forehead like whipcords."[73] He returned to the golf course but soon experienced the symptoms of indigestion that he attributed to his luncheon menu, and departed for his mother-in-law's residence. Most cardiologists on the case agreed that Eisenhower probably had suffered his heart attack on the golf course during the afternoon of 23 September, rather than on 24 September when the actual diagnosis of myocardial infarction was made.[74]

The President worked briefly on a painting after reaching home and then entertained guests at a roast lamb dinner. He had nothing to drink, however, since he did not feel well and decided to retire early. Around 2:30 A.M., Mrs. Eisenhower heard the President tossing and turning in his bed and asked him if he was having a nightmare. When he replied that he was not, she returned to her bedroom. Ten minutes later, the President came into her room, complaining of chest pains but not telling her how intense they actually were.[75] She gave him milk of magnesia since he had complained earlier of indigestion, and then telephoned Dr. Snyder who detected a "particular note of alarm in her voice."[76]

Shortly thereafter, Snyder arrived at the Doud residence, bringing with him, for reasons he never explained, oxygen and the various drugs he would need to fight a heart attack. If Eisenhower had had no history of heart disease, it is difficult to understand why Snyder would have arrived so equipped, especially since what he had always feared was an intracranial, rather than a cardiac, accident.[77]

He found the President agitated and with pain in his lower chest. After listening to his heart and taking his blood pressure, Snyder quickly and correctly diagnosed Eisenhower's condition as a serious heart attack. He gave the President amyl nitrate to sniff, then injected him with papaverine in order to dilate his heart arteries. There soon followed injections of morphine to reduce pain and heparin to stop blood clotting.

The President was very restless and would not tolerate an oxygen mask. Snyder points out that Eisenhower's pulse had steadied somewhat, but that the President "was incoherently insistent that I give him further relief from his pain."[78] He administered another injection of morphine at 3:45 A.M.; but soon after this, Ike's blood pressure collapsed, and his pulse rate shot up alarmingly. Although one of Eisenhower's aides was rubbing him with pure alcohol, and hot water bottles were placed around his body, his skin showed signs of cool perspiration, and he went into a state of shock.

Although Snyder claims that he was "disturbed," "alarmed," and even "shaken" at Eisenhower's condition, he made no effort at this time to summon outside assistance. Instead, he asked Mamie at 4:05 A.M. to slip into bed with the President and wrap herself around him "to see if this would quiet him and assist in warming his body."[79] Almost immediately after she had done so, Eisenhower became calm and then fell asleep.

By 8:00 A.M., Snyder felt that the President had survived the crisis and was "improving with every moment." He still declined, however, to call for help, a controversial decision on his part. Had Eisenhower died, Snyder would undoubtedly have faced an avalanche of criticism and almost certainly been accused of malpractice. Even when the President began to recover, reporters raised questions about the wisdom and propriety of Snyder's actions. The doctor became so upset at press criticism that at one point "he was actually in tears."[80] Snyder consistently defended the way in which he oversaw Eisenhower's treatment during this initial period: "I simply could not justify disturbing him simply to satisfy a diagnostic demand. The hours he slept during that period from early morning until twelve noon were more responsible for the ultimate recovery of the President than the entire remaining course of treatment."[81]

Shortly after Eisenhower awakened, Snyder telephoned the commanding general of Fitzsimons Army Hospital and requested him to send a cardiac specialist to the Doud residence in order to take an electrocardiogram. Colonel James Pollock soon arrived, took the tracing, and judged Eisenhower to have suffered "a massive infarct"—a diagnosis Snyder shared.[82]

Snyder had told Eisenhower's assistant press secretary at 7:00 A.M. that the President had had an attack of indigestion, because he didn't want the news of a heart attack to disrupt the calm and peace of his departure from the Doud residence—a decision that, he later wrote, "limited the heart damage to the minimum."[83] Eisenhower's press aide dutifully announced to reporters that the President had indigestion, and that it "wasn't serious; it is the kind of 24 hour stuff that many people have had."[84] Snyder later admitted that had Eisenhower not been President of the United States, he would have been treated at the Doud home under false diagnosis of a gastrointestinal disorder;[85] but, since he was President, and the attack serious, hospitalization was the appropriate course.

Surprisingly, the President was allowed to walk to his limousine after being carried down the stairs of his mother-in-law's home. After being driven to Fitzsimons Army Hospital, he was put to bed and, since he was experiencing mild respiratory distress, placed in an oxygen tent. This was upsetting to the President, Snyder reporting that "tears were as near there [his eyes] as I ever had seen."[86]

At 2:40 P.M., the press was finally informed that the President had suffered a "mild coronary thrombosis." This same report was again given at 3:05 P.M., even though the attending physicians Pollock and Snyder were agreed that Eisenhower's heart attack had been "massive." Finally, at the 10:20 P.M. press briefing, the word "mild" was deleted from the description of Eisenhower's condition.[87] Soon after, the press was informed that the President's heart attack had been "moderate," a 3 on a 5-point scale. This announcement of a life-threatening presidential illness had immediate repercussions: the Dow Jones index fell by more than thirty points, reducing the value of stocks by some twelve billion dollars, in the most serious collapse since the crash of 1929.[88]

Other physicians, notably Dr. Thomas Mattingly, Eisenhower's cardiologist, and Dr. Paul Dudley White, a civilian cardiologist from Boston, were flown to Denver to join the team of doctors attending the President. Dr. White became the leading spokesperson for the group and soon emerged as something of a celebrity because of his unique position in disseminating information about the President's condition and care.

Upon examining his patient, White found that the scar on Eisenhower's heart muscle was "about the size of a large olive, in the anterior wall of the left ventricle." The President's heart sounds were mediocre, and his pulse was a little fast with many premature beats. There was, however, no sign of heart failure. White reported that he didn't like the heart sounds or fast pulse, and felt that the next few days would be critical.[89]

Eisenhower at first seemed to rebound quickly from his coronary. On 28 September, his doctors felt that he had improved to the point where he could be lifted from his bed and allowed to sit up in a chair for increasing periods of time each day. Encouraged by this, the President told one of his doctors at the time, "I feel so good, if I didn't think you knew what you were doing, I would suspect you of having the wrong patient in bed."[90]

However, a few days after being allowed out of bed, the President's electrocardiogram showed negative changes, and he experienced a new episode of chest pains. The White House press secretary announced to reporters that the President is "a little tired this evening and did not feel as well as usual. Otherwise, his condition is good. When I say he is a little tired, that is a change from the usual."[91]

The President's physicians were considerably more alarmed than the press briefing suggested. Mattingly was of the opinion that there was a possibility of "either an extension of the initial infarction," or that a new infarction had developed.[92] Snyder believed that "there was no question but that there was an extension around the periphery of the primary lesion," and that "the President developed a pericardial adhesion in this area."[93] White agreed that "there was at least poor healing and slowed healing of the initial infarction," and that a slight possibility existed that an extension of the infarct may have occurred.[94] He told the press and members of the Eisenhower family, however, that no complications had developed. But to a medical colleague, White was considerably more forthcoming. On 25 October, he wrote Dr. E. Cowles Andrus that Eisenhower

did have a right smart attack and has undoubtedly (and confidentially) had a larger area of infarction than might be interpreted from some of the earlier reports at least. . . . He has gotten along remarkably well, in fact much better than I would have thought likely on looking at his electrocardiogram.[95]

Eisenhower was discouraged when doctors told him that his heart was more badly damaged than he had thought. His faith in Dr. White may have been undermined somewhat since White had strongly advocated the course of treatment which may have produced the President's sudden deterioration. Yet none of the President's cardiologists had objected to or opposed the program of exercise White had recommended. All, therefore, were deemed worthy of some criticism by Eisenhower. Snyder recounts that "each time he discussed this matter with his intimate friends, he seemed to be saying to me that he felt that I was guilty of a grave error in judgement in not protecting him from this abuse." Snyder never defended himself from Eisenhower's criticism because he feared to anger him, and felt that arousing "the President's anger would seem like committing murder to me."[96]

Subsequent electrocardiograms convinced Eisenhower's doctors that either an extension of his heart injury or a new injury to his heart had, in fact, occurred. Also, Mattingly detected a new and grave area of concern in these heart tracings: specifically, that the transverse diameter of Eisenhower's heart had increased by 5 percent to 10 percent, with a bulge appearing along the left ventricular border. Mattingly believed this bulge to be an aneurysm of the left ventricle, a condition he anticipated would lead to further complications. Such aneurysms often resulted in congestive heart failure and death: in fact, studies at the time revealed that almost 90 percent of patients whose myocardial infarctions were complicated by ventricular aneurysms died within five years, with 70 percent of these succumbing to congestive heart failure.[97]

Eisenhower's other doctors did not concur in Mattingly's diagnosis. Neither Snyder nor White were convinced that an aneurysm had developed in Eisenhower's heart, and their commitment to the anticoagulant therapy Mattingly advocated was only lukewarm. Also, no public announcement was made of Mattingly's findings. The 1956 campaign was, after all, already on the horizon, and Mattingly's diagnosis put the President at greater risk of death than his supporters would have liked.

After Eisenhower's death of cardiovascular collapse in 1969, his autopsy revealed "a large, thick and calcified walled aneurysm . . . , the highly calcified wall indicating it had been present for years"—and thus fully confirmed Mattingly's position. He relates that "the pathologist agreed that it had probably existed since 1955."[98]

In 1955, however, despite the fact that Mattingly's interpretation of the condition of the President's heart differed in an important and alarming respect from that of his other doctors, the public was informed that Eisenhower had suffered a heart attack without any complications. News of a possible aneurysm in Eisenhower's heart was actively suppressed, not only because his doctors disagreed on this point but also out of political considerations.

Ironically, Eisenhower himself believed in 1955 that a full account of his physical condition should be made available to the public. Long before suffering his heart attack, he had told his press secretary, Jim Hagerty, that if he ever became ill, Hagerty should tell the public "everything." When told after his heart attack that Hagerty was en route to Denver, Eisenhower said, "Good, tell Jim to take over."[99] These words have sometimes been misinterpreted. The President did not mean that his press secretary should run the executive branch of government in Eisenhower's absence; he meant, rather, that Hagerty should "remember our conversation and follow the orders I have given him."[100] As soon as Hagerty arrived in Denver, he began skillfully to control the flow of news about the President. This may well have made him the most powerful press secretary in history, since he was the most senior official on the scene and the President's only authorized spokesperson.[101]

In some respects, but certainly not all, Dr. White was only too ready to comply with the President's wishes about public disclosure. At the physicians' press conference which he had chaired, the Boston cardiologist went so far as to announce that the President had had "a successful bowel movement." He made this rather startling revelation because he was convinced that "doctors around the country would see this as a good prognostic sign."[102] Eisenhower was, however, not pleased, and is reported to have "grimaced" when he learned of White's words.[103] Later, Eisenhower admitted that he had suffered "acute embarrassment," and had told White that "I thought he and Jim were carrying 'realism' a bit too far." Yet he concluded that "it's too late to object now; forget it."[104]

Some Republican strategists as well as a number of Eisenhower's associates were convinced that the excessive candor regarding Eisenhower's heart attack was unwise. On 28 September 1955, C. D. Jackson, special assistant to the President, wrote Richard Nixon expressing concern that the openness about Eisenhower's heart attack "has actually played right into Democrat hands by giving the appearance that the President is permanently incapacitated and that his powers have to be 'divided'." Nixon wrote back almost immediately and pointed out that he had been "knocking down the idea of delegating powers whenever an opportunity has been presented. In view of the President's remarkable recovery, I see no need whatsoever for such a delegation."[105]

The President was indeed recovering. On 6 October, the practice of chair sitting was resumed; and on 23 October, the President stood for the first time since being stricken a month earlier. Three days later, he took his first unaided steps. By early November, he was allowed to walk freely; and by the end of the first week of the month, he was even climbing a few stairs. He was now considered ready for discharge from the hospital, but Eisenhower, ever concerned with the image he would project, delayed his departure by a week so as to be able to walk to his limousine rather than being pushed there in a wheelchair.

On 11 November, he thanked "the medical staff, the nurses, the clinical technicians, the enlisted men," and even the people who "clean out the hospital" for having done so much for him, and then flew to Washington, D.C., where a crowd of five thousand people—including former President Hoover, Vice President Nixon, members of the cabinet, and congressional leaders—welcomed him at the airport. To them, the President announced that "the doctors have given me at least a parole if not a pardon and I expect to be back at my accustomed duties, although they say I must ease my way into them and not bulldoze my way into them."[106]

For the trip to the White House, Eisenhower had requested an open car so that he could stand and wave to the crowds lining the route. However, the limousine provided him was closed, forcing him to " 'squeegee' around from window to window with considerable physical strain" in an effort to acknowledge the crowd's greetings, and even to kneel on the floor "in order to make myself seen."[107] He arrived at the White House tired and annoyed.[108]

The President soon left Washington for his Gettysburg farm, where his recuperation continued without serious interruption. Gettysburg was close enough to Washington to permit easy access to official duties yet far enough "to discourage the casual visitor."[109] At the farm, however, Eisenhower lapsed into a state of depression not uncommon to heart attack victims. He felt bored and useless as he bided his time away from the nation's capital. On one occasion, he referred to himself as "an old dodo"[110] and as a man whom time had passed by.[111] He would sit passively for long periods, brooding silently about the future,[112] and his dark mood reflected his frustration.

On 22 November, the cabinet met at Camp David with the President presiding. Chief of Staff Sherman Adams described this as "a moving event for all of us." He wrote that the President was a little thinner but "his eye and his glance were sharp and he showed, perhaps a bit consciously and deliberately, an added force and energy in his comments and expression of opinion."[113]

At the conclusion of the meeting, the President thanked his colleagues for the fine way they had conducted themselves while he was away. He told them that their behavior had "made him proud of his own selections and grateful for the way the group proceeded." Their thorough dedication to a set of broad principles was noted and Eisenhower indicated that his illness had given him a chance to observe that dedication.[114] Although the President expressed his gratitude to the cabinet for operating smoothly in his absence, he did not thank anyone personally for his or her performance. Nixon attributed this to the fact that "he felt that all of us . . . were merely doing our duty."[115]

On 3 December, the President became alarmed when he experienced an episode of chest pains; these, however, were found to have resulted from indigestion caused by a franks-and-sauerkraut luncheon.[116] A few days before Christmas, Eisenhower was back at the White House, pushing his aides to bring him "the hard ones" to tackle.[117] He was now capable of conducting the affairs of his office without undue fatigue, although he did complain of pressure in his chest after shaking hands with seven hundred White House staff members at a holiday reception.[118]

As a result of his heart problems, doctors indicated that Eisenhower would have to modify his work routine. They preferred him to stay out of his office until at least 8:30 A.M. each day[119] and also advised him to follow a fat-free diet, lie down for thirty minutes before lunch, spend the hour after lunch talking with friends and associates about noncontroversial subjects or working on light paperwork, and take a ten-minute rest at the end of each hour during cabinet and National Security Council meetings. In the event that he had to attend a social gathering in the evening, his day's work should be reduced correspondingly.[120] Excessive fatigue was to be avoided at all costs, especially if accompanied by overheating.

The President was told to keep his weight at 172 pounds, 6 pounds lower than his customary weight. Eisenhower found it difficult to keep his weight at the desired level since he enjoyed food so thoroughly. But he resented, in particular, the period of midday rest he was instructed to take each day before lunch because it caused "inconvenience . . . in planning a day's schedule."[121]

The President was also warned against losing his temper.[122] One of his aides recounts that Eisenhower was both dutiful and successful in following his doctors' orders to control his emotions. By 1956, "his capacity for anger was newly and markedly disciplined: not once in these months did there explode one of those outbursts of raging impatience so familiar in the past." The President told this aide, "Emotions are the things you got to watch out for. So all the doctors say. The worst is anger. . . . you notice I don't get angry any more—like I used to, just don't let myself. Can't afford to."[123]

THE DECISION TO RUN AGAIN

As Eisenhower recuperated from his 1955 heart attack, considerable attention became focused on his possible candidacy for re-election in 1956. Immediately after he was stricken, most of the press corps thought that he would not run again. Vice President Nixon was convinced that he would not.[124] The campaign for another term and the four additional years as President would subject Eisenhower to considerable strain and put him at risk of further heart problems. This, coupled with the fact that he would be sixty-six years of age in 1956, seemed to argue against another candidacy, and many people in Washington and elsewhere counted him out. Even the President seemed to share their concern, telling his vice president, on the day after Christmas 1955, that "he did not see how he could run in good conscience with that 'sword of Damocles' hanging over his head."[125]

Also, rumors had circulated even before his heart attack that Eisenhower was determined to be a one-term President. In fact, he had wanted to include in his 1953 inaugural address a pledge that he would not run for a second term, but had been warned that he would have less influence as a lame-duck President and should, therefore, be silent on the likelihood of another term. While Eisenhower had acceded to this advice, he later told associates that he would suffer a similar loss of influence in any second term because the Twenty-second Amendment made it impossible for him to run again in 1960.[126] This, therefore, became a political argument—at least, in his own mind—against another candidacy in 1956.

Eisenhower's personal predisposition seems to have been for one term. As early as December 1953, he told his brother Milton that "if ever for a second time I should show any signs of yielding to persuasion, please call in the psychiatrist—or even better the sheriff."[127] In April 1954, he offered to bet House Speaker Joseph Martin that he would not run for a second term: "I don't want a second term. Four years in the White House is enough for one man."[128] Three months before his 1955 heart attack, he told a friend that he had now fulfilled his "special duty," and, in late summer 1955, warned the Republican national chairman, Leonard Hall, "I've given my adult life to my country. I've done enough. I'm not going to run again."[129]

The pressure on Eisenhower to change his mind was substantial, and some of it came from an unexpected source. Mamie Eisenhower became convinced that her husband's work as President was not yet finished. She also worried that premature retirement might do more to bring on premature death than all the stresses of the presidency combined. Among key family members, however, she stood alone. His brother Milton and his son, John, both felt that retirement in January 1957 would add years to the President's life,[130] and John was particularly bitter about what the pressures of the presidency had done to his father.[131]

Republican party leaders, of course, wished Eisenhower to seek another term, as did loyal aides and associates. The former group was alarmed that without Eisenhower at the head of the Republican ticket in 1956, their party might well lose the presidency as well as some governorships and a number of seats in the House and Senate. One Republican state chairman answered a question about what should be done if Eisenhower declined to run again by saying, "When I get to that bridge, I will jump off it."[132]

Eisenhower was vulnerable to this argument since he had often expressed concern to his friends that "the country might fall into the hands of persons who had no real principles and who just believed in 'give away' for the purpose of trying to buy votes and favor at home and abroad."[133] Moreover, Eisenhower had indicated that although he wished that a successor to himself could be found within the inner circle of his administration, "he was not sure that he could see around him a person who had the desired youth and vigor, and who at the same time was respected by the country as having maturity and judgment."[134] In March 1956, he confided to a boyhood friend that he actually had a "guilty feeling" because he had failed to develop a suitable candidate who could succeed him in the White House.[135]

Most of his close associates also urged him to seek re-election to another term. General Clay was convinced that if Eisenhower did not run again, he would die,[136] and tried to mobilize the President's associates into a lobbying force behind another term. Secretary of State Dulles worked to convince the President that he was the principle force for peace in the world, and that without him, the cause for which he had worked so hard would be endangered. Treasury Secretary George Humphrey took a more practical approach in trying to convince the President to run again, telling him that "he had demonstrated so well his ability to delegate authority that it would be a shame to break the continuity of progress he had initiated both at home and abroad."[137]

At a press conference on 8 January 1956, the President indicated that he found the presidency to be "the most taxing job, as far as tiring of the mind and spirit" was concerned, but then admitted that it has "its inspirations which tend to counteract each other." Asked then whether "a sense of duty" might persuade him to seek another term, Eisenhower replied:

Well, I certainly sincerely trust that all of my actions with respect to public duty over the past forty years have been inspired and directed by my own sense of duty. So, of course, that would have something to do with it . . . but where does the sense of duty point, and who determines what the duty is?[138]

On 13 January, Eisenhower convened a dinner meeting of his closest aides and confidants and asked their advice on his possible candidacy for a second term. The group included Milton Eisenhower, Sherman Adams, John Foster Dulles, Herbert Brownell, George Humphrey, Henry Cabot Lodge, Leonard Hall, Arthur Summerfield, Wilton Persons, James Hagerty, Howard Pyle, and Tom Stephens. Not surprisingly, all those present with the exception of his brother urged him to run again. Prominent among the many reasons they offered for their affirmative recommendation was that he was the only Republican who could win in 1956, and it was his duty to lead the party once again to victory. The President felt that this conviction on their part "presented a challenge that I could not ignore."[139]

A month later, on 14 February, his doctors announced that the battery of tests they had conducted on Eisenhower indicated that he had made a good recovery from his heart attack. No symptoms suggested either weakness of the heart muscle or insufficient cardiac reserve. They concluded that "we believe that medically the chances are that the President should be able to carry on an active life satisfactorily for another five to ten years."[140]

At least two of his doctors, however, preferred for medical reasons that Eisenhower not seek a second term. As indicated earlier, Dr. Mattingly fully expected serious complications from the aneurysm he had detected in Eisenhower's heart, and Dr. White remarked that "if I were in his shoes, I wouldn't want to run again, having seen the strain."[141] White recommended to the President privately that, instead of running for re-election, he should become "a World Ambassador" for peace, working as a former President to promote peace among nations. This advice irritated the President and seems to have made him even more disenchanted with White. Soon after, he termed the Boston cardiologist a "publicity seeker" and indicated that he no longer wished to be under his care.[142] Despite his doctors' misgivings, Eisenhower announced on 29 February, both at a press conference and during a speech to the nation, that he would indeed accept the Republican nomination for the presidency once again. He admitted that his heart attack had changed his life, but assured the country that "my answer would not be affirmative unless I thought I could last out the five years."[143]

A number of factors persuaded Eisenhower to seek a second term. His work was unfinished, and he needed more time to accomplish his objectives. Having failed to groom a logical successor to himself in the Republican party, he felt he had to stay on to do the job himself. The Democratic party's candidates were uniformly unsatisfactory: He had developed a definite dislike for Stevenson,[144] felt that Harriman was "a complete nincompoop,"[145] and regarded Estes Kefauver of Tennessee as incompetent to run the office of President.[146] After surveying the field of possible successors in both parties, he simply determined that it would violate his sense of duty to turn the White House over to one of these "lesser" men. His vice president felt that there would certainly be risk to Eisenhower's health if he served another four years as President, but "there would be even greater risk to him from a physical, emotional and mental standpoint if he consciously turned his back on a clear call to national service."[147]

Shortly before his heart attack, the President had told his brother that commentators were claiming that his words and actions over the past several months had given his good friends the clear impression that he would again be a candidate for election in 1956. He then confided that "next to my own concepts of duty, one of the most decisive purposes that has ruled my life is a determination never to give any real friend the right to believe that 'I had let him down.' "[148] Once again, Eisenhower was stressing the importance of duty in his life—in this instance, his duty to his friends, which required that he not disappoint them.

Finally and significantly, far from dissuading him from seeking another term, Eisenhower's 1955 heart attack played a vital role in convincing him to become a candidate for re-election. His lengthy convalescence had bored him greatly. Even his enforced rest at his Gettysburg farm, where he would pace the living room "like a caged tiger,"[149] had shown him all too clearly what his life as a former President would be like, and he did not much care for the picture. He admitted to the press that he had felt "strange" while away from the White House at Gettysburg.[150] He had apparently missed the activity of the presidency and came to realize firsthand the drawbacks associated with retirement. The President's press secretary was convinced that his convalescence persuaded him to run for a second term because it was then that he faced "the complete and utter boredom of Gettysburg."[151] His vice president, viewing the President from a close vantage point, believed that his heart attack had been the key element in Eisenhower's decision to seek re-election.[152]

Asked by a reporter on 29 February 1956 whether he had made up his mind previous to his heart attack to run for another term, Eisenhower replied, "That is one secret I don't think I will ever tell anybody."[153] However, the President's chief of staff later revealed that Eisenhower had once told his aides, "You know, if it hadn't been for that heart attack, I doubt if I would have been a candidate again."[154]

ILEITIS SURGERY: JUNE 1956

Shortly after deciding to run for a second term, Dwight Eisenhower was once again stricken. For more than three decades, he had experienced stomach pains of considerable intensity, whose source doctors had never been able to locate. His appendix was removed in 1923, and his gall bladder examined on several occasions, all without effect. He was treated for amoebiosis in 1929, examined for gastric or duodenal ulcers in 1931, and diagnosed as having acute enteritis in 1937. Despite his strenuous attempts to locate a medical remedy, his stomach pains continued unabated into the years of his presidency. In fact, at the 1952 convention which nominated him for President, Eisenhower was suffering from severe abdominal discomfort;[155] and during his first term, stomach problems were frequent and troublesome. He was told to follow a bland diet at all times and to drink bottled water, and only bottled water, wherever he went.[156]

A thorough physical examination in May 1956 disclosed the existence of a "burned-out terminal ileitis," which is a serious constriction of the intestine. This finding was not revealed at the time, ostensibly because doctors feared that it would cause the President excessive anxiety.[157] Instead, the press was told that "barium studies showed a normally functioning digestive tract." The President was later said to have taken great exception to the deception practiced by his doctors in this instance.[158]

On 7 June, Eisenhower attended the White House news photographers dinner. Although he had just come through a "succession of very, very tough meetings" which would have killed "a lesser man,"[159] the President seemed in good spirits and ate his dinner with great enjoyment. Later that evening, however, Dr. Snyder was summoned to the White House because the President was in great pain. He found Eisenhower's abdomen to be distended and tender and his pulse rapid. He had considerable heart arrhythmia; but, otherwise, his heart sounds were good. Snyder learned to his dismay that Eisenhower had eaten a Waldorf salad for lunch that day, contrary to his doctor's warning that raw vegetables were difficult for him to digest. The President's physician suspected that pieces of undigested celery were lodged in the President's constricted intestine and were responsible for the blockage now evident.

Eisenhower was given quinidine sulfate, but his condition worsened. At 7:50 A.M. on 8 June, Snyder informed the President's secretary that Eisenhower had a headache and a digestive upset, and that all appointments were to be canceled except the cabinet meeting, which was to be rescheduled for 2:00 P.M. It soon became evident that the President's condition was more serious than Snyder had at first thought. By 8:15 A.M., he told Sherman Adams and Jim Hagerty that Eisenhower had "chronic ileitis" and was not improving. It was around this time that the White House physician came to realize that an operation would be necessary on his most famous patient.

By 10 A.M., the President was experiencing muscle cramps in both legs; and at 10:30, he vomited a substantial amount of fluid. Within forty-five minutes, he was perspiring heavily, especially his forehead and hands. Finally, at 1:25 P.M., Eisenhower was taken by stretcher to an ambulance and driven to Walter Reed Hospital, where he was examined by Dr. Leonard Heaton and several other physicians. The President was now listless, apathetic, and perspiring freely, and his skin was cool and clammy. He was experiencing mild but intensifying discomfort over his entire abdomen. Quite nauseated, he occasionally vomited and showed some shocklike symptoms of low blood pressure. The vomiting was controlled through "intravenous therapy," but there was abdominal distention and cramplike pain that was becoming increasingly severe.[160]

Initially, it was decided to treat the President conservatively. Whether doctors really believed that conservative treatment would suffice, or whether they were afraid to be the ones to "cut open" the President of the United States, is unclear. Whatever the reason, they procrastinated for a dangerously long time. Heaton later claimed that he wanted a unanimous decision from attending physicians before surgery was undertaken. By 8 P.M., all but one doctor favored an operation; and while they waited for the holdout to capitulate, fears began to be expressed that the delay was putting Eisenhower in danger of death. Snyder was concerned, in particular, about the possible onset of intestinal gangrene and urged that surgery be performed without delay. He later wrote that the nerves of the participating physicians had been "rubbed raw."[161]

At midnight, all doctors concurred that surgery was indicated after the

President's abdomen continued to swell. Strangely, Mamie Eisenhower remained unconvinced that surgery was necessary, and refused to sign the necessary consent papers. Her son finally signed them in her place.[162] When told of his doctors' unanimous decision, the President simply said, "Well, let's go." Apparently, however, his work was very much on his mind for, as he was being given the anesthetic, Eisenhower remarked to Dr. Heaton, "You know, Leonard, I have a lot of bills to sign and I am going to have to be able to sign them within three or four days." He then muttered something about the Constitution and nodded off to sleep.[163]

Surgery commenced at 2:57 A.M. on 9 June and lasted until 4:51 A.M. When doctors opened the President, they found that a plug of undigested celery was obstructing his constricted intestine. Furthermore, they discovered "dense adhesions" and that the involved area was grayish-red, thickened, inert and contracted with claw-like projections."[164] Also discovered was a condition known as Crohn's disease, an ailment that gradually narrows the intestine and eventually produces a bulge that must be removed.

Surgeons performed an ileotransverse colostomy in which about ten inches of the President's ileum was surgically bypassed and the healthy intestine connected to the right side of the transverse of the large intestine. The diseased intestine was not removed but rather bypassed and allowed to remain in the President's body. The nature of the surgery performed on the President stirred some controversy in medical circles. Some doctors believed that resectional surgery, which would have removed the constricted intestine, should have been performed. Eisenhower's doctors have since explained that resectional surgery would have required two operations, too much surgery for a patient who had recently experienced a heart attack. Also they were candid in admitting that resectional surgery would have required a three- to four-month recuperation period, which would have made it difficult for Eisenhower to run for another term that fall.[165]

It was clear from the outset that information about the President's condition would not be as plentiful in this instance as it had been after his heart attack. Press Secretary Hagerty explained that "a President's heart attack is the property of the people. But we did not consider the ileitis something that endangered the President's life." Since he was certainly not in critical condition, press briefings would not be as frequent, and doctors not as accessible to the press, as they had been after the heart attack. Soon after the President went under the knife, however, Dr. Heaton assured the press that "there is no relationship between ileitis and malignant disease. I want you to know that there was nothing suggesting a malignant disease found at the operation."[166]

Despite these hopeful words, Eisenhower's aides felt considerable concern over the President's condition. His chief of staff reported that he was told "by a surgeon that the chances are six or eight to one against a man of Eisenhower's age recovering from an ileitis operation."[167] Another aide wrote simply that "the outlook—if not completely gloomy—was certainly not bright."[168]

His surgeons have since reported that the President's condition at no time gave rise to any anxiety, but Eisenhower had to endure a most difficult postoperative convalescence. He was unable to absorb food and lost a considerable amount of weight. He suffered severe pain and developed a wound infection eleven days after surgery. When his son visited his hospital room, he found that "Dad was suffering severely and was really in no mood for visitors."[169]

In one sense, however, he could take great comfort from his ileitis operation: his abdominal surgery had provided his heart with its sternest test since the attack of 1955, and it had passed that test with flying colors. Within a week of the operation, Eisenhower was said to be working several hours each day. He was visited in his hospital room by administration officials as well as by West German Chancellor Konrad Adenauer, but was still in considerable discomfort. His vice president found that Eisenhower "suffered more pain over a longer period of time" and "looked far worse than he had in 1955. He hobbled about, bent over, during his postoperative convalescence, but he was determined to carry out the responsibilities of his job as he saw them." Indeed, the President had told Nixon that this period of illness had increased his fears concerning the constitutional ambiguities on presidential disability: he had been under anesthesia for two hours, and while he was unconscious, "the country was without a chief executive, the armed forces without a commander-in-chief."[170] He was more determined than ever to try to remedy this unfortunate constitutional gap, either by amendment or by some stopgap measure.

Three weeks after undergoing ileitis surgery, the President was discharged from the hospital and went to his Gettysburg farm to recuperate. There he regained his strength, but only slowly. Despite the difficulty of his recovery, he never seriously reconsidered his decision to be a candidate for another term. At a meeting with legislative leaders on 10 July, he promised that he would campaign vigorously. He could not help but know that concerns over his health would necessarily be heightened after this latest bout with illness, and he realized that he would have to dispel these fears by election day in November.

In mid-July, Eisenhower began an abbreviated schedule of office work, but his aides found that a "great physical and psychological depression" was still evident.[171] As a self-imposed test of strength, the President was determined to travel to Panama to attend a meeting of hemispheric heads of state which had been postponed for a month because of his illness. He was convinced that such a journey would demonstrate to the world that his health had returned, and show Latin Americans that the United States was interested in their well-being and held them in respect. Dr. Snyder, aware of the "close relationship between the President's physical condition and his mental outlook,"[172] encouraged Eisenhower to make the trip.

But even as late as 18 July, just a few days before his scheduled departure from Washington, the President was discouraged at his progress and uncertain whether he would be able to make the journey. According to one of his closest aides, Eisenhower was "a sorry sight" just before he left for Panama, and so frustrated that he warned friends that "if I don't feel better than this pretty soon, I'm going to pull out of this whole thing."[173] Within a day, however, he felt better and decided to attend the hemispheric conference after all. The trip proved to be excellent therapy for the President, even through it greatly taxed his strength.

Eisenhower left Washington at midnight on 20 July, wearing a surgical drain.[174] At 8 A.M., he arrived in Panama City and went immediately to a plenary meeting of the eighteen presidents. Afterward, he participated in a wreath-laying ceremony where he "stood bareheaded at attention in a driving rainstorm."[175] Throughout the day, he took six automobile tours and stood in an open car waving to large crowds. That night, he held four conferences with individual presidents before attending a reception at the presidential palace. During the following two days, he delivered his first speech since his surgery, listened to other speakers for more than three hours, held ten private conversations with other presidents, and toured the Panama Canal for more than an hour.

When he returned to Washington, he had, of course, not recovered completely from his recent surgery, but he seemed a remarkably changed man. His depression had vanished, and he appeared to be more vibrant and robust than just a few days earlier. Nixon greeted him at the airport and found that, although he "had left looking like an invalid—sick, tired and in pain— . . . he returned more the old leader, full of bounce and ready to plunge into work." The vice president concluded that "the trip, despite all of its strain upon his weakened body, renewed his physical vigor as well as his mental well-being."[176] The President's physician strongly concurred, feeling that the Panama trip had given Eisenhower "a new lease on life."[177]

THE PAINFUL RE-ELECTION CAMPAIGN OF 1956

During August, the President felt reasonably well but continued to experience abdominal discomfort.[178] He still felt under par after the Republican convention adjourned at the end of the month.[179] Republican strategists were anxious to avoid overtaxing Eisenhower lest he collapse in mid-campaign, and built a campaign designed to protect his health as much as possible. It was decided that the campaign would not begin in earnest until late September, and that Eisenhower would follow a minimum personal speaking schedule. Since he had proven four years earlier that he was a proficient television campaigner, the President would rely on television in 1956 to spare himself the rigors of barnstorming. He would deliver several nationwide TV addresses from the White House, and these would be supplemented largely by Republican spot commercials that would blanket the country.

This strategy, however, served only to heighten fears that Eisenhower was seriously ill and might not survive another term if re-elected. The campaign plan was modified: now Eisenhower would have to leave the White House and "show himself" to the voters. In addition to a limited number of speeches he would deliver on the stump, the President would ride in motorcades, standing in an open car and waving to the cheering crowds. The intent, of course, was to project Eisenhower's vitality to voters and dispel the notion that he was too ill to carry out his responsibilities during a second term. Even his brother, who was deeply concerned about the President's health, advised him to "get out and show the people how healthy you really are. . . . It doesn't even matter what you say."[180]

The motorcades achieved their purpose, even though Eisenhower complained that they were "killers."[181] The people saw their President smiling and waving as he rode in parades in different parts of the country, and television news—as well as Republican spot commercials—underlined the subliminal message: the President was alive, alert, and vigorous; and suggestions that he was near death's door were visibly untrue.

Despite the image projected by television, however, the President was plagued by health problems throughout the campaign period, although these were not made known to the media or the public. On 2 October, soon after the campaign got under way, he developed "a worrisome cough without expectoration." Two days later, his physician detected considerable heart arrhythmia and exaggerated heartbeats. During a motorcade in Pittsburgh on 9 October, Eisenhower's pulse was "rapid and skippy." After drinking two cups of hot coffee and a glass of whiskey, he calmed down, and his pulse returned to normal. He experienced abdominal distress on 14 October and, four days later, felt fatigued and dizzy and had an irregular pulse rate during a West Coast campaign swing. Snyder gave him a nitroglycerine tablet as Eisenhower requested—"presumably as a preventative medication."[182]

On 25 October, the President suffered abdominal pain and, on the following day, developed a case of diarrhea which lasted a month. He again experienced abdominal distention on election eve. On the day voters went to the polls, the President was concerned about some bulging in his abdominal scar, and his surgeon found that it was tender, inflamed, and swollen, conditions that persisted into December.[183] During the campaign period, Eisenhower also suffered from elevations of blood pressure, a recurrence of bursitis, and an upper respiratory infection that was still with him long after the campaign came to a close.[184]

Throughout all of these personal setbacks, Eisenhower fought on, pretending to the nation that his health was sound, and that his illnesses were safely behind him. As with any battle, he wanted to triumph here, too, telling one associate, "I want to win the whole thing . . . six or seven states we can't help, but I don't want to lose any more." From initially respecting his Democratic opponent in 1952, he had finally come to regard him as "a bigger faker than all the rest of them."[185]

Desperate for an issue that might damage his great popularity, the Democrats were stressing the theme of the President's ill health, almost intimating that he was terminally ill and raising simultaneously the "Nixon issue." In fact, on election eve, Stevenson went so far as to say, in one of the most tasteless campaign speeches ever delivered by a candidate for the presidency, that medical evidence strongly suggested that Eisenhower was unlikely to survive four more years as President, and that "a Republican victory tomorrow would mean that Richard Nixon would probably be President of this country within the next four years."[186]

Eisenhower's robust image, projected so powerfully by television, deflated these fears, however; and the popular President swept to another landslide victory. This time he carried forty-one states and captured 57 percent of the popular vote. His victory gave him great satisfaction; but, by campaign's end, he was visibly exhausted. On Inauguration Day, his cardiologist was given a seat in the reviewing stand in front of the White

House just outside the President's own box—a location that Mattingly felt reflected the President's unstable health and his concern that his cardiologist be readily available should his "assistance be needed."[187]

Eisenhower went on to defy Stevenson's gloomy prediction by serving out his second term in office. Irony of ironies, he also outlived both Stevenson and Stevenson's vice-presidential running mate, Estes Kefauver. They died in 1965 and 1963, respectively, whereas Eisenhower survived until 1969, more than eight years after retiring from the presidency and more than twelve years after the 1956 campaign passed into history.

The second term was a difficult one, however; and there are indications that Eisenhower did not enjoy it as much as he had the first. This had an impact on both his morale and his tolerance for the physical indispositions that beset him.[188] Eisenhower was then in his late sixties and fell ill, both seriously and frequently, throughout the 1957–61 period.

The Second Term and After: 1957–69

Dwight D. Eisenhower's second term was filled with many tensions, crises, and disappointments. The summer and fall of 1957 were particularly difficult for him. In July, he lost one of his closest associates when Treasury Secretary Humphrey left the administration. Two months later, he had to send federal troops into Little Rock in order to enforce school desegregation there. In October, the Soviets successfully launched a space satellite, casting doubt on U.S. scientific and technological expertise. Soon after, Attorney General Brownell resigned and returned to private practice. An economic recession seemed to be getting under way, and the administration's legislative program was still incomplete. Writing to a boyhood friend, the President said that for the last year, "his life had been a succession of crises."[189] He also complained to several associates of the tensions of office, saying that doctors had "let him in for something that he was not physically competent to handle."[190] He even confided to his diary that he felt he had made a mistake in deciding to seek a second term.[191]

As one sign of his frustration with his second term difficulties, the President began to show again explosive flashes of his temper which one aide described simply as "awesome, to say the least."[192] On one occasion, he flew into a rage "because his tray of food didn't have a shaker of regular salt."[193] On another, he threw a golf club at his doctor, Howard Snyder, having taken strong exception to the latter's congratulating him for making a "fine shot." Snyder reported that "the staff of the club wrapped itself around my shins and the heavy iron wedge missed me; otherwise I would have had a fractured leg."[194]

In addition to contributing to his outbursts of temper, the crises and aggravations of his second term exacerbated his vulnerability to illness. Just ten months after his second inauguration, the President fell seriously ill; and toward the end of his second term, his cardiovascular problems were so pronounced that had it not been for his determination, strong constitution, and vigilant medical care, he might not have survived his presidency. If, of course, Eisenhower had died in October or early November 1960, Vice President Richard Nixon would have succeeded him immediately as President and would then almost certainly have won the close 1960 election against John Kennedy.

THE STROKE OF NOVEMBER 1957

On 25 November, President Eisenhower confronted the first cardiovascular crisis of the second term. He had gone to the airport that morning to greet the king of Morocco and felt particularly chilled in the raw wind. When he returned to the White House and retired for his noon rest, the President asked for an extra blanket and a hot water bottle. Later, at his desk, he felt dizzy, had trouble picking up some papers, and found that the words on the top sheet "seemed literally to run off the top of the page." Eisenhower dropped his pen and failed, after two or three attempts, to pick it up. When he got to his feet, he had to grab hold of his chair for support. He rang for his personal secretary, Ann Whitman, but could only speak "gibberish" to her. He later wrote, "Words—but not the ones I wanted—came to my tongue. It was impossible for me to express any coherent thought whatsoever. I began to feel truly helpless."[195]

Despite his frustration at his inability to speak coherently, Eisenhower refused to leave the Oval Office and return to his White House living quarters. Instead, he buzzed his appointments secretary, Robert Gray. Gray reported that when he entered Eisenhower's office, the President "looked up at me slowly. It seemed an effort for him to raise his head. He blinked his eyes as if trying to focus his vision" and then called him by his predecessor's name.[196]

Dr. Snyder had been summoned by Whitman and told of the President's difficulty in speaking and his seeming disorientation. Whitman had also reported to him that she had noticed that day that the President was "inclining a little to one side as he walked."[197] When Snyder appeared at Eisenhower's desk, the President became quite irritated. Apparently he resented this unwelcome interruption as he tried, without success, to dictate a letter. He was finally persuaded to return to his living quarters and go to bed. There he again experienced dizziness and had difficulty in moving his legs.[198] These symptoms—which strongly suggested a stroke—so alarmed his chief of staff that Adams told Vice President Nixon, "This is a terribly difficult thing to handle. You may be President in the next twenty-four hours."[199]

In the meantime, immediate decisions had to be made. It was determined that the President would not attend the state dinner in honor of the Moroccan king that evening, but that Mrs. Eisenhower would attend as expected and Vice President Nixon would stand in for the President. However, as Mrs. Eisenhower and her son were talking with Dr. Snyder, the President walked casually into the room and indicated that he intended to go to the dinner after all. He told them with some feeling that "if I cannot attend to my duties, I am simply going to give up this job. Now that is all there is to it."[200] The First Lady responded that if he did go, she would not, and the President reluctantly agreed to go back to bed. Apparently this was the first time he realized the seriousness of his condition. At 6:20 P.M., the press was informed that Eisenhower had "a chill" and would not be able to attend the state dinner that evening.

On the following day, the President was better but still experienced difficulty in verbalizing his thoughts. This frustrated him greatly, as did the fact that he was unable to name his favorite painting on his bedroom wall. So frustrated did he become, in fact, that he actually beat the bedclothes with his fists.[201] As the day progressed, the President's condition improved; and at one point, he was even able to chat with the king of Morocco "without much difficulty."[202]

When it was finally revealed to the press that Eisenhower had suffered a slight stroke, four consulting neurologists announced:

The President had an occlusion of a small branch of a cerebral vessel which has produced a slight difficulty in speaking. There is no evidence of a cerebral hemorrhage or any serious lesion of the cerebral vessels. The difficulty in speaking has improved over the period of the last 24 hours and is now manifested only by a hesitancy in saying certain difficult words. Reading, writing and reasoning powers are not affected. The President's disability is mild and transitory in nature.[203]

Calvin Coolidge, accompanied by his wife Grace,
leaving the cemetary in Plymouth Notch, Vermont, following
the funeral of their younger son, July, 1924.
(Courtesy of the Coolidge Collection, Forbes Library)

ABOVE: A beaming Franklin D. Roosevelt visited a Civilian Conservation Corps Camp in Big Meadows, Virginia, on August 12, 1933. His physical appearance at the time conveyed health and assurance.

LEFT: The President "walking," May 4, 1941. Roosevelt rarely allowed photographs of this revealing sort to be taken.

BELOW: At Yalta, February 4, 1945, shortly before his death. The strains of office and the effects of illness clearly can be seen on Roosevelt's ravaged face.

(All photos courtesy of the Franklin D. Roosevelt Library)

One of the first photographs taken of President Eisenhower in the hospital after his 1955 heart attack.

Eisenhower on June 7, 1956, just a few hours before his ileitis attack and subsequent surgery.

(Photos courtesy Dwight D. Eisenhower Library, National Park Service)

A gaunt Eisenhower is photographed
with Mamie on June 30, 1956,
just after his release from the hospital.
(Courtesy Dwight D. Eisenhower Library, National Park Service)

President Kennedy at a press conference on April 21, 1961.
(Courtesy of the John F. Kennedy Library)

Kennedy meets the press on July 19, 1961.
The effects of cortisone are readily apparent in his swollen face.
(Courtesy of the John F. Kennedy Library)

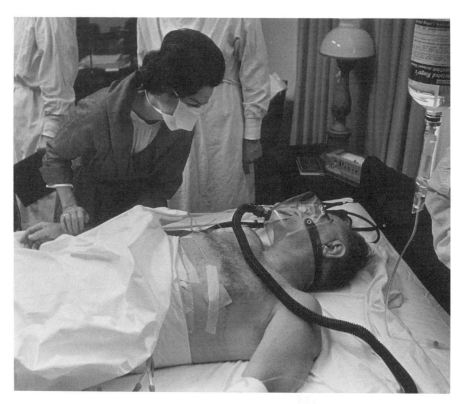

President and Lady Bird Johnson, immediately after his gall bladder surgery,
October 8, 1965.
(Courtesy of the Lyndon B. Johnson Library, Yoichi Okamoto)

Showing the anguish of office, President Johnson listens to a briefing on the
Vietnam War on July 31, 1968.
(Courtesy of the Lyndon B. Johnson Library, Jack Kightlinger)

President Ronald Reagan at his
Second Term Inaugural Celebration,
January 21, 1985, Landover, Maryland.
(*Courtesy of the Ronald Reagan Library*)

President Reagan at the White House,
slowly recovering from prostate
surgery in early 1987, at the height
of the Iran-Contra scandal.
(*Courtesy of the Ronald Reagan Library*)

President Bush, recovering from a bout of atrial fibrillation, is visited by his
grandchildren at Bethesda Naval Hospital.
(*Courtesy of the George Bush Library*)

President Clinton, on crutches after leg surgery, visits the new Franklin Delano
Roosevelt Memorial in Washington.
(Courtesy of the White House)

Although medical bulletins stated that the President's present illness had no relationship to his 1955 heart attack, the President's cardiologist disagreed. Mattingly believed that Eisenhower's cerebral thrombo-embolism was caused not by elevated blood pressure but rather by the ventricular aneurysm that he, Mattingly, had detected some two years earlier. Although the President seemed to be recovering quickly from this latest incident, Mattingly was convinced that his stroke was of major importance since it represented a complication of his heart attack.[204] Indeed, since the aneurysm was still very much present, this might be only the first of a series of strokes that could cripple, incapacitate, or even kill the President.

The mood at the White House was gloomy, and the tension even greater than at the time of the 1955 heart attack. The cerebral "spasm" seemed more ominous than the other two publicized illnesses since it had the potential of affecting the President's mind and reasoning powers. Influential columnists, such as Walter Lippmann, argued that the President should delegate his responsibilities to his vice president.[205] A number of commentators and newspaper writers suggested that the President should resign, with the *New York Post* editorializing that it preferred having Nixon as President to having no President at all.[206] Senator Wayne Morse of Oregon, who had switched from the Republican to the Democratic party in 1952, suggested that Eisenhower should step aside.[207]

Despite their own private concerns, administration spokespersons did their best to assure the country of the President's recovery and to deny that he would resign. The vice president announced that he saw

no reason whatsoever to believe that the President is considering or will consider resigning. . . . I would like to scotch once and for all if I can any rumors to the effect that the President, first, is in a condition that would make it necessary for him to consider resigning and second, that the President himself or anybody in the President's official family have discussed or are considering the possibility of resignation.[208]

On Thanksgiving Day, only three days after suffering his stroke, the President attended church services with Mrs. Eisenhower and on the next day left for a weekend at his Gettysburg farm. His doctors had recommended that Eisenhower have sixty days of complete rest.[209] They were concerned that his frustration at not being able to speak as clearly and as freely as before might bring on another stroke, and wanted him to put down the burdens of office for a two-month period. The President, however, had ideas of his own. While in Gettysburg, he had been somewhat bothered by a newspaper article that described how Vice President Nixon was "taking over" the government, and told the White House physician, "Howard, there can't be two Presidents in the United States. I think I'll go down to the Cabinet meeting on Monday morning."[210]

When Secretary of State Dulles learned of this decision, he read it as a dangerous omen and told Vice President Nixon that "we are liable to run into a situation where the President is incapable of acting and does not realize it." Nixon agreed that the President's judgment seemed impaired, and felt that "the people around him are not able to exercise judgment or control." The secretary of state worried about the "Woodrow Wilson problem": after suffering his stroke in 1919, Wilson had remained severely incapacitated and emotionally impaired for the remainder of his term. At this time, Dulles sought medical advice, and was told that "it was not such a bad idea for Eisenhower to return to work because 'continued frustration' would be worse than 'active participation.' "[211]

On Monday, 2 December, Eisenhower dutifully went to the Oval Office and later presided over a cabinet meeting for almost two hours— despite the fact that he had told Dr. Snyder that morning that he had been suffering from "a mild headache or feeling of dullness off and on during the several days we were at Gettysburg" and that he still had it now after returning to Washington.[212] One cabinet observer noticed that, although the President looked "a little tired" and had still "a trace of difficulty in his speech, his "mind was clear as crystal. He knew exactly what was going on and wanted to have a part in it."[213] Secretary Dulles agreed. Despite his earlier strong misgivings, the secretary of state became convinced, as he watched Eisenhower's performance firsthand, that the President's health was good.[214]

On the following day, Eisenhower participated at a meeting for legislative leaders. Although some aides—and even the White House physician—would have preferred for the President to avoid this potentially contentious meeting, Eisenhower told Nixon that he

had felt it was essential for him to come for personal reasons. He said he had to prove to himself that he was able to do the job. If he had been unable to come back for this meeting and the one the day before, it would have been necessary for him to do some "very hard thinking" about the future.[215]

Afterward, Nixon assured the President that the meeting had gone extremely well. One senator had even remarked that he was unable to detect any speech impediment whatsoever. Since Eisenhower had been upset by, and perhaps overly conscious of, his generally minor mistakes in word pronunciation, he was both pleased and relieved to get this report.[216]

In an effort to speed the President's complete recovery, his chief of staff took some tentative steps to lighten Eisenhower's workload. Adams told White House staff members, at a meeting on 6 December, that conferences with the President should be held on a "when needed" basis rather than regularly. Also, he directed each staff member to "stick to his own field and not carry in letters and suggestions extraneous to the general area of his own responsibility." Finally, he recommended that the agenda for cabinet and National Security Council meetings should be organized in such a way as to permit the President to leave when items "he doesn't really need to hear" are discussed.[217]

On 7 December, after the United States failed in its attempts to launch a satellite into space, Dr. Snyder found that Eisenhower's blood pressure and pulse were "booming."[218] This was disturbing to his doctors, particularly since the President wanted very much to attend a mid-December NATO meeting in Paris. Some of his doctors thought such a trip unwise if not foolhardy. Mattingly felt it would be hazardous to Eisenhower's well-being since the cause of his recent stroke had not been definitively determined and his anticoagulant therapy required close monitoring.[219] As his doctors debated whether he should travel to Paris, the President experienced so much tension that his blood pressure rose still further, and his pulse rate accelerated.[220]

Staff members also strongly opposed Eisenhower's making such an arduous journey. Vice President Nixon was prepared to go in his place, and Secretary of State Dulles voiced no objections to Nixon serving as the President's stand-in.[221] Nevertheless, the President was adamant, telling intimates, "I'm going to take this trip if it kills me. This is my job. I am going to run this damn show."[222]

Throughout this illness, Eisenhower seemed particularly anxious and determined to remain in command of his administration. He was sensitive to any intimation that he was incapacitated, and "reacted belligerently when anyone tried to shield him from an important issue." He said that he preferred to "die with his boots on"[223] and jealously guarded his presidential prerogatives. After the heart attack, he had instructed Nixon to call meetings of the cabinet and National Security Council. This time, he instructed him not to do so. The President pointed out to his vice president that "most people" would feel that it was not necessary for him or "any others in the White House staff to undertake any of the responsibilities of holding meetings." He even reminded Nixon that it was in his own best interests to avoid the appearances "of stepping in and exerting authority." When Nixon suggested at one point that Eisenhower use him and staff members more extensively in order to lighten his workload, and that cabinet members need not bother the President every time they had a decision to make, the President gave no indication "what he would do with regard to this recommendation."[224]

Driven by his determination and strong will, Eisenhower left Washington for Paris on 13 December and attended the NATO conference, which began three days later. Upon arriving in France, he stood in an open car for most of the trip into and through the capital, waving to throngs of people lining the route. Afterward, he felt great relief when he was able to read a public proclamation without distress or embarrassment, viewing this success as the first stage of a self-imposed test.[225] Reportedly, he told British Prime Minister Harold Macmillan while in Paris that if his physicians had forbidden him from making the journey to France, he would have resigned.[226] Instead, he had been allowed to go and had exceeded all expectations, both in Paris and at Marly, where he paid a nostalgic visit to the Supreme Headquarters of NATO which he had vacated five and a half years before. Mattingly seemed almost alone in finding that during this journey, the President "showed a noticeable hesitancy in his speech."[227]

Eisenhower was well satisfied with his performance in Paris, both during public appearances and during the private negotiating sessions in which he engaged. When he returned to Washington, he wrote an understated letter to Swede Hazlett, his boyhood friend, telling him that "all in all, the experience was pleasant and I think all to the good."[228] On the following Monday, he presided over a meeting of the National Security Council, during which his performance was "magnificent." No sign of a speech impediment could be detected nor any other indication that he had been ill.[229]

On 9 January, the President delivered his State of the Union Address to Congress. Unlike his 1956 State of the Union address following his heart attack which was read to Congress by a clerk, the President delivered this address personally, as another sign of his recovered health. The fact that he was able to speak for forty-five minutes with little difficulty gave Eisenhower another important psychological lift.[230] When he entered the cabinet meeting on the following day, the President received a standing ovation. Eisenhower flashed his famous smile and quipped, "Quite a matinee idol."[231]

A team of neurologists, who examined the President on 1 March 1958, determined that he had "completely recovered from the minor speech disturbance which he suffered on November 25, 1957" and that there was "no damage to his central nervous system."[232] Despite this positive prognosis, Eisenhower continued to have a slight weakness in the lower half of the right side of his face.[233] Nevertheless, his recovery—even if not quite complete—had been strikingly quick, and his resilience had again served him well. Not only did Eisenhower's recovery convince him that he had the physical ability to carry out his duties, but he later confided that "during the remaining three years of my Presidency, no question of the kind again occurred to me."[234]

THE FINAL WHITE HOUSE YEARS, 1958–61

Although free of self-doubts during the remainder of his second term, Eisenhower experienced a variety of medical problems before leaving the White House in 1961. Some of these were, though serious, not announced to the press. Dr. Mattingly actually believed that additional periods of hospitalization would have been appropriate during the second term, but that Eisenhower and Snyder had decided to forgo them lest they damage the President politically.[235]

In early 1958, some two months after suffering his stroke, Eisenhower developed a lingering respiratory infection as well as a sore throat and laryngitis. His abdomen was distended and painful on 10 March and again on 18 March. On 8 May 1958, Snyder administered five minutes of oxygen to the President and recommended that he take it regularly. By the middle of June, Eisenhower was taking oxygen twice a day and soon thereafter three times. On 19 July, the President once again suffered from a distended abdomen.[236] On 10 September, Dr. Snyder noted elevated blood pressure, which he attributed to the fact that several congressmen had urged Eisenhower to fire Sherman Adams for taking gifts from the Massachusetts industrialist Bernard Goldfine.[237]

In February 1959, the President developed another respiratory infection and sore throat. A few weeks later, he experienced chest pains for several days. His abdomen became obstructed on 31 March. In late April, he again developed a respiratory infection and sore throat.[238] On 4 June, his ear bled, upsetting him greatly because he thought that his blood was thin, and that he might have "hemorrhages such as General Marshall has." In late August, the First Lady reported to Snyder that Eisenhower had had shortness of breath while sleeping, which she attributed to his having overeaten the previous evening. The President had also complained that evening that his stroke "still bothered him in verbalizing his thoughts." Several weeks later, Eisenhower developed active peristalsis in his abdomen and came down with an inflamed throat.[239] In October, he suffered from a case of bronchitis. Two months later, during a visit to Kabul, Afghanistan, Eisenhower badly frightened his companions by collapsing after walking up a flight of twenty-four steps.[240] The Secret Service administered oxygen, and the President quickly revived. Kabul's high altitude seems to have been responsible.

Although some of these physical ailments brought the President pain and discomfort, his most critical, but unpublicized, health crises occurred in 1960 and were seriously life threatening. In May 1960, the Paris summit conference collapsed. This greatly disappointed the President since his term in office was rapidly coming to a close, and his chances for participating in another summit were extremely slim. When he returned to Washington, Eisenhower was fatigued, showed abnormally elevated blood pressure, and also developed a troublesome respiratory infection. Mattingly described him as having emphysema at the time.[241] The President actually stayed for several days in the presidential suite at Walter Reed Hospital to rest and to recuperate from his physical indispositions.

Within months, the 1960 campaign got under way, and Eisenhower entered the fray on behalf of his vice president, who was seeking to succeed him in the White House. Initially, his participation was only sporadic, with the President making several "nonpolitical" appearances around the country in mid-October. Finally, he began stumping intensively for Nixon during the first week of November in New York, Pennsylvania, and Ohio. The President's intervention seemed to help reverse Nixon's slide in the polls[242] and may well have contributed to making the 1960 election the closest in modern times.

Several postelection analysts have speculated about the outcome had Eisenhower intervened earlier and stumped for Nixon in such close states as New Jersey and Texas; and also, in wondering why Eisenhower was not used more extensively in the campaign, suggested that Nixon had either wanted to win on his own or been too proud to call on the President for help. We know now, however, that Eisenhower's health was a vital factor in limiting his involvement in the 1960 campaign. Indeed, at times during the campaign period, the President was actually in danger of death.

On 17 October 1960, the President traveled to Detroit on behalf of Nixon. When Dr. Snyder took his blood pressure in midafternoon, he found that "it was all over the map," and that his pulse rate was erratic. Snyder attributed this to the fact that Eisenhower had become upset when he had seen a union leaflet that was being circulated widely, and that proclaimed, "A vote for Kennedy is a vote for liberty; a vote for Nixon is a vote for bigotry."[243] He gave the President medication (quinidine sulfate) and sent him to bed for a nap. Later that afternoon, his pulse rate was even more irregular, and Snyder gave him additional medication which seemed to bring about improvement.

That evening, however, the President's condition worsened dramatically. Upon returning to his hotel after a speaking engagement that lasted for more than a half-hour, Eisenhower went immediately to his bedroom and summoned his physician, who found his blood pressure both faint and alarmingly irregular. Snyder also discovered that the President was experiencing ventricular fibrillation: that is, the rhythm of his heart would go out of control and, instead of pumping blood, would simply vibrate, a condition he described as "very dangerous."[244] Snyder gave the President oxygen for some twelve minutes, after which his pulse "which had been running away steadied down to where it was 82 with about 10 skips per minute." The doctor reports that he went to bed but kept the door between his room and the President's open. At 5 A.M., after Eisenhower summoned him, Snyder took the President's blood pressure—which had stabilized—and then gave him ten minutes of oxygen. Later that morning, while en route to Minneapolis, Snyder gave the President another eleven minutes of oxygen. The President's condition caused his doctor considerable concern. In an interesting footnote to history, Snyder relates that he almost missed the plane to Detroit, and that if he had, he just would not have gone out there at all: "Had this been the case, the President unquestionably would have been in extreme danger because of the episode he had with his heart action."[245]

On 28 October, the First Lady begged Snyder to warn the President that he had to stop campaigning for Nixon. She was afraid that "he might pop a cork." Snyder relates that he had been cautioning Eisenhower in this regard for several weeks. He followed this up on 31 October, just as the final campaign push was beginning, by advising the President to "take extra oxygen with all his work."[246] During the final week of the campaign, Eisenhower experienced dangerous episodes of ventricular fibrillation both in Chicago and New York just as he had in Detroit two weeks earlier, along with "definitely an increase in the frequency of transient elevations of blood pressure."[247] Eisenhower later understated the case when he wrote that his doctors had been concerned that he had "temporarily used up all his available cardiac reserves" in the closing weeks of the campaign.[248]

On the day after the election, the President was bitterly disappointed at Nixon's defeat and so upset that his blood pressure was elevated and his pulse irregular. Snyder later reported that the muscular and joint pains Eisenhower experienced around this time were caused by "the shock to the President's emotional system as a result of the election."[249] A few weeks later, Eisenhower's abdomen was badly distended once again, and he was in great discomfort.

The list of Eisenhower's ailments, both major and minor, over the years demonstrates beyond doubt that illness was one of his closest and most frequent companions. It is not surprising, given the number, frequency, and ongoing nature of his physical infirmities, that Eisenhower became something of a hypochondriac, and that manifestations of his hypochondria became more evident as the years passed. He was "hyper-concerned" about his rapid and irregular pulse beat and worried that he might have prostate cancer.[250] He suspected that his cardiovascular problems were more serious than his doctors thought, and, even though he continued to prefer his steaks marbled with fat, worried constantly about his cholesterol levels. So obsessed was he with his cholesterol count that his doctor would occasionally give him a false reading to ease his fears.[251]

Eisenhower's obsession with his own health continued after he left the White House. He was seventy years old when he retired from the presidency and anxious to prolong his active years as much as possible. He underwent frequent overnight physical examinations at Walter Reed Hospital and tried to get the exercise his doctors recommended through frequent golfing excursions. For several years, his health remained relatively good, although he suffered temporary limitations from recurrent respiratory and musculoskeletal problems.[252] But in late 1965, his health began to deteriorate progressively, with complications from both his cardiovascular and gastrointestinal ailments.

In the spring of 1965, former President Eisenhower developed congestive heart failure for the first time and then suffered two mild heart attacks the following November. A year later, he underwent gallbladder surgery, at which time his anticoagulant medication, vital to his cardiovascular well-being, was discontinued. In April 1967 while playing golf, Eisenhower experienced a period of transient cerebral confusion, not knowing where he was or what he was doing;[253] and his prostate gland became so enlarged that it began to obstruct his bladder. Because of his cardiac condition, however, his urologist declined to operate.

In April 1968, shortly after visiting his son's grave in Abilene, Eisenhower suffered another heart attack, which was complicated by congestive failure and critical arrhythmia and was viewed by some of his doctors as the beginning of his terminal illness.[254] Two months later, he experienced still another—and more serious—cardiac infarct; but once again, his resilience pulled him through.

In early August 1968, the former President delivered a taped message to delegates at the Republican national convention, appearing on the nation's television screens as a ghost of his former self. On the following day, he suffered still another heart attack, this one of such massive proportions that he had to receive electrical shocks to his heart on fourteen separate occasions over an eight-day period. His doctors later explained that "it is scarcely an exaggeration to state that he 'died' 14 times."[255]

On 21 February 1969, Eisenhower underwent abdominal surgery to relieve blockage caused by scar tissue resulting from his 1956 ileitis operation, and afterward developed periods of confusion, transient hallucinations, and increasing somnolence.[256] Within a month, his heart began to deteriorate precipitously, and Eisenhower confided to his son that he knew the end was near and hoped that it would come "the sooner the better." He told his family on the morning of 28 March 1969 that "I want to go, God take me."[257] Several hours later, at 12:25 P.M., former President Dwight D. Eisenhower was dead.

The Political Effects of Eisenhower's Illnesses

Not only, as I have discussed, was President Eisenhower's heart attack crucial in his decision to run for another term, but his ill health in general had a number of important effects on the way his administration functioned and even laid the foundation for a change in the American constitutional system. Although Eisenhower's resilience allowed him to rebound quickly from each illness, each nonetheless took a toll on the President's stamina and energy. His heart attack effectively removed him from the scene for several months in 1955, and his ileitis surgery for several additional months in 1956. Particularly after his stroke, aides found that the President's active workday became shorter, and that his performance was below par, especially as the day neared its end.[258] Even the President admitted to an associate that he was "beginning to feel a bit tired late in the afternoon, which was when we usually got most of our work done."[259] Sherman Adams confided to members of the White House staff, "This man is not what he was."[260]

Indeed, Eisenhower was then well into his sixties, and the effects of advancing age were undoubtedly compounded by his repeated illnesses. Like his 1955 heart attack, the President's stroke had a serious psychological effect on him. His vice president noticed that "he was depressed by the fear that he could no longer bring to the Presidency the physical and mental qualities it required and this was a serious blow to his morale."[261] As the President slowed down, his reduced energy levels not only caused concern and frustration in some administration circles, but also brought on attacks by the opposition party that he was essentially in retirement and not doing the job. Such charges greatly troubled the President, who was obsessed with doing his duty.

Somewhat ironically, Eisenhower's ability to respond to these attacks was impaired by the limited communication strategies available to him after he suffered his stroke. Indeed, the style of presidential communications and the nature of the President's discourse with the public during the second term were shaped, at least in part, by the aftereffects of his cerebral occlusion. Throughout his administration, Eisenhower's performance at press conferences was mixed. Unable to control the flow of questions, he found that many questions did not touch on areas of vital interest to him. Often his answers would be passive, cursory, and uninspiring. However, when questions touched on matters close to the President's heart, he could be forceful and eloquent.[262]

Early in his second term, the head of the U.S. Information Agency, Arthur Larson, suggested to Eisenhower that he make a series of televised chats, discussing a variety of issue areas with the American people just as Franklin Roosevelt had done on radio during the 1930s and 1940s.[263] Although the President had enthusiastically agreed to the suggestion and begun to implement it, his stroke brought the plan to an abrupt halt. Even though he recovered rapidly from that medical crisis, Eisenhower remained very self-conscious of his ability to speak properly and thus could not undertake with confidence a series of full-length television presentations.[264] Since a number of Eisenhower's formal speeches, such as his 1961 farewell address, were memorable, termination of his fireside chat plan may well have been a real loss to the administration and to the country.

Even more fundamentally, Eisenhower's ill health put the concept of team government—a concept based on the proposition that the top echelons of the executive branch should function on the basis of group, rather than presidential, effort—to its sternest challenge and gave his secretary of state a period of unchallenged influence in foreign policy making, just as a key crisis in the Middle East was unfolding. More indirectly, but no less importantly, the President's illnesses precipitated a move, finally achieved in 1967, to add a "presidential disability" amendment to the Constitution.

THE CONCEPT OF TEAM GOVERNMENT

Perhaps the most obvious effect of Dwight Eisenhower's illnesses on his presidency was that they put to the test his carefully crafted plan of team government. Steeped in military tradition, Eisenhower sought to establish in the executive branch a bureaucratic structure that minimized disruption caused by the absence of the chief executive. A firm believer in cabinet government, he wanted his cabinet to serve a major policy role in his administration.[265] He viewed members of the cabinet as generalists rather than specialists and expected them to become involved in the formation of overall government policies and to serve as general advisers to the President. The purpose of cabinet meetings was to resolve interdepartmental disputes at the highest level while providing for direct and frequent dialogue between the President and his department heads.[266]

At the same time, Eisenhower tried to establish in the White House a staff system that would protect the President's time and energy and serve as a buffer between the President and outside forces. Keenly aware of his own fierce temper, the President was anxious to establish effective buffers between himself and people who were likely sources of anger and frustration.[267]

His chief of staff had considerable power. Sherman Adams, who held that position for almost six years, shielded the President from work of secondary importance, guarded him from many unwelcome visitors, and served as a lightning rod deflecting criticism from the chief of state to the chief of staff. He also supervised other staff members, trying to make certain that they "would boil down, simplify and expedite the urgent business that had to be brought to his [Eisenhower's] personal attention,"[268] and provide him with recommended solutions for the problems that actually reached his desk.

Eisenhower intended for his administration to be a genuine group effort, rather than a one-man show, and wanted his time, as well as his disposition to be protected. Both cabinet and staff would serve as artfully designed buffer zones for the President.[269] During Eisenhower's absences, regardless of their cause, both cabinet and staff would continue to function in usual ways. Adams would preside at the White House, and Nixon would preside over the cabinet, both playing facilitating, rather than deciding, roles. This organizational construct was tested most seriously by Eisenhower's 1955 heart attack, since the period of recuperation following it was the most protracted.

Almost immediately following Eisenhower's coronary thrombosis, administration officials ranging from Vice President Nixon to Secretary of the Treasury Humphrey met to discuss the manner in which the business of the executive branch would be conducted in the President's absence. Their task was made considerably easier by the fact that the President's illness had come at precisely the right moment, if it had to come at all. No foreign policy crisis confronted the nation, Congress was not in session, the economy was strong, and presidential decision or intervention was not required either at home or abroad.[270]

Because of the relative calm that prevailed at the time, Eisenhower's aides decided quickly that no formal delegation of his powers had to be made.[271] This conformed to the legal opinion of Attorney General Brownell that, under the terms of the Constitution, the President was not so incapacitated that the vice president should assume his duties and powers.[272] Eisenhower was fully conscious, in control of his faculties, and his doctors had given favorable reports on the likelihood of his making a speedy recovery. In fact, one of those doctors had estimated that Eisenhower might be able to participate in conferences within two weeks.

The provisions of the Constitution dealing with presidential succession were considerably more vague, confusing, and incomplete at the time than they are today. They did not indicate, for example, how presidential disability was to be determined, what bodies or individuals would be involved in the determination of disability, or whether a President who regained his health could regain his office after being "replaced" by his vice president. Fortunately, the nature and timing of Eisenhower's heart attack meant that the ambiguities would not have to be resolved immediately.

Vice President Nixon felt it inappropriate for him to try to "replace" the President or even provide any overt leadership at all. Sensitive to political realities, he recognized that he must avoid even the appearance of being too anxious to supplant the ailing but still popular chief executive.[273] Nixon stressed that the business of the executive branch would be carried out by the President's "team," and explained to the press that Eisenhower had "set up the Administration in such a way that it will continue its policies, which are well-defined, during his temporary ab-

sence. The President has always made it clear that the business of government should go ahead. He set it up in such a way that it can go ahead
despite the temporary absence of anyone."[274]

The vice president later told Eisenhower that there had not been "one
iota of jealousy" among team members,[275] and all had worked together
harmoniously to advance the administration's interests. Sherman Adams
likewise asserted that "there was never a move on the part of any of us
to seize power."[276] Despite the sugar-coated words, however, a struggle
for power did go on behind the scenes not only among the strong
personalities involved but also between moderate and conservative factions within the Republican party.

John Foster Dulles, the forceful leader of the moderates, was neither
anxious nor willing to increase the vice president's power. The moderates feared that if Eisenhower did not run for re-election in 1956, a
strengthened Nixon would emerge as the Republican standard bearer
and carry the party down to defeat. Dulles, then, argued that Sherman
Adams should be stationed in Denver to serve as Eisenhower's voice
and ears, while Nixon would remain in Washington and preside over
meetings of the cabinet and National Security Council. The wily secretary of state warned that "certain people outside the government"
might attempt to establish themselves as authoritative spokespersons for
the President; and that to prevent such persons from succeeding in their
devious purposes, Sherman Adams's position as the one official channel
of information between the President and the outside world should be
reinforced. As a nationally recognized public figure closely identified
with Eisenhower, Dulles argued, Adams should be positioned in Denver, returning to Washington each week for the Friday morning cabinet
meeting.[277]

Understandably looking upon himself as "a nationally recognized public figure closely identified with Eisenhower," Nixon hoped to be stationed in Denver himself, since there he would play the most visible and
central role during the President's illness. The conservative faction of the
party did not wish the "White House clique" to take command,[278] and
preferred Adams to remain in Washington at the White House where he
would continue to direct the White House staff while Nixon stood on
center stage, and close to the President, in Denver.

Members of the cabinet, however, tended to side with Dulles. It was
quickly agreed—with Nixon's reluctant concurrence—that Adams
would go to Denver and serve as the conduit of all matters intended for
Eisenhower's attention. The vice president would remain in Washington

and preside over meetings of the cabinet and the NSC, helping them move their agendas and working to resolve any conflicts.

In addition, an informal coordinating committee—consisting of Dulles, Adams, Nixon, Brownell, Humphrey, and Wilton B. Persons (chief of staff in Adams's absence)—began to meet regularly in order to oversee government operations.[279] Attorney General Brownell later remembered that the members of this élite group never disagreed among themselves and considered themselves responsible only for overseeing implementation of the President's policies during his illness.[280]

The cabinet and the National Security Council served as coordinating mechanisms in the policy process. This was quite appropriate since Eisenhower had deliberately set out in 1953 to strengthen both bodies. The cabinet met an average of thirty-four times a year[281] and was even given a staff secretariat so that its meetings would be more productive. The NSC met some forty-four times a year, and Eisenhower spent significant time in presiding over its sessions, perhaps his favorite official function but also his most time-consuming.[282]

It was not uncommon for Nixon to preside over meetings of these bodies. Even before the President had suffered his heart attack, the vice president had been asked, on occasion, to "sit in" for Eisenhower.[283] Therefore, when Nixon replaced Eisenhower during his illness as presiding officer at cabinet and other meetings, the executive branch was actually following well-established precedent.

On 29 September 1955, less than a week after the President was stricken, the National Security Council met with Vice President Nixon presiding from his own, rather than the President's, chair. Nixon urged the council to make those decisions that needed to be made in accordance "with our best concept of the President's own wishes in the matter." Those matters that individual members of the NSC would normally take up directly with the President, rather than with the council as a whole, should now be discussed in a plenary session of the NSC. Moreover, Nixon said that the council should make those decisions that the public believes should be made, because "if it did not, the public would be 'wondering' if important actions are stalled by the President's absence."[284]

Key members of the council quickly concurred. The attorney general pointed out that there were no legal obstacles to either the NSC's or the cabinet's functioning in the ways Nixon had outlined. That, after all, was the manner in which President Eisenhower had asked the executive branch to function at least twice before in his administration—during his vacation in 1954 and during the Geneva summit in 1955. Also, concerned with keeping the President's future workload within manageable proportions, Brownell asked council members to give him a list of things normally done by the President that could reasonably be delegated to someone else.[285]

Secretary of State Dulles shared Brownell's view concerning the role of the NSC and cabinet during the President's illness. He stressed the necessity of avoiding the impression that "the statutory and constitutional status" of the NSC and cabinet was being changed from a deliberative to a decision-making body.[286]

Treasury Secretary Humphrey urged that the President be freed from as much mental and physical pressures as possible by making the NSC and the cabinet clearinghouses where members could discuss their problems and air all controversial matters. Defense Secretary Charles Wilson added that it was essential that all members keep one another advised, especially in taking any action on any matter that might impinge on the responsibility of any other member of the council or of the cabinet.[287]

On 30 September, Vice President Nixon chaired a meeting of the cabinet. As he had done the day before, Nixon urged that government business should be carried on expeditiously and warned against delays that would create backlogs waiting for the President's return. He indicated that major new policies would have to be postponed until the President returned, "but existing policies should continue to be implemented by each agency as long as those policies are strictly the business of the agency." Members should continue to submit those actions to the cabinet that ordinarily have been submitted in advance to it "by courtesy." Finally, those actions that were taken only after discussion with the President, and were related to NSC matters, should be reviewed in the NSC "in lieu of or as a preliminary to discussion with the President."[288]

The attorney general, just as he had done at the NSC meeting the day before, requested each cabinet member to submit a list of actions within his department that required presidential approval but that the member thought might be delegated. He emphasized, however, that delegations of this sort were not extraordinary since they "had frequently been accomplished in the past."[289]

Sherman Adams then reported his discussion with Dr. White the preceding evening. White and Adams had agreed that the medical experts should determine in each instance whether routine documents might be given to the President for approval. No document submitted in the near future could be controversial or require such close attention on the part of the President so as to tax his strength.[290]

General Persons, Adams's second in command, expressed concern that charges could be made that government business was being held up in the President's absence. He suggested that in order to forestall this criticism, cabinet members should retain in their departments those papers "which did not merit early action rather than letting them wait at the White House."[291]

As both the NSC and the cabinet meetings make clear, a "team government," sensitive to both political and medical realities, would drive the executive branch in Eisenhower's absence along lines the President himself had outlined during the previous two and a half years of his administration. To highlight his concurrence in the uninterrupted functioning of "the team," the President wrote Nixon a well-publicized letter in early October, saying, "I hope you will continue to have meetings of the National Security Council and of the Cabinet, over which you will preside in accordance with the procedure which you have followed at my request in the past during my absence from Washington."[292]

There was to be no repetition of the unhappy Woodrow Wilson experience of several decades earlier. When in 1920 that President's secretary of state convened a meeting of the cabinet during Wilson's illness, Wilson fired him. Rather ironically, Wilson's secretary of state, Robert Lansing, was the uncle of John Foster Dulles, secretary of state under Eisenhower. One commentator found that "Lansing's unfortunate experience played a central role in shaping Dulles' attitudes."[293] Eisenhower's secretary of state went out of his way, in 1955 and later, to make certain that history would not repeat itself.

Eisenhower, of course, remained captain of "the team," temporarily sidelined by heart injury. Doctors quickly determined that his recovery would be aided if his involvement in affairs of state resumed. Dr. White told the President's press secretary that "he's not so much of an invalid as he is President of the U.S. lying in there. He wants to do his job."[294]

Within two weeks, Eisenhower signed two documents, an indication to the public that he was on the road to recovery. The decision was then made to begin flying members of "the team" to Denver for conferences with their leader. Such conferences would provide the President with a sense of participation in the activities of his government and communicate to the world that he was, in fact, active and "in command" once again.

On 6 October, Adams announced to the National Security Council that Nixon would be the first to visit the President, and that Dulles would be second—Eisenhower having vetoed his doctors' recommendation that the heads of the least controversial departments confer with him first, and the "heavy hitters" afterward. Adams, however, warned all administration officials that

there should be no controversial problems placed before the President in the forth-coming week nor, indeed, problems which will require too much exercise of the President's reasoning powers and powers of judgment. On the other hand, he could go over general matters of National Security Council interest by the first of the following week by which time he could get into actual differences of opinion and into matters which would require the exercise of judgment.[295]

Beginning on 8 October, officials began traveling to Denver to visit the President. Nixon found him alert but "startlingly thin and pale."[296] On 11 October, Dulles thought the President to be in very good form. Shown a draft letter to Soviet Premier Nikolai Bulganin, Eisenhower reminded Dulles that missing from it was something that he, the President, had told Bulganin in Geneva: namely that the United States would be willing to accept the Soviet proposal for an on-site inspection team within each country.[297] Dulles revised the letter, and Eisenhower signed the new version that afternoon.

Subsequent visits by administration officials revealed a President who could be both impatient and statesmanlike. Defense Secretary Wilson was told by the President that he wanted cuts in the defense budget and that Wilson "should get on with it," being tough and not expecting the President to decide "where each little cut could be made." Eisenhower urged Agriculture Secretary Ezra Taft Benson to get congressional legislation that would allow the United States to sell wheat to the Soviet Union. Also, the President reminded him that "we are as much trustees of the soil and water for future generations as we are trustees of the liberties we are trying to pass on," and indicated his interest in a half-billion dollar program he wanted to call "a Soil Bank."[298]

Within some five weeks, Eisenhower saw sixty-six official visitors in Denver. The process went smoothly, with each visitor faithfully testifying to the press about how well the President looked and how alert he was. Thus, the country was reassured that affairs of state were being handled expeditiously, and that the President was recovering nicely.

Although the President's press secretary did a masterful job in arranging and orchestrating each visit for maximum publicity value, there were a few slip-ups. Dulles, for example, revealed that the President was unaware of the French-Algerian crisis over Algerian self-government. On another occasion, Hagerty was seen giving a cabinet member a prepared statement on the President's physical appearance before he had actually seen the President.[299]

Other problems surfaced as well. Although Eisenhower began meetings in his hospital room with members of "the team" just two weeks after being stricken, the President's role necessarily remained limited, and the façade of team government showed discernible cracks. Any team only functions effectively when it is led by someone who can resolve disputes among members and make authoritative and binding decisions. In the absence of such a person, the team may disintegrate, especially during times of conflict and crisis.

In health, Eisenhower tended to dominate the team. A cabinet member later said of his leadership style: "His work with the Cabinet as a collegial group did have an effect on the evolution of policy. Nothing was ever put to a vote and it was clear we were there talking about these matters as general advisors to him. He is the only person who voted. He is the only person who made a decision."[300]

But during Eisenhower's ill health, Vice President Nixon simply did not have the stature or the authority to exert similar leadership. Indeed, some officials found that he seemed unsure of himself and even excessively deferential. Agriculture Secretary Benson, for example, thought that Nixon's tentative behavior at cabinet meetings called into question "whether Sherman or Dick was running the meeting," and concluded that Eisenhower's firm hand was sorely missed.[301]

During the President's lengthy convalescence, policies that had already been formulated could continue to be implemented by the team. In the case of programs *not* previously adopted, however, the team spirit occasionally became badly frayed. Thus, it took "the team" some six weeks to hammer out the outlines of a stopgap farm program and to secure the agriculture secretary's agreement to have it even discussed at a cabinet meeting.[302] The absence of Eisenhower's authoritative voice necessarily resulted in protracted and contentious negotiations as well as considerable delay among administration officials.

The first political effect, then, of Eisenhower's 1955 illness was to demonstrate that committee government is an imperfect mechanism, regardless of the theories and good intentions on which it may be based. It encourages rivalries without providing a reliable means for controlling them, and its policy output tends to be minimal.

Committee government is even more inadequate in the international sphere and particularly during times of international crisis. A committee simply cannot conduct American foreign policy. In the absence of the President, a voice other than his must speak for the country, or the country's external relations will be in paralysis.

THE ASCENDANCY OF THE SECRETARY OF STATE

The President's 1955 and 1956 illnesses clearly strengthened the hand of John Foster Dulles in the conduct of U.S. foreign policy. It did this by removing the President as the central force in the foreign-policy-making process and by putting at a distinct disadvantage Dulles's rivals within the administration. One of these was Nelson A. Rockefeller, appointed by the President in 1954 to the position of special assistant for cold war strategy and given the mandate to "work for increased understanding and co-operation among all peoples."[303] Rockefeller took that mandate seriously and came up with several foreign policy recommendations that Dulles regarded not only as unwise but also as invasions of his turf. For example, Rockefeller's open skies proposal, which would have allowed international aerial inspection of all countries in order to prevent clandestine preparations for atomic warfare, intrigued the President but was regarded with considerable distaste by his secretary of state, who did all he could to kill it.

After Eisenhower was stricken in 1955, Rockefeller's influence within the administration declined sharply. The role he played depended on his close association with the President, and that dwindled dramatically during the latter's convalescence. Whereas Dulles served as a member of "the team" during Eisenhower's recuperation and began visiting him in the hospital as early as 11 October 1955, Rockefeller did not get to see the President until 5 December, a sure sign of his diminished standing and of Dulles's clear pre-eminence. It was only a few days afterward that the special assistant for cold war strategy resigned for "personal reasons," leaving Dulles without this dynamic rival for the President's attention.

The emergence of John Foster Dulles as essentially the sole architect of U.S. foreign policy during the President's convalescence had major ramifications. The most serious was that it contributed to a major upheaval in the Middle East and to a serious degeneration in the relationship between the United States and its allies—developments that might never have occurred if Eisenhower had not been ill at the time.

It was precisely during the period of the President's recuperation from both his heart attack and ileitis surgery that a major foreign policy initiative was moving toward culmination—that of the Aswan Dam project in Egypt. During the fall of 1957, the United States—with Eisenhower's concurrence—had made a tentative offer of fifty-six million dollars toward construction of the Aswan Dam, with additional millions to follow in subsequent years. In the intervening months, however, Egypt appeared to be moving closer and closer to the Soviet bloc despite its insistence that it was neutral in the East-West struggle. Particularly offensive to Dulles was the fact that Egypt had followed up the arms deal it had made with the Soviet Union in September 1955 by recognizing Communist China in the spring of 1956.

Egypt's action may also have intensified congressional opposition to the Aswan Dam project—although that opposition, at least in the Senate, seems to have been confined to the Appropriations Committee and might well have been overcome. No effort was made to overcome it, however. Dulles was unprepared to try; and Eisenhower, still recovering from his illnesses, had "neither the energy not the political desire to make the fight."[304]

In the absence of full-scale participation by the ailing President, Dulles was much freer than usual to play his own hand. Convinced that neutralism was immoral, the secretary of state was decidedly cool toward Egypt's leader, Gamal Abdel Nasser, and such personal feelings may well have shaped Dulles's decision with regard to financing the Aswan Dam.

Since at a meeting with Eisenhower on 16 July Dulles received no instructions to withdraw the offer,[305] the decision was his. The secretary, giving in to his negative predispositions, apparently determined that "it was necessary to demonstrate to friendly nations, by act rather than by oral explanation, that U.S. tolerance of nations which felt it necessary to stay out of Western defensive alliances could not brook the kind of insult Nasser presented in his repeated and accumulated unfriendly gestures."[306]

Although his official statement made reference to "Egypt's affinity for Soviet arms agreements,"[307] even some State Department officials were puzzled over the reasons for Dulles's actions. Deputy Secretary of State Robert Murphy later admitted that despite all of Dulles's explanations to the staff and to him, he still did not know why Dulles refused to make the Aswan Dam loan, "unless it were that Dulles did not like the ultimatum tone in [Egyptian Ambassador] Hussein's message."[308] This explanation seems on target. Dulles not only told the National Security Council privately that he did not intend to be blackmailed by Nasser but he also told the Senate Foreign Relations Committee publicly, "I do not believe in the U.S. being blackmailed, and any time I sense a purpose on the part of any country to try to get money out of us by threatening that if we don't pay it money, it will do something, at that point I say, 'Nothing doing.' "[309]

Nasser was infuriated by Dulles's actions. A week later, he responded by seizing the Suez Canal, an action that precipitated an invasion of Egypt by Great Britain, France, and Israel as well as a massive split in the Western alliance. The invasion of Egypt has been described as Secretary of State Dulles's greatest disappointment during his six years in office."[310] Ironically, it may well have been brought on by Dulles himself—as well as by the President's ill health.

Eisenhower was very confident of his knowledge of world affairs and, contrary to the conventional wisdom at the time, held Dulles in close check and modified his more extreme tendencies.[311] In this instance, however, Eisenhower, recovering from back-to-back illnesses, did not play a determining or a moderating role. Even his son later surmised that "in good health, Dad might well have exercised a restraining influence on Secretary of State Dulles in making this move."[312] Instead, Dulles acted essentially alone, and a major foreign policy debacle ensued.

PROPOSED CONSTITUTIONAL AMENDMENT

Eisenhower's illnesses made him acutely aware of the constitutional problems surrounding presidential disability. In 1955, concerned, in particular, that constitutional gaps in respect to a President's disability could have disastrous consequences in the nuclear age, the President, from his hospital bed, directed the attorney general to formulate a constitutional amendment to remedy the situation. Brownell put together a research team that consisted of himself, a law school dean, and two political scientists; and together, they prepared an amendment for submission to Congress. The amendment would, first of all, make clear that a vice president served as acting president only during the period of a president's disability, and that a President, upon recovery from illness, would recover his office.[313]

The amendment prepared by the "Brownell Commission," submitted to the appropriate committees of Congress in early 1957, contained the following provisions:

Section 1   In case of the removal of the President from office, or of his death or resignation, the Vice President shall become President for the unexpired portion of the then current term.

Section 2   If the President shall declare in writing that he is unable to discharge the powers and duties of his office, such powers and duties shall be discharged by the Vice President as Acting President.

Section 3   If the President does not so declare, the Vice President, if satisfied with the President's inability, and upon approval in writing of a majority of the heads of executive departments who are members of the President's Cabinet, shall discharge the powers and duties of the office as Acting President.

Section 4   Whenever the President declares in writing that his inability is terminated, the President shall forthwith discharge the powers and duties of his office.[314]

In submitting his proposed amendment to Congress, Brownell had been careful to avoid any attempt to change the order of succession to the presidency, since he wanted to avoid complications and minimize the likelihood of congressional opposition.[315] Thus, the Speaker of the House and President pro tempore of the Senate, both Democrats, would remain second and third in line of succession, immediately after the vice president. Nevertheless, members of the Democratic leadership team indicated immediately that they either opposed the amendment or thought additional study was needed. House Speaker Sam Rayburn was stoutly opposed, arguing that the proposal would "shock the country since it would be received as an indication that President Eisenhower was about to turn over his duties." Senate Majority Leader Lyndon Johnson "noted the need for extensive study prior to any congressional action."[316] Democrats seemed to fear that if the amendment were enacted, it would enhance the status of Richard Nixon, possibly even helping him win the 1960 election. They reasoned that if Nixon became acting president during an Eisenhower illness, he would be running in 1960 with the advantages of incumbency. Democratic leaders, unwilling to contribute to such a scenario, were determined to block the amendment.

Recognizing that the process of constitutional amendment would be lengthy, Eisenhower drafted a letter to Vice President Nixon which he hoped would greatly lessen the constitutional uncertainties about any possible disability of his own during the remainder of his term. The draft was submitted for review to the attorney general who found it to be not only in accord with the intent of the Framers of the Constitution but also as "good a drafting job as any constitutional expert could have done."[317] With the attorney general's imprimatur, the President sent his letter to Nixon, with a copy also going to Secretary of State Dulles. That letter, dated 5 February 1958, contained the following terms of understanding between the President and his vice president:

1. In any instance in which I could clearly recognize my own inability to discharge the powers and duties of the Presidency, I would, of course, so inform you and you would act accordingly.

2. With the exception of this one kind of case, you will be the individual explicitly and exclusively responsible for determining whether there is any inability of mine that makes it necessary for you to discharge the powers and duties of the Presidency, and you will decide the exact timing of the devolution of this responsibility on you. I would hope that you would consult with the Secretary of State, Governor Adams and General Heaton,* and, if possible, with medical experts assembled by him, but the decision will be yours only.

3. I will be the one to determine if and when it is proper for me to resume the powers and duties of the Presidency.

4. If any disability of mine should, in the judgment of any group of distinguished medical authorities that you might assemble, finally become of a permanent character, I will, of course, accept their decision and promptly resign my position. But if I were not able to do so, and the same group of consultants would so state, then you would take over not only the powers and duties but the perquisites of the Presidency including the White House itself.

5. In temporary cases of my inability, we agree that you should act for the necessary period in your capacity as Vice President and additionally, as Acting President.[318]

Since a constitutional amendment on presidential disability did not win enactment in the Eisenhower administration, Eisenhower's letter to Nixon remained the operative document on disability until the President left office in 1961. Indeed, his letter became the basis for similar letters written by President Kennedy to Vice President Johnson and by President Johnson to Vice President Humphrey on the same subject. Such letters do not have the force of law, however, and depend for their effectiveness on the good will of the parties involved.

In 1967, the Presidential Disability Amendment became the Twenty-

*Sherman Adams had been governor of New Hampshire, and Leonard Heaton was one of Eisenhower's doctors.

fifth Amendment to the Constitution. Its language is similar to that used by Attorney General Brownell in the amendment he had submitted to Congress for consideration ten years before. While it does not resolve all constitutional problems related to presidential disability, it is clearly superior to the complete constitutional void that preceded it. The Twenty-fifth Amendment, therefore, has its roots in the Eisenhower administration and reflects, in part, the reactions of President Eisenhower to his life-threatening illnesses and to the dangers such illnesses pose to the nation.

Eisenhower's Obsession with Duty

Dwight D. Eisenhower grew up, as I have indicated, in a household in which humility, hard work, and doing one's duty were of paramount importance. Above all, his pious mother, whose life he once described as one of "almost ceaseless work,"[319] served as the most powerful force shaping his character. Ida constantly preached the virtues of self-discipline and meeting one's responsibilities, and Dwight sought to remain true to her teachings throughout his adult life. Although he would come to know many of the world's greatest leaders, he always regarded his gentle but strong-willed mother as the finest person he had ever known. He delighted in her presence, saying that he found conversation with her to be among the most valuable moments of his life,[320] and greatly valued her approbation and love. Thus, Ida's principles served as the cornerstone of Dwight's life, and adherence to duty always ranked first among his priorities. His mother had, after all, stressed to her sons that they should behave properly because it "was the right thing to do."[321] This message was reinforced strongly during Eisenhower's West Point years as well as during his years of advanced officer training. As a cadet and as a young soldier and officer, Eisenhower was taught to be loyal to country and deferential to superiors, and oriented toward the ideal of fulfilling one's duty.

A close scrutiny of Eisenhower's adult life suggests, however, that his drive to do his duty was so obsessive as to be compulsive. A compulsive personality not only thinks and acts "as if compelled," but also places a high value "on the sacredness of obligation"[322]—a notion that seemed to guide Dwight Eisenhower's every step, as the word *duty* seemed to dominate his vocabulary.

In his early military life, whenever given unchallenging assignments, Eisenhower persevered in carrying them out, being firmly resolved "to perform every duty given to me to the best of my ability—no matter what its nature."[323] Later, as Eisenhower moved toward the pinnacle of his distinguished military career, duty remained central to his life. He even told his wife at one point that "my country comes first. You come second."[324] In February 1943, he wrote Mamie that "when you remember me in your prayers, that's the special thing I want—always to do my duty to the extreme limit of my ability."[325]

Even his deep and enduring grief over the death in 1921 of his first son can be read against this backdrop. It was his duty as a father to protect his son's well-being, but he had failed to do so just as his own father had failed to do so years before. Dwight had hired the maid from whom the young boy had contracted his fatal case of scarlet fever. No wonder Eisenhower regarded his son's death as the greatest catastrophe of his life. No wonder his stomach disorders began to become severe soon after the boy died. Such physical disturbances often result from anxiety and despondency. In his mind, he had failed to carry out his duty as a parent; he blamed himself for taking the child for granted and for bringing into his household the person who would give him a deadly disease. As a result, he admitted that he was on the verge of a nervous breakdown for a long time after the boy's death. Oliver Spurgeon English and Gerald H. J. Pearson, of the Temple University Medical School, have written that "there are certain crises in every life. At these points, the vulnerable personality tends to break down. In the past we have been prone to think of a neurosis or 'nervous breakdown' as it is often called as resulting from a major catastrophe such as the death of a relative."[326]

Eisenhower blamed himself because he "had often taken his [son's] presence for granted," and he and his wife were "completely crushed."[327] As often happens in such tragic situations, the relationship between husband and wife became strained, and they seemed to be growing apart if not moving in opposite directions.[328] The birth of a second son, John, in 1922 helped heal the breach; but the future President never fully recovered from his first son's death, which he described as "the greatest disappointment and disaster in my life, the one I have never been able to forget completely." He added, "Today, when I think of it . . . the keenness of our loss comes back to me as fresh and as terrible as it was in that long, dark day soon after Christmas, 1920."[329] Mamie Eisenhower once said, "it was as if a shining light had gone out in Ike's life. Throughout all the years that followed, the memory of those bleak days was a deep inner pain that never seemed to diminish much."[330] Every year, Eisenhower would send flowers to Mamie on Icky's birthday, usually yellow roses because yellow was the boy's favorite color.

In 1966, the Eisenhowers had Icky's body moved to the chapel at the Eisenhower Center in Abilene and reburied at the site of their planned entombment. A year later, the former President visited his son's grave and soon after suffered a heart attack. John Eisenhower recounted, "He left [the gravesite] upset, an emotion brought on not by concern for himself but by the sight of the tiny plaque on the floor where the body of my older brother had been placed."[331]

Icky's death had occurred when Eisenhower was thirty years of age—a vulnerable period of his life, as his responsibilities, both personal and professional, were mushrooming. Most adult neuroses break out between late adolescence and the age of thirty-five,[332] but all of them have their roots in childhood.[333] Icky's death, which, in Eisenhower's mind, may well have represented a failure of duty similar to that of his own father years before, seems to have made him more resolute, indeed more compulsive, in meeting subsequent duties, whatever those happened to be.

Adherence to duty undoubtedly was responsible for the punishing work schedule that Eisenhower followed in military life, and that almost certainly contributed to the frequency and intensity of his physical ailments. Seven-day workweeks and fourteen-hour workdays were not uncommon for him, and several times he found himself on the point of utter exhaustion. He would take vacations, however, only when ordered to do so by a commanding officer.[334]

When in 1947, after some hesitation, Eisenhower accepted the presidency of Columbia University, he did so "almost as a duty"[335]—a duty so burdensome that it contributed to his serious collapse in 1949, possibly his first heart attack. Then in 1950, when President Truman asked him to leave Columbia and accept appointment as commander of NATO forces, Eisenhower insisted that Truman order, rather than simply request, that he accept this post. Such an order would be a clear and unambiguous call to duty from which he, good soldier and good son, could not shrink, regardless of the consequences. Then, when approached by political leaders about a possible presidential candidacy in 1952, Eisenhower responded that he could never seek nomination to political office but "would consider a call to political service by the will of the party and the people to be the highest form of duty."[336] Shown a film, in February 1952, of a Madison Square Garden rally at which the crowd—"the people"—

chanted, "We want Ike! We want Ike!" Eisenhower bowed to duty and indicated that he was going to run.[337]

As President, Eisenhower was ravaged by the cares of office. He became very ill in 1953, possibly suffering from the cardiac difficulties that would strike him down some two years later. Yet he persevered in doing his duty. In fact, he went so far as to cite duty as the reason for his generally being a good patient for his doctors and for his having learned to control his temper more tightly than earlier in his life. He told reporters that "my reasons for obedience to the medical authorities are not solely personal. I must obey them out of respect for the responsibilities I carry."[338] The controlling of his temper, he explained, was due to the fact that "leaders are charged with responsibilities and must suppress personal impulse if duty so dictated."[339]

Early in his first term, Eisenhower had confided to one of his brothers that he did not intend to seek re-election in 1956: "I feel there can be no showing made that my 'duty' extends beyond a one-time performance."[340] But, when asked in early 1956, after the 1955 heart attack, whether he would run for another term, the President replied that he would make an announcement on the subject "as soon as I feel that the whole thing is completely clarified and that I can see where the path of duty is."[341] As I have discussed, that path of duty finally beckoned Eisenhower to seek another term. After formally announcing his candidacy for re-election, he remarked to his associates, "At least I can say that I have done my duty."[342]

When questioned in March 1956 about the impact of ill health on a possible second term, Eisenhower pledged that "there is going to be no neglect of the duties of the Presidency of the United States. When I feel that I can't carry them on, I won't be there." He also reiterated a promise he had made earlier to the American people: "unless I felt absolutely up to the performance of the duties of the President, the second that I didn't, I would no longer be there in the job or I wouldn't be available for the job."[343]

After suffering a stroke only ten months into his second term, Eisenhower initially contemplated resignation, fearing that he could no longer carry out his presidential responsibilities. A week later, he insisted on attending various meetings as a test of his ability to do his duty, saying that he would "have to do some hard thinking about the future" if he could not. Some sixteen days after suffering his stroke, the President, despite the contrary advice of his doctors and advisers I described earlier, attended a NATO meeting in Paris. One of his aides recounts that Eisenhower was determined to make this trip because he felt that "his presence was necessary to save the organization."[344] The President told one Allied leader that he would have resigned if his doctors had forbidden him to make the journey, because they would have been forbidding him to do his duty.[345]

About this time, Eisenhower lamented to a friend that "when I consider how many times I have been driven away from personal plans, I sometimes think I must be a very weak character."[346] The President was, of course, being excessively hard on himself. His character was not weak. It was, however, compulsive. In his actions as military leader and as President of the United States, he was compelled to be true to the lesson he had been taught back in Abilene, one reinforced in early military life. Duty must come first; all else comes after.

It is ironic that while always following the path of duty, Eisenhower often complained bitterly about where that path led him. In addition to grumbling about the unchallenging chores he was given early in his professional life, he professed to be unenthusiastic about, even oppressed by, some of the high positions he later held. For example, after being appointed chief of staff in 1945, he wrote: "No personal enthusiasm marked my promotion to Chief of Staff, the highest military post a professional soldier in the United States Army can reach. When President Truman broached the subject I told him that I'd much rather retire but he said he had a special need of me at the moment."[347]

And when Eisenhower accepted appointment as president of Columbia University in 1947, he complained that an educator would have been better suited for the job.[348] Although he soon seems to have concluded that he had made a serious mistake in accepting the Columbia appointment, since he found the position frustrating and the demands on his time severe,[349] he stated unequivocally that he did not want to leave Columbia in 1950 to become commander of NATO forces as President Truman wished. Describing this new position as a "thankless job," the reluctant Eisenhower nevertheless told Truman, "I had been a soldier all my life and by law was still an active soldier and I would report any time he said."[350] In the presence of Truman's order, his own wishes had to give way, even though he complained that leaving Columbia was "a tremendous personal disappointment."[351]

When approached about becoming a candidate for President, Eisenhower seemed at first to offer firm resistance. He argued that he had already reached his historical peak,[352] was too old,[353] and did not want "any type of political career."[354] He promised Senator Robert Taft of

Ohio, who was hoping for the Republican nomination, to withdraw from the race if Taft would, once nominated, agree to an internationalist foreign policy. When Taft remained noncommittal, Eisenhower edged closer to candidacy.[355] Then, too, he became convinced that he was the only person who could undo the belief that the state must guide all of our steps from the cradle to the grave.[356] Viewing himself as the nation's only savior from both isolationism and paternalism, Eisenhower felt that the "burden" of running for President was inescapable even though he professed himself distraught at the very thought of political office. He later wrote, "I have always been particularly sensitive to any insinuation that I might recoil from performance of any duty, no matter how onerous."[357]

Four years later, when pressured to run for re-election, Eisenhower initially refused to even entertain the thought, telling the Republican national chairman that he had given his entire adult life to his country and should not be asked to do more. Although he told a friend in August 1955, "I have seen many a man hang on too long under the definite impression that he had a great duty to perform and that no one else could adequately fill his particular position,"[358] six months later the President decided that, despite the heavy burdens of the presidency, he was still an indispensable man and would have to continue to serve his country in the White House.

Eisenhower's conscience, therefore, convinced him to accept appointment as chief of staff in 1945, although he said that he did so without enthusiasm. It convinced him to become president of Columbia University in 1948, although he said that others would have been better for the job. It convinced him to become commander of NATO forces in 1950, although he insisted that Truman order him to take on this "thankless task." It convinced him to run for President in 1952 and again in 1956, although he trumpeted his reluctance to enter both campaigns and spend four and then eight years of his life in an onerous political career. His conscience demanded in each instance that he do his duty, but his voice proclaimed at the same time his unhappiness at having to do so.

Perhaps the political scientist James David Barber has explained this paradox best: "Psychologically, one suspects the demands of conscience are met in part by maintaining the feeling of sacrifice—the person confirms that he is doing his duty by the fact that he does not enjoy it."[359] Erik Erikson put it even more succinctly: "[T]he adult compulsive would, deep down, have a stubborn wish for punishment."[360]

Thus, the parameters of behavior established by his parents—especially his mother—remained powerful long after Eisenhower had left home. As the psychoanalyst Dr. Otto Fenichel has pointed out,

a constant watchman has been instituted in the mind, who signals the approach of possible situations or behavior that might result in the loss of the mother's affection. This watchman fulfills the essential function of the ego: to anticipate the probable reactions of the external world to one's behavior. A portion of the ego has become an "inner mother," threatening a possible withdrawal of affection.[361]

As an adult, Eisenhower sought to live his life according to his mother's principles, so that she would be approving and her affection secure. Although he rose to positions of power and prestige in both military and political life, he tried to remain true to his Kansas roots, offering a modest and humble face to the outside world. Even his nickname (Ike) suggested a lack of pretension, and his campaign slogan ("I Like Ike") projected a degree of folksiness rare in the highest echelons of political activity. This was as his gentle and unpretentious mother would have liked. High office came about as a duty, Eisenhower often insisted, and not as a product of ambition. He simply bowed to the demands and urgings of all those who pointed out where his duty lay, no matter how burdensome that duty happened to be or how personally reluctant he might profess himself to be in accepting it. As Karen Horney tells us:

the neurotic has the feeling of not being a moving force in his own life. . . . When a person feels that he must do everything that is expected of him, he is actually set in motion by the pushes and pulls of others, or what he interprets as such. . . . Or, if somebody has become scared of his own pride and has set a taboo on ambition, he must deny—to himself—his active share in his doings.[362]

Clearly, Dwight D. Eisenhower was a complex man, perhaps one of the most complex ever to occupy the White House. He was keenly, perhaps excessively, sensitive to appearances[363]—but in his case, appearances did not often correspond with reality. He appeared to be an amateur politician, but his political skills were well honed. He appeared to be a smiling father figure but had a fierce temper (probably a sign of inner tension) and maintained a rather formal relationship with his own son.[364] He appeared to be verbally maladroit but had a masterful command of the English language, once describing himself as being, all his life, "an incorrigible reviser of written material."[365]

Even more interesting perhaps, Eisenhower appeared to be a man without an overwhelming ego, but a very large ego was often visible. He is reported to have wanted to design a distinctive general's uniform for himself,[366] and reveled in the adulation of the crowds after his victorious return to the United States in 1945. He described his welcome home in words that are revealing:

I was amazed at the number of people who met us in the streets and the wild enthusiasm of their greeting. The trip to Washington was so overwhelming I thought everything to follow would be anticlimax. When we went to New York, however, the entire city seemed to be on hand. Hour after hour, we traveled avenues jammed with people, with incalculable others hanging out the windows of towering office and apartment buildings.[367]

Ego was again much in evidence when he wrote that as president of Columbia University he was told by the head of the New York Transport Workers Union (who represented Columbia's maintenance workers) that "I've got more sense than to be taking on an opponent who is as popular as you seem to be in this city."[368] Also, when as President of the United States he was told by Secretary of State John Foster Dulles that "he was the most trusted leader and the greatest force for peace," Eisenhower's reaction was to note in his diary that "I suspect Foster's estimate concerning my own position is substantially correct."[369]

The unassuming "Everyman," therefore, gave clear evidence of having a well-developed and well-defined ego. Though seemingly modest, he delighted in the adulation of the crowds. Though seemingly reluctant, he enjoyed being pursued by political figures intent on making him President. Though seemingly without guile, he reveled in his great popularity and protected it with great care.

Also, although Eisenhower's adherence to duty often was accompanied by loud complaints that the duty was burdensome and/or unwelcome, he was far more willing to take on these responsibilities than he appeared. For example, while he claimed to dread political office, several American and British military officers who worked closely with him in 1944 were certain that he very much wanted to be President of the United States, even at that early date.[370] And years later, as President, he described his position as "probably the most taxing job, as far as tiring of the mind and spirit." Nevertheless, he admitted on more than one occasion that the presidency had "its inspirations."[371] Indeed, despite his many protestations to the contrary, many associates were convinced that this President actually enjoyed the presidency and found a number of his responsibilities to be rewarding and even exhilarating.

It was far more difficult for Eisenhower to admit this fact, however, than to bemoan his "fate" in life—that of being an irreplaceable man bearing a succession of burdensome responsibilities. As Fenichel writes, "the fear of losing the parent's affection may mean that one pretends to feel 'bad' at times when one actually feels 'good.' "[372] Dwight Eisenhower's ambition as well as his strong sense of pride may well have created severe inner conflicts, and these almost certainly intensified his physical indispositions.

The high positions he achieved did not bring him inner peace—not surprising, since "the neurotic lives between the two alternatives of pride and self-contempt" and "is at war with himself." A component of self-contempt is self-frustration, and "a most insidious form of self-frustration is the taboo on any aspiration."[373] As the record clearly indicates, Eisenhower was perpetually reluctant to admit that he aspired to any high office, and instead described many of the offices he held as burdensome, unpleasant, and having been "forced" on him. It was as though he viewed ambition as unacceptable and felt compelled to insist that the positions he occupied came to him as a result of duty rather than aspiration.

Self-hate culminates in "pure and direct self-destructive impulses and actions." These may remain unconscious and yet be actualized in such ways as engaging in dangerous activities or in "a rash disregard for physical disabilities."[374] Dwight D. Eisenhower accepted various heavy responsibilities during his lifetime even though—perhaps because—he must have known that they would intensify his cardiovascular and gastrointestinal ailments. This may well have represented an attempt to punish himself for his "sinful ways."

Whether his 1949 illness was a heart attack or a severe intestinal disorder, it seems to have been due to the pressures of the positions he held at the time. It was foolhardy, therefore, for him to become President of the United States a few years later since the burdens of office would be much heavier and the danger to his physical well-being much greater—unless, of course, he welcomed that danger.

After suffering a heart attack in 1955 (and possibly also in 1953) because of the pressures and frustrations of the presidency, Eisenhower nevertheless ran again in 1956, even though four more years of those pressures and frustrations would be punishing and even life threatening to him. Perhaps it was precisely for this reason that his heart attack emerged as the key factor determining him to seek another term. While some of Eisenhower's associates felt that retirement would pose greater health risks to him than another term in the White House, *he* may have viewed things differently, unconsciously gravitating toward the option that, to him, appeared the most punishing.

Eisenhower's decision to disregard his doctors' advice soon after his stroke in 1957 and fly to Paris for a NATO conference, perhaps believing that he would die there "with his boots on,"[375] seems to have demonstrated a well-defined death wish. And, although stricken on 17 October 1960 in Detroit with a dangerous episode of ventricular fibrillation which put his life at considerable risk, Eisenhower did not return immediately to the White House, his Gettysburg farm, or to Camp David to rest and recuperate. Instead, he flew to Minneapolis within hours of this severe cardiac disorder in order to fulfill another speaking engagement. Though he arrived on a raw, windy, and cold day, he still took off his overcoat and hat before speaking at the airport.[376] Once again, Eisenhower had chosen to follow the more dangerous course, thereby risking physical calamity, instead of the path dictated by prudence and reason.

These repeated instances of self-destructive behavior may represent the strangest paradox of this most paradoxical of presidents. The positions of power he occupied undoubtedly exacerbated his many physical ailments. Yet this may well have been the subconscious reason he accepted these high positions—as a punishment for his pride and ambition and for his "allowing" his son to contract scarlet fever so many years before. In short, Eisenhower may well have viewed the physical and emotional stresses of these positions as punishment for losing his mother's approval and love, and may have accepted them for precisely that reason. And although the pressures of high office undoubtedly contributed to his frequent and life-threatening illnesses, he may have accepted—indeed, subconsciously desired—those illnesses as punishments for the error of his ways. In short, when Dwight David Eisenhower told the American people on the eve of his retirement as President that he had done his duty for fifty years, he may well have been trying to reassure himself of that fact even more than he was reminding his countrymen of it. At stake was nothing less than his mother's love.

Chapter FIVE
Illness at Camelot:
John F. Kennedy

 t is both sad and ironic that an enduring symbol for the President who urged "vigor" on his countrymen, and is credited with inspiring the physical fitness craze that swept the country during and after his administration, is a rocking chair. The symbol, however, is, in some ways, entirely fitting since John F. Kennedy, a young and dynamic President whose persona and oratorical skills thrilled the nation and much of the world, was a man beset by illness and pain throughout his life. In this chapter, I will examine those illnesses, their political and psychological dimensions, and the possible impact of medication on Kennedy's behavior as President of the United States.

The Early Years

Born in Brookline, Massachusetts, on 29 May 1917, John Fitzgerald Kennedy was the second of nine children of Joseph and Rose Kennedy. Joseph was a strong-willed entrepreneur who became a millionaire by the age of thirty-five[1] but resented deeply the Boston Brahmins' condescending treatment of him.[2] One report had it that Joseph Kennedy was himself interested in the presidency of the United States before finally transferring that dream onto his sons.[3] Rose, the daughter of Boston's Mayor John Fitzgerald, was the steadying influence in the family and such a devoutly religious Roman Catholic that one of her daughers-in-law has referred to her as a "saint."[4]

The Kennedy children were brought up to be intense competitors,[5] and their parents took every opportunity to sharpen their interest in public affairs. They required them to read news stories or even *The Federalist Papers,* which they would collectively discuss at dinner.[6] A family friend recounts his recollections of dinnertime at the Kennedy household: "It wasn't like any other dinner table. The children had to be in their places five minutes early and the father kept the conversation on a high level. If you didn't talk about world affairs, you just didn't talk."[7]

When Joseph was away from home on one of his frequent business trips, Rose directed the family's uplifting conversations in her husband's place. She was a strict disciplinarian[8] and a strong-willed guardian who provided her children with purposeful direction and a sense of individuality.[9] Rose once described her maternal responsibilities in these words: "When I held my newborn baby in my arms, I used to think that what I said and did to him could have an influence not only on him but on all whom he met, not only for a day or a month or a year, but for all eternity—a very challenging and exciting thought for a mother."[10]

In an effort to develop a sense of individuality and self-worth, the Kennedy children were encouraged to play intensely and competitively. Touch football games, tennis matches, baseball games, and bicycle races were common pastimes, with the Kennedy children battling their companions as well as each other for supremacy. Their father, after all, was reported to have given them dual advice: "Don't play unless you can be captain," and "Second place is failure."[11] John Kennedy once said of his father that "he held up standards for us and he was very tough when we failed to meet those standards."[12] Even Rose was unrelenting in her efforts to push her children to excel. Her former secretary recalls being told by a nun that Rosemary Kennedy, the mentally retarded daughter, was still resentful years later of "how her mother tried to push her to keep up with the others when they were children."[13] One family friend remarked:

They are the most competitive family I've ever seen. They fight each other, yet they feed on each other. They stimulate each other. Their minds strike sparks. Each of them has warm friends. But none they like and admire so much as they like and admire their own brothers and sisters.[14]

Thus, John Kennedy grew up in a tightly knit and supportive family, with parents who worked hard to make their children self-assured and even aggressive toward each other and the outside world. At one point, he claimed that he could not remember any unhappy times during his childhood.[15] This however, seems to have been an exaggeration.

With so many children in the Kennedy household, parental affection had to be dispensed widely—and probably unevenly. John once confided to a friend that "my mother never really held me and hugged me. Never! Never!" He also remarked that living at home as a child was "like living in an institution . . . with all the toothbrushes lined up in a row."[16]

His parents were away from home frequently, and their absences did not always sit well with their offspring. Even though both parents took a great interest in their children's activities,[17] Jack complained on one occasion that "my mother was either at some Paris fashion house or else on her knees in some church. She was never there when we really needed her."[18] Rose reportedly confessed as much when she told one of her daughters that "I had no time to spend with you children. Your father was always gone, or we were having dinner at the embassy or attending formal affairs." The daughter to whom she made this admission is said to have responded, "That's why I'm still trying to get my head on straight."[19]

In addition to tensions with his parents, John Kennedy's relationship with his older brother was difficult. Joe, Jr., was taller, heavier, stronger, and more of an extrovert than Jack. He was something of a bully as well; and occasionally there were bitter fistfights between the two, from which Joe regularly emerged victorious. Jack later admitted of his brother, "He had a pugnacious personality. Later on it smoothed out but it was a problem in my boyhood."[20]

There may have been something of a symbiotic relationship between the two brothers. Some observers believe that John Kennedy's political career became inevitable on the day his older brother was killed in combat during the Second World War. His father expected his eldest son to enter political life. With Joe, Jr., removed from the scene, the mantle fell by necessity on John, the second son.

This was an unexpected development since, throughout his early life, John Fitzgerald Kennedy seemed an unlikely prospect for national and international leadership. He was a "rather frail little boy"[21] and almost died of scarlet fever at the age of three.[22] Moreover, his mother has told us that this was "only the beginning": "almost all his life, it seemed, he had to battle against misfortunes of health."[23] The family used to joke that if a mosquito bit Jack, the mosquito would surely die.[24] In addition to the usual childhood illnesses of bronchitis, measles, chicken pox, whooping cough, and german measles, John Kennedy suffered from diphtheria, allergies, frequent colds and flu, hives, an irritable colon,[25] a weak stomach which required a bland diet most of his life, and asthma which caused him considerable difficulty as a teenager.[26]

In 1930, he wrote his mother from boarding school complaining of blurriness and color blindness in his right eye—years later he would become hard of hearing in his left ear as well—and told his father that he had gotten dizzy and had fainted at Mass.[27] He underwent an appendicitis operation in 1931, had his tonsils and adenoids removed and came down with an enervating case of jaundice two years later, and in the mid-1930s developed a severe case of pneumonia. Approximately one year later, he had to end his studies at the London School of Economics after coming down with another case of jaundice so severe that it required hospitalization. After returning to the United States and beginning studies at Princeton, where he would be close to the New York doctors who were treating him,[28] the jaundice recurred and forced Kennedy to spend two months in Boston's Peter Bent Brigham Hospital and then move to Arizona to recuperate. In the fall of 1936, he entered Harvard University where he was closer to his family, but illness followed him. A bad case of the flu prevented him from making the swimming team which was to compete against Yale;[29] and in 1940, he developed a case of urethritis which recurred with some frequency throughout the remainder of his life. His bladder and prostate difficulties were so persistent, in fact, that shortly before his marriage he questioned one of his physicians about his ability to have children.[30] During these early years, he was described as "a slight, very slight, young man."[31]

Apart from his various illnesses, John Kennedy endured so many physical mishaps that some of his friends wondered whether he was accident-prone.[32] After a bicycle collision that left his older brother unhurt, young Jack required twenty-eight stitches. While traveling in Europe in 1937, he developed "the most terrible rash and his face blew up"[33]—probably an allergic reaction. In the war, his ship was rammed and sunk. Later, on the eve of his wedding to Jacqueline Bouvier in 1953, he cut his face on a rosebush.[34] More ominously, long before as a sophomore at Harvard, he had injured his right knee[35] and ruptured a spinal disk[36] playing football. While not the beginning of Kennedy's long bout with serious, painful, and almost fatal back ailments, the latter injury did compound them.

Kennedy's Bad Back

Dr. Elmer Bartels, one of the physicians who treated John Kennedy at the Lahey Clinic, reports that JFK had been born "with an unstable back."[37] Dr. Janet Travell, who began treating Kennedy for his bad back in May 1955 and became White House physician in 1961, has since revealed that

Kennedy "was born with the left side of his body smaller than the right; the left side of his face was smaller, his left shoulder was lower . . . and his left leg was appreciably shorter. . . . This was true all his life."[38]

Because of the malformation of his body, Kennedy was subject to back and spinal discomfort that was often intense. His "disparity in leg length created an abnormal seesaw motion in sacroiliac and lumbarsacral regions with each step and was a potential source of low back pain."[39] Moreover, muscle spasms were not uncommon and occasionally so severe as to almost completely incapacitate Kennedy. These muscle spasms apparently were caused, in part, by thyroid insufficiency. Dr. Travell explained that Kennedy suffered from hypothyroidism, and that a vast proportion of people who have underactive thyroid function "are extremely subject to persistent and recurring attacks of skeletal muscle spasm—painful and debilitating."[40]

The future President's medical problems were clearly compounded by the serious injury he suffered while playing football at Harvard. His mother believed that that injury "marked the beginning of troubles with his back that were to haunt him the rest of his life."[41] To be sure, Kennedy's football injury made his back problems more acute, but it was his wartime injury that eventually brought him to the surgeon's knife and to the point of death.

As the Second World War loomed on the horizon, John Kennedy tried to enlist in the army but was rejected because of his bad back. He was, however, accepted into the navy; his father is alleged to have intervened to have him pass the physical.[42] He emerged from navy service a war hero, explaining later with characteristic humor that heroism had been thrust on him involuntarily when "they sank my boat."[43] A cynic might argue that John Kennedy owed his successful political career to his bad back: had he entered the army instead of the navy as he initially planned, he might have remained an anonymous soldier and might never have succeeded in politics as a hero of the Second World War.

Regardless of the future political advantages that may have come to him, Kennedy paid a heavy personal price for his heroism. When his PT boat was rammed and sunk by an enemy destroyer, his bad back was "torn" by the "shock of the collision"[44] and he is reported to have thought to himself, "This is how it feels to be killed."[45] With his ruptured spinal disc, he spent many hours in the water, holding one of his wounded shipmates in his arms and even in his teeth so that he would not drown. This, of course, strained his muscles and his damaged back, as well as causing numerous coral lacerations which became infected. After this ordeal, Kennedy came down with a mild case of malaria[46] and an agonizing case of sciatica.[47] He also suffered from colitis, which was so painful and persistent that a duodenal ulcer was long suspected and later confirmed.[48]

On 23 June 1944, at the Lahey Clinic, Dr. James L. Poppen performed a lumbar disc operation on Kennedy's spine, removing some abnormally soft disc material.[49] The pain did not disappear as Kennedy had hoped, however, but instead grew steadily worse. Compounding the problem was the fact that Kennedy suffered from exceedingly severe abdominal pain which became almost constant after his back surgery. A spastic colon and gall bladder dysfunction were both diagnosed at the time and cited as contributing factors in his pain. His discomfort was further intensified when he underwent a hemorrhoidectomy in August.[50]

Kennedy was soon discharged from the navy not because of his bad back but because of his chronic colitis[51] and went to Arizona once again to recover. During the summer of 1945, he traveled to Europe, where he suffered a flare-up of malarial fever. One of his friends commented that "I've never seen anyone so sick in my life. . . . It scared the hell out of me. I thought he was going to die. I've never seen anyone go through the throes of fever before."[52]

Elected to the House of Representatives in 1946, the twenty-nine-year-old Congressman was so skinny,[53] gaunt,[54] and pale that "his colleagues feared for his life."[55] Lyndon Johnson said of Kennedy that House Speaker Sam Rayburn thought him "a very young-looking man who might be going to die of malaria."[56] In 1951, he went on a world tour to increase his knowledge of foreign affairs but became gravely ill during a visit to Korea. He was flown to a hospital in Okinawa where his temperature soared, according to his brother Robert, to "about 106 or 107°," and doctors "didn't think he could possibly live."[57]

By the time he ran for the Senate in 1952, chronic back pain caused him to be "tense and irritable" with his associates and required that he travel

with crutches, which he concealed in his car when he arrived at the hall where the audience was waiting. Dave [Powers] would notice him gritting his teeth when he walked with a determined effort from the car to the door where the chairman or the committee members were waiting to greet him, but then when he came into the room where the crowd was gathered, he was erect and smiling, looking as fit and healthy as the light-heavyweight champion of the world. Then after he finished his speech and answered questions from the floor and shook hands with everyone, we would help him into the car and he would lean back on the seat and close his eyes in pain.[58]

Within two years, Kennedy's back pain had become so intense that he was forced to use crutches constantly, and two of his closest associates report that he "hated being seen on crutches more than he hated the pain."[59] As a result, he hid his crutches before visitors entered his office, and also remained to do regular office work at his seat in the Senate chamber instead of returning to his office after roll calls since he wished to conceal the fact that he could not walk unaided.[60]

Kennedy's disposition reflected the intensity of his discomfort. He became so disagreeable that his personal secretary considered resigning from his staff and seeking another position on Capitol Hill.[61] Some observers have even attributed one of Kennedy's rare political blunders to his excruciating pain. Despite his not feeling well, he agreed to get involved in the 1954 Senate race in Massachusetts.[62] During a televised appearance, Kennedy failed to mention the name of the Democratic party's candidate for the Senate, leading some observers to conclude that he was indirectly endorsing the Republican incumbent instead.[63] This gaffe contributed to complaints that Kennedy was interested only in his own political fortunes and not in those of his party or his party colleagues, complaints that bedeviled him for several years.

Shortly after this episode, Kennedy entered the New York Hospital for Special Surgery, where he underwent lumbar fusion surgery in which an attempt was made to stabilize his spine by means of a bone graft and a metal plate.[64] Some physicians had disagreed that surgery should be performed and recommended more conservative treatment.[65] Others cautioned that the surgery would be extremely dangerous and might not ease the pain at all.

Kennedy was, however, determined to have the surgery, saying of the risks, "I don't care. I can't go on like this."[66] Although his New York doctors suggested that two separate operations be performed on Kennedy's back, he insisted that both operations be conducted at one time.[67]

The senator almost died of postoperative complications, including a grave staphylococcal infection;[68] and on two occasions, he was given the last rites of the Roman Catholic Church. Even after the immediate crisis passed, Kennedy's convalescence was lengthy and difficult, and still another operation had to be performed a few months later in order to remove the plate in his back which was causing recurring infection.

Unfortunately, the back operations that caused him so much difficulty actually made his back condition worse.[69] There was some fear that he would never walk again, and that he might have to resign his seat in the Senate.[70]

In early 1955, one of his closest friends was called by a Kennedy family member and asked to visit Jack Kennedy in Florida. This friend reported, "The family was worried about Jack and didn't know whether he was going to live. The doctor felt he was losing interest, and a visit from someone closely associated with happier times might help him regain his usual optimism and enjoyment of life."[71]

Kennedy's depression was understandable. A close political associate recounted that, in addition to continuing pain, he had a gaping hole in his back as a result of his 1954 and 1955 surgeries.[72] Another aide described the period of Kennedy's convalescence as "torture."[73] The situation was perhaps best described by one of the Senator's closest friends: "[i]t was a terrible time. He was bitter and low. We came close to losing him. I don't just mean losing his life. I mean losing him as a person."[74]

Nevertheless, John Kennedy used this difficult period in his life to work on his prize-winning book, *Profiles in Courage*. The journalist Arthur Krock, who visited the senator while he was recuperating, later reported that

he was lying on a board in his bed, absolutely flat, with one of those lecterns, bed lecterns, in front of him and pinned on that was a block of yellow paper, and there he sat writing the introduction to the Profiles in Courage *and some of the biographical material. I was deeply touched by this gallant performance of a man in his situation, in his pain, to be working on this.*[75]

In that book, Kennedy wrote of courage, defining that quality, in Hemingway's words, as "grace under pressure." He warned that "a nation which has forgotten the quality of courage which in the past has been brought to public life is not as likely to insist upon or reward that quality in its chosen leaders today—and in fact we have forgotten."[76] Although the considerable grace Kennedy brought to public life may not have been the political courage about which he wrote in *Profiles*, it reflected impressive personal courage in the face of his many physical ailments and unrelenting pain.

In May 1955, Senator Kennedy sought relief from his severe back spasms, and also from a flare-up of the knee injury he had sustained while playing football at Harvard, and consulted Janet Travell, a New York physician. Travell has recounted her first impressions of her most famous patient:

He was thin, he was ill, his nutrition was poor, he was on crutches. There were two steps from the street into my office and he could hardly navigate these. His major complaint was pain in his left low back with radiation to the left lower extremity, so that he couldn't put weight on it without intense pain. But he also had . . . a right knee which was, at that time, very stiff and painful. . . . He had a low basal metabolic rate of about minus 20, a high cholesterol running about 350 and . . . thyroid insufficiency. . . . He was really anemic. He had impaired vibration sense which is indicative of peripheral neuritis.[77]

She was able to help Kennedy almost immediately. Through vapocoolant therapy, she increased the range of motion of his right knee joint by some 50 percent. She also checked him into New York Hospital, where she initiated treatment of his back pain by giving him "local procaine or novocaine injection of trigger points."[78]

To correct his vitamin-B deficiencies, Kennedy was put on a regimen of vitamin B, vitamin B_{12}, and B-complex injections. Since deficiencies in vitamin B "are accompanied by neuromuscular irritability with tendencies for muscle cramps and muscle spasm,"[79] Kennedy's back problems were exacerbated by muscle spasms caused by both his thyroid condition, as previously noted, and deficits in vitamin B.

It was in Dr. Travell's office that John Kennedy discovered that a rocking chair provided some relief to his constant backache. Seated in her chair, he remarked, "This is so comfortable; why can't I have one of these?"[80] As a result, he had a rocking chair installed in his office, both as a senator and as President. That chair—intended to supplement Kennedy's back therapy rather than simply to provide him with ordinary relaxation—remains perhaps the single most prominent artifact of the Kennedy era and is now on permanent display at the Kennedy Library in Boston.

In order to compensate for the fact that one of Kennedy's legs was shorter than the other, Travell attached to the heel of his shoe a lift slightly over a quarter of an inch thick. When this was later found to be insufficient, Kennedy's shoe was "built up a little more by a small felt lift on the inside of the shoe which probably added an eighth of an inch or three-sixteenths of an inch more correction."[81] Kennedy was advised to wear no shoes—not even beach shoes—that did not have the heel lift, and to refrain from going barefoot.[82]

Moreover, Kennedy was instructed to use a firmer mattress so that he would have more support for his back as he slept. Since he was very allergic to horsehair, tightly tied cattle hair was used to produce a very firm mattress. In addition, a heavy bedboard was inserted beneath the mattress to provide him with even greater support.[83]

Despite these efforts, Kennedy was forced to re-enter New York Hospital in the fall of 1957 because of severe back pain, redness and swelling in the lumbar region, and fever. Doctors drained a localized abscess, but no bone diseases were discovered. Travell reports that this was the only occasion in their association when her patient was "really discouraged."[84]

Shortly after this setback, Kennedy's condition improved markedly. He began playing golf and, according to Dr. Travell, "was in wonderful condition. He had very little difficulty."[85] In fact, when he re-injured his back in his early months as President, forcing a return to crutches, he told Travell that he had become so accustomed to not thinking about his back that he "forgot to take care."[86]

In May 1961, in a tree-planting ceremony in Canada, President Kennedy stood too rigidly as he wielded his shovel, and sprained his back once again. Historian and White House aide Arthur Schlesinger wrote, "A premonitory twinge deepened after a few hours into an acute and nagging ache. . . . The pain did not leave him for more than six months, and in the weeks of travel immediately ahead, it was often sharp and exhausting."[87]

Even when, a few days after returning home from Canada, the President tried to escape the pressures of Washington by visiting the family compound on Cape Cod, he was in considerable discomfort. A chauffeur who saw his back during this visit described his scar as "vicious" and reported that the President kept massaging his back as he sat in his father's kitchen trying to relax. The chauffeur summarized his reactions by writing that Kennedy's "was no cheap Purple Heart."[88] Kennedy's back pain eventually became so intense as a result of the tree-planting mishap that he could not avoid being seen and photographed hobbling on crutches and even being transported up to and down from the door of Air Force One by hydraulic lift.[89]

A month after re-injuring his back, Kennedy became gravely ill, his temperature rising to 105°F. He had a very acute sore throat, coughing, and chills; and Dr. Travell diagnosed him as being "really quite sick" and not with a "simple viral infection."[90] After he was treated with intravenous infusion, large doses of penicillin, and alcohol sponge baths, his temperature returned to normal. A New York physician was brought to Washington, however, in order to examine Kennedy's back and ascertain whether infection had recurred and was causing his present difficulties. He found that it had not. This was the only day during his White House years that Kennedy was too ill to work. But by evening, he had left his sick bed and was playing host to guests at the mansion.[91]

Throughout the few remaining years of his life, Kennedy did not often forget to take care of his back. In the summer of 1961, the period immediately following the Canadian tree-planting episode, he began a physical therapy program at the White House with Dr. Hans Kraus of New York. This has been described as "a very hard period" for Kennedy since his back pain was again almost unbearable.[92]

Dr. Kraus prescribed a rigorous series of daily calisthenics, which the President followed faithfully,[93] and clearly strengthened his back.[94] Also, Kennedy began to swim regularly in the White House pool; though it had been redecorated at his father's expense, he had not used it previously, perhaps because it was so unlike the waters off the Kennedy compound at Cape Cod. Kennedy's initial refusal to use the pool was in direct contradiction to his White House physician's advice that he much needed this form of exercise[95]—unusual behavior in this normally good patient.

During the summer of 1961, the President began swimming each day in the White House pool heated to 90°F.,[96] shortly before lunch and then again in the evening. After lunch he would rest on a heating pad and each day would take three hot baths.[97] At all times, the President wore a brace across his back, even for the short walk from the dressing room to the pool.[98] One of his doctors described the brace as

a canvas lower abdominal belt, of very light material . . . [which] had no actual stays. It had a thickening in various portions where there were double or triple the number. They were not metal stays or bone stays or anything of that sort. You could hardly call it a brace. It was just a small support rather than any special brace.[99]

In the last six months of his life, Kennedy also began wearing mustard plasters on his back which had been recommended by his mother.[100] These had been particularly helpful to him during his tumultuous visit to Europe in June 1963. After his return, he wrote his mother that "those plasters of yours really helped. I only wish I had known about them sooner."[101]

Despite Dr. Travell's view that the exercise program with Dr. Kraus did the President "an inestimable amount of good,"[102] conflict apparently developed among his physicians. Dr. George Burkley, whom Kennedy appointed as head of the military medical unit at the White House on 1 February 1961, has reported that after Dr. Kraus entered the picture, Dr. Travell was instructed not to "attempt to interfere in any way."[103] Burkley has stated that his "management of the President's health was more general and not limited to the use of procaine injections which Dr. Travell advocated at all times."[104] More pointedly, Burkley believed that the procaine injections were "actually harmful or actually not beneficial in that after an injection the exercise should be curtailed and gradually built up again, and this would really set him back."[105] Burkley had the view that the injections may have lessened Kennedy's pain temporarily but did nothing to improve his basic physical condition.

It would appear that an arrangement was worked out under which Dr. Travell essentially cared for Jacqueline Kennedy and her children,[106] while Drs. Burkley and Kraus managed the President's care. This arrangement did not, however, prevent Dr. Travell from changing the height and shape of the lectern used at press conferences in July 1961, or from approving a redesign of the President's cabinet chair in early 1962 so as to minimize back strain.[107]

During the final months of his presidency, John Kennedy's back showed improvement but remained a potential, and occasionally an actual, source of difficulty for him. In addition to the frequent pain it caused, Kennedy's bad back prevented him from doing things he very much wanted to do. As an example, Ben Bradlee, one of his friends, related that the President kept urging him "to pick John-John up and throw him in the air because he loves it so and because Kennedy himself [couldn't] do it because of his back." According to Bradlee, the President said of his son, "he doesn't know it yet but he's going to carry me before I carry him."[108]

In May 1963, as he celebrated his forty-sixth and last birthday, the President was suffering from such severe back pain that his wife asked Dr. Travell for an injection to alleviate the pain, if only so that he could enjoy his birthday party. Although Travell was not able to help him in this instance,[109] the President's back "was almost miraculously better" a few days later.[110] When he left for his tragic visit to Texas on 21 November 1963, he told his aides, "I feel great. My back feels better than it's felt in years."[111]

After the President's assassination in Dallas, suggestions circulated that had it not been for the fact that he was wearing his back brace,[112] Kennedy might have survived his assassin's bullets. The first wound Kennedy received would not have been fatal. But his back brace held him in an upright position, keeping him from collapsing onto the seat of his limousine where he might have avoided further injury. Instead, he remained in an upright position, and another bullet shattered his skull and ended his life.

Addison's Disease

In addition to back problems so grave that his brother Robert said of him that "at least one half of the days that he spent on this earth were days of intense physical pain,"[113] John F. Kennedy suffered from a debilitating, potentially life-threatening disease for at least the last sixteen years of his life. Had Kennedy contracted it even a few years earlier than he did, he almost certainly would have died.

While on a visit to London in the fall of 1947, Congressman Kennedy became so seriously ill with weakness, nausea, vomiting, and low blood pressure that he was given the last rites of the Roman Catholic Church.[114] The physician who examined him diagnosed his condition as Addison's disease and told one of Kennedy's friends that "he hasn't got a year to live."[115] Arthur Krock, however, remembered being told by Joseph Kennedy, even before his son first ran for Congress in 1946, that Jack had Addison's disease and was probably dying. Krock related that Joseph Kennedy "wept sitting in the chair opposite me in the office."[116] If Krock's memory was accurate, it would appear that John Kennedy contracted Addison's disease somewhat earlier than previously thought. Indeed, this might well explain Kennedy's illness during his first campaign for the House of Representatives, when he collapsed during the final campaign event, a parade in Charlestown, sweating heavily and his skin discolored.[117]

One of the common symptoms of Addison's disease is a discoloration or bronzing of the skin.[118] Although several of Kennedy's biographers indicate that he did not have skin discoloration and/or that he insisted he did not,[119] other observers found that he had a surprisingly deep tan,[120] or yellowish skin,[121] or skin of a greenish tinge.[122] One who saw him during the 1960 campaign reported that his face was "lined and tanned to the extreme- and rough-looking, like the surface of a steak."[123] Theodore Sorenson, special counsel to the President, related that Kennedy once responded to a suspicious reporter's question about his year-round tan "by exposing a part of his anatomy that had not been burned by the sun."[124] This, however, was no proof that his tan was natural, since

Addisonian bronzing is "usually more marked on the exposed portions of the skin."[125]

Earlier, when a journalist had asked him about the unusual tinge of his skin, Kennedy replied with uncharacteristic candor, "The doctors say I've got a sort of slow motion leukemia, but they tell me I'll probably last until I'm forty-five. So I seldom think about it except when I have the shots."[126]

Addison's disease involves a failure of the adrenal glands. These glands are attached to the kidneys and produce adrenalin and the cortisone that maintains proper levels of minerals in the bloodstream.[127] Adrenal failure produces a disruption in salt and water metabolism and disturbs the utilization of body carbohydrates. Addison's disease also diminishes cardiac output, leads to immune deficiencies which make the body less resistant to bodily infection,[128] and often produces gastrointestinal disorders.[129]

When Addison's disease was first discovered in the mid-1800s, it was regarded as fatal. Before 1930, 90 percent of persons with the disease died within five years; but in the late 1930s, researchers developed a synthetic substance, desoxycorticosterone acetate (DOCA), which greatly reduced the mortality rate. However, it remained important for those with the disease to avoid great stress, since stress increases the body's need for steroids which the Addisonian's adrenal glands cannot provide.[130]

Classic Addison's disease has been caused by tuberculosis.[131] Since John Kennedy never suffered from tuberculosis of any kind, he and his spokespersons maintained that he did not have Addison's disease in the classic sense. Rather, they attributed his adrenal insufficiency to the physical strain of having to spend many hours in the water after his PT boat was sunk and to the case of malaria he contracted soon afterward.[132]

Nevertheless, Kennedy was wholly dependent on the cortisone therapy that Addisonians rely upon for survival. Initially, he took 25 milligrams of cortisone by mouth; then took it through injection.[133] Also, he had implanted in his thighs DOCA tablets of 150 milligrams, which were replaced several times a year.[134] There are even reports that the Kennedy family kept a reservoir of DOCA and cortisone in safety deposit boxes around the country so that Jack would have ready access to these medications wherever he traveled.[135] One of his closest aides recounts that Kennedy "used (and carried with him around the country) more pills, potions, poultices and other paraphernalia than would be found in a small dispensary."[136]

Addison's disease often produces severe muscular cramping[137] and thus may well have compounded Kennedy's back problems. Clearly, the disease played an important role in heightening the dangers associated with his back operations in 1954. In the case of Addisonians at the time, even such a simple procedure as a tooth extraction might have been followed by death. The disease was so serious that occasionally patients who did not appear to be in any immediate danger would die suddenly.[138] Surgery, therefore, was extraordinarily dangerous in Kennedy's case.

An article that appeared in a 1955 issue of the *AMA Archives of Surgery*, and examined the case of a thirty-seven-year-old male Addisonian who underwent spinal surgery at the New York Hospital for Special Surgery on 21 October 1954, is widely believed to have John Kennedy as its subject. Kennedy, after all, was a thirty-seven-year-old male Addisonian who had undergone surgery on the date and at the hospital specified. This article pointed out that the surgical procedures performed on JFK, a lumbosacral fusion and a sacroiliac fusion, were considered dangerous because of his adrenocortical insufficiency due to Addison's disease. Throughout the more than three-hour operation, the patient received hydrocortisone intravenously. In the postoperative period, this treatment was supplemented by added dosages of desoxycorticosterone, salt, and cortisone given intramuscularly.[139] Except for a urinary tract infection which arose three days after the operation, a mild reaction to a transfusion, and a wound infection, the patient did not develop a full-scale "Addisonian crisis," even though he suffered from "marked adrenocortical insufficiency."[140]

It was precisely the danger of an "Addisonian crisis" that led doctors at the Lahey Clinic in Boston to refuse to perform the operation in the first place, since they feared that Kennedy might not tolerate the surgery well and die. Although their worst fears were not realized, Kennedy's convalescence following his back surgery was protracted and painful. Dr. Travell, in fact, estimated that he suffered from a chronic infection in the soft tissues of his back for three and a half years after the back operations were performed.[141] Addison's disease, with its proclivity to render patients more susceptible to infection, almost certainly played a role in making Kennedy's recovery so slow and agonizing.

By the time John Kennedy launched his presidential campaign in the late 1950s, new treatments for Addison's disease (meticorten and the flouro-hydrocortisone derivatives or the gluco-corticosteroid compounds) had been developed,[142] the adrenal problems associated with the ailment had become entirely manageable and a normal life span had become possible for the first time.[143] Nevertheless, Kennedy's physical condition was made an issue in the campaign, despite a statement by one of his physicians that he was "fully rehabilitated from the depletion of adrenal function which he had suffered as a result of his wartime injuries."[144]

As he battled Lyndon B. Johnson for the Democratic presidential nomination, some of Johnson's allies made reference to Kennedy's Addison's disease and used it as an argument against his nomination. India Edwards, a southern Democratic party leader, told a group of reporters that "Kennedy was so sick from Addison's disease that he looked like a spavined hunchback."[145] She also asserted that doctors had told her that were it not for cortisone, Kennedy would be dead.[146] Another prominent Johnson ally, campaign manager John Connolly, charged that, if nominated and elected, Kennedy "couldn't serve out the term" since "he was going to die."[147]

The Kennedy forces responded to these attacks by asserting that "John F. Kennedy does not now nor has he ever had an ailment described classically as Addison's disease, which is a tubercular destruction of the adrenal gland. Any statement to the contrary is malicious and false."[148] In addition, Dr. Travell spent three or four hours with Dr. Eugene Cohen hammering out a statement on Kennedy's health; it was dated 11 June 1960 and sent in letter form to Kennedy for release to the press. The two doctors found the statement difficult to write. In fact, Travell later admitted that they "fought over every word of it."[149] The statement read in part:

We wish to point out that the fact that your adrenal glands do function has been confirmed by a leading endocrinologist outside of New York City.

With respect to the old problem of adrenal insufficiency, as late as December, 1958 when you had a general check-up with a specific test of adrenal function, the result showed that your adrenal glands do function.[150]

After Kennedy won the presidential nomination of his party on the first ballot, there was considerable interest in the choice of his vice-presidential running mate. Highly revealing is a generally overlooked comment made by Philip Graham, late publisher of the *Washington Post* in a memorandum concerning Lyndon Johnson's selection for second place on the 1960 ticket:

I told LBJ Jack would be phoning him and then . . . I returned to the vacant bedroom to call Adlai [Stevenson, the Democrats' 1952 and 1956 presidential nominee]. In our prior talk he had argued for [Missouri Senator Stuart] Symington on pure expediency grounds and I had been a bit testy in pointing out that any VP was likely to be President. (Emphasis added)[151]

During the general election campaign, an attempt was made to steal Kennedy's health records;[152] and the office of Dr. Cohen, the co-author of the statement on his adrenal insufficiency, was actually vandalized.[153] Also, prominent Republicans raised new questions about Kennedy's health. Congressman Walter Judd of Minnesota, a former medical missionary and the 1960 Republican keynote speaker, stated unequivocally:

For one thing I would like a flat answer to rumors in medical circles that Case Number Three in the American Medical Association's Archives of Surgery, Vol. 71, relates to Senator Kennedy. If so, this represents information which Senator Kennedy is duty-bound to make fully available to the consideration of every voter.[154]

Republican questions about Kennedy's health were diffused largely by the vigorous campaign he waged and by the image of vitality he projected. Except for the flu, acute sinusitis, and a case of laryngitis that "completely unnerved" him,[155] he was well throughout the campaign period, and Dr. Travell saw him only once or twice.[156] One of his closest aides expressed relief that the nominee's "history of bed-confining fevers did not recur."[157] At one of his first press conferences after his election, Kennedy made an extraordinarily rare reference to the rumors of his ill health: he insisted to reporters, "I have never had Addison's disease. I have been through a long campaign and my health is very good today."[158]

We know now that Kennedy's Addison's disclaimer was untrue, even though he may not have fully realized it at the time. Kennedy maintained that his adrenal insufficiency was a side effect of the malaria he contracted after the war. This is a possibility since "malaria has been known to cause lesions in the adrenal cortex."[159] Since Kennedy did not suffer at any time from tuberculosis, his adrenal insufficiency seems likely to have resulted from atrophy of the adrenal glands. One medical specialist has reported that about half of all Addisonians he treated suffered from adrenal gland atrophy rather than from tuberculosis.[160] Nine years after Kennedy's death, his autopsy photographs were viewed by Dr. John Latimer who found that "no abnormal calcification could be seen . . . to suggest tuberculosis or hemorrhage of the adrenals. It is [my] firm belief that the President suffered from bilateral adrenal atrophy."[161]

Dr. Travell later stated for the record that John Kennedy did indeed suffer from Addison's disease. Asked in 1966 whether it would be fair to say "for a secret historical record" that Kennedy had had Addison's disease, Travell responded:

The term Addison's disease has been extended at the present time to include all degrees of adrenal insufficiency and all causes of adrenal insufficiency. So that I would say yes to your question. At the present time, the broader meaning of this diagnosis would now cover his condition, although even fifteen years ago it would not have. [162]

As early as 1953, however, a physician associated with the Lahey Clinic had indicated that Kennedy had been suffering from and treated for Addison's disease since the late 1940s. While that physician pointed out that Kennedy had been a patient of the Lahey Clinic since 1936 and had had "quite a variety of conditions," he described his Addison's disease as the most serious of Kennedy's many ailments.[163] Apparently, Travell did not speak for all of Kennedy's doctors.

The Impact of Illness on Kennedy's Presidency

The pain and illness that were with John F. Kennedy during his formative years as well as later significantly affected his political personality and political predispositions in several ways. Although it is difficult to establish firm causal relationships in all instances, a number of likely linkages may at least be suggested.

First, Kennedy had to spend so much time alone, recuperating from his various ailments, that he developed, even as a boy, an impressive affinity for reading and learning. Reading became an early and comfortable part of his life, and he devoured books and magazines, especially those dealing with history, government, and biography.[164] By the time he was in his early twenties, he was impressing visitors with the breadth and depth of his knowledge. A university faculty member who spent time with the Kennedy family in 1941 wrote later:

It was clear to me that John had a far better historical and political mind than his father and older brother; indeed that John's capacity for seeing current events in historical perspective and for projecting historical trends into the future was unusual. [165]

As President, Kennedy was a compulsive reader. In addition to perusing many newsmagazines from the United States and abroad, he scanned more than a dozen newspapers each day. His press secretary revealed that when "he came into my office and saw one he hadn't read on my desk, he would inevitably walk out with it. No one on the staff was safe from his shoplifting."[166] The First Lady reported that the President read just about everywhere, so much so, in fact, that "his eyes were 'giving out.' "[167]

A "newspaper habit" is important to presidents,[168] and Kennedy's enabled him to become familiar with a broad range of issues and keep in touch with a spectrum of opinions useful to him as President. General Lucius Clay, a Republican, recollected that "I never met with him on any subject that he hadn't done his homework before the meeting. He was always well informed on the subject that he was meeting you about. . . . How he found time to do it, I don't know—but he did."[169]

In assessing Kennedy's international accomplishments as President, another observer wrote, "He had a large perspective, a sense of the ebb and flow of events, that permitted him to look beyond the immediate crisis. Both of these qualities helped him in dealing with the untidiness, the inconsistencies and internal contradictions of foreign affairs."[170]

Owing to the large quantities of information he had available at his fingertips, his press conferences were masterful, as he responded effectively to a wide variety of questions. His knowledgeability was transmitted to both the press and the public, and his press conferences drew large audiences and became an important adjunct of presidential power. Thus, developed from childhood, Kennedy's ease in reading and absorbing information, and his consequent broadened perspective, played a key role in his conduct of office. His illnesses, then, contributed to an intellectual life that left a clear imprint on his presidency.

Second, the combination of Addison's disease and a bad back negatively affected Kennedy's work in the House of Representatives and his reputation in Congress. After first taking office in 1947, Kennedy was highly regarded, winning praise from both national and Massachusetts commentators.[171] But after his adrenal insufficiency was diagnosed, Kennedy's absenteeism grew, and he compiled a generally mediocre record in the House.

During his first term in the Senate, his back surgery and lengthy convalescence caused him to be away from Washington for approximately a year. This was the period when the battle against Senator Joseph McCarthy was reaching its climax, and Kennedy missed the vote on the resolution censuring the Wisconsin Republican for violating the rules of the Senate. Some of his critics never forgave Kennedy for failing to cast his vote against McCarthy or at least to pair his vote with that of another absentee senator wishing to vote in favor. Although two of his closest aides have argued that "everyone in the Senate knew that Kennedy had been planning to vote for the McCarthy censure,"[172] the fact that he had not, in some way, made his position clear haunted him for years. Questions about Kennedy's stand on McCarthyism shadowed his brief quest for the vice-presidential nomination in 1956 and surfaced again during his presidential campaign in 1960.[173] Eleanor Roosevelt criticized the Massachusetts senator for failing to condemn McCarthyism, as did the liberal Americans for Democratic Action.[174] Had Kennedy not been absent when the vote was taken, he almost certainly would have voted with the Democrats against McCarthy, and liberal opposition to his advancement would have been ameliorated. Instead, he attempted to use his illness as the reason for his noninvolvement; and critics never accepted this rationale and attacked him vigorously for lack of courage in refusing to take a more public stand on the issue.

Third, there was an urgency to Kennedy's political life that may have been caused, even if subconsciously, by the fear of premature death. In 1946, when he was only twenty-nine, he ran for a seat in the House of Representatives despite the life-threatening illness and intense pain of those years. In 1952, when he was only thirty-five, he challenged the venerable Republican Henry Cabot Lodge for his Senate seat, even though he was seriously incapacitated and hardly able to walk. In 1956, at the age of only thirty-nine, Kennedy, not yet fully recovered from his nearly fatal back operation in 1954, attempted to become Adlai Stevenson's vice-presidential running mate. And in 1961, at the age of only forty-three, Kennedy became the youngest elected President in American history.

His was an activist presidency; and although his term was relatively brief, Kennedy took actions in both foreign and domestic policy that were striking departures from the past. Having promised in his campaign to get the country moving again, he surrounded himself with youthful, activist associates who shared his commitment to the "New Frontier." Kennedy's activism may have resulted from the need he perceived to bring about change in the status quo. Perhaps, however, it also resulted from his fear that time was running out for him, and that much had to be accomplished quickly. One of his favorite poems, after all, was Alan Seeger's "I Have a Rendezvous with Death."[175] A friend related that "illness and death . . . was seen by Kennedy as always waiting for him. . . . So whenever he was in a situation, he tried to burn bright, he tried to wring as much out of things as he could."[176] His personal secretary agreed that he was eager "to crowd as much living as possible into every single hour."[177]

Fourth, Kennedy's lifelong battle against illness and pain made him particularly sensitive to the issues of health and health care while he was president. At one point during his administration, he indicated that he wanted to "blaze new trails in health"[178]—and, in fact, he did.

Because his own childhood was marred by illness, he had, in the words of one of his sisters, "a rather sympathetic outlook about children."[179] Within nineteen days of his inauguration, he directed the surgeon general to organize a child health center in the Public Health Service to deal with health problems of children, calling them "a matter of particular interest to me." Two months later, he convened a major White House Conference on Disease and, later in 1961, announced that he had "substantially increased over the Eisenhower budget the amount that we requested for the Department of HEW, including research."[180] In early 1962, he urged Congress to increase federal involvement in the expansion of medical education in the United States by providing scholarships and grants to entering students and matching grants for the construction of new medical schools.[181]

The most prominent reflection of Kennedy's keen interest in issues of health was seen in his long battle for the enactment of his Medicare proposal. In February 1963, he sent a special message to Congress insisting that "a proud and resourceful nation can no longer ask its older people to live in constant fear of a serious illness for which adequate funds are not available. We owe them the right of dignity in sickness as well as in health." He pointed out on 15 November 1963, in one of his final speeches, that "I cannot tell whether we are going to get this legislation before Christmas but I can say that I believe that this Congress will not go home next summer to the people of the United States without passing this bill. I think we should stay there until we do."[182] Although Kennedy did not live to see his Medicare proposal become law, he clearly set the stage for its enactment a few years later during the Johnson administration.

Finally, Kennedy's long bouts with illness seem to have given him strength of character, a sense of stoicism, and a cool detachment that served him well as President. He had ample time during his convalescences to plan his life and develop his political philosophy. When asked in 1960 whether he agreed with the Indian prime minister Jawaharlal Nehru that "there is nothing like an illness . . . to do some thinking and develop a political philosophy," he responded wryly, "Yes, it's the hard way, however."[183]

Kennedy, who could have chosen to lead the life of a wealthy semi-invalid, opted instead for one of intense political activity, driving himself to the very top of the American political establishment. He rarely complained of his ailments and did not even want to bother his doctors with them unless they had become very acute.[184] His mother remarked, "Although he was seldom, if ever, really free of pain, he bore it with such few outward signs that nobody but his doctors, the family and a few close associates realized his condition."[185] His father once remarked, "I can tell Jack's sick by looking at him but not by listening to him."[186] His brother Robert reported that those close to him would realize "he was suffering only because his face was a little whiter, the lines around his eyes were a little deeper, his words a little sharper. Those who did not know him well detected nothing."[187] The closest he ever came to complaining about his physical problems, according to his press secretary, was when he would "ease into a warm bath with a sigh of relief."[188]

Curiously philosophical about his afflictions, Kennedy accepted them without rancor, telling the country:

There is always inequity in life. Some men are killed in a war, and some men are wounded, and some men never leave the country. . . . It's very hard in military or personal life to assure complete equity. Life is unfair . . . Some people are sick and others are well.[189]

Despite pain that must have caused him considerable stress, Kennedy was the quintessentially "cool" President, seemingly in total command of himself at all public functions. With his cool personality, he was the perfect leader in the age of "telepolitics" and used the medium of television to great effect.

Kennedy's sense of detachment also allowed him to stand back from crises and calmly survey them. In the early weeks of his administration, not only did his blunder at the Bay of Pigs humiliate and infuriate him because he had failed to challenge, as he usually did, "the experts";[190] but it also served to reinforce his innate sense of caution, moderation, and balance. Thus, for example, during the Cuban missile crisis in the autumn of 1962, in order to be free to exercise independent judgment in resolving it, he refused to participate regularly in the deliberations of the Executive Committee (Ex Com), which he had established to deal with the issue of Soviet missiles in Cuba. One of the most astute analysts of this tense U.S.–U.S.S.R. confrontation writes:

In a highly sensitive domestic political context where his opponents demanded some action against Soviet interests in Cuba, Kennedy was following a policy of reason and responsibility. He demanded that Khrushchev be given time, again and again delaying the Ex Com's preference for quick, forceful U.S. action.[191]

Although the joint chiefs of staff felt that a naval blockade was "far too weak a course," and argued that an air strike and an invasion were the only steps that "the Soviet Union would understand,"[192] the President opted for a naval blockade. He was convinced that a blockade would demonstrate American resolve but at the same time leave respectable avenues of retreat open to the Soviets.

Throughout the crisis, Kennedy remained master of events. Every time the Soviet premier, Nikita Khrushchev, tried to delay or go back on his word, Kennedy would apply an appropriate amount of pressure, always pushing but never bludgeoning the Soviet leader, and always remembering that Khrushchev was a politician like all others and must not be put in a position where he risked discredit and humiliation at home.[193]

As the crisis reached its peak, Khrushchev sent a message to Kennedy in which he agreed to remove Soviet missiles from Cuba if the United States promised not to invade the island. However, on the following day, he sent a new and disturbing message, this time agreeing to remove Soviet missiles from Cuba if the United States withdrew its missiles from Turkey. Although the U.S. State Department prepared a strong response flatly rejecting the Turkish missile removal demanded in Khrushchev's second message, Kennedy decided to respond positively to the Soviet leader's first message and to ignore the second message completely. The Soviets publicly agreed to Kennedy's acceptance of the first Khrushchev proposal on the next day, and the crisis essentially was resolved.[194] After the Soviet capitulation, Kennedy warned his associates against gloating and instead congratulated Khrushchev on his statesmanship.[195] A Laborite member of the British Parliament described the entire operation as "a model in any textbook of diplomacy."[196]

Kennedy's penetrating and detached mind generally gave him a sense of caution and moderation throughout his political life. Though surrounded by activist advisers, he often took the middle ground among them, eschewing ideas that might be excessively aggressive.[197] One observer has called him "a rationalist with a critical intelligence."[198] He once referred to himself as "an idealist without illusions."[199] Kennedy was, after all, the President who spoke stoically of a "rhythm to personal and international life" which "flows and ebbs." He was also the President who told the press and the nation that "I hope our restraint or sense of responsibility will not ever come to an end." And in the speech he was to deliver in Dallas on the day of his assassination, Kennedy intended to conclude by saying:

We ask . . . that we may be worthy of our power and responsibility, that we may exercise our strength with wisdom and restraint, and that we may achieve in our time and for all time the ancient vision of "peace on earth, good will toward men." That must always be our goal, and the righteousness of our cause must always underlie our strength. For as was written long ago, "except the Lord keep the City, the watchman waketh but in vain."[200]

The Impact of Medication on Kennedy's Presidency

Despite his pain and illnesses, John F. Kennedy generally took no painkillers since he did not want them, and he had no need for sleeping pills since he slept so well.[201] Nor did he drink alcoholic beverages to any extent. A journalist who socialized frequently with him reported that "normally he sipped at a scotch and water without ice, rarely finishing two before dinner, sipped at a glass of wine during dinner, rarely had a drink after dinner, and he almost never had a drink in the middle of the day."[202]

Kennedy was, however, on heavy medication during much of his life. One of his friends related, "Wherever Jack went, an aide carried a special little bag because he had to have medical support all the time."[203] This raises the question, then, whether Kennedy's medication affected his judgment, his perceptions, and/or his moods, as he carried out his presidential responsibilities.

In order to deal with Addison's disease, Kennedy received a regular dosage of cortisone as well as desoxycorticosterone. Both medications have definite side effects, some quite dangerous. In the case of desoxycorticosterone, for example, an overdose of this adrenal steroid causes hypertension, weight gain, heart failure, and occasionally death.[204] Physicians have to monitor carefully the combination of medications which all Addisonians receive—probably a difficult task in Kennedy's case, because he was under the care of several physicians.

Kennedy's dosage of cortisone was increased in 1961.[205] This is not surprising, since the presidency involves enormous stress and, in times of stress, Addisonians are instructed to double and triple the amount of cortisone taken.[206] Kennedy's physical therapist, Dr. Kraus, found that the President took it "all the time."[207]

Fluid retention is a common side effect of steroids, and the medication often made Kennedy's face appear fuller and puffier than normal. At some public appearances, his face was obviously swollen, a condition that bothered the President. One of his friends related, "Vain as always, it bugged him if he appeared a bit jowly at press conferences, which he often did, not because he overate, but because he was taking some form of cortisone."[208]

In addition to causing bodily swelling, cortisone has been found to increase one's sense of well-being, energy, cheerfulness, optimism, concentrating power, and hyperactivity.[209] The mood swings caused by the medication tend to be in the direction of euphoria rather than depression. Since, however, Kennedy took cortisone as replacement therapy for his malfunctioning adrenal glands, the effects of the drug may well have been less pronounced in his case than in that of people who have healthy adrenals but take the drug for other reasons. Travell insisted that "the record should be perfectly clear that the things that he did take were normal physiological constituents of the body, almost entirely."[210] Too much cortisone, however, can produce the side effects noted previously, and one of Kennedy's daily tasks was to avoid overdoses.

There is one report that, before becoming President, Kennedy suffered an attack of steroid psychosis. This condition is a result of large dosages of steroids taken over a lengthy period, and its symptoms include disorientation, agitation, memory disturbance, hostility, and mania. L'Etang states that the physician treating Kennedy at the time had been "discretely noncommittal rather than forcefully dismissive" about the episode.[211] Whether such an attack occurred is, in the first instance, unclear and unproven. But even if it did occur, it did not take place during Kennedy's presidency.

The subject of Kennedy's medications and how they may have affected his behavior as President is rendered considerably more complex by an additional factor. Besides being treated by Drs. Burkley, Kraus, and Travell, President Kennedy also saw, both socially and professionally, a controversial New York physician, Dr. Max Jacobson, who took an unconventional approach to the treatment of his patients—so unconventional, in fact, that in 1975 he finally lost his license to practice medicine in New York because he was found to have violated federal and state drug regulations.

Dr. Jacobson has admitted that he often combined amphetamines (speed) with vitamins and other medications and injected the mixture into his patients, ordinarily without telling them that he was giving them anything beyond vitamins and hormones. Furthermore, Jacobson insisted that the dosage of amphetamines was too low to produce a "kick" or lead to dependence when taken in the quantities he directed.[212] Despite Jacobson's disclaimer, his office staff admitted that the doctor bought amphetamines at the rate of 80 grams per month, enough "to make 100 fairly strong doses of 25 milligrams every day"; and many of his patients found that the injections gave them "boundless energy and more productive and pleasurable lives."[213]

When amphetamines are administered in large dosages and over a long period, symptoms resembling those of paranoid schizophrenia often result. The drug is addictive, and withdrawal symptoms include a deep and enduring mental depression. Some of Dr. Jacobson's patients experienced considerable difficulty with the injections he gave them. Truman Capote stopped seeing Jacobson after having a severe reaction to the shots; and another patient reported that he developed amphetamine poisoning from Jacobson's treatments and had to spend two years in a mental hospital as a result. The photographer Mark Shaw, a friend of the Kennedy family and a patient of Jacobson's, died in 1969 at the age of forty-seven; his post-mortem found his internal organs to be "laden with methamphetamine residue."[214]

During the Kennedy administration, Jacobson was a visitor at the White House and seems to have treated the President and the First Lady on occasion. Jacqueline Kennedy admitted to having been treated by Jacobson, but has not provided details. The President had a case of laryngitis just before he addressed the United Nations on disarmament, and it was apparently cured after Jacobson gave him an injection in his neck over his voice box. A New York doctor reportedly warned Kennedy not to take any more shots from Jacobson, and indicated that he told the White House that "if I ever heard that he took another shot, I'd make sure it was known. No President with his finger on the red button has any business taking stuff like that."[215]

Jacobson accompanied the President on some of his overseas journeys, including his 1961 summit conference in Vienna. Although Dr. Travell indicated that she was unaware that Jacobson was in Vienna at the time,[216] the controversial doctor's name appears on the hotel list for members of the President's party.[217] Jacobson was not, however, invited to the dinner given for Kennedy by the President of Austria, whereas both Dr. Travell and Dr. Burkley were on the guest list. Neither Burkley nor Jacobson were assigned space in the presidential motorcade in Vienna, but Travell was assigned to the twelfth car in line. Perhaps Jacobson's absence from both motorcade and state dinner explains why Travell failed to see him in Vienna, especially since the two were assigned rooms in different hotels.

Jacobson's relative anonymity in Vienna might suggest that the White House was trying to downplay his presence there. This notion finds some support in the fact that the airplane passenger list for the President's Vienna entourage is classified and, even today, not available for review at the Kennedy Library.

In any event, Jacobson has indicated that he treated Kennedy in Vienna for an infected hand. The treatment involved an intravenous injection that included antibiotics and immune globulin. Whether it included anything else will probably never be known. In fact, it is unlikely that it will ever be determined with certainty whether Kennedy, in Vienna or elsewhere, was injected with, or received, amphetamines. Also, since Jacobson typically prescribed dosages below those required to produce severe symptoms,[218] Kennedy was not likely to have exhibited a visible reaction to the drug, even had he been injected with it.

A few commentators have suggested that the Vienna meeting was "alarming" because of Kennedy's medications,[219] and that Kennedy's behavior there was "charged," the President barely sleeping for two days after the conference.[220] Those who so describe his behavior admit that it did not constitute proof that the President had taken amphetamines at the time, but add that "given his other physical problems . . . it is reasonable to speculate that the level of activity he sustained at Vienna . . . was attributable to something other than his natural sources of energy."[221]

However "reasonable" to indulge in such speculation, it is nothing more than that. Kennedy may have used Jacobson rather than the White House physicians, Burkley and Travell, because the former was the only one of the three who could be located in Vienna at the precise moment when the President decided to summon a physician. The possibility is interesting, but there is no evidence either way.

Transcripts of the summit conference have not been released, but Kennedy's behavior in Vienna seems to have conformed to his general pattern throughout his presidency. Although Robert Kennedy believed that his brother found Khrushchev to be "completely unreasonable . . . tough . . . and harsh" in Vienna,[222] available reports indicate that the President was firm, calm, and deliberate during negotiations with the Soviet leader, telling Khrushchev at one point that the civil war in Laos pitting communist and non-communist forces was not worth a war be-

tween the superpowers. He also spoke at considerable length of his desire
to avoid a nuclear war that resulted from miscalculation. He even went
so far as to admit that he had miscalculated during the Bay of Pigs episode,
and urged that both sides avoid critical situations that could lead to armed
conflict.[223]

Kennedy also demonstrated a wry sense of detachment as well as of
humor in Vienna. When Khrushchev, after becoming particularly com-
bative, told Kennedy that the decorations he was wearing were Lenin
Peace Medals, the President replied, "Well, I hope you keep them." And
when the Soviet leader indicated that he intended to sign a treaty with
East Germany that would endanger American rights in Berlin, Kennedy
remarked, in his typically understated way, that "it will be a cold winter."[224]

In his report to the American people on 6 June, President Kennedy
related that his meetings with the Soviet leader had been "very sober."
He also said that

*the gap between us was not, in such a short period, materially reduced but at least
the channels of communication were opened more fully, at least the chances of a
dangerous misjudgment on either side should now be less, and at least the men on
whose decisions the peace in part depends have agreed to remain in contact.*[225]

Even one of Kennedy's sharpest critics, political scientist Bruce Miroff,
describes a calm, rational, and measured President in Vienna:

*Kennedy expressed the hope that the two great powers could prevent direct confron-
tation in the future . . . and reiterated the need for both sides to avoid situations that
might lead to war. . . . Kennedy remarked that he did not oppose the fall of corrupt
or reactionary governments but, he insisted social changes must not involve the
prestige or commitments of America or Russia or upset the balance of world
power.*[226]

Indeed, Kennedy seems to have played such a subdued role in Vienna
that the White House was concerned that the general public had gotten
the impression that he had been weak.[227] Not surprisingly, American
hard-liners had the same impression.[228] It is difficult to conclude from
available evidence that Kennedy was euphoric, peculiarly cheerful, or
optimistic in Vienna, or that he showed an unusual "sense of power"—all
symptoms of heavy cortisone and/or amphetamine usage. Rather, his
Vienna summit meeting with Khrushchev seems characterized by the

same sense of balance, moderation, and perspective evident during the Cuban missile crisis and throughout most of his political career. In short, although the Vienna summit conference has been cited as an episode in Kennedy's presidency where the use of drugs may have affected the President's judgment and behavior, available evidence simply does not support this conclusion.

Kennedy's Drive to Excel

John Kennedy's sicknesses and disabilities affected his psychological outlook. Not only did he refuse to give in to his pain and illnesses, but he actually denied that he was at all sickly. His mother writes:

Even when he was laid out flat in bed from some new accident or disease, with his face thin and his freckles standing out against the pallor of his skin, he could always smile or grin about his own bad luck, as if he had been victimized once again by some absurd joke that he should have been on guard against. He went along for many years thinking to himself—or at least trying to make others think—that he was a strong, robust, quite healthy person who just happened to be sick a good deal of the time.[229]

Although this denial might be considered delusional,[230] it is not surprising in the child of a close and active family in which the children were encouraged to be competitive and vigorous. Not only had the Kennedy children been taught from birth to be self-reliant, tough, and assertive; but they had been told, too, that "Kennedys don't cry" and should "be as good as the spirit is."[231] John Kennedy did what had to be done to live up to these standards. Even when, as a boy, he had written his father that he had gotten dizzy and weak during Mass, he hastened to add "Joe fainted twice in church so I guess I will live."[232] The subliminal message to his father was clear: if sturdy and robust Joe, Jr., fainted twice in church, then Jack's dizziness during Mass was fully acceptable for a Kennedy. To admit or accept the fact that he was *unusual* in his sicknesses, or to give in to his pain, would run counter to the rules of Kennedy family life and might render him, in the eyes of his parents, less worthy than his brothers and sisters. For those who place great value on bodily strength and integrity, the most probable reaction to an incurred disability is denial of its existence.[233]

A child who does not feel that he belongs, that he is an accepted member of the family, becomes anxious and insecure and may even undergo a process of self-alienation. He may come to feel the need "to evolve artificial, strategic ways to cope with others," which may force "him to override his genuine feelings, wishes and thoughts. . . . He is no longer the driver but is driven."[234] Self-alienation produces a need for a self-identity that will provide feelings "of power and significance." In an effort to develop such a self-identity, the child creates first an idealized image of himself—what, in other words, he would most like to be. An idealized image "always entails a general self-glorification and thereby gives the individual the much needed feelings of significance and of superiority over others."[235]

The low self-esteem and depression brought about by feelings of rejection may lead, too, to a narcissistic personality disorder. The psychoanalyst Heinz Kohut writes that as children, persons suffering from this disorder "had felt emotionally unresponded to and had tried to overcome their loneliness through erotic and grandiose fantasies."[236] During adulthood, "the dramatic, intensely exhibitionistic aspects of the personality do not become securely alloyed with mature productivity; and the eroticized, excitedly pursued activities of adult life continue to be but one step removed from the underlying depression."[237]

Although Kennedy may not have suffered from such a disorder, he sought to be accepted as a full member of his family by being as strong, healthy, and vigorous as his siblings. Therefore, he rejected the notion that he was sickly, and viewed himself as healthy as the others. As a boy, Kennedy idealized and fantasized himself into the figure he wanted to be. Contrary to the belief that he decided to enter politics only after his older brother was killed in the war, he reportedly admitted, on the day of his inauguration in 1961, that he had seen himself as President of the United States "ever since the days of his youth."[238] Kennedy's political career may well have represented a compulsive search for glory by the sickliest and least robust Kennedy son: his aim, to "lift himself above others"[239] and prove his worth and mettle beyond any shadow of a doubt and for all time.

Kennedy's attempt to live out other aspects of his idealized image caused him to suffer considerable pain and physical discomfort. Although he "fought like fury when he had to," he still lost most of his frequent battles with his older and bullying brother. Although "he wasn't nearly heavy nor strong nor healthy enough for the varsity," he played football anyway and ruptured a spinal disk during a game, intensifying the back problems that tormented him the rest of his life.[240]

In his years as an adult and as a member of Congress, Kennedy took steps to conceal his various illnesses from the public. A close associate, Theodore Sorenson, reported that such concealment was due to Kennedy's fear that the public might think he was too ill to serve in political office:

Aside from his 1954–1955 spinal surgery, his confinements in the hospital for any cause, however minor, were never publicized during his career as Senator, even though it often meant my offering other excuses for cancelling or re-arranging speaking dates. On one occasion he checked into the New England Baptist Hospital in Boston simply as "Mr. K."[241]

Dr. Travell underscored the secrecy that surrounded Kennedy's hospitalizations while he was in the Senate: "[W]hen in New York Hospital seven or eight times for two or three days or nights, the last being in October, 1957, that fact was concealed—an assumed name would be put on his door, his chart was taken off the wallboard and locked in a drawer." Travell also related that when, on one occasion, he was being treated for an abscess, Kennedy told her, "You know, that's a very ugly word. I don't want to have an abscess." She announced to the press instead that he had a "virus infection."[242]

Not only did Kennedy conceal his illnesses from the public, he also tried to deny and/or conceal them from the people closest to him. He was unwilling to have Secret Service agents see his back brace, and even instructed his doctors to refrain from discussing his medical problems with his wife: "I don't want her to think she married an old man or a cripple." Evelyn Lincoln, his long-time personal secretary, has said that "it was hard for him to use his crutches even in front of me. He used them mostly when he was alone."[243] His press secretary, Pierre Salinger, indicated that when friends and aides saw that he was in pain and tried to offer comfort, Kennedy would usually "smile them off with assurances that everything was well."[244]

Also, Kennedy insisted to aides that he did not have Addison's disease, and went so far as to tell one of them in 1959 that "no one who has the real Addison's disease should run for the Presidency, but I do not have it."[245] When, around the same time, Dr. Travell tried to discuss his Addison's disease with him, Kennedy retorted, "But I don't have it, Doctor." Travell explained to him, without evident success, that he didn't have classic Addison's disease, but that "doctors disagree maybe because they aren't talking about the same thing."[246] In 1960, when one of his aides expressed unhappiness over the selection of Lyndon Johnson as his vice-presidential running mate, Kennedy replied, "Get one thing clear . . . I'm forty-three years old, and I'm the healthiest candidate for President in the country and I'm not going to die in office."[247]

Kennedy's concealment of disability and denial of illness, both from the public as well as from his closest aides and even his family and his doctor, may well have had its roots in the self-realization and self-idealization previously discussed. With regard to these processes, Karen Horney writes that an inevitable stage of self-realization is a "search for glory."[248] Moreover, striving for power and prestige is a way "frequently used in our culture for obtaining reassurance against anxiety."[249] The constituent parts involved in a search for glory include a need for perfection, a compulsive ambition for external success, and a drive toward "a vindictive triumph," although this drive is frequently hidden.[250]

Throughout Kennedy's life, he demonstrated a need for perfection— winning the Pulitzer Prize for a book he had written, becoming a war hero, marrying a rich and beautiful girl, and becoming the youngest elected President in American history. These were all public manifestations of his psychic needs. But private manifestations may also have existed. Reports of his incessant womanizing may be read as Kennedy's attempt to outshine his philandering father as well as his brothers in this most intimate sphere as well as in all others.

Ambition burned bright in John Kennedy, pushing him relentlessly to reach the very top of the political structure. This he did at an early age, possibly the most visible demonstration of external success that can be achieved. While he was publicly gracious in victory in 1960, there are reports that he did not like his opponent personally and felt that he had "no class" and even was mentally unsound.[251] Victory over Nixon took on, therefore, personal rather than simply political dimensions.

As presidential candidate and as President of the United States, Kennedy projected an image of strength and dynamism. He urged vigor and discipline on the American people and spoke to them often in terms of strength, courage, and endurance. In his 1960 campaign, he pledged frequently to get the country moving again. On 20 January 1961, he began his administration by emphasizing his youth ("the torch has been passed to a new generation of Americans—born in this century, tempered by war, disciplined by a hard and bitter peace") and by promising that "we shall pay any price, bear any burden, meet any hardship . . . to assure the survival and the success of liberty."[252] On 22 November 1963, in his final speech three hours before his assassination, Kennedy unwittingly concluded his administration by saying:

No one expects that our life will be easy, certainly not in this decade and perhaps not in this century. But we should realize what a burden and responsibility the people of the United States have borne for so many years. . . . I don't think we are fatigued or tired. [253]

He had not been fatigued or tired by the burden of pain and illness he had had to carry for so many years. Neither as boy nor as man had he been defeated by his afflictions. His presidency constituted his greatest glory and was the most visible sign that he had become the most powerful and prominent Kennedy of them all.

Conclusion

There is no evidence that John Kennedy's physical ailments had any negative impact on his conduct of the presidency. Indeed, Dr. George Burkley emphatically stated that "his back pain affected his normal conduction of the office of President in no way. He tended his office and went back and forth occasionally—at one point he was on crutches—but that did not deter him from his full duty as President."[254]

Burkley also asserted that adrenal insufficiency "was never a problem with the President when under my care."[255] Dr. Janet Travell agreed with this assessment, saying, "We had much smoother control of the problem of adrenal insufficiency while he was in the White House when he was in one place and not travelling around." She added, "I thought . . . that his health would be more than adequate for him to carry the duties and responsibilities of the presidency and indeed it was."[256]

Presidential physicians are not always completely candid in evaluating publicly—and sometimes even privately—the condition of their famous patients[257] (see also chapters 3, 4, and 6). But even if Kennedy's physicians tended to minimize the impact of his ailments, the President's actions spoke louder than their diagnoses. His presidency was characterized by measured activism; and the President clearly served, by word and by example, as the center of his administration, setting its tone and shaping it. One commentator, surveying a "fairly average day during President Kennedy's first year in office," counted twenty-three appointments with some thirty individuals beginning at 9:17 A.M. and running through 7:45 P.M.[258] In the thirty-four months of his tenure, Kennedy missed only one day of work because of illness.

The medications he received, while substantial, also do not appear to have interfered significantly or noticeably with his exercise of presidential power. His pattern of behavior as President seems consistent with that shown throughout his political life; and there is no authoritative evidence that his behavior at Vienna or during the Cuban missile crisis, two key episodes in his administration, was affected by medication and/or drugs.

Indeed, rather than adversely affecting him politically, Kennedy's physical ailments vitally contributed to the development of his character and to the formation of his political personality. Even more significant perhaps, John F. Kennedy's ailments may have led to his meteoric political career—so far as his drive toward the glory of the presidency was an attempt, however subconscious, to prove his worth and demonstrate his strength by rising above all others.

His parents must have been very proud. The frail little boy, who was the sickliest and most incapacitated of the Kennedy sons, became the most powerful leader in the world, a charismatic presence who inspired millions and became a hero, perhaps for all time.

Chapter SIX
Ambition and Torment:
Lyndon B. Johnson

H e was a towering figure, a man who became President of the United States at a moment of national weeping. Lyndon Baines Johnson, a master congressional politician, assumed the presidential office in late 1963 after John F. Kennedy's tragic rendezvous with an assassin. As a new President, Johnson quickly left the imprint of his personality on the office, dazzling the country he sought to lead. Within a year, he won election to a presidential term in his own right by the largest majority in American history. Relishing the use of his every power to achieve his every objective and pushing and prodding Congress and members of his Administration to do as he wished them to do, Johnson became known as a tormenting president. We know now, however, that he also was a tormented president—tormented by deep and punishing insecurities and by a debilitating pattern of ill health. In this chapter, I detail the self-doubts and illnesses of Lyndon Johnson—as well as their impact on his political life—and offer an explanation for the striking linkages between the state of his mind and the weaknesses of his body.

The Early Years

Lyndon Baines Johnson was born in Stonewall, Texas on 27 August 1908. He was the first child and first son of a bright, strong-willed mother, Rebekah Baines, and a caring but heavy-drinking father, Sam Ealy Johnson. At the very beginning, his mother saw omens portending a great future for her new son. She later wrote of the day of his birth that "... the light came in from the east, bringing a deep stillness, a stillness so profound and so pervasive that it seemed as if the earth itself was listening."[1]

Rebekah Baines Johnson was the daughter of a Texas Secretary of State, a graduate of Baylor University, and a woman whose educational attainments made her unusual for her era. She taught young Lyndon history and geography from an early age and encouraged him to achieve unusual things in his life just as she had in hers. Rebekah pushed her son to learn, to excel, and never, never to disappoint her. Years later, Lyndon could still remember the piles of books in her room which she discussed with him and her other children (Rebekah, Josefa, Sam Houston, and Lucia, born respectively in 1910, 1912, 1914, and 1916). When her children disappointed her, however, she could be cold and indifferent to them for long periods of time, not speaking to them and even pretending at times that they had died.[2]

Lyndon's father, Sam Ealy, was deeply interested in politics and served several terms in the Texas legislature. He has been described as an honest, well liked but contrary political figure.[3] He also was a stern disciplinarian who slapped and spanked his children often. Lyndon later confided that "he'd take a razor strap and just whip the hell out of us."[4] The relationship between Johnson's parents was far from perfect. Sam's drinking and carousing caused enormous tensions in the household and led to intense friction. Lyndon later explained:

there was nothing Mother hated more than seeing my Daddy drink. When he had too much to drink, he'd lose control of himself. He used bad language. He squandered the little money we had on the cotton and real estate markets. Sometimes he'd be lucky and make a lot of money. But more often he lost out. These ups and downs were hard on my mother. She wanted things to be nice for us but she could never count on a stable income. When she got upset, she blamed our money problems on my father's drinking. And then she cried a lot. Especially when he stayed out all night.[5]

Many years later, when he would discuss his early years, Johnson would speak lovingly of his mother whom he described as a "saintly woman to whom I owe everything."[6] When he mentioned his father, which he did less often, he sometimes would be quite critical. The family, after all, had had to endure difficult financial straits, so difficult, in fact, that when Lyndon left home at fifteen, he explained that "it meant one less mouth for my poor daddy to feed."[7] His mother's key role in his life, always to encourage and push him to succeed, was enduringly acknowledged by the former President in 1971 when he dedicated his memoirs to the four individuals "whose strength and love and courage have sustained me throughout my life." Among those mentioned—his wife (Lady Bird), his daughters

(Lynda and Luci), and his mother—his mother's name appeared first.[8] His father's name appeared nowhere.

Despite growing up in a somewhat contentious household, Johnson enjoyed generally good health as a child, except when he had to drop out of first grade because of whooping cough and spend the year at home. Later, at the age of twenty-seven, he came down with pneumonia for the first time. It was, however, after the beginning of his political career that his physical indispositions began to show themselves in earnest. Johnson's physical and psychological health were intimately intertwined. He was a man filled with deep insecurities, and each time he was stricken with the fear that his political career was in jeopardy, he would threaten to withdraw and/or would become physically ill.[9] Mary Rather, his personal secretary for many years, told an interviewer that he ". . . never, *ever* thought he would win in every race he ever had. . . . He was never a confident man as far as his elections were concerned. . . . I think he always ran scared."[10]

The Congressional Years

ENTRY INTO ELECTIVE POLITICS

At the age of twenty-nine, Lyndon Johnson became a candidate for the U.S. House of Representatives. During the campaign, he developed appendicitis, suffered intense pain, and vomited frequently. Just two days before voters went to the polls, his condition became acute. As he delivered a speech, Johnson almost doubled over in agony and felt that he was about to faint.[11] He was rushed to an Austin hospital and underwent emergency surgery, his appendix dangerously close to rupturing.[12]

Some of Johnson's foes accused him of faking his illness, which his doctors quickly denied. An aide later guessed that Lyndon actually won his first election to the House of Representatives due to his appendicitis surgery, "because it got us an unexpected top-page headline. This last-minute burst of publicity quite possibly gave uncommitted people a reason to go to the polls and vote for Johnson."[13] Others believed that the attacks by LBJ's opponents backfired and damaged *their* credibility rather than his. Attacking an opponent for becoming ill seemed vindictive and small-minded, hardly the behavior expected of genteel southerners.

Johnson had lost as much as forty pounds during his first campaign for the House. His strenuous campaigning, lack of sleep, and painful illness and surgery all contributed to the gauntness of his face and his shrunken appearance. It took him longer to regain his strength than his doctors expected. His wife worried out loud to a friend that he was "not progressing as [he] should."[14] Even when Johnson finally left the hospital two weeks after his surgery, he was still thirty pounds lighter than his normal weight of 180 pounds and was pale and in need of further rest. But he had won his first race for public office by a comfortable margin and his political career was underway.

As a new Congressman, Johnson suffered from such intense nervousness that he developed a severe rash on his hands. The cause of this condition may have been, at least in part, a form of post-traumatic stress following the delayed surgery for his dangerously advanced appendicitis, but his intense desire to succeed in his new position must also have been a major contributing factor. Whatever the precise etiology, Johnson was forced to wrap a small towel around his right hand whenever he signed correspondence, so that the oozing blood would not smear his letters.[15] He also began to smoke heavily at this time, as many as three packs a day. He worked very long hours, skipped and/or postponed meals, and drove himself without mercy or letup. These work habits—which he would follow and even intensify during his long political career—inflicted a heavy toll on his body.

ASCENT TO THE SENATE

In the spring of 1941, Lyndon Johnson decided to run for a seat in the United States Senate suddenly made vacant by the death of the incumbent, Senator Morris Sheppard. At first Johnson seemed assured of victory but then, quite unexpectedly, Texas Governor Pappy O'Daniel entered the race. At the news that O'Daniel had emerged as one of his opponents, Johnson was taken ill and had to be hospitalized. His condition was described to the press as pneumonia, but he suffered from deep depression as well. His wife alluded to this fact when she lamented that "he was depressed and it was bad."[16]

The realization that he might well encounter defeat and rejection at the polls produced such severe physical and psychological reactions in Johnson that he had to spend two weeks in the hospital, not in Austin but, for reasons of secrecy, in Temple, Texas, some sixty miles away. For a week, Johnson's illness was kept secret, and he was described by various stand-ins as being tied up with organizational work.[17] During the second week, however, news of his illness leaked out and rumors circulated that he would use this illness as an excuse to withdraw from the race, particularly if he did not get out of the hospital quickly. Johnson, however, soon resumed his barnstorming across Texas. In an election in which vote-stealing seems to have been rampant, Lyndon Johnson went down to a narrow defeat at the polls, the only electoral rejection he would ever suffer as a candidate for public office.

Later that year, Congressman Johnson applied for a commission to the navy. At the time he suffered from chronic tonsillitis, which required treatment at the Mayo Clinic,[18] sinusitis, and a kidney ailment. While stationed in New Guinea, Johnson admits to having experienced "chest trouble," and he also contracted bronchiectasis,[19] a dilation of the bronchial tubes. He suffered from a very high fever and was delirious for several days.[20] His bronchial difficulties led him to be awarded disability pay after the Veterans Administration determined that "residuals of pneumonia and bronchitis were service connected."[21] Johnson apparently was much more interested in securing the determination of service-related disability than he was in the disability pay itself, which he promptly rejected.

Johnson left navy service after President Roosevelt issued an order directing incumbent congressmen in military service to return to inactive duty. While four congressmen resigned their seats and remained in uniform, LBJ was one of four members of Congress who returned to Washington.[22] He remained in the House of Representatives, waiting impatiently for another opportunity to run for the U.S. Senate.

In the mid-1940s, Johnson suffered from a number of debilitating ailments and had to be hospitalized on several occasions. Early in 1946, he developed a somewhat mysterious illness which put him in Austin's Seton Infirmary for a month. The announced cause of his hospitalization was pneumonia, but two of his aides indicated that he was suffering from "nervous exhaustion." Echoing Lady Bird Johnson's description of her husband's condition in 1941, long-time aide Walter Jenkins said of Johnson's 1946 condition that "it was bad."[23]

After a slow recovery, the Congressman was hospitalized again in March, this time for kidney stones, an ailment that would be a recurring one. Seven months later, he spent several weeks at the Seton Infirmary and then in the Mayo Clinic for a severe bronchial infection. Johnson, at this time, was overweight, had a double chin, and looked much older than his thirty-eight years.

Johnson's physical indispositions, however, did not prevent him from seeking political advancement. In 1948, he ran again for the U.S. Senate. This time his principal opponent was Coke Stevenson, the man who had succeeded Pappy O'Daniel as governor of Texas in 1941, after O'Daniel had defeated Johnson in his first try for the Senate.

During this second senatorial campaign, Johnson again fell ill with a painful case of kidney stones. Even at the party held to celebrate his announcement of candidacy, the Congressman was in considerable discomfort. A physician who gave him several shots of painkillers that night told one of Johnson's aides that "he didn't know how in the world a man could keep functioning in the pain he was in. . . ."[24] Lyndon, however, gave the speech announcing his candidacy and appeared to be in glowing good health.

Despite intense pain, Johnson refused to seek medical treatment. He was convinced that he would pass this kidney stone as he had passed others. He told aides "You just leave me alone, I can take care of it and I'll pass this stone, and when that is done, why, everything will be clear."[25] As he continued to campaign, aides noticed that he was beginning to perspire and that he appeared to be burning up with fever. They gave him aspirin and whatever medication they were able to find, but his condition worsened steadily. One of those aides later described Johnson's discomfort:

[He] was suffering alternately from chills in which he would literally freeze to death or fever in which he would literally burn up. And they would come in waves. . . . When he was hot, he'd say "get this window down." Then the chill would come and he'd call for the extra blankets. Finally, one time he asked me to get in the berth with him, and I actually got in the berth with him on two occasions that night to try to give him some heat from my body over to his and try to keep him warm because he was literally just racked with fever and chills.[26]

Johnson refused to be examined by a doctor because he feared that his campaign would suffer if voters viewed him as a sick man.[27] Whenever he canceled an appearance because of his illness, the weather would be blamed. At long last, however, he was in so much pain that he agreed to have a doctor called. The doctor wanted to hospitalize him immediately but Johnson refused. He only agreed to undergo tests at the Medical Arts Building in Dallas at the urging of the Secretary of the Air Force, Stuart Symington, who happened to be visiting in Texas.

It was during that overnight hospital stay in Dallas that Johnson had a major falling out with his friend and political ally John Connolly. Johnson wanted Connolly to withhold news of his hospitalization from the press since he expected to "pass the stone during the night." Connolly responded that "This is ridiculous. . . . We can't do that. . . . We've got to release this and tell the press."

Johnson instructed one of his aides to tell Connolly that "I order" that this not be done. The aide has since admitted that:

at this point, I think, it must be said that his fever was such that he really was not in complete control of his thinking processes because there was an element of delirium. . . . He really wasn't capable of making a judgment of this type in his physical condition. . . .[28]

In any event, Johnson's "order" had reached Connolly too late, although he probably would have ignored it anyway. He had already informed the press that Johnson was ill and had been hospitalized. When LBJ learned of this, he was calm but livid, telling associates "Well, if I can't run my own campaign, I guess I might as well [withdraw]; now is the time to get out." He dictated a statement of withdrawal from the 1948 Texas Senate race to an aide, but the aide, realizing that Johnson was too sick to be fully rational, wisely suggested that Lady Bird, then en route to Dallas, be consulted before the withdrawal statement be made public. After Lady Bird arrived and took control, the idea of withdrawing from the race "seemed to kind of fade into the background."[29] But Johnson and Connolly did not speak to each other for several weeks and instead relayed messages through Walter Jenkins.[30]

Johnson finally agreed to fly to the Mayo Clinic in Minnesota, to be examined by a famed urologist visiting from England, despite his initial fears that this might be interpreted as an insult against Texas doctors. Perhaps he changed his mind after his Texas doctors told him that he was not going to pass this stone, "because it was lodged very high up," and that surgery was going to be needed.[31] This news frightened Johnson, since a lengthy post-surgery recuperation period would force his withdrawal from the race.

At the Mayo Clinic, Johnson's fever was brought under control and, in an effort to remove the stone without surgery, he would be taken on bumpy rides on the back roads of Minnesota and walked up and down the stairs of the hospital in order to "jar the thing loose." When this therapy failed to produce the desired result, Johnson was taken into an operating room and the stone was successfully removed through a cystoscope. An aide explained that the procedure "involved going way up the urethra and attempting to crush the stone. . . . After 45 minutes, the procedure succeeded. Doctors said that the stone 'was as far up as it was possible to go and still get it.' It was one of the few times they had been able to reach and crush a stone."[32] No incision had been necessary and within three or four days, the candidate had returned to the campaign trail and soon was elected to the United States Senate by a very narrow margin.

SENATE LEADERSHIP AND CARDIOVASCULAR CRISIS

The Senate was a comfortable home for Lyndon Johnson. His interpersonal skills, hard work, dedication, and ability to move toward a consensus impressed his colleagues and propelled him upward in the Senate hierarchy. In January 1953 he became Democratic Minority Leader and two years later became Majority Leader of the Senate, at forty-six the youngest in history.

Within a day of becoming Majority Leader, Johnson was again hospitalized for kidney stones. This episode had begun the previous month when sudden and sharp back pains had prevented him from traveling to New Orleans to play a role in the selection of the new Democratic Party National Chairman.[33] Unlike 1948, this time Johnson required surgery at the Mayo Clinic. Despite his doctor's view that "he got over it quite rapidly and got along quite well,"[34] Johnson's recuperation period lasted for some two months. Even then, doctors advised further rest, and the new Majority Leader had to wear a steel brace for about a month because of the pain.[35]

By the spring of 1955, Johnson was working some eighteen hours a day.[36] He still chain-smoked packs of cigarettes, and, in the words of his brother, continued "to drive himself at a furious pace. . . ."[37] His weight rose to 225 pounds, an ominous development for someone who was part of a family that had seen its male members die at an early age of cardiovascular disease. Not surprisingly, Lyndon Johnson soon experienced the most serious health crisis of his life. On 18 June 1955, he suffered what appears to have been a mild heart attack.[38] Two weeks later, he suffered a heart attack so severe that he was in danger of death.

On 2 July, the Majority Leader had an unpleasant confrontation with one of his Senate colleagues and then held a small press conference with a few reporters. He was nervous and irritable throughout and actually lost his temper at one of his questioners. Then, after visiting a sick colleague, Johnson left Washington for the home of a friend, George Brown, in Middlebury, Virginia. En route, he developed symptoms of indigestion and, when he arrived at the Brown residence, complained of severe discomfort, saying that "I feel like somebody's sitting on my chest."[39] He was first given Amphojel and then carbonated soda, neither of which relieved his symptoms.[40] Another party guest reports that their host had also given Johnson a digitalis pill, which "we later found out could have killed him."[41] Despite the entreaties of his host, Lyndon refused to allow a doctor to be called. He was beginning to be mentioned by the press as a 1956 presidential possibility and wanted to do nothing to dampen his prospects.

When Senator Clinton Anderson arrived at the party, Johnson told him that he had eaten "some bad food," but Anderson told the Majority Leader that he thought he was having a heart attack.[42] This diagnosis made Johnson "frantic," but he still resisted medical assistance. It might be noted here that Johnson's refusal to admit the possibility, much less the likelihood, of a heart attack is a not uncommon coping mechanism even in persons who have no political ambitions at all. Yet in Johnson's case, his reactions were heightened and sharpened by his intense drive and lofty political ambitions. He would risk even death before allowing anything to interfere with his rise to power.

Finally, however, a doctor was summoned, who confirmed that Johnson had "every symptom of a heart attack and a bad one."[43] An ambulance (actually a hearse since there was no ambulance in Middlebury) was summoned, and Johnson, in severe pain but "as mad as hell" that he was being hospitalized,[44] was driven to Bethesda Naval Hospital. Expecting to die, he told aides that he wanted Lady Bird to get everything he had.[45]

At the hospital, Johnson turned parchment gray as he was placed in an oxygen tent, and his blood pressure dropped to zero over forty.[46] Contrary to so many accounts, including that of Johnson himself,[47] Dr. James Cain has said that "he was not actually in shock at any time. He had been quite ill. His blood pressure was down, but he always had a relatively low blood pressure. But he was not in shock. . . ."[48] Cain's judgment in this instance is supported by Dr. Willis Hurst, Johnson's cardiologist. Hurst maintains that, after his heart attack, Johnson suffered not from cardiogenic shock but rather from hypotensive bradycardia syndrome. This condition implies low blood pressure and a slow pulse rate. Commonly associated with Johnson's type of heart attack, the condition is viewed as "troublesome."[49]

It was uncertain whether Johnson would live or die. This was the crisis that he had always expected. His father had suffered two heart attacks and died at sixty. Two of his uncles had died at similar ages, also of cardiac problems. Lyndon was still not yet forty-seven, but he realized that his life might now be coming to an end. He told his wife that his tailor should continue to make his new blue suit, because "I need it whichever way it goes."[50]

Slowly Johnson began to recover, but he remained subject to deep moods of depression. One day he was visited in the hospital by his brother, who found him in tears. "I'll never get a chance to be President now," he complained, certain that political advancement was now shut off to him.[51] Walter Jenkins has admitted that Johnson had periods of real despondency:

Of course, I think he, more than just the average patient, felt this. If he had any chance to be president or vice president or something, that this had ended it. I think he felt that and he became quite despondent at times during the next two or three weeks when he wouldn't talk to anyone very much. . . . He just wouldn't talk. . . . They gave him some despondency medicine; I don't know what it was. And he'd be all right then for a while and then he'd have another period of despondency.[52]

On 7 August, Johnson left the hospital and then returned to his Texas ranch on his birthday, three weeks later. His long-time secretary, who spent the period of his convalescence with him there, found that "he was the thinnest thing you have ever, ever seen, and his clothes were just hanging on him."[53] He continued to suffer from depression and from frightening nightmares. He told one confidant that "I knew then how awful it was to lose command of myself, to be dependent on others. I couldn't stand it. But at least I was home with my family and friends. These were the people I could trust."[54] Ironically, to family, friends, and aides, Johnson was often impatient and given to outbursts of temper. He was unsure now whether his health would permit him to reach his highest goal, and his outward demeanor often reflected his inner turmoil. The pressures on those around him were so great that Lady Bird once admitted, "when this is over, I want to go off by myself and cry for about two hours."[55]

Once again, Johnson began talking about leaving politics. He told a friend that "I've thrown away the whip. That heart attack taught me to appreciate some things that a busy man sometimes forgets. . . . Essentially it all means, I guess, that I'm learning all over how to live."[56] At other times, however, Johnson was not so positive about the lessons of his illness. His wife reports that he would just sit and stare into space.[57] Walter Jenkins worried that "he would kind of give up, maybe wouldn't really make the effort to recover."[58]

Johnson's doctors had warned those around him that there might be sharp changes in his character and behavior. But one of his closest aides, George Reedy, confides that:

It would not be accurate to say that his personality changed. . . . But before the heart attack, his darkest side was kept under a modicum of control. After the heart attack, he stopped just short of supreme disaster—and not very short at that. Some-

times it seemed as though he really wanted to get caught doing something outrageous so he would no longer have to make decisions or accept responsibilities.[59]

He did, however, follow the medical advice given him by his doctors and even tried to set a better record than the one they laid out for him. They ordered that he stop smoking, which he did, but he kept a pack of cigarettes on his night stand just to prove that he had conquered the habit. They wanted him to reduce his calorie intake to 1500 a day but he aimed at 1200. They recommended that he reduce his weight to 180 pounds but he aimed at 170.[60] One area which did *not* change in the desired direction was his drinking, which seems actually to have increased after his heart attack. Although he pretended to drink bourbon, a solid American drink, Johnson actually consumed large quantities of scotch, despite its impact on his weight.[61]

After five months of recuperation time, Lyndon returned to the Senate. His doctors claimed that they did not want him to retire from politics after his heart attack, since politics was such an important part of his life. Dr. Cain advised Lady Bird that "this had been his life; it was what he knew; it was what he liked" and we have "no evidence that continuing working with a degree of moderation would shorten his life a bit."[62]

In this instance, Johnson may have fallen victim to the "celebrity effect," which has surrounded other prominent and powerful personalities.[63] His doctors may simply have deferred to the preferences of their famous, high-status patient, no matter how harmful or dangerous those preferences might have been. Moderation—as his doctors surely knew—was not in Lyndon Johnson's vocabulary, and almost immediately he resumed the same long hours and killing pace that had preceded his severe heart attack. Perhaps he thought he had little time left to him and that he had to move quickly.

The Vice Presidency

In 1960, with the impending retirement of Dwight D. Eisenhower from the White House, the Democratic Party's presidential nomination was an attractive prize, but Lyndon Johnson seemed reluctant to enter the fray. He told friends that a southerner could not be nominated but also claimed that his health would not allow him to compete actively for first place on the ticket.[64] Some of Johnson's allies were convinced that his 1955 coronary prevented him from waging the kind of campaign that was necessary for victory. While John F. Kennedy and Hubert H. Humphrey battled it out in the early primaries, Johnson remained in Washington, carrying out his responsibilities as Senate Majority Leader, refusing to be enticed into entering even those primaries (e.g., West Virginia) where he might be expected to do well and hoping instead that his contact with party leaders might win him the nomination if a deadlock should develop at the convention.

Johnson reportedly was surprised at Kennedy's emergence as the 1960 front-runner. He later said "here was a young whippersnapper, malaria-ridden and yellah, sickly, sickly. . . . Now, I will admit that he had a good sense of humor and that he looked awfully good on the goddam television screen and through it all he was a pretty decent fellow, but his growing hold on the American people was simply a mystery to me."[65] On 5 July, long after the primaries had ended and less than a week before the Democratic convention was set to begin, Johnson finally announced that he, too, was a candidate for the office of President of the United States, telling reporters that his electrocardiogram tracing, which he carried in his wallet, was the sign of "a perfectly healed heart."[66]

At the convention, there was considerable tension between Johnson and Kennedy, and much of it surrounded the health issue. Some of Kennedy's supporters raised questions about the state of Johnson's health, pointedly asking whether Johnson's serious heart attack only five years earlier precluded his taking on the burdens of the presidency.[67] Johnson's allies responded in kind, charging that Kennedy had Addison's Disease and that without cortisone he would be dead. At least one of these went so far as to predict that if Kennedy were nominated and elected, he would die in office of his various maladies.[68]

After Kennedy's first-ballot victory, he surprised almost everyone by offering the vice presidential nomination to Lyndon Johnson. Since the Catholic Kennedy needed a powerful bridge to the Protestant South, his tapping of the Texas Senator was not really so surprising as it first appeared. Johnson's *acceptance* of the offer, though, has provoked considerable speculation. Some of Johnson's close friends have explained that he considered the vice presidency as a promotion and a step up on the ladder of power[69] and/or as his duty to the party. One of them explained, "you just have to understand this man's sense of duty. I have heard him say 'you can't accept all the benefits of the party . . . all the good things of the party and then when they ask you to do something that you might not prefer to do, you can't say, No, I am going to turn my back.' "[70]

Interestingly, Lady Bird Johnson, one of her husband's shrewdest and most influential advisers, counseled him to accept the vice presidential nomination for a quite different reason. She reportedly felt that the slow pace of the vice presidency would protect Lyndon's health and well-being whereas the burdens of being Majority Leader were so all-consuming that they might well bring on another health crisis.[71]

Sam Rayburn, Speaker of the House of Representatives and Johnson's close friend and mentor, also advised acceptance of the vice presidential nomination. Rayburn despised Richard Nixon for what he interpreted years earlier as an attack on his patriotism and was strongly committed to Nixon's defeat in the 1960 presidential election. Although he initially opposed Johnson's joining the Kennedy ticket, Rayburn finally relented and urged him to run as Kennedy's running-mate in order to save the country from a Nixon victory.[72]

Johnson's acceptance of second place on the ticket might also be interpreted as a much colder and more calculating personal decision. Afraid that his power as Majority Leader might shrink if a Democrat should be elected president or that he would be blamed by northerners for Kennedy's defeat if he refused to join the ticket and then Nixon won, Johnson may well have decided that he *had* to run for vice president in 1960 if he had any hopes of running for president in some future year.[73] Also, prior to and during the Democratic Convention, rumors about Kennedy's health were common. Whispers about fearsome ailments were heard so widely in political circles around the country that Johnson may have accepted the number two spot on the ticket because he believed that Kennedy's physical problems might well end his life before his term expired, whether in 1965 or 1969, and that his Vice President would then be catapulted into the Oval Office.[74] In any event, Johnson surprised many observers when he accepted the vice presidential nomination, telling Kennedy aide Larry O'Brien that:

I'm going to do everything physically and mentally that I'm capable of doing in the interest of this campaign and this ticket. . . . You're going to find that I am everything that you want me to be in terms of being a running-mate.[75]

During the 1960 campaign, Johnson worked hard for the ticket and his wife worried about his fatigue.[76] Aides also worried about his drinking habits, which almost burst out of control. George Reedy has since revealed that "the 1960 campaign was a nightmare for the staff—a weird collage of beratings, occasional drunken prowls up and down hotel corridors and frantic efforts to sober him up in the mornings so he could make speaking engagements."[77] Haunted by the specter of losing Texas, Johnson became so overwrought that Kennedy actually warned him that "I believe you're cracking up."[78]

After Johnson became Vice President, he found the unaccustomed lack of power to be frustrating. Perhaps trying to set a record in the one constitutional duty assigned to vice presidents, Johnson presided over the Senate, his former home, for long hours,[79] but he clearly no longer led it. A conversation he had with a friend about his vice presidential chauffeur tells much about his feelings at the time. He explained that:

That's a smart man, my chauffeur. He's been driving Senate Majority Leaders since Joe Robinson and when I got elected Vice President, I asked him to come with me. At first he said no. I said, "why?" He said he liked to drive the Majority Leader because there was a man with real power. He said the Vice President doesn't have any power at all. . . . He's a pretty smart fellow, my driver. I wish I'd had him with me in Los Angeles [the site of the 1960 Democratic Convention].[80]

Johnson once said that the only useful purpose the vice president served was to remind the president of his own mortality and admitted that "every time I came into John Kennedy's presence, I felt like a goddam raven hovering over his shoulder."[81] Once again, he spoke about quitting politics and ruminated about whether he might be happier "living at the ranch, perhaps lending a hand to better education in Texas, helping the small colleges he believed in so strongly. . . ."[82] Later, he said of the vice presidency that "in the end, it is nothing. I detested every minute of it."[83]

On 22 November 1963, in the midst of a tumultuous motorcade in Dallas, Lyndon B. Johnson's vice presidential tribulations came to an end. With the assassination of John F. Kennedy, Johnson suddenly ascended to the presidency of the United States and achieved his highest ambition. He had long prepared for this moment and now turned his considerable talents to the leadership of his country.

The Presidency

Despite its abruptness and the national trauma that accompanied it, the elevation of Lyndon Johnson to the office of President of the United States was impressively sure and smooth. The new President moved quickly to reassure the nation that he would carry on for his assassinated predecessor and to establish himself as a Chief Executive who was experienced, able, and in charge. Despite his early political successes as President and the high approval ratings given him by his constituents, the new Chief Executive, mindful of the severe heart attack which he had suffered in 1955, began to worry that the unrelenting pressures of the presidency might bring on another serious breakdown in his health. He hinted to family members and friends that he would not run for election to the presidency in 1964, later explaining that:

there was the constant uncertainty as to whether my health would stand up through a full four-year term. The strain of my work in the Senate had helped to bring on my severe heart attack when I was only forty-six. Now I was nine years older. . . . I felt a strong inclination to go back to Texas while there was still time—time to enjoy life with my wife and daughters, to work in earnest at being a rancher on the land I loved, to slow down, to reflect, to live.[84]

Although it was not widely known, Johnson secretly prepared a statement of withdrawal from the 1964 presidential election-contest, leaving space for his doctors to insert medical items at the appropriate time. Before that could happen, however, the First Lady intervened. She feared that retirement from politics would be the worst course for Johnson to take and might well lead to "depression and frustration as he watched Mr. X running the country and thought what he would have done instead." Apparently his doctors agreed. Lady Bird writes that Drs. Cain and Hurst "thought that inaction, idleness, lack of command would be a harder role for him than the long hours and heavy responsibility he now shoulders. They both really thought that he should continue for now."[85] The First Lady advised the President to run in 1964, admitting to him that the cares of his office might result in his earlier death but warning him that being semi-idle on the ranch would not be enough for him at the age of fifty-six.

Even as late as the summer of 1964, Johnson flirted with political retirement. In mid-July, his wife wrote in her diary that she saw him "going through the throes of what may be the last desperate turning away, the desire to escape being the Democratic candidate this Fall. But the trouble is he can't find any honorable escape." A month later, she sent him a frank memorandum, warning him that "to step out now would be wrong for your country and I can see nothing but a lonely wasteland for your future. Your friends would be frozen in embarrassed silence and your enemies jeering." She further recommended that Johnson announce in February or March 1968, that he would not run again for the presidency, since "by that time . . . the juices of life will be sufficiently stilled" for him to return to the ranch in contentment.[86]

Johnson later revealed that he did not "fully and finally" decide to run in 1964 until after the Democratic National Convention opened in Atlantic City in late August.[87] Nevertheless, his actions on 30 July 1964—when he publicly announced his removal of Robert F. Kennedy and the rest of his Cabinet from consideration as vice presidential possibilities—suggests rather strongly that Johnson had made up his mind "fully and finally" to run for President somewhat earlier than he later claimed. The most important point, however, is that in his final campaign for public office, Johnson flirted with withdrawal from the race, in part for reasons of health.

Elected in a great landslide, Lyndon Johnson embarked on what would become one of the most turbulent presidencies in American history. It was also a presidency marred by a number of presidential illnesses, some of which were concealed from the public, others announced publicly at some point but downplayed in their seriousness. In fact, even when Johnson was moving out of the vice presidential residence into the White House in the fall of 1963, he was suffering from a severe cold and a chest condition, but no public mention was made of this indisposition.[88]

More serious, just three days after his inauguration in January 1965, Johnson was rushed to the hospital at 2:26 A.M. suffering from chest pains and a hacking cough. Vice President Humphrey was telephoned at 3:30 A.M. in Minnesota with the news that the President had been hospitalized with chest pains. Humphrey was not alone in his fears that Johnson had suffered another heart attack, a prospect he found "particularly frightening because Lyndon had suffered a serious one ten years before." Many years later, Humphrey complained that Johnson, "for some bizarre reason, refused to let any medical facts be given to me immediately. Instead the orders came to me that he wanted me to fulfill my scheduled weekend commitments so that no one would think his illness was serious." When Humphrey left home later that morning, he still did not know whether Johnson had suffered another heart attack, how critical his condition might be, or whether he would soon be succeeding Johnson as President. He later wrote that "it was an awesome prospect, a terrible shock, compounded by not knowing what precisely was happening."[89] Perhaps the shock was further compounded by the fact that although Johnson had intended to enter into a disability arrangement with his vice president, he had not, at that time, done so.

That day, Humphrey told a hushed audience that after he had received the phone call about the President's hospitalization, he had just walked around the house for a while and then had a long talk with his wife.[90] He appeared to be particularly grim and apprehensive, unusual for the normally ebullient vice president. In Washington, however, tests on Johnson revealed that he had not had a heart attack. The White House physician, Dr. George Burkley, diagnosed his condition as that of a "common cold with tracheal and bronchial irritation." and the White House insisted that "there certainly is no cause for alarm."[91] The First Lady, however, described the situation as one in which doctors "skimmed around the word 'pneumonia.' "[92] The President's temperature at one point soared to 104.4°; he coughed frequently and experienced considerable pain in the throat and upper chest when he did so.[93]

It was while Johnson was hospitalized that Winston Churchill died in Great Britain. Dr. Wilbur Gould, a consulting physician, indicated that Johnson's temperature rose immediately after learning of Churchill's death. His doctors strongly advised him not to attend the funeral in his weakened condition and in the damp British weather, and Lady Bird strongly concurred, fearing the emotional impact on her husband if he attended.[94] The President's absence from the funeral occasionally has been misunderstood and misrepresented. One critic, for example, complained that "possibly because very few British votes are cast in the U.S. elections and because British officials can do him very little good, Johnson could not find time to attend the funeral of Winston Churchill." Yet, he continued, the President managed to slip away "from Washington to attend the funerals of Senator Richard Russell's nephew in Georgia and Congressman Emmanuel Celler's wife in New York and Senator Harry Byrd's wife in Virginia. . . ."[95] In point of fact, Johnson was simply too ill to travel abroad at the time of Churchill's death and was following doctors' orders in remaining at home.

Released from the hospital after 83 hours, Johnson was still not completely recovered. He continued to cough and at night sweated profusely, once drenching two or three pairs of pajamas. The First Lady described this condition as "an old enemy" which has been "a symptom of his illnesses for all the years I have known him."[96] He continued to work, though, while he recuperated and within days had resumed his killing pace. As president, Johnson's schedule was a punishing one. He normally awakened at 6:30 A.M. and, in an effort to conserve his strength,[97] worked in his bedroom for two hours before meeting with aides on the day's business. At around 10 A.M. he proceeded to the Oval Office for more formal appointments and meetings. Frequently he took a late lunch break, went for a swim, and/or took a nap, and, then, around 5 P.M., began his "second day." He worked for another five or six hours before having dinner and then retired to his bedroom where often two or three hours' worth of night reading would be waiting for him. It is rumored that he took more than a hundred phone calls a day and that Mrs. Johnson used to pin notes to his pillow, warning him to take it easy.[98]

Johnson even instructed aides to wake him in the middle of the night with news that he wanted to have shared with him. Congressional aide Larry O'Brien has reported that when a vote in Congress went against him at 3 or 4 A.M., he decided not to call the President until 6:30 or 7:00. When Johnson learned that the actual vote had occurred several hours earlier, he complained to O'Brien: "God, you should have called me right then and there. When you're bleeding up on that hill, Larry, I want to bleed with you."[99]

Even periods of vacation at the Texas ranch were packed with activity. The First Lady wrote that "rest at the ranch is a complete misnomer to me. The airport stays busy, with planes disgorging Cabinet members with important, difficult decisions, budget estimates, crises. . . . Visitors pour in and news pours out. And these old walls are bursting at the seams."[100] No President can fully escape the burdens of the presidency no matter what his location, and Lyndon Johnson rarely even tried. An aide once explained that Johnson believed that "the essential margin he has over other men is his capacity to work harder—to work and work and work all through the day and night, beyond any other man's capacity."[101]

GALLBLADDER SURGERY AND CARDIAC DIFFICULTIES

On 7 September 1965, the President was stricken once again. This time he developed severe stomach pains, waking Lady Bird at 4 A.M. to tell her he was in agony. Although they both feared that he might be having another heart attack, they did not summon help until several hours later for fear of causing too much alarm. The First Lady later explained "there was a necessity to be calm while frightened, to bridle anxiety whenever you opened your mouth—a familiar feeling."[102]

Dr. Burkley finally was called, and he thought that the problem was catfish poisoning, since the President had consumed large quantities of deep-fried catfish on the previous evening. Since Johnson's urinalysis was completely normal, Burkley did not believe that a kidney stone was causing the problem. Dr. James Young, a White House Physician, suggested to Burkley that in light of the President's elevated temperature of 100.8 as well as his normal urinalysis, the gallbladder might well be the culprit.[103]

After the President returned to the White House, he was given a gall-bladder x-ray series which clearly showed a large gallstone as well as a poorly functioning gallbladder. Dr. Cain recommended to the President that he have his gallbladder removed but only after an interval of three or four weeks so that it would "cool off a little bit."[104] Johnson readily agreed, but no public announcement of his illness or impending surgery was made at the time.

President Johnson initially believed that no one need know about his surgery until it was over. When he discussed this idea with former President Eisenhower, Eisenhower demurred and urged complete candor. It was not until 5 October, however, a full month after he was stricken, that Johnson announced to the press that he would have his gallbladder removed on 8 October, emphasizing that a poorly functioning gallbladder was the only physical problem uncovered by the medical tests he had just undergone.[105]

Also on 5 October, the White House described the disability arrangements that would be in effect during the President's hospitalization. Press Secretary Moyers announced that "in the event of an inability which would prevent the President from communicating with the Vice President, the Vice President, after such consultation as seems to him appropriate under the circumstances, would decide upon the devolution of the power and duties of the office and would serve as Acting President until the inability had ended." The vice president would not be acting president "unless the particular situation arises in which the need for him to accept the powers of the acting presidency is apparent." Since Johnson "won't be able to inform him of this while under anesthesia, Humphrey will have to determine if the national interest requires further action by him."[106]

At his own news conference, Vice President Humphrey announced that "The President has fully discussed the situation with me and with the Cabinet, and we are clear as to the procedures to be followed during his short absence if necessity arises. I shall, of course, be available in Washington at all times during the President's absence from the White House."[107]

The President went to great lengths to make it clear that he would be neither slowed nor stopped by his physical indisposition. On the eve of his hospitalization, he participated in the signing of a regional medical center bill, took a walk with his beagles around the White House grounds, greeted and shook hands with tourists, taped a speech, met with a group of people from Appalachia, attended the National Press Club luncheon for cartoonists, and met with his economic advisors.[108]

Johnson's doctors had told the press in early October, just before the surgery, that the risks associated with it were "very low" for a person of his age and that his cardiac history did not increase those risks, "since he has done extremely well, with no symptoms whatsoever for the entire ten years." The press was assured that the President "would have full intellectual capacity to carry out the job," that he would be sedated for "a surprisingly short" period, and that the sedation would "absolutely not make the President inactive or render his judgment slightly cloudy."[109]

In private, doctors worried about pancreatic cancer. Dr. Cain asked Lady Bird what should be done if, during the surgery, "we found a cancer in the pancreas? What should we do? The operation to remove the pancreas is a tremendous operation and a very dangerous operation." The First Lady directed him to remove the pancreas in that eventuality, despite the risk. "This is what we want. I want him around for many, many years."[110]

At 7 A.M. on the morning of 8 October, several Secret Service agents in surgical masks and gowns joined ten doctors in the operating room at Bethesda Naval Hospital. In a procedure that lasted two hours and fifteen minutes, surgeons made a twelve-inch incision in the President's abdomen, removed his gall bladder and, at the same time, removed a kidney stone. There was no sign of malignancy. According to Dr. Cain, Johnson went through the operation "beautifully as expected,"[111] which, as we shall see, was not entirely accurate. Thirty minutes after surgery ended, the White House—following the President's orders—sent a message to General Westmoreland in Saigon, informing him of Johnson's progress, so that American forces in Vietnam would know that their Commander in Chief was still firmly in control.

At 5:22 that afternoon, the White House Press Secretary described Johnson as "fully capable of making any necessary decisions," and at 6:35 the following morning Johnson moved to dispel any doubts as to who was in charge by signing the Interest Equalization Tax Extension Bill.[112] On 10 October, the President met with reporters and told them of his pleasure at the passage of the beautification bill and that he had signed "some judgeships, a bunch of Ambassadorships, some foreign service officers, District Attorneys and Marshalls" and that he had made his first official phone call since his surgery two days before.[113]

On the following day, he met with the vice president, discussing with him intelligence reports, legislation, and a possible visit to the United States by the West German chancellor. That evening, however, sedation was not used and he spent a very restless and unpleasant night. The following morning, he was in considerable discomfort.

The President had embarked on a much slower and more difficult recuperation than his doctors had expected. He developed gas pains, which caused him great distress, his incision and muscles were very sore, and he tired easily.[114] Contrary to his doctors' predictions that he would feel like himself within six weeks, Johnson's recovery took at least twice that long.

His doctors stressed the positive, however, telling the press of Johnson's "unusual recuperative powers" and stating that "the President's condition is . . . every bit as good, perhaps a little bit ahead of what one would expect with any patient of his age. . . ."[115]

In a moment of unusual candor, however, Bill Moyers admitted to the press on 14 October that "I think he is weaker than anyone thought. I think the pace of the last 20 months has accumulated weariness that was not evident until the operation. . . . I think he is gaining his strength more slowly than anyone thought. In that regard, he is probably proving to be an average patient."[116]

Four days later, Moyers again presented a candid view of Johnson's condition. He told the press that "I still observe that the President is wearied by his activities, whether they are of a peripatetic nature . . . or signing bills or reading reports or affixing his signature to mail on his desk. . . . I also think it is going to take the President longer to regain his strength and to recover and return to the peak of activity . . . than anyone thought." Moreover, he indicated that Johnson's doctors would agree with his assessment.[117]

Another point now agreed to by Johnson's doctors was that they had been considerably more concerned with the President's heart status at the time of the surgery than they had admitted. On 22 October, with the operation safely behind them, the President's physicians now indicated that "the chief concern we had and would have with any patient . . . because of his past history was . . . cardiac arrest." Despite their earlier assurances that Johnson's 1955 heart attack did not increase the risks associated with his 1965 surgery, they later revealed that two meetings had been held to discuss possible ways of dealing with any cardiac crisis that might develop while Johnson was on the operating table. They were prepared to use external heart massage, electrical methods for starting the heart, and even direct injection of medicine into the heart if serious cardiac problems arose during surgery.[118]

Their fears were not unwarranted. As he was being given anesthesia, the President developed a supraventricular tachycardia, which means that his heartbeat increased significantly. This condition is potentially quite dangerous, but it was quickly detected by Drs. Hurst and Young, who were monitoring his continuous electrocardiogram. Dr. Hurst suggested an intravenous dose of atropine to the anesthesiologist, who then administered it to the President. Johnson's rapid heartbeat subsided quickly, converted to a normal rhythm, and a crisis was averted.[119]

Soon after surgery, the President returned to work, at least on a part-time basis, but initially resisted resuming the full burdens of the job. An aide who asked that he respond to a detailed memorandum elicited a tersely written reply: "I'm sick."[120] Johnson left the hospital on 21 October for the White House and then proceeded to the Texas ranch, where he continued to make slow progress. In late November, Moyers announced that "because of health considerations, the ceremonial and desirable but unnecessary functions of the presidency will have to stay at an absolute minimum."[121]

Johnson suffered, too, from post-operative depression and actually wanted to draw up papers of resignation from the presidency.[122] He was further depressed at the uproar that resulted when he tried to prove, by showing his surgical scar to reporters, that he had undergone gallbladder rather than cancer surgery and that he had not suffered another heart attack.[123]

As late as mid-December, the President was reported to be suffering occasional discomfort, and it was revealed that his doctors expected him to have it "a good while longer." On 29 December, doctors pronounced him "fully recovered," despite sporadic twinges of pain.[124] For several additional weeks, however, Johnson experienced pain, discomfort, and fatigue.

THROAT SURGERY AND OTHER AILMENTS

A little more than a year after his gallbladder surgery, the President was back again at Bethesda Naval Hospital, both for throat surgery and to repair a hernia in his gallbladder incision. In early November, his doctors had found a growth in his throat that had to be removed. There was some possibility that it might be cancerous, and members of the Johnson family experienced great tension over the possibility. In a one-hour operation, doctors removed a sessile polyp from the President's right vocal cord, a process that required four stitches with fine steel wire. It had extended downward about five millimeters, and doctors expected that its removal would lead to three or four weeks of pain and anywhere from four to six weeks of hoarseness.[125] The polyp was soon discovered to be benign, but public speaking was discouraged for a short time. Doctors then turned their attention to repairing a protrusion in his gallbladder incision. Johnson had experienced difficulty with his scar soon after surgery in October 1965, but Dr. Cain felt that the problem could be easily corrected.[126] It was not. Instead, a new two-inch incision had to be made and the muscular connecting tissue brought together by interrupted sutures and stitches.[127] Dr. Cain later explained:

the gallbladder operation was a difficult operation. He had a kidney stone at the same time. . . . While fixing the gallbladder we decided . . . we would try to see if we could get this kidney stone out. . . . It meant a slightly unusual kind of operation. . . . But . . . having to make a little bit of an unusual incision, we did get a small incisional hernia that is of no consequence except that it did mean that it had to be closed later on.[128]

When Johnson awakened from the anesthesia, he asked Lady Bird to turn on all three television sets in his room. A few hours later, he met with reporters at his bedside. On 19 November, three days after surgery, he left the hospital, telling the press that his throat had "some ache."[129] Once again he returned to his Texas ranch to regain his strength, but, again, recovery was slow. He was not able to return to Washington for several weeks.[130]

During Johnson's years in the White House there were other illnesses and medical problems besides the surgeries of 1965 and 1966. He had as many as forty skin lesions removed from his body, one of which was malignant.[131] He developed sties on his eyes which his wife described as "red, swollen and painful"[132] and which caused concern to one of his doctors.[133] He complained of "foot trouble"[134] and fever blisters.[135] In 1966, John Steinbeck found that the President did not look well; he was "too drawn and too taut." At White House receptions, he sometimes looked exhausted and pale. In the fall of 1967, Dr. Hurst warned the First Lady that he was greatly concerned over her husband's health.[136] Around the same time, Lady Bird wrote in her diary:

the fear that haunts me is that if Lyndon were back in office for a four-year stretch— beginning when he was sixty years old—bad health might overtake him, an attack, though something not completely incapacitating, and he might find himself straining to be the sort of President he wanted to be—to put in the eighteen-hour days—and unable to draw enough vitality from the once bottomless well of his energy. A physical or mental incapacitation would be unbearably painful for him to recognize, and for me to watch.[137]

It was during 1967 that Johnson had arranged for preparation of a secret actuarial study on his life expectancy, telling intimates that in light of his family history and 1955 heart attack, "I'd never live through another four years. The American people had enough of presidents dying in office."[138] The stresses of the office clearly were taking their toll on Lyndon Johnson, and Vietnam, in particular, came to consume and torment him. Even as early as February 1966, the First Lady confided to her diary that "Lyndon talked about Vietnam—in fact, this is about two-thirds of what we talk about these days. He talked about the individual feelings of every mother who has a son in Vietnam. . . ."[139] Eventually, the President became so overwrought because of the war that Georgia's Senator Richard Russell stopped going alone to visit him in the White House, because, Russell explained, Johnson would start crying uncontrollably and the senator could not stand being subjected to that kind of emotionalism.[140]

In February 1968, the President's brother found him to be distressed, almost disconsolate. He recounts that one morning, at 2 A.M., Johnson invited him to play dominoes. As they began to play, the President appeared to be "very tired and deeply worried. He was having one of those sleepless nights that makes an old man out of anyone who becomes President." Sam Houston remembers that Lyndon was tormented that morning by Vietnam, by not knowing "whether I'm making the right move" and by having to choose "between my opposing experts." After expressing the wish that he "could really know what's right," the President, in his bathrobe, shuffled "down the hall toward the elevator on his way to the Situation Room in the basement to get the 3 o'clock report from Saigon." "He looked," his brother recalled, "tired and lonely as he pushed the down button."[141]

In addition to appearing tired and lonely, Johnson showed signs of a far more serious problem—at least to one or two of his aides. As the war, and the controversy surrounding it, escalated, these aides found that the President began to show increasing signs of unreason and irrationality. To them, his outbursts at the "Kennedy crowd," the press, the communists, the liberals, the "Harvards," and the intellectuals revealed a pattern of paranoid behavior and a growing instability. When they described to psychiatrists Johnson's behavior patterns, his condition was diagnosed—but only from afar—as "paranoid disintegration."[142]

The revelations of paranoia did not come, however, until 1988, long after Johnson's presidency, and even his life, had come to an end. Whether the President was, in fact, paranoid or simply venting his anger privately and colorfully at his opponents will likely never be known. Nevertheless, even the suggestion by one or two close aides that a president of the United States is irrational and unstable is rather chilling.

In any event, on 31 March 1968, Lyndon B. Johnson, described by associates who watched him speak on television that evening as "old," "weary," "battered," "drained," "pallid," and "aged,"[143] announced to the nation that he would not be a candidate for re-election. His inability to extricate the country from Vietnam, his fear that he could not unite the nation, and his concerns about his health were important motivating factors in his decision. On that historic day, the First Lady confided to her diary that the President's face "was sagging and there was such pain in his eyes as I had not seen since his mother died."[144] But the President told Defense Secretary Clark Clifford that day that "I never felt so right about any decision in my life."[145]

Although the White House Physician claims to have been unaware of any health reason for Johnson's withdrawal in 1968,[146] Johnson himself has emphasized the importance of health factors in his decision to leave the White House. He told Vice President Humphrey at the time that "even if I should run and be re-elected, I most likely would not live out my term."[147] Later he spoke very eloquently of health considerations in his 1971 autobiography:

two hospitalizations for surgery while I was in the White House had sharpened my apprehensions about my health. My heart attack of 1955 seemed well behind me, but I was conscious that it was part of the background of my life—just as I was conscious of my family's history of stroke and heart disease. I did not fear death so much as I feared disability. Whenever I walked through the Red Room and saw the portrait of Woodrow Wilson hanging there, I thought of him stretched out upstairs in the White House powerless to move, with the machinery of the American government in disarray around him.

Johnson also described the work of the presidency as "demanding and unrelenting" and ". . . always there to be done." He wrote:

Of all the 1886 nights I was President, there were not many when I got to sleep before 1 or 2 A.M. and there were few mornings when I didn't wake up by 6 or 6:30. It became a question of how much the physical constitution could take. I frankly did not believe in 1968 that I could survive another four years of the long hours and unremitting tensions I had just gone through.[148]

Even as a lame-duck President, Johnson continued to work at a feverish pace. His wife believed that, if anything, he actually "accelerated his activity" since he was determined "to push with every power he has toward peace abroad and toward furthering his programs at home."[149] When Senator James Eastland told her that he hoped the Democratic Convention would draft Johnson in August, she told him that even if he was nominated, "he wouldn't accept."[150]

In August, a physical examination revealed that Johnson had two kidney stones in his left kidney. These had been detected previously but showed no change. His doctors also pointed out that since 1960, diverticula were present in his large intestine. These were non-inflamed protrusions in the colon wall which are fairly common and which reportedly caused the President no real discomfort at the time.[151]

On 16 December, Johnson awakened in the middle of the night with chills and fever. At 4 A.M., a doctor arrived at his bedside and insisted that he go to the hospital. Understandably, the President thought it best to wait four or five hours because "to go in the night" would have negative effects on the stock market and would set off the "rumor machine." When he finally was hospitalized, the First Lady reported that he had just lain in bed for several days "not talking, not reacting, just lying still"—a very untypical posture for Johnson and the measure of his misery.[152] Lady Bird must have been greatly relieved when her husband's presidency ended four weeks later. She had been deeply worried about him throughout his term in office as his periodic ailments appeared and disappeared, all reflecting the uncertain state of his health.[153]

The Final Years

On 20 January 1969 Lyndon Johnson left Washington and retired to his Texas ranch. The former President initially seemed to be in stable health and threw himself into his new life as a rancher and teacher. Unfortunately, he began to stray from his diet and gained a considerable amount of weight. As time went on, he resumed smoking cigarettes, after many years of abstinence. In the spring of 1969, he was laying pipe on his property when he experienced chest pains and shortness of breath.[154] The following March, he was hospitalized because of severe chest pains.[155] A month later, he told staffers at the *Washington Post* that his condition was far more serious than the public knew.[156] In April 1972, he suffered a massive heart attack while visiting his daughter Lynda in Charlottesville, Virginia. After spending only a few days in intensive care there, Johnson insisted on being flown back to Brooke Army Hospital in Texas. For the remaining months of his life, he experienced sharp angina pains on a daily basis. Friends have said that he knew that he was dying. He told at least one of them, "I've got an instinct."[157] In the fall of 1972, Johnson privately consulted Dr. Michael De Bakey about the possibility of a heart operation but was told that it would simply be too risky.[158] To Senator George McGovern he confided that

". . . every day I start out pretty well, but then by afternoon, these damn chest pains start bothering me, and at four o'clock, I'm pretty well through. I go lay down."[159]

Not only did Johnson often need an oxygen machine during this period but he also suffered from several painful bouts of diverticulitis.[160] An aide working with him at the time writes that "his intestinal system was in continuous turmoil."[161]

On 11 December, against his doctors' orders, Johnson attended a civil rights symposium at the Johnson Library in Austin. He had been ill the night before and had gotten little sleep. As he spoke to the crowd, he experienced chest pains and, in full view of the cameras, took a nitroglycerine tablet before proceeding with his remarks. A former aide comments that the crowd knew that "the giant was clearly not so strong as he once was."[162]

At 3:50 P.M. on 22 January 1973, the former President desperately called the ranch switchboard, seeking the head of his Secret Service detail. Agents rushed to his bedside with a portable oxygen machine and found him lying on the floor beside his bed. He had suffered another heart attack, fallen, and bruised his head.[163] Efforts to revive him failed. He was taken to San Antonio where he was pronounced dead at 4:33 P.M. His autopsy showed that he had been suffering from severe coronary arterial disease. Two of the three major arteries to the heart were completely occluded; the third was 60 percent occluded.[164] Although he had almost never wanted to be alone, he died alone at the early age of sixty-four.

The Political Effects of Johnson's Illnesses

While it is sometimes difficult to establish firm linkages between personal health and political behavior, several such linkages seem clearly to emerge in the case of Lyndon B. Johnson. First, intimates have pointed out that both the Johnson family history and Lyndon's own illnesses, particularly his 1955 severe heart attack, made him a driven man, thoroughly committed to accomplishing objectives quickly since he might not have the time to accomplish them over a long period. George Reedy believed that "the heart attack speeded LBJ up if anything,"[165] and Clark Clifford estimated that ". . . his heart attack had only made Lyndon Johnson feel more impatient, as though he now feared that he might be felled by another before he could achieve his goals."[166] Even Johnson's irritability and temper flare-ups—those intense personal qualities that led one of his closest aides to describe him as "a bully, sadist, lout and egotist,"[167] may have had their roots in the fear that death might overtake him at an early age. As President, Johnson drove himself relentlessly, pushing himself beyond the point of exhaustion. There was, after all, so much that he wanted to do and only limited time in which to do it.

Second, Johnson's 1955 heart attack seems to have had an important impact on the timing and duration of his post-senatorial career. Specifically, it may have led him to avoid the exertion of the primaries in 1960 and hope instead that either a convention deadlock or the vice presidential nomination would eventually propel him to the presidency. In 1964, he apparently flirted with the idea of leaving the presidency the following January out of health concerns. Then, in March 1968 he withdrew from the presidential race after concluding that he could not survive four more years of presidential tensions. His health, then, appears to have played a role in shaping the strategy he adopted in 1960 for moving onto the presidential stage and contributed to his "surprise" decision to remove himself from that stage in January 1969.

Third, Johnson's gallbladder surgery, and his slow recovery from it, had a negative impact on his congressional leadership at the time. Although legislative aide Larry O'Brien estimated that with the gallbladder surgery "nothing changed as far as the White House and its operations were concerned,"[168] others disagreed. During Johnson's hospitalization, the House of Representatives reversed itself and voted down a program of rent subsidies to low-income families that Johnson supported. A lack of intense personal lobbying by the President seems to have been crucial in this reversal. Around the same time, the Senate voted to continue a filibuster against repealing a section of the Taft–Hartley Act which labor—and Lyndon Johnson—wanted repealed. During his illness, the President could not maintain the efficient intelligence operation so crucial to the Johnson system. Moreover, his absence from center stage during the last three months of 1965 encouraged in Congress an "ugly mood of growing revolt."[169] He had long since become known for the "Johnson treatment" in dealing with congressional leaders and others with whom he came into contact. The treatment included cajolery, flattery, indifference, coldness, insult, and even intimidation. At the time of his illness and long convalescence, however, the Johnson treatment, so important a part of his legislative strategy, was suspended. The result was legislative defeat and disappointment for the Administration.

Fourth, Johnson's fears of ill health and premature death made him especially alert to the issues of presidential disability and succession. His own sudden elevation to the presidency on 22 November 1963 heightened that sensitivity, particularly since it left the vice presidency vacant until the next election and subsequent inauguration of a new vice president. This meant that if Johnson should die at any time during the ensuing fourteen months, the presidency would pass into the hands of House Speaker John McCormack, seventy-two. Should McCormack also die before the next election and inauguration, the person next in line of succession to the presidency would be eighty-nine-year-old Carl Hayden, President Pro Tempore of the Senate. This undoubtedly troubled the new President, particularly in light of his own cardiac history. Larry O'Brien has since revealed that:

It was a general concern, a recognition, let's put it that way, of the facts of life, and a feeling that we'd better have that in order. Part of it clearly was the age of both Hayden and McCormack. I think it alerted everyone . . . to the fact that a procedure should be established and not be subject to question or scrutiny.[170]

Not wanting to offend either McCormack or Hayden, Johnson tread softly around the issue of presidential succession in the early days of his presidency. He did remark at one point, however, that "I think it is important to find a way to replace a vice president when the vice president succeeds to the presidency."[171]

Johnson also sent a letter to Speaker McCormack outlining procedures to follow in the event that the new President should become incapacitated. McCormack later recalled that "the letter represented an understanding of minds between us and it was clear and specific as to what course of action I should take, and whom I should consult in relation to legal questions. . . ."[172] In order to prepare the Speaker for possible accession to the presidency, Johnson invited him to attend Cabinet meetings as well as meetings with the Joint Chiefs of Staff.

As soon as he and Hubert Humphrey swept to victory in 1964, the President moved swiftly to see the Twenty-fifth Amendment to the Constitution adopted. On 10 December 1964 he discussed the matter of presidential disability with a key senator, saying that "I know it's a problem that needs to be solved. . . ."[173] A few weeks later, in his 4 January State of the Union Address, Johnson announced that "even the best of government is subject to the worst of hazards. I will propose laws to insure the necessary continuity of leadership should the President become disabled or die."[174]

On 28 January 1965, in a special message to Congress, Johnson emphatically endorsed passage of the Twenty-fifth Amendment. He declared that:

our stability is more superficial than sure. While we are prepared for the possibility of a President's death, we are all but defenseless against the probability of a President's incapacity by injury, illness, senility or other afflictions. A nation bearing the responsibilities we are privileged to bear for our own security—and the security of the Free World—cannot justify the appalling gamble of entrusting its security to the immobilized hands or incomprehending mind of a Commander-in-Chief unable to command.[175]

Within six months, both Houses of Congress voted to adopt the Twenty-fifth Amendment, and it was then sent out to the states for ratification. In February 1967 the amendment was formally added to the Constitution, and Lyndon Johnson held a public ceremony in the East Room of the White House in order to give recognition to the importance of the amendment to the political health of the nation.

Finally, Johnson's long history of pain and illness seems to have made him, like Kennedy, particularly sensitive to the issue of health care for the American people. Just two and a half months after becoming President, he delivered a special message to Congress on the nation's health, committing himself to the best of health care for all Americans and recommending such steps as federal mortgage insurance and loans to help build group practice medical facilities and grants to build and expand schools of nursing.[176]

Johnson also set up at this time a Presidential Commission on Heart Disease, Cancer, and Stroke, composed of physicians and laymen and headed by heart specialist Dr. Michael De Bakey, to recommend steps that could be taken to reduce the disability and death rate from those diseases and to plan for a "life span and a work span for the average man or woman of 100 years."[177] When the Commission met for the first time on 17 April 1964, Johnson told its members that "the work which you have begun today is work in which I have the keenest and most personal interest."[178] De Bakey later pointed out that LBJ "had understood the needs of people in terms of their health needs. . . . I always had the impression that President Johnson had an . . . emotional, sort of, gut reaction to this matter. . . ."[179]

In August 1965, the President announced plans for a two-day White House Conference on Health that would convene on November 30. In his message to participants, Johnson indicated that he had called the conference "to bring together the best minds and the boldest ideas to deal with the pressing health needs of the nation." He then set forth several goals for conference members to consider: increase life expectancy, achieve a healthier environment, decrease infant mortality, improve the care of the mentally ill, and eliminate such diseases as whooping cough, measles, and tuberculosis.[180]

Most important, perhaps, Johnson was strongly committed to passage of President Kennedy's Medicare proposal and announced that health care legislation was "just the top of the list in legislative goals for 1965."[181] Larry O'Brien agreed that LBJ "was wedded to civil rights and wedded to Medicare, that's a given."[182] The President himself wrote that "the overriding importance of Medicare to me was that it foreshadowed a revolutionary change in our thinking about health care. We had begun, at long last, to recognize that good medical care is a right, not just a privilege."

During Johnson's administration, forty national health measures, including Medicare, were recommended to and passed by Congress "more than in all the preceding 175 years of the Republic's history." Federal expenditures for health programs more than tripled (from $4 billion to $14 billion). Johnson cited these initiatives with pride and described them as a salute to what the people "demand of their government and to the system that makes it possible to meet the demand."[183] They perhaps represented some of his greatest legacies to the nation he led.

The Fear of Rejection

Lyndon B. Johnson was stricken at almost every key moment of his political career as he ascended the ladder of power. Whether he suffered from appendicitis, pneumonia, nervous exhaustion, depression, kidney stones, or heart attacks, the pattern is both clear and striking. Even after reaching the very pinnacle of power, he was often ill and in pain and tried hard to conceal many of his indispositions then, just as he had earlier in his life.

In order to have any understanding into this unusual pattern of ill health, one should look back at Johnson's childhood years. His relationships with both his mother and his father were complex and difficult and left him with a fear of failure and a sense of self-doubt that he was never able to overcome. This was vital in Johnson's subsequent development. As Leon Saul suggests:

The childhood pattern of interacting with others . . . affects the person's adult behavior, either facilitating the development toward maturity if favorable or hindering or warping it if unfavorable. This pattern, if it contains elements of distorted human relationships, contains a nucleus of psychopathology.[184]

Lyndon B. Johnson's deep insecurities led him to fall ill whenever he feared that his political career was in danger and that he faced rejection by his constituents. It is not surprising, then, that his political life was punctuated at key points by painful, debilitating and even life-threatening ailments. Viewing these as further jeopardizing his political advancement, Johnson tried to ignore them until they could no longer be ignored and then concealed them until concealment became impossible.

Despite his enormously successful political career, Johnson remained obsessed with failure until the end of his life. Even during his retirement in Texas, he once responded to a problem at the ranch by telling an aide: "It's all been determined. Once more I'm going to fail. I know it. I simply know it."[185]

Johnson's obsession with failure likely had its roots in his childhood, particularly in his interaction with his parents. As a young boy, Lyndon was close to both of them. At the age of three, he tried to follow his father everywhere, even sitting in a barber chair next to him while he got a shave.[186] Later, at twelve, he was described as "his father's shadow in Austin" since he would often accompany Sam to sessions of the state legislature and listen to debate.[187]

Ben Crider, a long-time friend, once remarked that Lyndon "was very proud of his daddy's record as a member of the Texas House of Representatives. I have heard him speak of it a lot."[188] Johnson himself later pointed out that "The Ku Klux Klan was at its height when my father was in the Texas legislature. . . . They threatened him. . . . I was fearful that my daddy would be taken out and tarred and feathered. . . ." Later, he compared his own record on the Klan with that of his father: "my father fought them many long years ago in Texas and I have fought them all my life because I believe them to threaten every community where they exist." Not surprisingly, Johnson admitted that "I wanted to copy my father always, emulate him. Do what he did. He loved the outdoors and I grew to love the outdoors. He loved political life and I followed him."[189] Former Congressman Wright Patman, a friend of both father and son, once said of Lyndon, "he was so much like his father it was humorous to watch."[190]

However, as Lyndon entered adolescence, his father's failures in business began to accumulate. Sam lost the family farm and kept his own home only because his brothers agreed to guarantee the mortgage.[191] As failure mounted on failure, his drinking increased sharply, his disposition began to worsen, and Lyndon's attitude toward him began to sour.[192] The distance between the two became wider and wider, and Lyndon's rebelliousness and disdain became more and more evident. Their relationship would never fully heal. This, perhaps, is best shown by a story recounted by Sam Houston Johnson, Lyndon's younger brother. When their father died in

1937, the Johnson family gathered to distribute some of his personal belongings. As the elder son, Lyndon reached out to take his father's gold pocket watch but was stopped cold by one of his sisters. She told him ". . . you can't have the watch. That belongs to Sam Houston now. Daddy wanted him to have it. We all know that." Sam Houston reveals that "it was an embarrassing moment for Lyndon, and I felt sorry for him. . . . He was the older brother." Years later, Sam Houston gave Lyndon his father's watch as a gift and reports that he accepted it "with a kind of sad smile." Interestingly, when the family section of the Lyndon B. Johnson Library was being prepared, the watch was nowhere to be found.[193]

Lyndon's relationship with his mother, on the other hand, seems to have been stronger and more enduring. He once described her as "faith, pure gold, the greatest female I have ever known, without any exceptions."[194] Rebekah was a refined and genteel woman who found life in rural Texas to be difficult, lonely and limiting. Since her husband was often away from home, Rebekah had to spend many hours alone, a situation which she found disconcerting. Lyndon later revealed the first memory he had of his mother, when he was only three or four years old. His father was away, and his mother "was crying, it was nine or ten o'clock . . . she was frightened, afraid. I told her I'd protect her."[195]

Lyndon's mother also taught him to love politics. Her father, to whom she had been devoted, had been Secretary of State of Texas and she told Lyndon often that he had laid the cornerstone of the Texas Statehouse forty years earlier and had been a great man.[196] Her husband, on the other hand, often disappointed her, and throughout her marriage, she had shed frequent and bitter tears over his various failings. Her tears had deeply touched her elder son.

Perhaps to compensate in part for her husband's failures, Rebekah pushed and prodded Lyndon always to succeed and never to disappoint her. Her guidance was firm, unrelenting, and occasionally overbearing. He later said of his mother that she was "the strongest person I ever knew. When she gets an idea in her head, she never gives up."[197] This single-minded determination led her to be a stern taskmistress indeed. Whenever Lyndon, her first and favorite child, had "failed," she excluded him from her affection, ignoring him to the point of pretending that he was no longer among the living. Her love, then, seems to have been conditional, focused not so much on his person as on his successes. The pattern in Lyndon's relationship with his mother was both uneven and frustrating. As Doris Kearns points out:

[T]he "love" whose experience, denial or withdrawal is basic to the configuration of a given psychic structure must be, psychoanalysts tell us, perceived as a response to one's own being, unqualified by success or failure, by mental or physical defects, or by relationships with the external world. When this fundamental love is denied, or, as in Johnson's case, attached to external performance, then no recognition of personal qualities and gifts, such as integrity, warmth, energy and talent can suffice to satisfy inward needs. Performance alone must be continually displayed since past effectiveness is swiftly erased and soon counts for nothing at all.[198]

Striving hard to please his mother, in part by greatly outstripping the meager accomplishments of his father, Johnson set lofty goals for himself and labored hard to achieve power and domination. Failure on his part might result in rejection, a fear that plagued him throughout his life and periodically made him ill. As Dallek wrote, "he was a difficult, overbearing personality who struggled with inner demons that drove and tormented him. He had to be the best, outshine all the competition, and win at almost any cost."[199]

Once again, the work of Otto Fenichel affords us with a pertinent explanation for Lyndon Johnson's inner demons. As noted in Chapter 4, Fenichel wrote of the "internalization of the mother" and warned that some individuals are always subconsciously sensitive to situations which might result in the loss of their mother's affection and approval and, at the same time, to opportunities which might win it. They anticipate the likely reaction of others to their behavior, linking those reactions to those of their mother. "A portion of their ego," he wrote, "has become an 'inner mother,' threatening a possible withdrawal of affection."[200]

At the beginning of his political career, Lyndon's mother had written to her "darling boy," telling him that "I expect great things of you."[201] At the end of his political career, it was almost inevitable that Johnson would conclude his memoirs by writing that he had achieved the greatest of those great things—"the majesty and the power and splendor of the Presidency"—and that he had given it everything that was in him.[202] Nothing less was expected of him and nothing less would be accepted.[203] After all, as his mother once explained, at Lyndon's birth, the earth itself had listened.

Chapter SEVEN
Scars in the Teflon:
Ronald Reagan

n 20 January 1981, Ronald Reagan became the oldest man ever inaugurated as President of the United States. At the time, he was just three weeks short of his seventieth birthday. Reagan's physical appearance, however, seemed to belie his age. His hair was thick and dark, he walked with a spring in his step, and he was erect and well built. He seemed a robust and healthy chief executive. Indeed, in sharp contrast with Jimmy Carter, his immediate predecessor, Reagan appeared to be so blessed with good luck that his administration became known as the "Teflon presidency." Whereas other presidents have aged noticeably in the White House, Reagan seemed largely unscarred by the cares of office. He retired in 1989 looking essentially the same as he had eight years earlier and appearing, as one former aide wrote, to have discovered the "fountain of youth."[1]

During his presidency, however, Reagan underwent two life-threatening medical emergencies—an assassination attempt in 1981 and surgery for cancer in 1985—which significantly affected his administration. The success of his first term, in which key portions of his legislative program were passed, was largely owing to the assassination attempt and Reagan's heroic response to it. On the other hand, it is likely that his cancer surgery contributed to the Iran-Contra scandal which devastated his second term. Throughout his two terms in office, as throughout his life, Ronald Reagan responded to events and emergencies in an unconscious effort to transcend the dark shadow cast on him from birth as the child of an alcoholic father.

Early History

On 6 February 1911, Ronald Reagan was born to John and Nelle Reagan in Tampico, Illinois. He weighed ten pounds at birth, and his delivery was so difficult that his mother was advised to have no more children.[2] When his father saw his second son for the first time, he said that he looked like "a fat little Dutchman," and the nickname "Dutch" attached to Ronald Reagan from that time forward. Since as a child he did not think the name Ronald was "rugged enough" for a "red-blooded American boy,"[3] he encouraged people always to call him by his nickname.

Of Irish background, Jack Reagan was a Catholic who did not practice his religion. His firstborn son, Neil, claimed that he had not known that his father was a Catholic until he, Neil, was a young adult.[4] Jack's Catholicism was unusual in the heavily Protestant section of Illinois where the Reagans lived, and seems to have caused problems for his younger son. Dutch claimed to have engaged in fistfights over his father's religion.[5]

Reagan's mother, Nelle, was a member of the Disciples of Christ Church, into which he was baptized at the age of twelve. A descendant of Scots-English parents, she was an inveterate do-gooder who brought food to families in need and visited the sick and the incarcerated.[6] Described by one of her granddaughters as a fiery Bible thumper,[7] Nelle played a positive role in her younger son's life. It was she who held the family together in difficult times.[8] Although she had never progressed beyond elementary school, Dutch viewed his mother as fundamentally wise, and his feelings toward her were unambiguously positive. His brother once remarked, "I always say that Ronald is my mother's boy and I'm my father's boy."[9]

In one important respect, Ronald Reagan clearly was his mother's boy. She enjoyed putting on morality plays that projected the tenets of her faith,[10] and Ronald frequently played a role in them. It is likely that he acquired his love of being on center stage from his mother, a frustrated actress whose first love was performing. When one of his performances was applauded, Ronald relished the experience, writing that "for a kid suffering childhood pangs of insecurity, the applause was music."[11] This feeling was enhanced by Reagan's experiences as a lifeguard from his fifteenth to his twenty-second summer, a job he loved because the guard stand "was like a stage. Everyone had to look at me."[12] For the rest of his life, Ronald Reagan sought career paths that would satisfy the craving for attention and applause that may well have been planted in him by his mother, the center of his childhood universe. It was his mother about whom Ronald would talk in future years, almost never his father; and when she died in 1962, it took the normally cheerful Reagan several months to bounce back.[13]

Ronald's attitude toward his father was wholly ambivalent. Maureen Reagan later described the relationship between her father and grandfather as "strange."[14] The strangeness was due to the fact that while Ronald knew that he was supposed to respect his father, he nevertheless felt repulsion at his father's often out-of-control drinking problem. An unreformed alcoholic, Jack went on drinking binges throughout his adult life. The family was forced to relocate frequently during Ronald's boyhood, largely because of Jack's drinking. The Reagans moved from Tampico to Chicago when Ronald was three, to Galesburg when he was four, to Monmouth when he was seven, back to Tampico when he was eight, and to Dixon when he was nine. While living in Dixon, the Reagan family moved on five separate occasions.[15] It is not surprising that a child would feel resentment toward a parent who was responsible for such upheaval.

Also, in large part due to Jack's excessive drinking, the Reagan family was not financially secure. Jack and Nelle never owned their own home, and money was hard to come by. Ronald's clothing came to him as hand-me-downs from his brother after the latter had outgrown them. Yet years later, the former President would write that he had not known that his family was poor in comparison with others in town, or that they had been at all disadvantaged.[16]

Reagan tended to view his boyhood through rose-colored glasses, remembering the days of his youth as being a "sweet and idyllic" Huck Finn/Tom Sawyer existence.[17] In reality, those days were filled with jarring unpleasantness. Jack's alcoholic binges, which would continue until two weeks before his death in 1941 at the age of fifty-eight, took a heavy toll on the members of his family, including his younger son. One of Ronald Reagan's most powerful memories was that of finding his father lying drunk and unconscious in the snow outside their house one cold and snowy night. Dutch was eleven years old at the time, and the memory clearly lasted a lifetime. In his 1981 autobiography he discussed this sad incident, describing his father's arms as "outstretched as though he were crucified" and his hair as "soaked with melting snow," and poignantly explaining his own feelings:

I stood over him for a minute or two. I wanted to let myself in the house and go to bed and pretend he wasn't there. Oh, I wasn't ignorant of his weakness. I don't

know at what age I knew what the occasional absences or the loud noises in the night
meant but up till now my mother . . . or my brother handled the situation and I was
a child in bed with the privilege of pretending sleep. [18]

Reagan wrote again of this night in his 1990 postpresidential memoirs
and this time displayed a young boy's embarrassment at his father's public
drunkenness: "When I tried to wake him he just snored—loud enough,
I suspected, for the whole neighborhood to hear him. So I grabbed a piece
of his overcoat, pulled it and dragged him into the house, then put him
to bed and never mentioned the incident to my mother." [19]

Although his mother always urged her sons not to be angry toward
their father since his alcoholism was a sickness beyond his control, [20]
Ronald clearly viewed his father as a weak man. After all, he could not
help but notice that while his father stressed that every individual must
stand on his own two feet, he himself often was unable to stand at all.
And when the politically liberal father told his sons that all men are
created equal, and that it is man's own ambition that determines what
happens to him the rest of his life, [21] young Dutch could not help but
realize that by his own teaching, his father was branding himself a failure.

Also, despite Nelle's advice to her sons to be patient and understanding
toward their alcoholic father, Ronald could not fail to see and even hear
her anger toward her husband when his drinking got out of hand. The
young boy heard "some pretty fiery arguments through the walls of our
house." [22] Ronald later wrote that Jack was not the kind of alcoholic who
was abusive to his family, but could become "pretty surly"; and that he
and his brother heard "a lot of cursing from my parents' bedroom when
my mother went after him for his drinking." [23]

During his early years, Ronald Reagan was essentially in good health
but for several physical indispositions. His first serious illness was bronchial pneumonia at the age of three. As a boy, he was extremely near-
sighted and had trouble seeing the blackboard even from the front row of
his classroom; only through his near photographic memory did he manage to keep up his grades. One day he happened to put on his mother's
glasses and "shouted with delight." [24] He was fitted for glasses of his own
but hated the look of the huge black horn-rimmed spectacles. When he
got to Hollywood, he changed to contact lenses, which at that time "were
big, rigid and fit over the whites of your eyes like a pair of football
helmets." [25] At the time Dutch Reagan entered his teenage years, he was
short and thin. Four years later, however, he had grown to nearly six feet

and had gained some thirty pounds,[26] much closer to the image he would later project on screen.

Likely in reaction to his home life, Dutch was a somewhat introverted, introspective boy who spent long hours in his own company, reading or playing with toy soldiers. Looking back many years later, his older brother remembers him being quiet and "not one you would expect would end up as an actor or a politician, even."[27]

In 1930, Reagan entered Eureka College, a seventy-two-year-old Illinois school financially backed by the Disciples of Christ Church, on a needy-student scholarship which paid a portion of his tuition. One of the most significant things to happen to Reagan at Eureka occurred early in his freshman year. He became part of a strike committee formed in opposition to the college president's plans to economize by firing faculty and cutting programs. The president was finally forced to resign; more important, Reagan gave a speech to the college community and discovered that "an audience has a feel to it and in the parlance of the theater, the audience and I were together."[28] He later wrote, "[F]or the first time in my life, I felt my words reach out and grab an audience and it was exhilarating."[29] Soon afterward, Dutch joined the Eureka Dramatics Society and, by the time he was a senior, had made up his mind to become an actor. In his senior year, he was also elected president of his class. These two paths—acting and politics—converged for Reagan while he was still in college, as they would again and again throughout his life.

SHOW BUSINESS

After graduation from Eureka, Reagan sought a job in Chicago as a radio announcer. This was in the midst of the Depression when jobs of all kinds were hard to come by, and the recent graduate encountered rejection because he was both young and inexperienced. He later wrote that his spirits hit bottom and he felt completely defeated by his unsuccessful job search.[30] Following one station manager's suggestion that he acquire experience by working at a station "in the sticks,"[31] Reagan applied for a job at station WOC in Davenport, Iowa. This led to his being hired to broadcast football games on a part-time basis, which, in turn, led to a full-time job as a staff announcer.

When WOC folded, Reagan moved on to station WHO in Des Moines, where he spent four years and he established a reputation as an articulate and colorful sports announcer. He was able to broadcast sports events from a booth, using brief wire-service bulletins and pretending that he was witnessing events as they occurred on the playing field. At times he would "invent" action in order to keep hold of his audience, once going so far as to describe a fictitious tussle between two young boys over a foul ball.[32] Reagan was so believable as a storyteller that those who listened to their radio sets never suspected the deception. As one observer suggests, this shows "just how comfortable he can be with illusion."[33]

In 1937, Reagan was given a screen test by Warner Brothers and then put under contract. During his movie career, he played in more than fifty mostly "B" movies, many of which he admitted were "pretty poor."[34] He consistently sought roles that depicted him as a hero and only once played a screen villain. Of all his movie roles, he felt that his performance in *King's Row* (1940), in which he played a man whose legs had been amputated, was his finest, and believed that it elevated him to the rank of real movie star. The title of his first autobiography—*Where's the Rest of Me?*—came from that film, a sign of the high regard in which he held it.

During the Second World War, Ronald Reagan was assigned to Army Air Force Intelligence, where he made training films and documentaries. Although he achieved the rank of captain, he declined to be considered for promotion to major, since he had not been involved in military combat.[35]

In 1947, Reagan became president of the Screen Actors Guild. He served in that post for five terms and made his mark principally by fighting efforts by the Communist party to make inroads into the entertainment industry. With Reagan's support, the guild voted to require noncommunist affidavits of its own members. At the same time, he became an informant for the FBI.[36]

It was also in 1947 that Reagan experienced two serious health problems. First, he contracted viral pneumonia while filming *That Hagen Girl* with his co-star Shirley Temple and had to be rushed by ambulance to the hospital. He was so ill with fever and chills that he later claimed that he had decided simply to stop breathing; a nurse coaxed him into resisting the temptation. Reagan lost seventeen pounds during this ordeal and was plagued for many weeks by lack of strength, shortness of breath, and clammy perspiration.[37] While he was in the hospital, his first wife, Jane Wyman, gave birth to a premature baby girl who died after only one day of life. This would have been the couple's third child. Their first, a daughter named Maureen, was born in 1941; and they adopted a son, Michael, soon after his birth in 1945.

Not long after, Reagan suffered a multiple fracture of his left thigh while playing in a charity baseball game. The injury was a bad one, with his bone shattered into six separate fragments. He had to spend two uncomfortable months in traction and additional months in a cast, and then to wear a steel and leather brace, use crutches and canes, and spend almost a year in therapy before his leg would function and his knee recover most of its ability to bend.[38]

To make matters worse, while Reagan was in the hospital he had an allergic reaction to his bandages, which caused his eyes to swell, his teeth to hurt at even the slightest touch, and his skin to itch and peel. For a week he received massive doses of histamines that kept him only semi-conscious. Weeks of discomfort followed, since the bandages to which he was allergic could not be removed. During the same period, he suffered severe muscle spasms whenever he tried to move.[39]

Reagan's medical difficulties were not his only problems in the late 1940s. His marriage to Jane Wyman came to an end in 1948, and his career as a movie star went into decline. Though he was still only in his thirties, the better roles began to go to other actors. With his movie career fading, he looked to television for salvation and in 1954 became host of the TV series, "General Electric Theater." For eight years he hosted this program, becoming a major television celebrity. As a spokesperson for General Electric, he visited GE plants and spoke to some 250,000 GE employees. Reagan later described his experience with General Electric as "not a bad apprenticeship for someone who'd someday enter political life."[40]

Soon after General Electric Theater was canceled in 1962, Reagan agreed to host and occasionally act in another series, "Death Valley Days." In one of the most momentous decisions of his life, he also agreed to co-chair Barry Goldwater's 1964 presidential campaign in California. During the summer and fall of that year, he spoke at many fund-raising functions and was finally asked by several major Republican contributors to deliver a nationwide television address on behalf of the Republican ticket.

Shortly before election day, Reagan made a speech for Goldwater that won considerable acclaim, electrifying conservatives and bringing in eight million dollars for Goldwater and the Republican party. As he later admitted, "That speech was one of the most important milestones in my life—another one of those unexpected turns in the road that led me in a path I never expected to take."[41]

GOVERNOR OF CALIFORNIA

Within six weeks after delivering his Goldwater speech, Ronald Reagan was approached by a group of wealthy California businessmen and urged to run for governor in 1966. One biographer writes that, from that moment on, Reagan was thinking of the presidency.[42] Although he himself denies such lofty ambitions, saying that he even hoped another candidate for governor would be found, Reagan announced on 4 January 1966 that he would run. He won a bitter primary campaign against the former San Francisco mayor George Christopher by a 2-to-1 margin and then went on to defeat the incumbent governor, the Democrat Pat Brown, by a margin of 58 percent to 42 percent.

As governor, Reagan developed the management style that he would essentially follow as president. He was rarely involved in the details of government and instead presided over his administration in a detached, even remote, fashion. Whenever feasible, cabinet secretaries tried to iron out their differences alone and then present them to him to ratify.[43] Only rarely did Reagan reject a decision the cabinet supported, a fact that magnified the role of the cabinet but diminished that of the governor in the policy-making process.

The governor's associates recognized that Reagan's approach to politics was both nonchalant and anecdotal. He had no intention or inclination to read long position papers or voluminous written reports, preferring instead brief memoranda. The cabinet secretary, William Clark, directed all department heads to boil down their policy proposals to one-page mini-memos, each consisting of no more than four paragraphs.[44] One commentator has succinctly summed up Reagan's role as California governor:

> *In the Hoover Institution's Reagan archives, box after box contains the story of an administration full of controversy and often rich in ideas. But Reagan initiated few of them . . . not much is seen of Reagan's participation in those struggles, nor is his imprint on the vital internal debates that shaped his administration's policies.*[45]

Although removed from the day-to-day activities of his administration, Reagan could not completely escape its pressures. After just a few months in office, he developed a painful stomach ulcer. When his stomach first began to hurt, he told his wife, Nancy Davis—whom he had married in 1952 and with whom he had two children (Patti, born in 1952, and Ronald, born in 1958)—that "I spent thirteen years at Warner Brothers and they couldn't give me an ulcer, but I think I'm getting one now."[46] Reagan suspected that the ulcer might have begun to develop while he was contemplating the race for governor, but was convinced that the problems his administration had confronted in its early days, particularly the battles with the legislature and the campus unrest, contributed greatly to the problem. After a year of pain, during which he watched his diet and took a "daily dose of Maalox," the pain suddenly disappeared, and doctors could find no trace of the ulcer. Instead of attributing his recovery to his dietary regimen, however, Reagan suspected that the power of prayer—both his and those of his supporters—was responsible.[47] When he retired from the governorship in 1975, he was in excellent health, except for a growing deafness in both ears and severe allergies. Although almost sixty-five years of age, he reports that he "didn't feel old" and "never gave a thought to retiring."[48]

THE RACE FOR THE PRESIDENCY

Almost immediately after leaving the governorship, Ronald Reagan launched a serious bid for the 1976 Republican presidential nomination and, in so doing, had to do battle against an incumbent president of his own party, Gerald R. Ford. While he may have been reluctant to try to unseat a Republican incumbent, Reagan feared that, if he waited until 1980, he might be too old to become President.[49]

The battle between Ford and Reagan was extremely close, each man winning a string of primary and caucus victories. At the convention, Reagan received 1,070 delegate votes to Ford's 1,187. Although he failed to unseat Ford, Reagan came the closest in modern times to a successful intraparty challenge to a sitting president.

In 1980, Ronald Reagan made another bid for the Republican presidential nomination. Then sixty-nine years old, he was considered by many to be too old for the presidency. The only other man in American history who became president at such an advanced age was William Henry Harrison, and he had survived only one month in office. Although Reagan claimed that he didn't feel any older in 1980 than he had always felt,[50] the age issue was an important one in the campaign. Two astute observers wrote that "primary voters had never been confronted with a candidate with that much mileage on him and no one knew how they might react."[51]

Reagan's public persona did much to weaken such fears. He appeared much younger than his age and campaigned, in public at least, with vigor. In private, however, some observers found the former governor to be lethargic[52] and worn-out. The fact that he regularly went to bed by eight or nine o'clock in the evening[53] reinforced the insiders' view of his fragility and his dwindling energy reserves.

After winning the presidential nomination of his party, Ronald Reagan faced the incumbent but ill-starred Democrat Jimmy Carter. In their one televised debate, Carter tried hard to label Reagan as a dangerous right-wing extremist, but Reagan remained so cool, calm, and collected throughout the encounter that he emerged as a reasonable alternative to the beleaguered President. His genial retort ("There you go again") to Carter's negative comments about him became the single most memorable line of the entire debate, and was repeated again and again by all of the mass media. On election day, Ronald Reagan captured 51 percent of the popular vote and carried forty-four states with 489 electoral votes. On 20 January 1981, he was inaugurated the thirty-ninth President of the United States, just a few days short of his seventieth birthday.

The First Term: 1981–85

Early in Ronald Reagan's first term, he came dangerously close to death. On an early spring day, he was stalked and then shot by John Hinckley, a twenty-six-year-old man who fired his weapon repeatedly at the President in the hope of attracting the attention and winning the love of the movie star Jodie Foster. Just hours before trying to kill the President, Hinckley had written to Foster:

I would abandon the idea of getting Reagan in a second if I could only win your heart and live out the rest of my life with you. . . . The reason I'm going ahead with this attempt now is because I cannot wait any longer to impress you. I've got to do something now to make you understand in no uncertain terms that I am doing this all for your sake.[54]

What Hinckley did that spring day, of course, did not win Jodie Foster's heart or make it possible for him to live out his life with her. But his actions stunned the world, precipitated a grave medical crisis for the President of the United States, and left an indelible mark on Reagan's presidency.

THE ASSASSINATION ATTEMPT OF MARCH 1981

After little more than two months in the White House, Ronald Reagan came close to becoming the fifth American president to lose his life to an assassin. That he escaped that dubious distinction is due largely to the

Secret Service agent in charge of his security detail at the time and to the skillful care of the medical personnel at George Washington University Medical Center.

On 30 March 1981, President Reagan delivered an address to the Construction Trades Council at the Hilton Hotel in Washington, D.C. Shortly before 2:30 P.M., as he left the hotel, smiling and waving to reporters and onlookers gathered outside, he suddenly heard what sounded to him like two or three firecrackers going off to his left. As he put it himself, it was "just a small fluttering sound, *pop, pop, pop.*"[55]

He did not see his assailant or realize that he had been shot. Nor did he know that his press secretary, Jim Brady, had sustained a grievous head wound or that a Secret Service agent and a District of Columbia policeman had also been hit. What he did know was that the head of his Secret Service detail, Jerry Parr, grabbed him around the waist, pushed him into the rear of his limousine, and then threw himself on top of his body.

The President, landing face down atop the armrest in the back seat, felt a pain in his upper back he later described as "unbelievable" and "excruciating."[56] He told Parr, with some feeling, that he had broken one of his ribs. Parr lifted himself from the President's body, gave him a quick onceover, and ordered the driver to return immediately to the White House. When Reagan tried to sit up, he found himself almost paralyzed with pain; and when he coughed, he saw that the palm of his hand was covered with dark-red blood. This led him to believe that his supposedly broken rib had punctured one of his lungs.

When Parr saw the blood, he made a decision doctors later claimed saved the President's life. He ordered the limousine to proceed not to the White House but to George Washington University Medical Center. The President was bleeding internally; and, as was soon discovered, his blood loss was massive. Reagan reports that his handkerchief was so soaked with blood that Parr gave him his to use. Also, as his car sped to the hospital, the President experienced difficulty in breathing. Unable to get enough air, he became frightened, even "a little panicky."[57]

Upon arriving at the hospital, the President, ever mindful of his media image, walked inside unaided. However, as he entered the emergency room, he was in a state of incipient shock and collapsed.[58] He was picked up and carried into a trauma unit, where his clothes were cut from his body as he complained to medical personnel, "I feel so bad."[59]

Since his bleeding was largely internal, with only a few drops of blood found on his shirt, no one knew at the time that he had been wounded. In fact, several of his aides and even the White House physician Daniel

Ruge, who was present in the trauma unit, feared that he might have suffered a heart attack.[60] Then, however, Dr. Wesley Powell, listening to the President's chest, detected crackling noises in one of his lungs and diminished breathing sounds, indications that air was not flowing in and out easily.[61] Powell then noticed a bullet-entry wound, between the size of a nickel and a dime but in the shape of a narrow slit, under the President's left armpit. There was no visible exit wound, which meant that the bullet was still lodged somewhere in his body. Immediately, he was given a tetanus shot to guard against infection and muscle spasms.

Dr. Benjamin Aaron, head of cardiothoracic surgery at George Washington University Medical Center, reports that when Reagan first arrived in the emergency room, he had no recordable blood pressure. He had been hemorrhaging into his chest cavity and may have lost nearly half of his body's blood supply.[62] His left lung had collapsed, causing the breathing difficulties that were so upsetting to him. He was breathing rapidly, but otherwise Aaron found that his vital signs were good. An endotracheal tube was inserted, and transfusions were begun at once. Soon the President's blood pressure began to rise, an absolutely crucial development. Had his blood loss continued without replacement for even five or ten minutes longer, he likely would have died, possibly of a heart attack or even a stroke.[63]

Dr. Joseph Giordano, head of the hospital's trauma unit, then made an incision between the President's ribs and inserted a tube so that the blood building up there could be drained off and X rays taken.[64] A substantial amount of blood was expelled through the chest tube, but the bleeding did not stop. Also, the dark ruby cast of his blood suggested to some of his physicians that the pulmonary artery had been damaged.[65]

The X rays disclosed that a piece of metal had penetrated the President's lung. Initially, doctors were not able to determine whether this constituted the entire bullet or was only a fragment. When they tried to learn from the Secret Service, and then from the FBI, what caliber of bullet had struck the President, they were told erroneously that it had been a .38.[66] This was bad news for the operating team, since the piece of metal seen on the X-ray screen was too small to be a .38-caliber bullet and thus must be a bullet fragment. In an effort to locate the rest of the bullet inside the President's body, Dr. David Rockoff, head of thoracic radiology at George Washington Medical Center, took X rays of his abdomen, but with negative results.[67] Dr. Giordano then made an incision below Reagan's navel and ran a liter of saline solution into his abdomen. When the fluid was withdrawn and analyzed, it was without traces of blood, leading doctors to conclude that no damage had been done to the President's abdominal area.★

After the bullet was removed from the body of the Secret Service agent who had also been shot during the assassination attempt, doctors learned it had been fired from a .22-caliber revolver after all. This meant that at least one needless procedure had been conducted on the President's body, since the abdominal X rays would not have been necessary if only a .22-caliber bullet had been involved. Also, the news about the actual caliber of the bullet caused one member of the medical team to fear some government agency complicity in the assassination attempt.

While doctors now knew that the piece of metal in the President's body constituted the entire bullet, they were later dismayed to learn that the bullet fired was a type known as a "devastator" and contained a capsule of lead azide. Lead azide is a toxic, volatile substance which usually produces an explosion on impact. Although the bullet had not exploded inside the President, doctors had to wonder whether the lead azide had seeped out into his body.[69]

The immediate objective of the three-hour surgery performed on the President was to stop his internal bleeding rather than to find the bullet lodged somewhere in his lung. Doctors have indicated that the President could have lived with the bullet inside his body, but since there was danger of its migrating and/or becoming a source of infection, a subsequent operation might well have become necessary to remove it. Also, knowing that the public would be concerned if the bullet were left inside the President's body, the doctors decided to try to remove it at once.

The President was anesthetized with a combination of valium, pentothal, and a synthetic narcotic.[70] A six-inch incision was made in his left chest, and rib spreaders were used so that surgeons could explore the chest cavity. (One of the resident physicians, Dr. David Gens, later described this procedure as among the most painful from which to recover.)[71] A sizable blood clot was encountered almost immediately, and blood was flowing from a wound in the President's lung. Dr. Aaron and his associates found that Reagan's lung wound was large enough for a thumb to fit inside. Aaron probed the damaged lung tissue and, after some difficulty, located and removed the bullet. After striking the presidential limousine, it had narrowed down to the shape of a flat, jagged-edged disk before penetrating the President's body. The flattened piece of metal had hit the President's seventh rib and then entered his lung, tumbling down through

★The procedure performed by Dr. Giordano is known as peritoneal lavage.[68]

it and coming to rest less than an inch from his heart.[72] Fortunately, the capsule of lead azide was still intact, which meant that the substance had not flowed into the President's body.

The fact that the bullet was lodged so close to Reagan's heart was not considered of particularly great moment by his doctors, since patients have been known to survive a bullet wound to the heart itself. The principal danger to Reagan came from his severe hemorrhaging and blood loss. Once the bleeding was brought under control, doctors were optimistic that he would survive. In fact, once the President's blood pressure stabilized, at least some of his doctors felt that he was in no real further danger.[73]

After the surgery was completed and Reagan transferred to the recovery room, Dr. Ruge met with the head of the White House political liaison office at the time, Lyn Nofziger, and the assistant hospital director, Dr. Dennis O'Leary, to discuss how to disseminate information about the President. Contrary to the experience of other administrations where there had been virtual power struggles over the flow of information about the President's condition, this time there was none. Dr. Ruge indicated at once that the George Washington University Hospital should serve as the official conduit of medical bulletins about the President, since the hospital was entrusted with his care. Each morning during Reagan's hospitalization, Ruge would confer with Dr. Aaron, other presidential physicians, and Dr. O'Leary on the President's condition. On the basis of those discussions, O'Leary would prepare and issue a statement to the press.[74] Later, hospital personnel were entirely laudatory of Dr. Ruge's performance during this period, commending him for avoiding any jealous safeguarding of his own "turf" and for allowing members of the hospital medical team to "do their thing."

Although several initial news reports on 30 March had been erroneous—for example, when Chris Wallace of NBC announced that Reagan was undergoing open-heart surgery[75]—subsequent bulletins were considerably more accurate. As has usually been the case with presidential illnesses, however, the positive was clearly accentuated. News releases issued by the hospital revealed none of the concern that some of his doctors later admitted they had experienced at various stages of the President's care.

News of the attempted assassination dominated the airwaves that spring afternoon. At first, it seemed to be 1963 all over again—shots fired at a president, pandemonium at the scene, the rush to the hospital, uncertain news reports of his condition. But this time there were important differences. The President was still alive and, although wounded, was cracking jokes to his wife and doctors. Reagan's gallant behavior helped assure the country that this time all would be well. And even family members were highly sensitive to the message that their actions would telegraph to the country, and took care to communicate only what they intended. The President's elder son, Michael, has reported that the Reagan children did not fly from California to Washington until nighttime "because if we were seen rushing to the airport, the press would have known that Dad was in serious condition."[76] The First Lady explained her reason for not spending the first night at the hospital by noting that if she had, "I'd be sending out a message to the world that Ronnie's condition was critical. It was, of course, but at that moment I didn't want people to know."[77]

Although the nation and the world received the message that Reagan was doing beautifully and being gallant in the face of adversity, enormous tension and uncertainty permeated the government itself. Initially, key members of the White House staff had arrived at the hospital soon after receiving reports of the shooting, and members of the cabinet had gathered in the Situation Room at the White House. Aides could only wait for word of the President's condition, not knowing how badly he had been wounded or whether he would live or die. Treasury Secretary Donald Regan later revealed, however, that "no one of us at any time thought that the wound was fatal, although we were all concerned about the President's ability to recuperate quickly."[78] As I will later discuss, the tensions and uncertainties of the moment led to some emotional flare-ups by administration officials, particularly by Secretary of State Alexander Haig; and those flare-ups would have lasting effects.

Despite the gravity of the President's condition and the fact that he was under anesthesia for three hours, no serious thought was given to invoking the Twenty-fifth Amendment.[79] When key aides met with Dr. Aaron to discuss Reagan's prognosis, they never once mentioned the Twenty-fifth Amendment to him.[80] However, in discussions with Dr. Giordano, they asked how effectively the President could be expected to function after the surgery, and Giordano saw this as an unspoken inquiry whether power should be transferred to the vice president, George Bush.[81]

Dr. Ruge met occasionally with members of the President's staff as well as with the cabinet and the congressional leaders in order to brief them on the President's condition. While he was never asked specifically about invocation of the Twenty-fifth Amendment, Ruge believes that it should definitely have been invoked: "[T]here was a period of 10–15 hours when Ronald Reagan was unable to function as President and could not have responded to a crisis. This was the period of time when the Amendment clearly should have been in effect."[82]

Visitors to the President's bedside may well have agreed with Ruge. Deaver reports that he looked in on Reagan while he slept, and "was shaken by how bad he looked. His skin was gray and drawn, his breathing labored." Deaver admits that he told his wife afterward that the President "will never be the same."[83] House Speaker Thomas P. O'Neill writes that he was shocked when he visited Reagan in his hospital room: "His condition seemed much more serious than what had been announced. He was clearly exhausted and in pain. I stayed only a moment as he obviously was in no shape to receive visitors."[84] And the deputy White House assistant Helene Van Damm, who visited Reagan the day after his surgery, was "not quite prepared for how weak he looked. Though there was some color in his cheeks, his eyes were lacking their usual light. It was obviously too painful for him to speak."[85] Even Defense Secretary Weinberger expressed shock at Reagan's appearance: "[F]or the first time in all the years I had known him, he looked exhausted and very ill. His face seemed almost collapsed."[86]

Despite Reagan's condition at the time, the administration's high command decided, for a variety of reasons, not to invoke the Twenty-fifth Amendment. It would have made the President's condition seem particularly critical, something his aides wanted very much to avoid. It had already been determined that the vice president and the secretary of defense would, under the National Command Authority System, assume the commander in chief's powers in the event of any military crisis during Reagan's physical inability, so there was no real worry on that score. And White House staffers did not want to involve the cabinet in the determination of presidential inability, as one section of the amendment provided. At least one high-level aide reportedly feared that "the Cabinet might actually seize the initiative."[87]

At the time of the shooting, Vice President Bush was in Texas—having gone there to unveil a national historic plaque at the Fort Worth hotel where John F. Kennedy had stayed the night before he was assassinated. Bush's plane was just leaving Fort Worth for Austin when he learned from a Secret Service agent of the attempt on Reagan's life. Soon after, Bush was called on open telephone lines by the secretary of state and the secretary of treasury, and urged to return to Washington immediately. He then received a coded teletype message which, when decoded, told him that Reagan had been shot and was undergoing emergency surgery.

Bush was advised by his air force military aide to fly to Washington and continue by helicopter to the White House—a step that would have dramatically reassured the country and demonstrated to the world that the executive branch was still functioning. Bush rejected the suggestion, however, telling his military aide that "only the President lands on the south lawn." Even though he was giving up "good television," Bush insisted that normal procedures be followed: his helicopter would land near the vice-presidential residence, and then he would drive to the White House.[88]

The vice president readily agreed that it would be appropriate for him to meet with the cabinet and the National Security Council, but felt that he must follow a basic rule: "The country can have only one President at a time, and the Vice President is not the one."[89]

At about 7:30 P.M., Bush arrived at the White House and presided over a crisis-management meeting in the Situation Room. He announced that he would hold cabinet and congressional leadership meetings on the following day, and told those present that "the more normal things are, the better. . . . We want to make the government function as normally as possible."[90] Bush's behavior during the crisis was widely praised. Education Secretary Terrell Bell went so far as to refer to him as "a perfect Vice President."[91]

It was around this same time that President Reagan awakened from anesthesia. He was on intravenous antibiotics, and his vital signs were being closely monitored. He had tubes in his chest for drainage, and Dr. Samuel Spagnolo, director of the hospital's Division of Pulmonary Diseases, was adjusting and controlling the volume ventilator which was being used to assist the President's breathing and provide additional oxygen.[92] At this point, Reagan required up to "80 percent oxygen compared to 20 percent in normal air."[93] The lower lobes of both his lungs had partially collapsed, and the President was in great discomfort.[94] He felt that he was not getting enough oxygen, and even signaled to family members that he could not breathe. After receiving an additional dosage of morphine, the President relaxed somewhat, and his breathing began to improve. Several hours later, he was taken off the ventilator and maintained on oxygen instead.[95] The First Lady found that after the ventilator tube had been removed from the President's throat, his condition was "slightly better," but reports that hospital personnel had to turn him onto his stomach every four hours and pound him on his back to "shake out the fluids and keep them from building up in his lungs."[96] He did manage—however shakily—to sign a minor piece of agriculture legislation on the morning after the shooting, an act that aides hoped would reassure the country.

Gradually, Reagan's blood oxygen levels began to improve, a sign that his lungs were functioning more normally. X rays taken on 1 April showed that his left lower lobe had partially expanded. Despite the improvement in his condition, doctors remained somewhat concerned about the level of oxygen in the President's blood and kept him on supplemental oxygen for about a week. There was some concern also about a small growth on Reagan's vertebra which the X-ray pictures had revealed, but this was later diagnosed as being of only minor significance.[97]

Although the President was clearly recuperating, he was considered to be in critical condition for several days.[98] Four days after undergoing surgery, in fact, he suffered something of a relapse: he began to cough up small amounts of blood, and his temperature rose to 102–103 °F. Dr. Ruge considered the temperature elevation normal for patients who had undergone surgery and transfusions, and suspected that clotted blood in Reagan's body may have become unclotted after an interval of several days, giving the appearance of renewed bleeding.[99] Dr. Giordano indicated that the elevation in temperature was "expected for this kind of operation," and said he felt "no real concern" over this apparent relapse; and Dr. Rockoff viewed the situation as "entirely manageable."[100]

Dr. Aaron and Dr. Spagnolo, however, admitted that the President's seeming relapse made them somewhat apprehensive. Dr. Aaron feared that a major blood vessel in Reagan's lung might have opened and bleeding begun again. Although Reagan had not needed lung resectioning at the time of his surgery, Aaron worried that he would have to operate on the President a second time and remove his lower lobe.[101] Also concerned that Reagan's bronchial tubes may have been filling with blood, Aaron decided to perform a bronchoscopy on the President. Although this procedure causes considerable discomfort, Reagan agreed to only minimal sedation since the tense international situation at the time required the commander in chief to remain conscious and alert. The test revealed that Reagan's bronchial tubes were clear of blood.

Dr. Spagnolo believed that the reappearance of high fever three nights after surgery and the renewed coughing up of blood were likely signs of infection, and recommended that a complete fever workup—consisting of a battery of blood, sputum, and urine tests—be conducted at once. Other members of the President's medical team seemed to resist this suggestion, until Spagnolo threatened to resign from the case.[102] Shortly thereafter, the workup was begun, and Reagan subjected to a range of medical tests. Although no bacteria were detected in the President's body, Spagnolo remained convinced that he was suffering from infection. Reagan was put on antibiotics (penicillin and tobramycin) as well as Tylenol in order to deal with this probable infection and to lessen the danger of pneumonia.

Spagnolo also recommended at this time that a number of outside specialists in various medical subfields be brought in to look the President over, but found that his suggestion "went nowhere." Medical access to Reagan remained tightly controlled and limited, a fact that Spagnolo considered unwise. He was convinced that "outside consultants should have been brought into the case simply to be on the side of safety and prudence."[103] Somewhat ironically, it was around the time that Spagnolo's recommendation for outside specialists was being ignored that some of Reagan's closest associates began to wonder whether "the Chief" would ever fully recover, and quietly reconsidered their decision not to invoke the Twenty-fifth Amendment.

The President's older daughter, Maureen, has since written that when Reagan suffered his relapse, he was "as close to death's door as I'd ever care to see him," and that "one look at him a week after the shooting and you'd know this was no routine recuperation."[104] Despite her fears and those of the White House staff, Reagan had not suffered a major setback and responded well to antibiotic therapy. His bleeding soon stopped, and his fever broke within a week. So well did his recuperation proceed that doctors decided that he would soon be able to leave the hospital and return to the White House.

Throughout his hospital stay, Reagan received only mild pain medication in addition to antibiotics. Initially, he was given small amounts of morphine, but this was replaced with Percocet, a mild pain medication, and Tylenol. The President's pain threshold was high, and he managed quite well on only mild sedation. Except for the period when he was under anesthesia, his mental processes were not materially affected by any medication he received.[105] The antibiotics, however, did contribute to a loss of appetite, and the President's weight dropped noticeably. Despite efforts by the First Lady to have his favorite foods brought from the White House to the hospital, Reagan had little interest in eating. However, after he stopped receiving the antibiotics, his appetite began to improve, and food tasted good again for the first time since the shooting.[106]

On 11 April, the President returned to the White House. He was able to walk unassisted from his car into the mansion, providing photographers with an excellent photo opportunity. Once back inside, Reagan never used oxygen again. He did use a respirex machine or, as it is called, an "incentive respirator" to expand his lung capacity, but needed no machine to inhale.[107] Since a portion of the President's left lung had been damaged, he was told to engage in a regular exercise program to help him regain his full lung capacity. The President proved to be a good patient, exercising for an hour every day. He had been in sound physical condition prior to the assassination attempt but afterward managed to add to his chest an inch and a half of muscle[108] and increase his biceps size as well.

Initially, the President followed a light schedule of work in the White House. For the first time since childhood, he took afternoon naps, a practice he followed for a month after leaving the hospital. He often met with his aides and even attended a National Security Council meeting dressed in pajamas and slippers, and confined himself for some three weeks to the living quarters. He said that he preferred working in his living quarters rather than in the Oval Office because he could make telephone calls to members of Congress without bothering to get dressed.[109]

After three weeks, the President began spending time in his office; and in late April, he delivered a nationally televised address to Congress. His energy and stamina were reduced sharply, however, and occasionally he would be "exhausted to the point of incoherence."[110] It would take the President more than six months to fully recover.

Although one author has written that after his return to the White House, Reagan walked "with the hesitant step of an old man" and "was pale and disoriented,"[111] his doctors—Aaron, Giordano, Rockoff, Ruge, and Spagnolo—are unanimous in their view that the President's recovery went extremely well, particularly given his age, and that he had probably recuperated more quickly than most men of his age group would have, following such a traumatic experience. All five physicians agreed that reports to the contrary were considerably exaggerated.

After Reagan recovered from his gunshot wound, he served out his first term in essentially good health. Despite his age and his brush with death, the President still appeared to be both rugged and vigorous. There seemed to be no chance that he would decline to seek another term in the White House.

In an interview with Hugh Sidey of *Time* magazine on 25 July 1985, Reagan admitted that, having come face to face with his own mortality after being shot in 1981, he had resolved to do "those things that I believed in doing, for whatever time I have left."[112] Later he wrote that he never doubted that he would run again since he wanted "to preserve what we had accomplished."[113]

Reagan's lead in the polls throughout 1984 was substantial, and his victory seemed inevitable. The campaign, however, was not uneventful, and Republicans were given a major scare by the President himself when he lent credence to the charge that he was too old to continue to serve in the nation's highest office.

THE RE-ELECTION CAMPAIGN AND THE POLITICS OF AGE

At seventy-three, Ronald Reagan was not only the oldest chief executive in American history but would, if re-elected, retire from the White House just three weeks before his seventy-eighth birthday. The second oldest President, Dwight D. Eisenhower, had been only seventy at the time of his retirement in 1961.

It was extremely fortunate for the President that unlike 1980, he faced no Republican challengers in 1984, since he could "sit out" the caucus and primary season and conserve his strength for the fall campaign. He had a comfortable lead in the polls, and the percentage of voters who regarded him as physically equal to the job of President was noticeably higher than it had been in 1980 when he was four years younger.[114]

Close observers, however, thought that the President was beginning to fail. Some felt that his reaction time had slowed, and that his proclivity to "wander off into anecdotes of questionable relevance" had increased. Asked whether he was too old to serve another term, Reagan joked, "I'm really not this old. They mixed up the babies in the hospital."[115]

On 7 October in Louisville, Kentucky, Reagan engaged in a televised debate against his fifty-six-year-old opponent, the Democrat Walter Mondale. The age issue was no longer a laughing matter. In that encounter, Mondale was alert, articulate, and aggressive; Reagan confused, inarticulate, and befuddled. For the first time ever, Reagan appeared on the nation's television screens to be an old man, almost pathetic in his inability to defend his record coherently. When the President tried to invoke against Mondale the same line that had been so devastating against Carter in 1980—"There you go again"—Mondale turned it sharply to his own advantage. He replied, "Now, Mr. President, you said, 'There you go again.' Right? Remember the last time that you said that?" Reagan, looking thoroughly confused and disoriented, stammered, "Mmm, hmmm." Mondale continued, "You said it when President Carter said you were going to cut Medicare. . . . And what did you do right after the election? You went right out and tried to cut $20 billion out of Medicare."[116] Unable to recover, Reagan rambled, misspoke, became tangled in his thoughts. The President who had previously seemed strong and resolute came across to many viewers as a confused, failing, almost senile old man. Later he tried to explain his poor performance: "I had myself so filled up with trying to remember facts and figures for whatever might be raised that I wasn't really thinking and responding to what [Mondale] was saying there when we were face to face."[117] His good friend, Senator Paul Laxalt of Nevada, agreed that the President had been "brutalized and smothered with details."[118]

Mondale was stunned at Reagan's performance and reportedly told one of his aides, "This guy is gone. It's scary. He's really not up to it."[119] Other observers were not nearly so stunned. House Speaker Tip O'Neill said of Reagan's poor debate performance, "[T]o me, that was the real Ronald Reagan."[120] Journalist Mark Hertsgaard well summarized this school of thought: "Senility had not been Reagan's problem in Louisville; . . . his misstatements and non sequiturs were less a function of aging than of being deprived of his teleprompter and having to think for himself."[121]

Whatever its cause, the media gave Reagan's poor debate performance heavy coverage. The strongly Republican *Wall Street Journal* asked in a front-page story whether Reagan, the oldest President, was now showing his age. It quoted a professor of medicine who said that Reagan was moving from the "young-old" category to that of being "old-old." The *Journal* pointed out that 10 percent of seventy-five-year-olds suffer from senility, and cited two doctors who thought it appropriate for Reagan to take some sort of formal mental-impairment test, with a summary of its results made known to the public. It also quoted a pro-Reagan psychologist who said, "I am very concerned . . . about his inability to think on his feet, the disjointedness of his sentences and his use of the security blanket of redundancy. I'd be concerned to put him into a corporate presidency. I'd be all the more concerned to put him into the U.S. presidency."[122] Newspapers across the country soon followed suit, prominently featuring the "age issue."

The three networks each did a story on aging, none of which was flattering to Reagan. They interviewed physicians on the subject of senility and its effects on those who suffer from it. One story included a close-up of the President's hands, their age spots clearly visible. The networks also aired several times Reagan's closing remarks during the

Louisville debate: "The system is still where it was in regard to the uh, the uh, the uh, the uh, progressivity as we said."[123]

A Gallup poll found that 54 percent of viewers thought Mondale had won the debate; only 35 percent saw Reagan as the winner.[124] The ABC/Washington Post survey showed that Mondale had cut Reagan's lead from 18 to 12 points. Mondale's own polls disclosed strong gains (10 percent) in his positive ratings and sharp drops (9 percent) in his negatives.[125] One observer wrote, "Something even more unexpected than a Mondale victory had happened: a Reagan defeat of such proportions that people began to wonder if the whole calculus of the election might change."[126]

In his second debate with Mondale on 21 October in Kansas City, Reagan turned in a much stronger performance. He simply "looked better" than he had in Louisville, whereas Mondale looked tired and under stress. Ironically, the pivotal question for Reagan that night centered on the so-called age issue, and his clever response got his campaign back on track. Asked whether "there was any doubt in his mind that he would be able to function in such circumstances as when President Kennedy had to go for days on end with very little sleep during the Cuban missile crisis," Reagan replied, "I will not make age an issue in this campaign. I am not going to exploit, for political purposes, my opponent's youth and inexperience."[127] That quip became the "sound bite" that dominated the news media in subsequent days. The networks showed and reshowed it, newspapers trumpeted it, and the public enjoyed it. Even though the President's closing statement of the debate was rambling and somewhat incoherent, many voters no longer had doubts about his ability to function as President. He had joked; therefore, he could lead. Chief of Staff James Baker remarked, "The age issue is dead. The President did what he had to do."[128]

However slim Mondale's chances for victory had been before the Kansas City debate, they were essentially nonexistent after it. Surveys revealed that once voters had been reassured that Reagan had not drifted toward senility, they were happy to stick with him.[129] On election day, Ronald Reagan won a landslide victory, capturing 59 percent of the popular vote and carrying forty-nine states—a victory that would usher in a second term marred by serious illness and serious scandal.

The Second Term: 1985–89

In May 1984, just before the campaign for re-election got under way, a small, benign polyp was found in President Reagan's descending colon. A polyp is a protruding growth in mucous membrane tissue caused by inflammation and usually is harmless. After being removed, the President's polyp was examined by Dr. Francis Tedesco, a prominent gastrointestinal specialist who, in 1985, became president of the American Society of Gastrointestinal Endoscopy. Tedesco diagnosed Reagan's growth as a totally benign, inflammatory fibroid polyp, which was not dangerous in any way, and recommended that nothing further be done.[130]

Ten months later, blood was found in the President's stool, leading to the discovery of another polyp, this one in his ascending colon. At the advice of Dr. Edward Cattau, six additional stool examinations were conducted, but all proved negative. Cattau also recommended an examination of the President's entire colon, but none was performed for four months.[131] An administration official later explained that "in April he [Reagan] had a trip to make to Europe; in May there was something else. So we penciled it in for mid- to late June. But then the hostage thing [the hijacking of TWA flight 847 by Shia Muslim gunmen] broke out and so we put it off to now."[132]

On Friday, 12 July, the President underwent a forty-three-minute colonoscopic examination during which a small, harmless polyp was removed from his colon. The procedure also revealed in the President's lower right colon the existence of a large, ominous growth that caused his doctors considerable concern. Since it was as large as a golf ball, the chances of malignancy were high. Doctors told the First Lady that the growth was probably cancerous or, at best, precancerous, and indicated that they were concerned about the surrounding areas, particularly the liver.[133] So certain was the assistant White House physician, Dr. John Hutton, that the growth was malignant that he told the acting press secretary, Larry Speakes, on that Friday, "It's cancer, it's big, it's black, it's ugly."[134]

The President was advised that he could go on to Camp David for the weekend as he had planned, and return to the hospital on Monday for surgery or else remain in the hospital and have the surgery performed the next day. Since Reagan abhorred the medicine that cleans out one's system prior to removal of a polyp, he opted to remain in the hospital and have the surgery performed as soon as possible.

It may be of passing interest that Nancy Reagan's astrologer, Joan

Quigley, maintains that the discovery that the President did, in fact, need an operation came on 10 July, and that doctors had wanted to operate immediately, but that she had told the First Lady that the astrological signs were more favorable for 13 July.[135] Mrs. Reagan insists that the growth was discovered on 12 July and removed on the following day, and that astrology played no part in the process.[136] However, the acting press secretary's admission that it had become apparent the previous week that Reagan would have to undergo major surgery,[137] may give some credence to Quigley's interpretation of events.

In part because of the criticism leveled at the President for not invoking the Twenty-fifth Amendment after the 1981 assassination attempt, Reagan decided to delegate his powers to Vice President Bush during the time he would be under anesthesia and immediately afterward. At 10:32 A.M. on 13 July, he signed a letter to the Speaker of the House of Representatives and the President pro tempore of the Senate, and in it wrote:

I am about to undergo surgery during which time I will be briefly and temporarily incapable of discharging the Constitutional powers and duties of the office of the President of the United States.

After consultation with my counsel and the Attorney General, I am mindful of the provisions of Section 3 of the 25th Amendment to the Constitution and of the uncertainties of its application to such brief and temporary periods of incapacity. I do not believe that the drafters of this Amendment intended its application to situations such as the instant one.

Nevertheless, consistent with my long-standing arrangement with Vice President George Bush and not intending to set a precedent binding anyone privileged to hold this office in the future, I have determined and it is my intention and direction that Vice President George Bush should discharge those powers and duties in my stead commencing with the administration of anesthesia to me in this instance.[138]

Bush, then, was designated as acting president, but Reagan seemed strangely reluctant formally to invoke the Twenty-fifth Amendment. Despite his statement that he did not believe that the amendment pertained to such "brief and temporary periods of incapacity" as his then, this became, in fact, the first time that the amendment was actually invoked. At 11:30 A.M., when anesthesia began to be administered to the President, Vice President Bush became acting president of the United States.

Surgery commenced at 11:48 A.M. and lasted for two hours and fifty-three minutes. A large, flat growth, about two inches in diameter, was removed from the President's colon, along with two small polyps and two feet of the President's intestines.[139] Although it was not known then whether the large growth was cancerous, it was a villous adenoma, a type that often is. However, no sign of cancer was found elsewhere in the President's body.

Dr. Dale Oller, one of Reagan's surgeons, described the operation as a right hemicolectomy, and the procedure by which the President's bowel was sewn back together as an ileotransverse colostomy. Surgeons also performed an exploratory procedure involving the entire length of the President's intestines, as well as his liver, spleen, and other parts of his abdomen. The large polyp was located in the cecum, the first portion of the large intestine. Since the doctors were reasonably certain, pending the outcome of biopsy, that the growth was cancerous, they treated it as though it were. The section of the intestine which contained the polyp was not opened while it was inside the President's body. Also, surgeons used a technique known as "no touch" and, as Dr. Oller explained, did not touch the polyp until after it had been removed, to avoid any inadvertent spread of the cancer cells into other parts of the body.[140]

Oller and Reagan's other physicians were pleased with the way the operation had gone, the way the President had withstood it, and the ultimate prognosis. They said the President was "doing beautifully," and Dr. Stephen Rosenberg told reporters that even if cancer was present in the polyp that had been removed, the operation which the surgeons had performed "could in and of itself be curative."[141] Chemotherapy would not be used, since it has not been found to help in cases of colon cancer.

Immediately after the surgery, to help ease his pain, Reagan was given morphine by means of a new technique that does not impair mental function. When the anesthesia wore off, he could, according to one of his surgeons, make any decision that needed to be made.[142] The President admitted that he awoke from anesthesia "feeling groggy and confused." He had an incision that ran up past his navel to his chest, his body was "laced by tubes of various dimensions," and his "stomach felt as if it had really been through something."[143]

Shortly after 7:00 P.M., aides visited the recovery room, bringing with them the letter by which the President reclaimed the powers and duties of his office. Not surprisingly, the chief of staff found Reagan looking "pale and drawn."[144] He asked the President how he felt, and Reagan responded, "Fine. Fit as a fiddle."[145] Aides had determined that if he was able to read the letter they had given him to sign, he was sufficiently lucid to take back his powers from Bush. Initially, Reagan experienced difficulty in reading the letter, giving rise to the concern that he might be seriously impaired. But then he put on his glasses and read the letter perfectly.[146] At 7:22 P.M., he signed it, informing the Speaker of the House and the President pro tempore of the Senate: "Following up on my letter to you of this date, please be advised that I am able to resume the discharge of the Constitutional powers and duties of the Office of President of the United States. I have informed the Vice President of my determination and my resumption of these powers and duties."[147]

For several days the President was in a good deal of pain and unable to sleep properly. On Monday, he received the bad news that the large polyp, removed two days earlier, had indeed been cancerous. Although he was told by his doctors that they had gotten it all, Reagan undoubtedly was upset. He described Monday night as "miserable," and indicated that he "kept waking up and felt I'd had no good sleep at all." Two days later, he reports that he felt better but "still knew I'd been through something."[148]

The President's doctors emphasized that his long-term survivability rate was very high. Cancer had not been found anywhere else in his body, and his lymph nodes were all clear. However, the doctors admitted that the cancer had penetrated the muscle wall of the bowel, and thus had grown to the second level (a Dukes B level) of seriousness.[149] (A Dukes A growth would involve just the very superficial layers of the bowel; a Dukes B would include penetration of the bowel wall muscles; and a Dukes C would signify that the cancer had spread into the lymph nodes.)[150] Dr. Rosenberg assured the President that "[his cancer was] confined to the wall of his colon or bowel; it had not spread in that local area outside of the bowel wall; all of the lymph nodes surrounding the colon had no evidence of tumor; there was no evidence of tumor that was invading any blood vessels or nerves."

Rosenberg's prognosis was entirely optimistic. He told Reagan, "I think the chances are excellent that this tumor will not occur again. . . . I think the weight of evidence would indicate that no further treatment is indicated."[151] Dr. Hutton agreed. Although he admitted to the President's family that he would have been happier if the cancer had been confined to the adenoma, he informed them that the malignancy had been contained within the adenoma and the intestine wall, both of which had been removed, and that the President's surgeons were "very sure they had gotten it all."[152]

During the cancer surgery, Reagan's doctors had also discovered that he suffered from diverticulitis, an inflammation of the intestine which can be aggravated by small particles of food.[153] The condition can be painful, and the President was warned to avoid eating such foods as peanuts and popcorn. His wife joked that this was his "worst moment," since he so much enjoyed eating popcorn: "You would have thought his whole world had come to an end."[154]

Also upsetting to the President and members of his family was the way in which the news media covered the story of his surgery. Soon after his cancerous growth had been removed, Reagan watched a medical expert on television predicting that he would not live five years, and was understandably distressed at this negative prognosis. Deputy Press Secretary Speakes revealed that Mrs. Reagan was "particularly upset by the sight of a detailed diagram of the President's intestines on national television and was appalled when CBS ran an actual medical school videotape of a proctoscopic instrument probing the insides of a colon."[155]

The President also felt that the press incorrectly reported the nature of his condition after his operation. He complained that news stories reported that he "has," rather than "had," cancer. In his autobiography, he later described his feelings:

Yes, doctors found an object in my body that was cancerous. But they removed it and because they couldn't take any chances that malignant cells might have penetrated beyond the polyp, they also took out a portion of my intestine. But they learned that no cancer cells had entered the rest of my body at all; there was no cancer beyond the polyp and it was removed.[156]

For its part, the press was not fully satisfied with the way it was treated. The White House tightly controlled the flow of information about the President's condition. His physicians were permitted to speak with reporters on only two occasions but not thereafter,[157] and reporters chafed at their inaccessibility. The release of photographs was also controlled and arranged for maximum political effect. Speakes described the first postoperative photograph of the President as being "artfully arranged to conceal the nasogastric tube that had been inserted in Reagan's nose and was held in place by tape." The photograph showed the First Lady kissing the President, with her face concealing both tube and tape. Speakes later admitted that the Reagans only wanted him to reveal what they felt the news media and the public absolutely had to know.[158]

News releases emphasized that the President was doing extremely well after his surgery. Dr. Oller announced that Reagan was "on a postoperative course that surpasses by 99.9 percent all patients who undergo this type of surgery. That includes all patients, much less one who is 74 years old. So far, it is a spectacular post-operative course."[159]

On 20 July, only one week after surgery, Reagan returned to the White House, dressed in a shirt and pair of pants smaller than his usual size so that his weight loss would not be noticed. Three days later, he attended a state dinner for the president of China, although he did not remain afterward for the entertainment. On 27 July, he was able to walk around the shallow end of the swimming pool in his bathing suit,[160] a sure sign of his speedy recovery.

Despite the President's rapid and complete recuperation, medical controversy surrounded the way in which his colon difficulties were treated by his doctors. Specifically, one line of reasoning held that if Reagan's colon had been carefully examined after the 1984 polyp had been detected and removed, his cancerous adenoma would have been found and removed before it had a chance to penetrate the wall of his intestine. Dr. Jerome Waye, a former president of the American Society for Gastrointestinal Endoscopy, has argued that the President should have had a complete colon examination in 1984 after the first polyp was discovered:

[I]f you find one polyp, there's at least a 50–50 chance that there are others. . . . Colonoscopy is best, but it is almost 95% certain that if performed a year earlier, a double-contrast barium x-ray would have detected a cancer similar to the President's. Detection of a polyp, including a benign polyp, is a marker to the potential pathology of that individual colon. Once you have discovered a polyp, you have something that is a step beyond a colon complaint or a colon symptom. You have a finding, and in my experience, that finding requires as a minimum standard the barium x-ray.[161]

Other specialists, also former presidents of the American Society for Gastrointestinal Endoscopy, disagreed. Dr. Melvin Shapiro pointed out that "if we find an adenomatous polyp, we do a colonoscopy; if we find an inflammatory or hyperplastic polyp, we do not in the absence of other findings do a colonoscopy. It's that simple. The [cancer] yield from colonoscopy on one hyperplastic polyp would be less than 1%."[162]

Dr. Tedesco, who consulted in the President's care in 1984, agreed. He maintained that the presence of a single, isolated inflammatory polyp in no way argues for a colonoscopy or a barium X ray; and thus had recommended in 1984, when Reagan's first polyp was removed, that nothing further be done.

Once, however, blood was found in the President's stool in March 1985, the experts agree that a colonoscopy should have been performed. The most common clues to colon cancer, after all, are blood in the stool and anemia. Reagan did not exhibit anemia in 1984 or 1985, but he did have blood in his stool in the latter year. Dr. Shapiro indicated that when "other findings" accompany the detection of an inflammatory or hyperplastic polyp, a colonoscopy is in order.

Even Dr. Tedesco expressed concern over the appearance of blood in the President's stool in 1985, and indicated that he "would probably have reacted to the blood . . . in the stool of a 74-year-old man." Moreover, Tedesco warned that the six negative stool tests Reagan underwent did not cancel out even one positive test since "cancers are known to bleed intermittently," but he did not find the four-month delay to be significant.[163]

Most experts, then, believe that the discovery of an inflammatory polyp in Reagan in 1984 did not call for a colonoscopy or barium X rays. However, Dr. Bergein Overholt believes that the finding of a *second* nonneoplastic polyp in the President's colon should have led to a colonoscopic examination within six weeks. Moreover, the finding of blood in a 1985 stool test certainly should have resulted in a thorough examination of the colon, although the four-month delay was not viewed by most experts as particularly important since such adenomas may take a decade to develop.[164]

Reagan's surgery for cancer on 13 July 1985 was, though his most serious medical problem during his second term, not his last. Just a few days after returning to the White House following his surgery for colon cancer, the President had a bump removed from the right side of his nose. It had been there for years but had become more inflamed in recent days, a fact Reagan attributed to the tape that had held his postoperative tubes in place. That he might again have cancer caused considerable upset in the White House. Mrs. Reagan, in particular, worried that the public might get the impression that the President was cancer-prone. In order to prevent news leaks, the nose tissue was sent for biopsy under the name of Tracy Malone, a sixty-two-year-old white female.[165] The biopsy disclosed that the bump was a basal cell carcinoma, almost certainly caused by exposure to the sun. Despite its minor nature, Mrs. Reagan refused to allow news of the President's skin cancer to be released. Instead, the White House announced, in a statement the deputy press secretary refused personally to endorse:

On Tuesday, July 30, a small area of irritated skin on the right side of the President's nose was removed. The irritation had recently been aggravated by the adhesive tape used while the President was in the hospital. It was submitted for routine studies for infection and it was determined no further treatment is necessary.[166]

Far from ending speculation about the bump on the President's nose, this statement almost certainly heightened it. Finally, on 5 August, Reagan met with a group of reporters and admitted that he had had a basal cell carcinoma removed from his nose. Speakes was sharply criticized by the press for not revealing this fact earlier. Sam Donaldson warned the deputy press secretary that "regardless of who had asked him to conceal the facts, it was his reputation on the line";[167] and the relationship between the two men was never afterward the same.[168] Even Nancy Reagan later admitted that she "shouldn't have done that to Larry, because it damaged his credibility with the press."[169]

Also, before retiring from the White House in 1989 Reagan had two additional basal cell carcinomas removed from his face, and each of these procedures was treated more openly by the White House, largely because of criticism over the handling of the earlier episode. He also had several additional polyps removed from his colon. In early 1987, the President underwent prostate surgery by means of a transurethral resection, a procedure that avoids a surgical incision but often has undesirable side effects.[170] This was the second such procedure Reagan experienced, the first being in 1967.[171] The latter resection, however, came in the midst of the Iran-Contra scandal, a time when the Teflon presidency had lost its invulnerability and Reagan's popularity had plummeted. Likely because of the pressure he was under and the fact that he was now almost seventy-six years of age, the President did not bounce back from his prostate surgery as quickly as his aides expected,[172] and had to follow a sharply reduced schedule. Also, at subsequent Cabinet meetings, aides reportedly kept the President well supplied with water, since "frequent drinks of water help keep the plumbing flushed out for those with prostate irritation."[173] Finally, during his last months as President, Reagan underwent surgery to alleviate an abnormality in his left hand. His ring finger had been in a flexed position for some time, but the condition had worsened. The surgery allowed the finger to appear and function normally.[174]

The Political Implications of Reagan's Medical Emergencies

Each of Ronald Reagan's medical crises had significant and far-reaching effects on his presidency. The assassination attempt, coming only two months into his first term, determined the basic structure of Reagan's administration for the duration of the 1981–85 period and, in part, even thereafter. It contributed to the early departure of its senior cabinet official, Secretary of State Alexander Haig, who had seemed only too anxious to take over the reins of government while the President was hospitalized and recovering from his wound. More broadly, the shooting of Ronald Reagan created an environment in which the troika concept of executive branch administration was born, and which determined the ideological configuration of the administration for the next several years. The assassination attempt also produced a second and more profound political honeymoon for the "Teflon" presidency, but it was not to last throughout the Reagan years. Indeed, during his second term, Ronald Reagan's cancer surgery and the Iran-Contra scandal coincided, with devastating results for the President's popularity, credibility, and effectiveness.

THE DOWNFALL OF A SECRETARY OF STATE

On 30 March 1981, the day President Reagan was shot, confusion and tension reigned supreme in Washington. Aides gathered at George Washington University Hospital where the President was being treated and in the Situation Room at the White House, waiting for word on Reagan's condition and trying to keep the government functioning. Secretary of State Alexander Haig, a former military commander of the North Atlantic Treaty Organization and a former chief of staff to President Nixon, took it upon himself to try to provide leadership. He began by sending messages to Vice President Bush, urging him to return to the capital as soon as possible, and by cabling U.S. ambassadors around the world with a message for the governments to which they were accredited. Haig also telephoned the Speaker of the House, the majority and minority leaders of the Senate, the minority leader of the House, and all former presidents, in order to brief them on the assassination attempt.

The press, of course, was clamoring for information, and it initially fell to the deputy press secretary, Larry Speakes, to try to provide it. Administration officials watched with growing dismay as Speakes responded to reporters' questions on the television screen in the Situation Room.

Asked whether the President was in surgery, Speakes replied, "I can't say." Asked whether U.S. military forces had been placed on a higher level of readiness, Speakes responded, "Not that I'm aware of." Asked "Who is running the government right now," Speakes admitted, "I cannot answer that question at this time."[175] Haig later expressed his own sentiments as he watched this press briefing: "The official White House spokesman was being asked who was running the government at a time of national crisis, and he was responding that he did not know. He was being asked if the country was being defended and he was saying that he did not know."[176]

Out of frustration but without informing their companions in the Situation Room, Haig and the national security adviser Richard Allen rushed upstairs to the press room. Speakes had just concluded his meeting with reporters as Haig took his place at the podium. His performance in the next few minutes would mark the beginning of the end of his tenure as secretary of state.

Haig announced that the President had, in fact, been wounded in his left lung and was undergoing surgery. He indicated that no military-alert measures were necessary, and that none had been taken. The secretary of state then offered to take questions and, not surprisingly, was asked, "Who is making decisions for the government right now?" In an answer that was a major blunder, far worse than anything Speakes had said moments before, Haig announced to the press and to the country:

Constitutionally, gentlemen, you have the President, the Vice President and the Secretary of State, in that order, and should the President decide he wants to transfer the helm, he will do so. He has not done that. As of now, I am in control here, in the White House, pending the return of the Vice President and in close touch with him. If something came up, I would check with him, of course.[177]

This statement was a public relations disaster on several fronts. First, in the line of succession to the presidency, the secretary of state stands behind not only the vice president but also the Speaker of the House and the President pro tempore of the Senate. Clearly, Haig appeared to be ignorant of the Presidential Succession Law and was publicly displaying that ignorance on national television.

Second, regardless of how they were intended, Haig's words smacked of a naked grab for power. His "I am in control" remark, in particular, struck some listeners as being an intimation of some sort of coup d'état. Even President Reagan later complained that Haig was trying to seize the reins of government: "[O]n the day I was shot, George Bush was out of town and Haig immediately came to the White House and claimed he was in charge of the country."[178]

As damaging as the words proved to be, Haig's demeanor was even more unsettling. Richard Allen described the secretary of state as being on the verge of collapse, and indicated that he was actually "prepared to catch him. . . . His legs were shaking as if they were gelatinous. It was extraordinary, absolutely extraordinary."[179] Haig seemed to be short of breath (undoubtedly from running up a flight of stairs to the press room), tense, and even panicky. Instead of projecting the reassuring image to the country he intended, his demeanor that afternoon suggested that he was dangerously close to being out of control. The presidential assistant Michael Deaver thought that the secretary of state looked "like a man about to crack."[180] Haig himself later admitted:

Perhaps the camera and microphone magnified the effects of my sprint up the stairs. Possibly I should have washed my face or taken half a dozen deep breaths before going on camera. The fact is, I was not thinking about my appearance. I was wholly intent on correcting any impression of confusion and indecision that Speakes's words may have inadvertently created. Certainly I was guilty of a poor choice of words.[181]

The secretary's "performance" was given heavy play by the news media, and his unfortunate "I am in control" remark became fodder for countless comedians, both amateur and professional. Over all, the episode badly damaged Haig's reputation for being a controlled and temperate leader and seriously undermined his relationship with associates in the administration at the very moment when the sixty-day-old administration was taking shape.

This change in relationship was immediately evident when, returning to the Situation Room, he confronted Defense Secretary Weinberger's unhappiness over his remarks on the alert status of U.S. forces. Weinberger had, in fact, ordered a slight increase "because of the incident and because I did not know whether it was simply an isolated incident or the opening episode of some coordinated plan and also because USSR submarines were closer to the U.S. than usual."[182] When Haig challenged him on this action, Weinberger informed him that the President had explicitly put him in charge of defense matters in such a situation as this and in the absence of the vice president.

Also, when cabinet members and others criticized Haig's assertion that he was second in line of succession to the presidency, the secretary of state angrily told them that they should "read the Constitution." Reportedly, the White House counsel Fred Fielding informed Haig that his understanding of presidential succession procedures was incorrect.[183] Weinberger claims that he "repressed an impulse to do so."[184]

Haig's intense turf-consciousness, and his insistence that he was the sole "vicar" of American foreign policy, had already created for him more enemies than usual in the administration, and they moved in "for the kill" after his unfortunate performance on 30 March. Education Secretary Terrell Bell got to the heart of the matter: "Haig's pressroom behavior unquestionably hurt his image. But the manner in which the White House handled the situation told the rest of us a good deal about how a cabinet member in trouble could be left to bleed a little if he was not perceived to be a good team player."[185]

Secretary Haig remained in office only for another fifteen months. On 25 June 1982, he resigned from the cabinet, complaining that the foreign policy of the United States was moving away from the "careful course" he and Reagan had charted at the beginning of the administration. A more accurate explanation for his departure was that the President simply was unwilling to give him the independence and power he sought, and his standing in the administration was in tatters. Haig's successor as secretary of state was George Shultz, a more congenial team player.

A major factor in Haig's fall from grace had been his inability to function as a "team player" and his proclivity for what was widely perceived as "grandstanding." The "I am in control" remark following the attempt on Reagan's life had been interpreted, both within and outside the administration, as a grandstanding effort *par excellence;* and the secretary of state's credibility was never fully rehabilitated in the months that followed.

THE "TEFLON" PRESIDENCY

Although Ronald Reagan won a decisive popular and electoral-college victory in 1980, many commentators attributed his showing to the unpopularity of Jimmy Carter rather than to Reagan himself or to his conservative principles. The Gallup poll taken some ten days after his inauguration revealed that only a bare majority (51 percent) approved of his performance in office.[186] Thus the "rally 'round the President" trend, which often occurs in American politics right after a new President takes office, was slow to materialize in the case of Ronald Reagan. His approval rating in early 1981 was the lowest of any President since public opinion polling was begun on a systematic basis,[187] suggesting that public expectations about the "actor-president" were low. These lowered expectations were also shared by Washington correspondents and by political insiders, many of whom viewed Reagan as a lightweight or even as "an amiable dunce."[188]

Although it might not seem like good luck in the traditional sense, the assassination attempt on 30 March 1981 provided Reagan with a dramatic and convincing "rebirth" as a national political leader. Public opinion surveys taken after Reagan was shot disclosed that 67 percent then approved his performance in office.[189] Indeed, the fact that Reagan had survived John Hinckley's bullet marked a dramatic reversal in fortunes for the presidency of the United States, an office that had seemed bedeviled for some twenty years: Kennedy had died of his wounds in 1963; Johnson had been fatally wounded by the war in Vietnam; Nixon had been destroyed by Watergate; Ford had been laid low by his pardon of Nixon and by his debate performance against Jimmy Carter; Jimmy Carter had been destroyed by the Iranian hostage crisis. Moreover, by becoming the first President in American history to survive being shot, Reagan seemed almost to have conquered death and to have "risen above mortality."[190] To his great good fortune, Reagan became like Teflon, impervious to damage; and it seemed "almost impossible to dislike" the President.[191]

Also, the endearing way in which Reagan reacted to his bullet wound transformed him into something of a folk hero. The President's well-publicized quips to his wife ("Honey, I forgot to duck") and to his doctors ("I hope you are all Republicans") catapulted him into the domain of the mythical—an aura that would never completely disappear.[192] The oldest President in American history seemed to bounce back quickly and effortlessly from his serious injury, acquitting himself of the charge that he was too old to be President[193] and projecting a grace and charm that captivated much of the country.

Government insiders were almost as deeply impressed as the general public. Senator Daniel Patrick Moynihan, a New York Democrat, reflected the dominant sentiment in remarks he delivered on the Senate floor on the day Reagan was shot and in a newsletter he sent out soon after: "In the history of the office has any man ever so triumphed over danger and pain and near death? We are surely proud of him. . . . I do not know that in our time we have seen so great a display [of grace under pressure]. It makes us proud of our president."[194]

The press was similarly taken by the President's heroic performance. Reporters gave heavy play to Reagan's jokes and to the courage he displayed in the face of death. Even hardened and hostile media personnel could not help but be impressed. This brought about a "tread lightly attitude within the news media as well as among the White House press corps who covered him most closely, a new respect for Reagan the man." David Gergen, the White House communications director, agreed that "the press held back a little more after the assassination attempt," and even Sam Donaldson believed that the assassination attempt was one of the factors that made the press easier on Reagan than it might ordinarily have been.[195] One interesting study has found that Reagan enjoyed unusually favorable coverage by news magazines after the assassination attempt. Specifically, 86.6 percent of news-magazine stories about Reagan in May 1981 was favorable—the eighth most favorable month in news-magazine coverage of a President since 1945.[196]

The White House decided early on to capitalize on Reagan's heroic image in order to achieve administration objectives. Almost as soon as the President's survival was assured, his closest aides, especially Baker and Deaver, devised a strategy for bringing the national public sympathy and respect for the recovering chief executive into play in dealing with Congress.[197] On 28 April, less than a month after sustaining his chest wound, Reagan appeared before a joint session of Congress and appealed for passage of his economic program. The drama of the moment exerted a powerful force in the legislative process and turned Reagan into a "can do" President.

During that appearance, he fully lived up to his new mythical image. He spoke well and forcefully and seemed completely recovered from his rendezvous with death. But some of those who watched and listened with particular care noticed subtle but understandable changes in Reagan's appearance and demeanor. He was a little thinner than before; and one of his physicians noticed that, as he spoke, he was still somewhat short of breath.[198] In all, however, the appearance on 28 April was a major Reagan triumph. Many members of Congress seemed overwhelmed by the President's courage, if not by his presence itself, and the hero of March became the legislative leader of April and May.

Reagan enjoyed heavy support from Republicans in both houses of Congress. Republican senators, in the majority for the first time in almost three decades, voted with their President 80 percent of the time in 1981, the greatest support given any president by members of his own party in the thirty-odd years of voting studies by the *Congressional Quarterly*.[199] Democrats in Congress were not only impressed by Reagan's refurbished image but also frightened by his surging popularity. David Stockman, then budget director, writes, "By the time the House voted on the budget, his already imposing strength in the Boll-Weevil districts had reached never-before recorded levels."[200] The Democratic leadership had seen the handwriting on the wall. Senate Democrats quickly threw in the towel; and in the House, the Democrat-controlled Rules Committee paved the way to easy passage of the Reagan budget by allowing the entire House to vote on both the President's budget and that offered by the Budget Committee chairman, James Jones. Stockman points out, "The up or down vote thus reduced the decision on U.S. economic policy for the 1980s to a political question: Whose side are you on?"[201] The answer was a resounding victory for Ronald Reagan.

The former House Speaker Thomas P. O'Neill has described this period of time as "the lowest point in my career":

For a while I was a solitary voice crying in the wilderness. To my distress, some of the weak-kneed members of my party were willing to desert our basic principles and vote with the Republicans. A few of them at least came to me and explained that the people back home really wanted them to support the President—which was undoubtedly true. . . . Many Democrats were scared stiff at the prospect of being out of step with the mood of the country. And for a while there, we were out of step.[202]

Congress passed the principal features of the Reagan administration's economic recovery program, accepting tax cuts that largely benefited the well-to-do and sanctioning a sizable defense buildup. Although Reagan had derided big government as being "the problem" in the United States, his legislative victories in 1981 convinced many people that government *could* work when entrusted to an effective leader. What Franklin Roosevelt had done in the 1930s and Lyndon Johnson in the 1960s, Ronald Reagan did during the early 1980s. Instead of deadlocked government at the national level, the United States seemed to be operating on the principle of majority rule. The "people" wanted Reagan's economic programs, and Congress was simply not prepared to stand in the way. As the Urban Institute researchers Lester M. Salaman and Alan J. Abramson wrote:

The administration's initial legislative victories restored a significant degree of confidence in the responsiveness of the system and the efficacy of the presidency. As one journalist noted, President Reagan had made a mockery of the conventional wisdom that the country was ungovernable.[203]

His legislative victories also made Reagan seem invincible. In fact, the less Congress—and the Democrats—opposed him, the more invincible he appeared.[204] Had Reagan not succeeded in getting his economic programs through Congress in his first few months in office, he would have appeared to be afflicted with the same malady of ineffectiveness from which so many of his predecessors seemed to suffer. Instead, in 1981, Reagan succeeded in proving that the political process could be made to work by a determined and popular President, especially when that President was engulfed in a wave of public sympathy and admired as a national hero because of his recent personal ordeal. Thus, seeing the President's physical invulnerability as political invulnerability, Congress gave him a great deal of what he wanted—an unlikely legislative outcome had Reagan not been shot.

Ironically, Reagan's popularity sagged just months after his summer legislative successes. His approval levels fell below 50 percent in mid-November 1981; and during much of 1982, his disapproval ratings were higher than his approval ratings.[205] In the 1982 midterm elections, Democrats won significant victories, picking up twenty-six seats in the House and thus shattering the façade of Reagan's invulnerability. He would never again duplicate his legislative successes of 1981.

GOVERNMENT BY TROIKA: VICTORY FOR THE MODERATES

The attempt on President Reagan's life left clear marks on the internal structure and modus operandi of the Reagan administration. Since the administration had been in office for little more than sixty days, it was still "settling in" and developing its own rhythm and working mechanisms. The shooting of the President and his press secretary necessarily altered the administration's rhythm, and the results of that alteration would endure throughout the first term.

Prior to the assassination attempt, the key player in the administration—apart from the President—had been Edwin Meese, Reagan's long-time associate from his California days. After Reagan moved into the White House, Meese became counselor to the President, overseeing cabinet administration and coordinating issue development for both national security and domestic policy.[206]

The person who initially stood second in influence was James Baker, Reagan's chief of staff and the man responsible for the overall supervision of White House units involved in the implementation of administration policy.[207] Baker was a newcomer to the Reagan camp. He was a moderate

Republican, much more pragmatic in political orientation than the staunchly conservative Meese, and widely distrusted by administration conservatives who felt that with Ronald Reagan they at last had one of their own in the White House. In fact, Baker had worked for both Gerald Ford and George Bush in their preconvention campaigns against Reagan, and Reagan had surprised and disappointed his conservative allies when he brought Baker into the White House. They would be even more surprised and disappointed as Baker's power within the administration mushroomed.

Following the assassination attempt, a third Reagan adviser, Michael Deaver—an assistant to the President in charge of scheduling, travel, and the First Lady's office—came into his own. Deaver was a close friend and confidant of the First Lady. When the President became temporarily incapacitated in March 1981, Nancy Reagan's presence became acutely felt, not only at the hospital but also in the councils of government. Through her influence, Michael Deaver's stature grew. Deaver had had practical experience in public relations; and as the administration worked to project to the world the image of a recovering President, Deaver's skills took on new significance. He began to emerge as a third powerful force within the administration, helping to shape the President's image at a time of great national uncertainty. The First Lady appreciated and welcomed Deaver's work. A White House aide has described Deaver as often being on the phone with Nancy Reagan, sometimes as much as a dozen times a day, and pointed out that "their friendship became a critical axis of power."[208]

The troika of Meese, Baker, and Deaver moved quickly to take control of the administration, although they met with the recuperating President in the hospital every day and tried to convey the impression that he was very much involved in running the executive branch. The journalists Jane Mayer and Doyle McManus write that one of the triumvirate later admitted that "the hospital visits had been window dressing. In reality, the troika paid only brief visits to the ailing President, spending the rest of the time in the hospital cafeteria, quietly keeping the government going for him."[209]

This was far easier during Reagan's incapacitation than it had been during Eisenhower's illness twenty-five years earlier. Even in good health, Reagan provided his subordinates with little direction and supervision. In contrast to the far better informed and more forceful Eisenhower, Reagan did not often speak at cabinet and other meetings and seemed even deferential to his subordinates. Except on rare occasions, he did not dominate meetings either by force of personality or by conviction. Deaver himself later revealed, "In truth, the government hardly skipped a beat during the president's recovery, in large part because of the Reagan style. He is a big-picture man who has never enjoyed immersing himself in details."[210] The same picture of Reagan has been painted by many other sources. For example, Donald Regan, secretary of treasury during the first term, has confided:

In the four years I served as Secretary of Treasury I never saw the President alone and never discussed economic philosophy or fiscal and monetary policy with him one-on-one. From first day to last at Treasury, I was flying by the seat of my pants. . . . I found myself in an environment in which there seemed to be no center, no structure, no agreed policy.[211]

Perhaps Clark Clifford, a long-time Washington attorney and former defense secretary under President Harry Truman, summarized it best: "Reagan showed less interest in the art of governance than any President since Calvin Coolidge."[212] Reagan had simply grafted his life as an actor onto his life as President. In a very real sense, he was playing a role—the most spectacular of his life—and did it as he always had—by passively accepting direction and following a script.[213] Actors simply do not lead—directors do—and Reagan was a consummate actor. In this kind of environment, the temporary absence of the President would cause only indirect administrative ripples.

One indirect ripple was the emergence of the troika which would remain powerful throughout the remainder of the first term. A second would soon make itself seen as well. When Deaver became part of the influential triumvirate, the relative power of Edwin Meese and Jim Baker also began to change. Although Meese and Deaver had worked together in California for several years, they did not work especially well together in Washington. Increasingly, Deaver began to ally himself with Baker, and the two men together began to outmaneuver Meese. A Reagan aide writes: "Deaver would usually side with Baker on the grounds that public relations would be better served by Baker's recommendations. In private, their cooperation and like-mindedness were even more visible."[214] As the alliance between Deaver and Baker slowly but surely eroded Ed Meese's power and influence within the administration, it weakened a conservative force and strengthened the hand of the pragmatists in charting the administration's direction during the first term.

Possibly these power shifts would have occurred eventually even if

Reagan had not been shot. But the assassination attempt clearly magnified the role of the First Lady in the formative days of the administration; and, through her, Mike Deaver emerged as a major power broker just as the administration was taking shape. The troika concept came into its own during the President's recovery, and the balance of power between the ideologues and the pragmatists was shaped by the Baker-Deaver alliance. Although the relationship among members of the troika, and between them and others in the administration, was sometimes strained, the troika concept worked reasonably well in the Reagan White House since it provided the President with a variety of viewpoints across the ideological spectrum. It was only after the troika disintegrated at the end of the first term that it became apparent how effectively it served the Reagan administration.

THE IRAN-CONTRA SCANDAL

By most accounts, Ronald Reagan was neither a diligent nor an attentive President. The hours he worked were fewer than those of any President since Calvin Coolidge—and, indeed, not only was Coolidge Reagan's favorite and most admired chief executive, but his portrait was prominently displayed in the White House during the Reagan years. The fact that Coolidge is widely regarded as one of our least successful presidents did not dissuade Reagan from admiring and emulating his "laid-back" working style and detached approach to the exercise of presidential power.

Ronald Reagan's management style— one not merely of delegation of power but also of abdication of responsibility—demanded that he surround himself with strong and competent advisers. During his first term, the triumvirate of Meese, Baker, and Deaver, along with the seven cabinet councils established to analyze specific policy areas, provided Reagan with invaluable assistance and protection. Although his style of delegating power to subordinates carried high risks, the administrative structure established during the first term minimized them and kept the President at least minimally in touch with his own administration.

At the end of the first term, however, all of that came to a sudden halt. Chief of Staff James Baker, tiring of his White House chores, indicated that he intended to leave the administration. Instead, he was reminded by Treasury Secretary Donald Regan about a conversation they had previously had about a job swap: Baker would take the reins at Treasury, and Regan become chief of staff. The two men finalized their plans for such an exchange in December 1984 but did not present them to the President until early January 1985. The President, as was his custom, asked few questions at the time and seemed not to realize the potential stake he would have in the proposed arrangement. Regan later claimed that the chief executive was "surprisingly passive" and "seemed to be absorbing a fait accompli rather than making a decision."²¹⁵ Within less than a half hour, Reagan agreed to the plan. It was one of his gravest political errors.

Donald Regan had been a businessman prior to his service in the cabinet. A long-time executive at Merrill Lynch, Regan admitted that his "involvement in political activity was marginal."²¹⁶ He was not a politician by temperament and had a somewhat abrasive personality which made enemies for him throughout the administration, to say nothing of Congress. His style, then, was quite different from that of the more diplomatic and politically astute Baker.

At the very time that Baker left the chief of staff position and moved to Treasury, the other two members of the troika were also in the process of moving on—Meese to become attorney general, and Deaver to pursue private business activities. Thus, the troika that had served President Reagan so well in his first term was now disbanded; and in its place was a powerful chief of staff who intended "to bring a semblance of managerial order to the affairs of the Presidency."²¹⁷ Within months, however, the presidency would be in considerable disorder and the President in danger of political destruction. During the summer of 1985, the Iran-Contra scandal began to take shape, and it would almost destroy Ronald Reagan as a political force in the United States.

It is significant that the beginning of the Iran-Contra affair coincided perfectly with Ronald Reagan's surgery for abdominal cancer. After his surgery, the First Lady controlled access to Reagan, and for several days Donald Regan was the only administration official to see him. On 18 July, however—five days after the President's surgery but only three days after he had learned he had had cancer—the National Security Adviser Robert McFarlane was allowed to visit the President in his hospital room. Chief of Staff Regan attended the meeting between Reagan and McFarlane, and the three participants had widely varying recollections of what actually transpired during that historic twenty-three minutes.

The President later told the Tower Commission—a three-member board which he appointed on 1 December 1986 to investigate the Iran-Contra scandal—that he "had no recollection of a meeting in the hospital in July with McFarlane and that he had no notes which would show such a meeting."²¹⁸ Although both Regan and McFarlane had clear recollections of such a meeting, they disagreed sharply about what was discussed at it.

McFarlane told the Tower Commission that, even before he was hospitalized, Reagan had given him permission to "explore the United States' willingness to talk to Iranians concerning hostages."[219] McFarlane further maintained that, during their 18 July conversation, Reagan did not approve of U.S. arms going directly to Iran but left open the possibility that Israel would supply Iran with weapons. Specifically, McFarlane asserted that when he told Reagan of the Israeli plan, the President replied, "Gee, that sounds pretty good" and, shortly thereafter, approved by telephone the Israeli arms sales to Iran.[220] There was, however, no record of such a phone call—unusual since McFarlane was normally careful about such things; and the President did not remember making the call.[221]

If actually given, Reagan's approval would seem to have violated the Arms Export Control Act of 1976, which prohibits the sale of U.S. arms to nations that sponsor repeated acts of terrorism, because Iran had been designated such a nation in 1984. Also, the act prohibits the President from allowing transfers of U.S. weapons to countries to which the United States cannot itself sell such weapons.[222]

Donald Regan had, however, no recollection whatsoever of arms sales being discussed by the President and his national security adviser at Bethesda Naval Hospital: "There is nothing in my notes or in my memory to suggest that the idea of swapping arms for hostages was mentioned by either man on this occasion." Regan also claimed that he later asked the President whether he had authorized the sale of arms during McFarlane's hospital visit, since the chief of staff had no recollection of any such authorization being made at the time. The President responded that he "had no recollection of ever having given verbal or written authorization for the transfer of arms to Iran."[223]

Reagan's behavior during the investigation of the Iran-Contra affair called into question not only his administrative style but also his general competence to serve as President. On 26 January 1987, he told the Tower Commission that he approved the shipment of arms to Iran by Israel, as well as the replenishment of those arms, sometime in August 1985, but that he "was uncertain as to the precise date." On 11 February 1987, however, he told commission members that he did not recall authorizing the August shipment of arms in advance, that his approval for replenishment of the Israeli weapons could have taken place in September, and that since he "had been surprised that the Israelis had shipped arms to Iran . . . this fact caused the President to conclude that he had not approved the transfer in advance." As if this backtracking were not damaging enough to his reputation, the President wrote the Tower Commission on 20 February 1987 a remarkable letter, in which he admitted:

The only honest answer is to state that try as I might, I cannot recall anything whatsoever about whether I approved an Israeli sale in advance or whether I approved replenishment of Israeli stocks around August of 1985. My answer, therefore, and the simple truth is "I don't remember—period."[224]

The Tower Commission concluded that the President "most likely" approved the Israeli arms sales before they occurred; and the congressional committees that also investigated the scandal agreed with this conclusion, stating that "McFarlane had no motive to approve a sale of missiles to Iran if the President had not authorized it."[225]

The scandal had many additional twists and turns, including direct participation by the United States in arms transfers, the clandestine funding of the Nicaraguan Contras from proceeds flowing from Iranian overpayments for the arms received, and the administration's ignoring of Congress until the entire matter burst into public attention in early November 1986. But it is not my intention here to recount the sad and often sordid details of a secret policy that went badly amiss. Rather, my concern is directed toward one important question: Why did Ronald Reagan approve of arms sales to Iran, an action even some of his closest aides viewed as paying bribes to terrorists?[226] While we may never have a definitive answer to this question, it is plausible, and indeed reasonable, to attribute part of Reagan's puzzling behavior and shocking memory lapses to the fact that the seeds of the scandal were planted shortly after his surgery for intestinal cancer. Reagan's later denial—puzzling and shocking in itself—that he had, in fact, negotiated with terrorists will be explored later in this chapter.

McFarlane's discussions with Reagan in his hospital room about the Iranian "initiative" came at a time when the President was in both physical discomfort and psychological distress. After all, he was seventy-four years old and had undergone a three-hour operation for cancer only five days before. He was having trouble eating and had spent several sleepless nights. He reports, for example, that "Monday night was miserable. I kept waking up and felt I'd had no good sleep at all."[227] Even in the best of times, Ronald Reagan was a distracted and inattentive chief executive. But July and August of 1985 were not the best of times for him, and his customary inattentiveness may have been greatly intensified by his discomfort.

In addition to his physical distress, Reagan undoubtedly was experiencing psychological distress as well. He learned on Monday, two days after the surgery, that his polyp had been cancerous, and that the cancer had invaded the wall of his bowel. Dr. Daniel Ruge, the White House physician during the first term, believes that Reagan may well have been emotionally distracted by his recent experiences, and that his physical problems may have come to consume the lion's share of his attention at the time.[228] Dr. Norman Knorr, professor of behavioral medicine at the University of Virginia, has pointed out that "once diseases get very severe and the person with the illness feels overwhelmed by them or becomes very self-centered so that all of their energy is wrapped up in their illness, it becomes a problem in terms of their ability to make decisions."[229]

Although Reagan was not heavily sedated in the period after his surgery, his consciousness was almost certainly dominated by that medical crisis and the bad news he had just received. To be sure, doctors told the President that they were confident that they had "gotten it all out," and that the prognosis was good. Nevertheless, to learn that a cancerous growth had been removed from his body, and that the cancer was at the second stage of development, must have touched the President deeply and makes more understandable his inability to focus clearly on McFarlane's words. Dr. Knorr and Dr. Daniel Harrington explain that "when a person's sense of security is threatened, psychic stress is felt and a psychological reaction occurs. . . . During this reaction period, from seconds to days, the individual's judgment may be temporarily clouded and decisions made which are not always in the best interest of the individual."[230]

It may well be argued that after Reagan left the hospital, he became an active participant in the arms-for-hostages arrangement, and that this fact takes precedence over his earlier role. Indeed, one consultant to the National Security Council at the time wrote:

Far from being a detached observer, or a laid-back overseer of the foreign policy process, the president played a very active role at the beginning of Iran-Contra and intervened as late as the winter of 1985–86 to insist, over the objections of his Secretaries of State and Defense, that the Iran initiative continue.[231]

This was unusual behavior for Ronald Reagan. Strong dissent by even one key player was usually a serious obstacle to action in the Reagan administration, and serious objections by two or more high-level advisers would "almost surely kill an idea."[232] Yet, in this instance, the President persevered, perhaps regarding the policy as having been set on its course by his own actions, either in the hospital or during his recuperation period afterward. The objections of Secretaries Shultz and Weinberger, therefore, may have come too late to derail a policy the President regarded as "ongoing" and building a momentum of its own.

The important point, of course, is that when the arms-for-hostages initiative was *first* proposed to him, the President was distracted and upset by life-threatening health problems and almost certainly found it difficult to fully process and absorb McFarlane's words. Defense Secretary Weinberger, who strongly opposed the Iranian arms sales, attributes Reagan's memory lapse to his physical condition at the time: "[E]ven if McFarlane ever did raise the subject with the President, it would have been when the President was in the hospital and in the weakened condition familiar to anyone who has had major surgery."[233]

The effects of the Iran-Contra scandal on the country were explosive. The President's popularity collapsed from a 67-percent approval rating to 46 percent, the sharpest one-month decline since such polling had begun fifty years before.[234] Americans of all political persuasions no longer believed what he said. This loss in personal credibility was even more serious than the growing belief that the President did not know what his subordinates were doing in his name or, at least, could not remember knowing.

Reagan had always been seen as a man who said what he meant and meant what he said. No longer would he be viewed in this light. As one commentator wrote: "Precisely because he communicated assorted personal or ideological visions with such sincerity and conviction, the contrast between what was initially expected and how it all finally turned out became particularly vivid."[235] Simply put, the scandal—and Reagan's complete inability to deal with it—badly damaged the President as a viable political leader for the remainder of his term. By March 1987, fully a third of the American people thought that Reagan should resign, and an impeachment resolution against him was introduced in the House of Representatives.[236] At the same time, his influence in Congress declined steadily, until his success rate in having his programs pass became the lowest since such ratings were first compiled in 1953.[237]

Within weeks of the November 1986 revelations about the diversion of funds to the Contras, President Reagan found himself in the hospital once again, this time for prostate surgery. The President was then under great stress, uncertain whether he would survive the growing scandal. As previously noted, he did not bounce back quickly from this procedure.

After being discharged from the hospital, he followed a sharply reduced schedule, working only an hour or so each day. To his chief of staff he seemed to be "in the grip of lassitude." Regan complained that the President "seldom, if ever, emerged from his office and wandered down the hall as he had done before. He seldom raised the subject of the Iran-Contra affair, and seemed uninterested in the fact that the field had largely been left to his detractors at one of the most crucial hours of his career."[238]

Reagan later wrote that his doctors had told him to take it easy for up to six weeks after the prostate operation.[239] The First Lady, however, more influential than ever because of the President's weakened condition, wanted an even longer recuperation. She insisted that no press conferences should be held for at least three months, and that no travel or other important outside activity be undertaken during the same period.[240] This brought her into sharp conflict with the chief of staff.

Throughout much of his tenure as chief of staff, Donald Regan had been brash and aggressive. After the President's cancer surgery, for example, Regan actually told the press that "we'll try to make as many decisions as we can without involving him. . . . Where we can't get agreement and it can't be ironed out, we'll make it crisp and succinct and take it in to him for a decision. We will try to spare him as many of the details as possible."[241] This remarkable public statement is revealing of the role Regan visualized for himself in the administration. He assumed the right to exclude the President himself from the "loop," and bragged to reporters that he intended to do so while the President was in ill health. Some administration officials believed that Regan supplanted Reagan even when the latter was in good health. Ed Rollins, Reagan's White House political director, estimated that 80 percent of the decisions during the Reagan presidency were made by Regan.[242] It is likely that his ultimate departure from the White House was hastened by the conflict that developed between him and Nancy Reagan over the President's schedule. Regan argued that the presidential invisibility she advocated would isolate Reagan from the American people during the most crucial period of his tenure in office. If the President continued to remain silent and withdrawn while his critics filled the newspapers and airwaves with negative stories, the administration would lose the battle for public opinion. The First Lady refused to back down, however; and the President acquiesced in his wife's wishes, which Regan later argued were shaped by her astrologer in San Francisco.[243]

Not surprisingly, the Tower Commission took great exception to

Regan's general behavior and outlook as chief of staff. Its report included this judgment:

More than almost any chief of staff of recent memory, he [Regan] asserted personal control over the White House staff and sought to extend his control to the National Security Advisor. . . . He, as much as anybody, should have insisted that an orderly process be observed. . . . He must bear primary responsibility for the chaos that descended upon the White House.[244]

Although Regan wished to postpone his resignation so that he would not appear to have been forced from office by the harsh words of the Tower Commission Report, the appointment of his successor, Howard Baker, was announced by administration officials on 27 February, the day after the report was issued, even before Regan had submitted his resignation. When the chief of staff heard this news, he became enraged, submitted a one-sentence letter of resignation to the President, and left the White House almost immediately, never to return.

The Tower Commission went on in its report to place ultimate responsibility for the Iran-Contra affair directly on the President:

The President should have ensured that the NSC system did not fail him. He did not force his policy to undergo the most critical review of which the NSC participants and the process were capable. At no time did he insist upon accountability and performance review. Had the President chosen to drive the NSC system, the outcome could well have been different. As it was, the most powerful features of the NSC system—providing comprehensive analysis, alternatives, and follow-up—were not utilized.[245]

Clearly, Ronald Reagan's place in history will be lower because of the Iran-Contra scandal. His inattentive, lackadaisical, and even irresponsible management style allowed the scandal to grow and fester and brought him into considerable disrepute. According to one of his aides, the President was "extraordinarily trusting and not very curious about the behavior of his subordinates, characteristics that contributed to the Iranamok affairs that seriously weakened his presidency."[246]

But Reagan's cancer surgery, with its physical and psychological implications, may well have allowed the seeds of the scandal to be planted in the first place. Had he not been so ill in the summer of 1985, the President's political instincts might well have led him to reject McFarlane's plans to swap arms for hostages, whether those arms came from

Israeli stocks or from our own. But he was ill and distracted at the time, his political instincts failed him, and he will never be able to escape the devastating consequences of what transpired. Although Reagan would eventually develop rationalizations to explain away the Tower Commission's findings, the Iran-Contra scandal resulted in the unmaking of an American hero. The destruction of his heroic image constituted another assassination attempt against Ronald Reagan, this one largely self-induced. If the rationalizations he constructed shielded him from this unsettling reality, President Reagan was simply doing in this instance what he had done many times before: trying, by building a dream world, to escape the sins of his father.

The Curse of Drink:
Reagan's Psychological Vulnerability

If from his mother Reagan acquired his love of the stage, it was from his father, an unrecovered alcoholic, that he acquired many key elements of his behavior in later life, including the years of his presidency. It was owing to his father's abject weakness, which he saw as a "black curse,"[247] that Reagan always wanted to play the role of a hero in his films. He simply did not want to resemble his unheroic father and, in fact, wanted to separate his "image" from his father's as much as he could. Later, as a high-level chief executive, as governor of California, and as President of the United States, he was the ultimate heroic figure and the very exemplar of success. What a contrast to his father, who could not hold even the job of shoe salesman!

During his early years, Ronald Reagan was a Democrat and regularly voted the Democratic ticket. His father was an outspoken Democrat, and Ronald followed his political lead.[248] A few years after his father died, however, Reagan began to vote Republican and, in 1962, formally switched parties. This almost certainly would have displeased his father, perhaps the very thing that Ronald intended, even though his father was no longer on the scene.

As a young adult, Reagan was, again like his father, a liberal who believed that government can solve all of the country's problems. Later, however, he became a staunch conservative, arguing that government cannot solve problems because government itself is part of the problem, and that people resent and suffer from dependency, even when that dependency is on government itself. Even as a lifeguard, he had come to believe that the drowning swimmers he rescued felt insulted by his having to save them because they had lost their sense of independence and self-control.[249] The historian Robert Dallek writes:

Reagan's program satisfies his own compelling psychological needs—to promote freedom and individual independence and punish government and ruling authority. . . . His insensitivity to the suffering of the poor has less to do with enriching himself or other wealthy Americans than it has to do with his antipathy to their dependence and their failure to achieve the self-reliance he gained for himself. The needy remind him of his dependent father, from whom he tried to separate himself all his life.[250]

Reagan was so appalled and offended by weakness of any kind that he even viewed illness as a sign of personal weakness and something to be denied. While governor of California, he developed an ulcer and actually felt shame at having done so: "I'd always regarded an ulcer as evidence of weakness. Now I had one. I didn't want anyone to know about it and so I kept it a secret from everyone except the family."[251]

Years later, after he had the cancerous growth removed from his intestines, Reagan admitted that he had had major surgery but still described the episode as "a minor situation."[252] Nancy Reagan writes that the President argued, "I didn't have cancer. I had something inside of me that had cancer in it and it was removed."[253] Apparently it was easier for Reagan to downplay the entire situation, even to the point of fantasy, than simply to admit that he had had cancer. His mother had described his father's alcoholism as an illness: alcoholism had made his father into a weakling. To Ronald Reagan, therefore, illness was a form of weakness, and he would not easily succumb to it or even admit its existence.

Other aspects of Reagan's behavior as an adult can also be attributed to his unhappy relationship with his father and to his having grown up in the household of an alcoholic. Parents are, after all, powerful role models, from whom their children take "cues." In a recent study, children of alcoholics were described as "a population at risk."[254] Thus, the adult children of alcoholics typically exhibit certain characteristics: they have difficulty with intimate relationships and are, therefore, emotionally detached and isolated.[255] They are either super reliable or super unreliable, "taking it all on or giving it all up." They are "extremely loyal, even in the face of evidence that their loyalty is undeserved." They often deny unpleasant realities, since "lying is basic to the family system affected by alcohol."[256] Finally, they constantly seek approval and affirmation,[257] since they have an impaired sense of self-worth as a result of their interaction

with their alcoholic parent. Ronald Reagan clearly exhibited these behavioral characteristics in his political life and was often affected negatively by them.

First, despite his great affability and gregariousness, Reagan had difficulty in establishing close relationships. His close associates generally saw
him as aloof and indifferent to those around him.[258] One of his aides
writes: "I think he must have suffered a terrible hurt in his youth, because
he closed himself off. He didn't become involved with people. The
people he worked with, they were all interchangeable. He didn't become
immersed in their lives, and they didn't touch him. He was closed off."[259]

At the same time, while he publicly stressed family values and the
importance of the family, Reagan's relationship with members of his own
family was markedly distant. On the day his older son was married in
Hawaii, Governor Reagan attended the wedding of Tricia Nixon in
Washington, D.C., an act his son describes as deeply hurtful. As President,
Reagan did not see his granddaughter until she was eighteen months
old,[260] even though he was in California frequently and could easily have
managed a visit.

Family members have commented on Ronald Reagan's self-imposed
isolation, even from them. The former First Lady has remarked, "There
is a wall around him. He lets me come closer than anyone else, but there
are times when even I feel the barrier."[261] His daughter Patti, from whom
he is currently estranged, has revealed, "I never knew who he was. I could
never get through to him." And his son Ron, Jr., has said, "You almost
get the sense that he gets a little bit antsy if you try to get too close and
too personal and too father and sonny."[262] This is all understandable in
light of the President's family history, since alcoholism "can cripple a
child's concept of legitimate relationships."[263]

Second, as a political leader, Reagan tended to be distracted and disengaged. In other words, he tended "to give it all up," rather than "taking
it all on." He did not just delegate, as all presidents must to some degree,
but, in fact, often abdicated his responsibilities and his power. He did not
supervise subordinates, asked for no progress reports on their activities,
held them to no accounting. As Donald Regan noted, the President "laid
down no rules and articulated no missions."[264] In short, he was often
removed from his own administration. Of adult children of alcoholics,
Janet G. Woititz, president of the Institute for Counseling and Training,
writes that "not having a sense of being part of a project, of cooperating
with other people and of letting all the parts come together and become
a whole, you either do it all, or you do none of it."[265] Reagan, as both

governor and President, did none—or very little—of it. As a result, his administration was often leaderless.

Third, although Reagan was not really close to his aides in a personal sense, he was intensely loyal to them, even when loyalty became dysfunctional. He found it extraordinarily difficult to fire or discipline those below him in the chain of command. Regan described the President as "all but incapable of firing a subordinate."[266] The intense and bitter infighting within the administration has been attributed largely to the fact that Reagan was almost constitutionally incapable of cracking down on his subordinates when he should have, and of instilling order in the White House. One of his closest associates admitted, "I have never known anyone so unable to deal with close personal conflict. When problems arose related to . . . the personnel in his office, Nancy had to carry the load."[267] Another aide reported that "in the Reagan White House it was backstabbing and knifing each other and anonymous sources killing each other with gossip. And you have to lay it on ol' Dutch. He wouldn't crack down. He should have stopped it. And he could have. But he didn't. It just wasn't his style to get involved."[268]

When subordinates were insubordinate, Reagan was tolerant and forgiving, even when he was deeply embarrassed by their actions. For example, when David Stockman, the head of the Office of Management and Budget, indiscreetly told a reporter (who then published the remarkable story in the *Atlantic Monthly*) that Reaganomics was just "trickle down" economics, and that the tax cut was a Trojan horse to disguise a giveaway to the rich, most senior advisers as well as the First Lady urged that he be fired. Reagan met with Stockman, however, and told him, "I want you to stay on. I need your help."[269]

Similarly, after Secretary of State Alexander Haig sent instructions to an American envoy overseas that had not been formally approved by the President, he visited the Oval Office and spoke with a perturbed Reagan about the episode. The President asked him what he would do if he were a general and one of his lower officers circumvented him and acted on his own. Haig replied, "I'd fire him, Mr. President." Instead of taking this proffered opportunity to rid himself of a secretary of state with whom he had had a somewhat difficult relationship, Reagan replied, "No, no, I didn't mean that. But this mustn't happen again."[270] The secretary of state soon left the administration, but Reagan seemed extraordinarily ill at ease throughout his leavetaking and prolonged it needlessly.

Since establishing a relationship was so difficult for Reagan, he preferred retaining relationships, if at all possible, once established. Woititz writes, "Of course, there is a lot of safety in an established relationship. It is known. The known is always more secure than the unknown. Change being extremely difficult, you would prefer to stay with what is."[271]

Fourth, Ronald Reagan was unusual, at least among recent presidents, in that he often denied unpleasant realities by fabricating rationalizations behind which he would hide and/or constructing dream worlds in which he would live. One of his children remarked that "he makes things up and believes them."[272] A more scathing indictment was that he had "an apparently pathological disregard for the truth."[273]

Dr. Stephen Rosenberg, one of President Reagan's surgeons, explained his claim that he had not had cancer—but had only undergone the removal of something inside him that had *contained* cancer—as "simply the President's way of dealing with cancer."[274] So he had dealt with difficult events long before. When Reagan's father died in 1947, for example, he claimed that he did not have to feel sad because his deceased father had spoken to him, saying, "I'm OK and where I am is very nice. Please don't be unhappy."[275] When his marriage to Jane Wyman ended in divorce, he maintained that since he did not initiate or want the breakup, he had not really been divorced at all.[276] Later, as President the same psychological mechanism was at work when Reagan denied the arms-for-hostages deal with Iran, or that it violated his own policy of never negotiating with terrorists. When the Tower Commission issued its highly critical report of his conduct, Reagan was reported to be "stunned and confused."[277] In fact, after his public approval ratings finally rebounded from the low point to which they had fallen at the height of the scandal, the President reacted by saying that "it was as if Americans were forgiving me for something I hadn't done."[278] Once again, he seemed unable to accept the reality of the situation in which he found himself, and insisted that he had done nothing wrong or inconsistent.

Referring to the alcoholic household, Woititz writes, "Lying is basic to the family system affected by alcohol. It masquerades in part as overt denial of unpleasant realities, coverups, broken promises and inconsistencies."[279] During the Iran-Contra affair, Ronald Reagan, the son of an alcoholic father, denied the unpleasant reality that his tough policy on terrorism had been rendered a joke by his own administration, and that terrorists, far from not being allowed even to hide, had been allowed to profit handsomely from their terrorist acts.

Finally, Ronald Reagan, like most adult children of alcoholics, constantly sought approval and affirmation. As a young man, he reveled in his position as lifeguard because he was "the only one on the guard stand" and everyone looked up at him.[280] As an actor, Reagan wanted to play the role of the hero so that his audiences would like and admire him. In political life, he avoided positions that would make him one of many (such as legislator) and sought those (governor, President) that would make him the center of attention and applause, first in California, then in the country as a whole.

In James David Barber's typology of presidents, Reagan would be categorized as a passive positive president—one who does not work hard at his job but who wants the presidency because it brings him popularity and love.[281] Reagan enjoyed being President, the greatest and most heroic of all his many roles. Even when he was shot, he responded as a hero would—walking unaided into the hospital and then making jokes to doctors, nurses, and members of his family, despite the seriousness of his condition. It was as if he were laughing in the face of death, and his heroism inspired the nation and brought him an outpouring of affirmation and affection.

Some associates, such as the former Senator Paul Laxalt, believed, however, that Reagan was deeply affected by the attempt on his life: "For quite a time afterwards, there was a certain sadness. You could see it in his eyes. It wasn't just the physical pain. I think that he was deeply hurt, emotionally, that this could happen to him, that someone would do this to him."[282] Thus, the man who saw the presidency as a vehicle for attracting attention and generating affection from his countrymen had some difficulty in accepting the fact that one of those countrymen had so little affection for him as actually to have tried to kill him. Even heroes can be saddened by unplanned and unanticipated events. Also, Reagan learned, in this instance, that being President of the United States was a far more difficult and dangerous role than any he had ever played before. Its dangers were real rather than contrived, its script often took unplanned detours, and there could be no stand-ins.

Many observers found aspects of Ronald Reagan's behavior patterns unusual and, at times, surprising. Those who have studied the effects of parental alcoholism on the lives of adult children would not agree. Robert J. Ackerman explains that "living with an alcoholic is a family affair. . . . To one degree or another all members of the family are affected."[283] Although all members of the family are not affected in the same manner and to the same degree, the behavioral tendencies described here are not at all uncommon for adults who have grown up in a household blighted by alcoholism.

Although Ronald Reagan was once described by his brother as "his mother's boy," he was inescapably his father's boy as well. For this President, the "black curse"—as he once described it—was an ever-present reality, and he has spent his entire life trying to break free from its dark shadow.

Chapter EIGHT
Prescriptions

s the experiences of the six twentieth-century presidents examined here make abundantly clear, the presidential office carries not only political dangers for those who occupy it but physical and psychological dangers as well. The two-hundred-year history of the presidency of the United States bears eloquent testimony to these same central facts. Most obviously, of the forty presidents whose terms are now completed, four (10 percent) have been assassinated, and many others have been plotted against and unsuccessfully stalked by potential killers. In recent years, Ronald Reagan became the first President to survive being shot while serving as the nation's chief executive, and Gerald Ford became the first President to escape two active assassination attempts during his two-and-a-half years in office.

Although the Secret Service tries mightily to protect the President, there is simply no failproof system for doing so, particularly in a country where some interaction between a President and his constituents is expected. Almost every would-be assassin must realize that the chances of killing the President and going unapprehended are extremely slight. However, many such persons *desire* to be caught, since assassination of a President represents their grand entrance into the history books.

Even when the President wears a bulletproof vest, he is still highly vulnerable to head and neck wounds. A bulletproof vest might well have spared Reagan and other presidents from being shot, but it would have meant essentially nothing to our most recently assassinated President, John F. Kennedy, whose fatal wounds were to his head. Physical harm to presidents will, therefore, remain highly possible, even though riding in open cars and walking into large crowds have become increasingly infrequent and wearing bulletproof garments has become rather common.

Apart from assassination and plots of bodily harm, the presidency is a complex and difficult office, and its pressures are debilitating. As we have seen, tension—and the inability to deal effectively with it—are related intimately to a wide range of diseases and physical indispositions. In addition to the four assassinated presidents, another four chief executives (10 percent) have died in office of illnesses that were likely job-related. William Henry Harrison caught pneumonia while delivering his inaugural address and died just thirty days later. Zachary Taylor and Warren Harding were two tormented presidents who died suddenly in office, most probably of cardiovascular disease. And Franklin Roosevelt died of a cerebral hemorrhage at the beginning of his fourth term in office, after serving during many years of economic depression and world war.

Presidential death was anticipated and provided for by the Framers of the Constitution who established the principle of vice-presidential succession. It was not clear, however, whether the Framers intended the vice president, in the case of presidential death, to assume the office of the presidency itself or only the "powers and duties" of the office as acting president. While it would certainly appear that the latter was the case,[1] this constitutional ambiguity was effectively resolved by the first vice president to replace a president who had died in office. In 1841, John Tyler insisted, after William Henry Harrison's untimely death, that he had inherited the office itself and was, therefore, President of the United States rather than acting president. He even took the presidential oath to symbolically demonstrate that he had become the tenth President of the United States.[2] When Tyler's assertion went essentially unchallenged by Congress, it created a powerful precedent which Millard Fillmore, Andrew Johnson, Chester Arthur, Theodore Roosevelt, Calvin Coolidge, Harry Truman, and Lyndon Johnson all followed upon the death of their predecessors.

In the event of presidential death, therefore, the path became clear even before the Twenty-fifth Amendment was added to the Constitution in 1967. By practice, the vice president succeeded to the office itself, followed by other officials as determined most recently by the Presidential Succession Law of 1947. The Speaker of the House of Representatives is second in line of succession, the President pro tempore of the Senate is third, and then members of the cabinet in order of departmental seniority, the oldest department (State) first and the newest department (Veterans Affairs) last. This arrangement explicitly repudiated that established by the

Presidential Succession Law of 1886, which provided that the vice president be followed in line of succession by members of the cabinet in order of departmental seniority. The prior succession arrangement was attacked by President Truman and other critics as being undemocratic, since cabinet members are wholly unelected. In 1947, Congress moved to remedy this situation by passing a succession law which places two elected officials—one from the House, the other from the Senate—behind the vice president in line of succession to the presidency. The "democratic" character of presidential selection is preserved, therefore, but only in a limited sense, since the constituencies of the Speaker and President pro tempore are only local.

While the succession process has been made more democratic, since it provides for elected officials to succeed a President who has died in office, it must be remembered that the stresses of the presidency produce and/or contribute to *nonfatal* physical ailments that occasionally incapacitate our chief executive. Presidential disability has been, and continues to be, an area of considerable uncertainty and concern. Bush suffered from atrial fibrillation; and, earlier, Reagan from colon cancer and a bullet wound, Johnson from gastrointestinal afflictions, Kennedy from Addison's disease, Eisenhower from gastrointestinal and cardiovascular ailments, Roosevelt from congestive heart failure, and Coolidge from a paralyzing depression. The impact of some of these presidential "indispositions" may be resolved, or at least ameliorated, by the enactment of the "Presidential Disability" Amendment of 1967. Some problems, however, remain both unresolved and troubling possibilities.

In this chapter I will assess the strengths and weaknesses of the Twenty-fifth Amendment in an effort to determine whether further constitutional "tinkering" is desirable. In addition, since the Twenty-fifth Amendment becomes operative only *after* the crisis of presidential disability or death has occurred, I will examine *political* steps that might be taken to lighten the administrative burdens on the President so that they will be somewhat less debilitating. Finally, recognizing that presidential disability and death are likely to remain recurring features of the American political system, I will suggest a practical way to upgrade the office of vice president, an office that is simply too important to be treated, as it often has been, as an afterthought.

The Twenty-fifth Amendment Revisited

The constitutional problems surrounding presidential disability were "finally" and authoritatively dealt with by the Twenty-fifth Amendment, which was added to the Constitution in February 1967 after years of debate. That amendment contains four sections, each of considerable significance.

Section 1. In case of the removal of the President from office or of his death or resignation, the Vice President shall become President.

Section 2. Whenever there is a vacancy in the office of the Vice President, the President shall nominate a Vice President who shall take office upon confirmation by a majority vote of both Houses of Congress.

Section 3. Whenever the President transmits to the President pro tempore of the Senate and the Speaker of the House of Representatives his written declaration that he is unable to discharge the powers and duties of his office, and until he transmits to them a written declaration to the contrary, such powers and duties shall be discharged by the Vice President as Acting President.

Section 4. Whenever the Vice President and a majority of either the principal officers of the executive departments or of such other body as Congress may by law provide, transmit to the President pro tempore of the Senate and the Speaker of the House of Representatives their written declaration that the President is unable to discharge the powers and duties of his office, the Vice President shall immediately assume the powers and duties of the office of Acting President.

Thereafter, when the President transmits to the President pro tempore of the Senate and the Speaker of the House of Representatives his written declaration that no inability exists, he shall resume the powers and duties of his office unless the Vice President and a majority of either the principal officers of the executive departments or of such other body as Congress may by law provide, transmit within four days to the President pro tempore of the Senate and the Speaker of the House of Representatives their written declaration that the President is unable to discharge the powers and duties of his office. Thereupon Congress shall decide the issue, assembling within forty-eight hours for that purpose if not in session. If the Congress within twenty-one days after receipt of the latter written declaration, or, if Congress is not in session within twenty-one days after Congress is required to assemble, determines by two-thirds vote of both Houses that the President is unable to discharge the powers and duties of his office, the Vice President shall continue to discharge the same as Acting President; otherwise, the President shall resume the powers and duties of his office.

Section 1 of the Twenty-fifth Amendment settles definitively the matter of vice-presidential succession, which occurs when the president is removed from office by death, impeachment, or resignation. In all such instances, the Framers' intentions notwithstanding, the vice president becomes President of the United States and not merely acting president. Thus, when Richard Nixon resigned the presidency in 1974 under threat of impeachment, his vice president, Gerald Ford, became President of the United States, and constitutional challenges to that fact were no longer feasible. The Tyler precedent is, in other words, now the law of the land.

Section 2 tries to fill the gap in the line of succession that exists when the vice presidency becomes vacant. Between 1789 and 1967, vacancies in the vice presidency were not uncommon. Seven vice presidents died in office during that period (George Clinton, Elbridge Gerry, William King, Henry Wilson, Thomas Hendricks, Garret Hobart, and James Sherman), one resigned (John Calhoun), and eight vacated the office to succeed to the presidency (Tyler, Fillmore, Andrew Johnson, Arthur, Theodore Roosevelt, Coolidge, Truman, and Lyndon Johnson).[3] During this time, therefore, the vice presidency was vacated on sixteen occasions, and it remained vacant until the next election. This meant, of course, that should the President have died, resigned, or been impeached at any one of these points in history, the Presidential Succession Law in effect at the time would have determined the identity of the new President. Since 1947, that person would be the Speaker of the House, and after him, the President pro tempore of the Senate.

Under Section 2, however, vacancies in the vice presidency are intended to be filled quickly and expeditiously. Specifically, the new president shall fill the vice presidency with his or her appointee, after that appointee has been confirmed by a majority vote of both houses of Congress. In the time since the Twenty-fifth Amendment was added to the Constitution, section 2 has become operative on two occasions. In October 1973, Vice President Spiro Agnew resigned from office under a legal cloud. Three days later, President Nixon nominated Congressman Gerald Ford for the vice presidency, and Ford was subsequently confirmed by Congress 54 days after his nomination. After President Nixon's resignation from office in August 1974, he was succeeded by Gerald Ford as President. Eleven days later, Ford nominated Nelson A. Rockefeller to serve as his vice president, and Congress finally confirmed Rockefeller to that post 121 days later.[4] Since Rockefeller never succeeded to the presidency, Gerald Ford remains the only appointed vice president ever to become President of the United States.

Section 2 does not address the simultaneous removal of the President and the vice president or the problems inherent in the sometimes lethargic confirmation process in Congress, but it is useful in correcting an unfortunate situation that has arisen fairly often since the Constitution was written. Although some members of Congress felt that section 2 undercuts the ideal of having an elected—and only an elected—vice president,[5] it still provides a useful and welcome mechanism for filling vice-presidential vacancies in the period between elections, and it fills them with persons of the President's own party. It does not guarantee that presidential succession will not extend beyond the vice presidency, but it comes much closer to that goal than was the case prior to 1967. Had the Twenty-fifth Amendment not been added to the Constitution in 1967, the thirty-seventh President of the United States would have been, following Richard Nixon's resignation, House Speaker Carl Albert, a Democrat, rather than Vice President Gerald Ford, a Republican.

Section 3 of the Twenty-fifth Amendment applies to those situations in which the President is able to inform congressional leaders in writing that he is, or is about to become, unable to carry out his presidential responsibilities. In such circumstances, it provides for the vice president to assume the office of acting president and allows the vice president to act in this capacity until the President reclaims his powers and duties, again in writing. Section 3 makes clear that the vice president is only acting president in such situations and that the President can reclaim his powers after his inability ends.

Since the Twenty-fifth Amendment was ratified, section 3 has been invoked on only one occasion. In 1985, President Reagan transferred his powers to Vice President Bush during the period of his colon surgery and for several hours thereafter. During this period of some eight hours, the President was under either anesthesia or medication and could not discharge his duties. Although apparently reluctant to do so, Reagan effectively invoked the Twenty-fifth Amendment, and Bush served as acting president for part of that day. Section 3 should have been invoked—but was not—in the period immediately after the assassination attempt against President Reagan in 1981 since he was not able to discharge his duties at the time, and the amendment was designed for just such a contingency. It would almost certainly have been invoked in 1991 if electrical shocks had had to be administered to President Bush's heart in order to bring under control his sudden episode of atrial fibrillation. When medication effectively stabilized Bush's heartbeat, the need for invoking the amendment was nullified.

Section 4 of the Twenty-fifth Amendment deals with one of the most difficult and awkward situations that could arise in American political life. When a President is unable or unwilling to inform Congress that he is incapable of discharging his duties, section 4 allows the vice president, acting in concert with a majority of cabinet members (or a majority of members of some other body established by Congress) to supplant him. In such circumstances, the vice president becomes acting president of the United States.

Under the terms of section 4, the President may reclaim his powers by informing the Speaker of the House and President pro tempore of the Senate that an inability no longer exists, unless the vice president and a majority of the cabinet (or some other congressionally created body) disagree, again in writing. In this unusual and dreadful situation, Congress is called on to decide the matter within a specified period. A two-thirds vote of both houses would be required to allow the vice president to continue to serve as acting president.

Section 4 clearly is the most controversial and potentially the most nightmarish provision of the Twenty-fifth Amendment. It provides for the removal, temporary or even permanent, of a President, possibly even against his will, if he becomes unable to discharge his duties for any reason. Prior to 1967, the only way to accomplish the removal of a disabled but resistant President was to impeach him, but impeachment properly pertains to high crimes and misdemeanors, not to ill health.[6] Section 4 provides a remedy considerably short of impeachment, but not a remedy that is easy or painless.

First, it puts the burden of initiation on the vice president, a person who owes his position to the very President he would be acting to replace. As has been clear throughout American history, the vice president is the last person who would be likely to move overtly to supplant his stricken leader. After President Garfield was shot and lay dying for six months, Vice President Arthur remained "sympathetic and self-effacing."[7] During President Woodrow Wilson's grave and lengthy illness, Vice President Thomas Marshall was largely silent and invisible. During the medical emergencies of presidents Franklin Roosevelt, Dwight Eisenhower, and Ronald Reagan, the sitting vice presidents leaned over backward to appear loyal to the President and reluctant to supplant him. The reason for their reticence is easy to understand. If they had appeared in the least bit anxious to replace their ailing chief, the media would likely have crucified them, the public would have been appalled at their ambition and insensitivity, and their political careers would likely have come to an end.

Section 4, therefore, puts the vice president in an excruciatingly difficult position. It requires public initiative from the most politically deferential of individuals. Had section 4 been in effect earlier than 1967, it is extremely unlikely that any vice president in history would have invoked it, just as they have not since 1967. Only in the case of the President's sudden and unexpected loss of consciousness—and only in the expectation of a lengthy period of unconsciousness—would the vice president even contemplate invoking section 4 and, even then, undoubtedly with great reluctance.

If, for example, Franklin D. Roosevelt had remained in a state of unconsciousness instead of dying after suffering a cerebral hemorrhage in April 1945, one can only imagine Vice President Truman's discomfiture at having to declare publicly that the stricken President was being replaced by himself as acting president. Conceivably, the dangers associated with successfully concluding the Second World War might have induced Truman to initiate a formal transfer of power; but even then, the difficulty of initiating such a procedure at such a delicate moment would have been formidable.

More recently, President Reagan's three-hour surgery in 1981 for removal of a bullet from his lung was not the kind of medical situation that typically would trigger invocation of section 4. The period of presidential unconsciousness was so limited that the vice president would understandably refrain from moving formally to take over the reins of power. What is constitutionally permissible is, after all, sometimes politically and/or logically prohibitive.

In addition, any assertion by a vice president that the President is unable to discharge the powers and duties of his office has to win the assent of the cabinet. If, as was reported, a Reagan aide in 1981 feared that the cabinet might actually seize the initiative in invoking the Twenty-fifth Amendment after the President was shot, he was needlessly worried. The cabinet's role is wholly contingent on the vice president: if the vice president is unwilling to invoke section 4 of the Twenty-fifth Amendment, it simply is not invoked.

Despite this fact, section 4 puts on members of the cabinet burdens almost as heavy as those it puts on the vice president. Cabinet members, also beholden to the President for their high positions, are unlikely to wish to appear so ungrateful as to vote to remove him from office, even if only temporarily. As political scientist Richard F. Fenno points out: "The Cabinet is his [the President's] instrument, to use as he sees fit. Its attachment to him and its consequent reliance upon him prevent the

Cabinet from developing a high degree of autonomous institutional strength."[8]

In recognition of this political fact of life, the Twenty-fifth Amendment allows Congress to set up another "body" to decide on the extent of a President's inability. The membership of such a body would be for Congress alone to determine. Whether this body would enjoy political acceptance, however, is another matter. Allowing members of Congress to serve on such a body might well be *politically* unwise since party differences and even past executive-legislative conflicts may well subvert public perceptions of objectivity and fairness. Allowing members of the Supreme Court to serve on such a body would be *constitutionally* unwise since the Supreme Court might well be called on to adjudicate some aspect of the Twenty-fifth Amendment, and the involvement of justices in the decision to remove the President might well compromise their future role on the Court.[9]

To appoint a "body" composed of medical doctors, as some have suggested, and to give that body the power to vote to remove or retain the President has a ring of simplicity and an aura of both common sense and infallibility. As we have seen, however, in the cases of several presidents, doctors are not always forthcoming about a president's physical condition since they, too, become loyal to him and occasionally duplicitous about the true status of his health. Also, doctors not infrequently disagree among themselves in diagnosing their patients' conditions, and medical disagreement in such a body might well paralyze the entire process.

After considering various alternatives, and despite the obvious difficulties involved, the cabinet seems the most appropriate body, in conjunction with the vice president, to make a determination of presidential inability. Not only do cabinet members observe the President firsthand, but also their judgment is likely to win the greatest public acceptance throughout the country. Their participation would also be likely to give the vice president the greatest political legitimacy as acting president, a significant contribution in itself.

Should the cabinet be reluctant or unwilling to act in the case of evident presidential inability, Congress could then "threaten" to set up another body to act in its place. Such a threat might "inspire" the cabinet to act in order to protect its constitutional prerogatives. If, however, it did not act, and another body was created by Congress to consider the matter, the cabinet then would forfeit its role in the process.[10]

A President could veto legislation creating a body outside of the cabinet to consider the matter of his inability, and such a veto would have to be overturned by a two-thirds vote in each house of Congress. If Congress should fail to overturn the President's veto, and if the cabinet remained immobilized for any reason in declaring the President unable to exercise his powers and duties, the vice president would remain vice president, and the President would not be replaced.

Although a commission of medical doctors should not be allowed to make the actual determination of presidential inability, medical consultation must be an integral part of this process. The President's primary physician should, and undoubtedly will, play a vital role. The Miller Center's Commission on Presidential Disability suggested that the President's physician "should abide by the views of the American Medical Association concerning patient–doctor confidentiality and those circumstances under which it can be abridged.[11] According to the American Medical Association's Council on Ethical and Judicial Affairs, a physician is freed from the strictures of confidentiality in the presence of "overriding social considerations" and where there is the "need to protect the welfare of the individual or the public interest."[12]

Commission members also recommended that the White House physician-designate should meet during the transition period with an incoming President regarding the potential use of the disability provisions of the Twenty-fifth Amendment: "[T]he physician should undertake during the transition with the president-elect, the vice president-elect and those who will become the president's chief of staff and legal counsel to establish, if possible, a written protocol regarding the use of these provisions."[13]

While worthy in intention and useful in theory, the latter recommendation might not be fully workable in practice. First, it is not clear when, during the transition period, the presidential physician will be chosen. Second, the President-elect will be primarily interested and, indeed, absorbed in putting together his administration and in preparing his legislative agenda. He will likely be unwilling to devote a substantial amount of transition time to discussions of his own possible disability, this almost certain to be his last priority at the time of his greatest political victory. Finally, in light of the fact that all issues of disability have been resolved nowhere since they are so complex, a disability "protocol" involving applications of section 4 of the Twenty-fifth Amendment would be difficult and time consuming to construct. It is, therefore, likely to be one of those things "put off" to a less busy time. Prudence dictates, however, that such a protocol should be prepared as soon as is practicable.

In the final analysis, the problem of presidential disability cannot be completely resolved by either statute or constitutional amendment. Disability comes in several forms, and legal remedies attach to only some of them. When a President anticipates being anesthetized, he can invoke the Twenty-fifth Amendment without difficulty. Should he become suddenly unconscious, remain so for a prolonged period, and be unable to invoke the amendment, thereby providing reasonably clear evidence of inability, the amendment provides a useful remedy that is legally and politically feasible. Should, however, a President be conscious and not acknowledge the seriousness of his physical condition, the situation becomes murky. If he has a good relationship with his vice president, a satisfactory solution may be found. If he does not, it probably will not be.

Even in the former situation, a President might be reluctant and unwilling to admit that he is, in fact, disabled, since such an admission might well damage his future authority and legitimacy. Presidents *must* concern themselves with public perceptions both at home and abroad. Public perceptions affect their ability to govern, and presidents are understandably reluctant to damage those perceptions.

Presidents even know that an invocation of the Twenty-fifth Amendment might well have negative effects on the nation's economy, for which their administration will be blamed. Rather than provoke a harmful economic downturn, presidents are likely to "muddle through," hoping their disabilities will be temporary and brief, and trusting that their subordinates will keep the ship of state on course during their illness or physical indisposition.

Finally, there are types of presidential inability that are almost impossible to deal with in a statutory or constitutional sense. Psychological rather than physiological inability is one such type, and there are several subtypes of psychological disorder. Calvin Coolidge's major depression, which undermined his presidency, posed an intractable and devastating problem for both the President and the country; but in today's world, such a depression could probably be treated with miracle drugs.[14] Even today, however, it is unlikely that such a condition would be publicly diagnosed by a President's physician, since mental impairment is considered prohibitive in terms of presidential politics. When Thomas Eagleton in 1972 was discovered to have received psychiatric treatment because of depression, he was removed from the Democratic ticket. In 1988, when rumors about the Democratic candidate Michael Dukakis's psychiatric "history" circulated in the media, he dropped 8 percent in public opinion polls almost overnight.[15]

Presidents, therefore, are unlikely to seek treatment for psychological impairment while serving in the White House, since they know full well that such treatment will almost certainly provoke negative public reaction. Also, even excluding this fact of political life, a President so afflicted might not even realize that he needs such treatment, and the vice president is unlikely to be the one to tell him that he does.

To deal with this awkward situation, a small mental health unit might be established in every administration as part of the White House medical office to assist the White House physician in diagnosing and treating psychological problems. Operating inside the White House, mental health specialists would observe the President at close range and might detect psychological problems about which they could approach him, perhaps through the good offices of the White House physician. They also could assist in treating possible alcohol abuse by the President, the First Lady, other members of their family, or even members of their staffs.[16]

This arrangement would make consultation with mental health specialists easier and more routine for a President and reduce the likelihood of public disclosure. Even the possibility of public disclosure would be an obstacle to treatment for most, if not all, presidents; but as attitudes toward mental dysfunction change in the United States, presidents might find the presence of mental health specialists in the White House increasingly useful. They would be able to receive treatment for psychological distress in a routine way, and the country might well be spared an emotionally disabled or impaired chief executive.

Except in instances of obvious and severe mental impairment (such as advanced senility or dementia), the Twenty-fifth Amendment is unlikely to be of much help in dealing with psychological illness. One can only imagine the public reaction if Vice President Charles Dawes had declared that President Coolidge was psychologically impaired because of his severe depression, and that he (Dawes) was initiating the process of removing Coolidge from office. "Silent Cal" almost certainly would not have remained silent in this instance, and Dawes would have become a political pariah!

Another "psychological" problem not addressed by the Twenty-fifth Amendment concerns the alteration of a President's mental processes by certain kinds of medication in various situations. As we have seen, presidents have taken such medicines as morphine, cortisone, and percoset, drugs that have as possible side effects depression, mood swings, euphoria, memory loss, disorientation, drowsiness, and anxiety. Such factors as dosage and even the size and weight of a patient determine the extent of the mood-altering effects of these medications.[17] However, even small doses of some of them (say, morphine) have been found to produce mood changes and mental clouding.[18]

In early 1992, a flurry of concern followed the First Lady's disclosure that President Bush frequently relied on halcion to help him sleep during extended plane trips. A commonly prescribed sleep medication, halcion has been found to have such disturbing side effects, after extended usage, as amnesia, anxiety, delusions, hostility, and hyperexcitability.[19] Regulatory agencies in several nations have either banned the drug outright or restricted its use. Dr. Anthony Kales, the head of the Psychiatry Department at Pennsylvania State University, has described halcion as a "very dangerous drug" with "a narrow margin of safety."[20] The knowledge that President Bush had taken the drug "frequently" provoked concern and even some alarm in the nation's news media. The White House physician, Dr. Burton Lee, soon announced that he would try to avoid prescribing the medication for the President's use because of the "public relations" problems involved.[21]

The ominous side effects of presidential medications, whatever their nature and purpose, pose potential problems for the nation, but the Twenty-fifth Amendment seems of little help in resolving them. Medication dosage would certainly appear to be a matter of discussion between a President and his doctors, but it does not seem to be a matter that lends itself to constitutional or statutory solution.

In all, then, the Twenty-fifth Amendment probably does the best that can be expected in providing for situations of presidential inability. It does not, and cannot, resolve all problems, however. It does not guarantee that a specific instance of presidential disability will be handled smoothly, or even that constitutional crises can always be averted. But it seems to be the best constitutional remedy at hand, and tinkering with it would be unwise.

The only alteration in the Twenty-fifth Amendment that deserves some consideration is whether to require explicitly that a range of medical advice be sought by the vice president, the cabinet, or the alternative body created by Congress to determine presidential inability. If so, the requisite medical advice should come not from the White House physician alone but from a panel of physicians that would include the White House physician and several other physicians chosen perhaps by him or her. It is important that any medical advisory group be perceived as having professional integrity and the ability to make an independent judgment on the status of the President's health. The public must be convinced, after all, that the process is legitimate, and that some sort of coup d'état has not occurred.

While medical input clearly would be necessary and appropriate in any determination of presidential disability, it does not seem prudent to try to set in advance its precise nature by adding to section 4 a detailed "medical consultation" clause. Instead, the nature of the medical involvement might better be left to the vice president and the cabinet in light of the particular circumstances at the time (for example, physical versus psychological impairment). Flexibility is clearly needed here, and any attempt to preordain the nature of the medical advice required in the process by means of a constitutional mandate seems unwise and counterproductive.

It is important to remember that the removal of a President, even temporarily, because he is unable to discharge his duties is, in the final analysis, a political rather than a medical process. The American people— and, indeed, the entire world—must be convinced that a medical emergency exists, as documented by competent medical advisers, and that its existence is accepted by the vice president and a majority of the cabinet. Precisely because the vice president and cabinet are beholden to the President, their involvement in his possible removal would make the process all the more legitimate and acceptable to the public. This, in itself, is a major advantage of the amendment as currently written. Since it almost goes without saying that the vice president and the cabinet would be certain to base their decisions on competent and extensive medical advice, the Constitution might well remain silent on this point.

Under section 4, it is a fairly simple matter for the President, once recovered, to reclaim his powers. As President Reagan demonstrated in 1985, he need only provide a written declaration that his inability no longer exists, and then resume the exercise of power. It is highly unlikely in any such circumstance that the President would be challenged. If, however, he should be, by the vice president and a majority of cabinet officers (or some other body created by Congress), section 4 provides a method for resolving the crisis that would ensue. Congress would make the final determination. Since Congress has not recklessly rushed to invoke its impeachment power against the President, neither will it recklessly rush to declare him unable to perform his duties because of medical impairment.

While the problem of presidential disability has not been finally and fully resolved, the Twenty-fifth Amendment does have several clear-cut virtues. It ensures the constitutional legitimacy of a President who has succeeded a deceased or removed predecessor; it allows a vacant vice presidency to be filled before the next election; it provides for a constitutional transfer of power to a vice president and creates the position of acting president; it provides for the President to resume his powers and duties after his inability ends, a process that was constitutionally uncertain prior to 1967. While the amendment provides only an awkward and imperfect solution to the problem caused by a President who does not acknowledge his inability, such a problem represents a constitutional crisis in any event, and the Twenty-fifth Amendment at least provides ways of dealing with it. This, in itself, is an important contribution to the American political and constitutional order.

Perhaps the most fitting way to conclude an analysis of the Twenty-fifth Amendment would be to quote the words of one of its principal authors and sponsors. Speaking to the Senate during the debate over the amendment's ratification in 1965, Senator Birch Bayh of Indiana pointed out with both frankness and accuracy:

I have never pretended to the Senate or to my colleagues that this measure is noncontroversial or that it would cover every possible, conceivable contingency that the mind of man could contrive. I have suggested that it is the best thing we have been able to come up with, and it is so much better than anything we have ever had before—namely, nothing. [22]

While the Twenty-fifth Amendment provides, for the first time, legal remedies for some of the contingencies to which Bayh referred, it does not deal in any way with the central fact that the stresses and frustrations of the presidency play a dramatic role in the illnesses and premature deaths of presidents. Though not suitable for constitutional remedy, this sobering fact must be addressed in political practice so that the stresses of the office may be made more manageable and the effects of presidential illness and death rendered less dangerous to the Republic.

The Executive Office Re-examined

Some of the stresses of the presidency result from the growing and unrealistic public expectations about presidential performance. These spring in large part from the dramatic increase in the size and range of activities of the executive branch. As that branch has grown, the President confronts new problems of supervision, duplication, and institutional overload that are both frustrating and debilitating. Ironically, the addition of new layers of assistants onto the presidency was meant to help those who held the office, but the "growth curve" continued to the point where it actually came to hurt them.

In 1789, George Washington confronted only four cabinet-level departments of government; in 1997, Bill Clinton confronts fourteen. Much of this growth was inescapable as the country industrialized and became more complex, but it remains for presidents to direct and coordinate the work of their cabinets so that the goals of their administration will be achieved. This is a daunting task indeed and is unlikely to become less so, even with major organizational restructuring.

The problem is greatly compounded by the enormous growth in other areas of the executive branch. With sufficient political will and determination, however, certain of these areas may be restructured and redesigned so as to alleviate some stresses and frustrations of the presidency.

In 1937, the Commission on Administrative Management (the Brown-law Commission) found the President to be in dire need of assistance. Its report pointed out:

A weak administration can neither advance nor retreat successfully—it can merely muddle. Those who waver at the sight of needed power are false friends of modern democracy. Strong executive leadership is essential to democratic government today. Our choice is not between power and no power but between responsible but capable popular government and irresponsible autocracy.[23]

Responding to its findings, Congress passed the Reorganization Act of 1939 which established the Executive Office of the President (EOP) and also expanded the President's personal staff in the White House Office. As the years passed, the EOP grew in size and range of activities. One critic wrote that the EOP became "a bloated command post that arrogated to itself many of the decisions formerly made in the departments and agencies."[24] In recent years, it has served as the administrative home for such bodies as the Office of Management and Budget, the National Security Council, the Council of Economic Advisers, the Office of the U.S. Trade Representative, the Council on Environmental Quality, the Office of National Drug Control, the Office of Administration, the Office of Policy Development, the National Critical Materials Council, the Office of the Vice President, the Office of Science and Technology, and the White House Office.[25]

During the past forty years, the number of employees in the EOP has fluctuated between 1,400 and 2,200, with the Johnson and Nixon administrations showing the highest growth rates in personnel. As of the mid-1990s, the EOP numbered approximately 1,700 employees.[26] The overall increase in the size and budget of the EOP led one observer to conclude that "the development of the presidential branch has been . . . one of the most significant innovations within the framework of American government over the last fifty years."[27]

Although the White House Office is a division of the EOP, it has remained functionally separated from the other components of the EOP and stands as a personal, intimate staff arm of the President.[28] However, the "intimate" nature of the White House Office has diminished as its size and range of activities have grown. As of the mid-1990s, the White House Office numbered approximately 400 employees, a tenfold increase since the Roosevelt administration.

One of the principal factors behind the growth in power and prestige of the White House Office was that its members tended to be close friends and long-time associates of the President from his prepresidential days. Since cabinet members generally were appointed for political reasons (such as geographical, ethnic, and/or gender considerations), they were members of the President's official family who often had policy preferences quite different from the President's. With close ties to pressure groups, cabinet secretaries often acted as "advocates for agency interests rather than as spokesmen for the President."[29] It was understandable, then, for presidents to look to their friends in the White House Office as a means of getting around uncooperative cabinet members. Indeed, presidents tended to bring more and more subject matters into the White House because they thoroughly distrusted members of their own cabinets.

Ironically, as the White House Office has grown in size and activity, it has taken on some of the very functions the cabinet formerly was intended to serve. Specifically, it has come to represent key interest groups in American society. During the 1960s and 1970s, a number of important interests demanded greater presidential attention; and in more recent times, it "now appears essential to interest groups to have their own man (or woman) right there in the White House."[30] Because of this trend, the White House Office has become increasingly bureaucratized, with many diverse and far-ranging subdivisions. Even though a contraction in the size and range of activities followed the Watergate scandal when the "President's men" were found to have engaged in illegal activities, the White House Office in the 1990s contains units dealing with such matters as legislative affairs, personnel, speechwriting, research, public liaison, media relations, management and administration, intergovernmental affairs, legal affairs, national security affairs, economic and domestic policy, national service, special activities and initiatives, and political affairs.[31]

Unfortunately for presidents, this proliferation in both the number and range of activities of their "personal" presidential assistants contributes to the stresses of office. It is the President who must supervise these subordinates, and that task has become increasingly burdensome. As both Richard Nixon and Ronald Reagan can testify, a President who fails to exert a supervisory role over those below in the chain of command may find himself embarrassed, endangered, and possibly even destroyed by their activities and/or inactivities. The former Kennedy aide Theodore Sorenson aptly points out that "if you have hundreds of people invoking the President's name, there is no way you can keep them out of mischief."[32]

Also, as the number of White House Office functions has grown, so have public expectations concerning the range of presidential activities and interests. The belief that an ever-expanding array of problems will be solved by the President avoids the reality that some of these problems would be better solved elsewhere. As more and more matters are brought into the White House, the President is stretched thinner and thinner as he tries to respond to them. This means, of course, that he will have lesser amounts of time and energy for matters central to his administration. The end result must be intensely frustrating to a President as he sees his own agenda becoming crowded, if not overwhelmed, with matters of only subsidiary interest. At the same time, public expectations cannot possibly be met, and the President's popularity suffers.

One astute commentator points out that the "managerial presidency ... becomes a trap, offering increased capacity and influence to Presidents but creating even greater expectations about presidential performance."[33] Another adds that "the centralization of responsibility in the person of the president has lessened his ability to perform the duties of the office."[34] In other words, the effort to provide the President with needed assistance has produced White House overkill. The chief executive can supervise only so many direct subordinates before the situation is beyond his control; the President can deal with only so many issue areas before his administration becomes afflicted with overload; and public expectations of presidential performance can rise only so high before they are dashed. In the 1990s, the President again needs assistance, but this time of a different sort. Fortunately, it is within the President's authority to provide, and he can do so, at least in part, by downsizing the White House and by securing the services of a competent chief of staff.

DOWNSIZING THE WHITE HOUSE

To ameliorate the tensions and frustrations that spring from presidential responsibilities that are literally impossible to fully execute, the size and scope of the White House Office should be reduced. While some units of that office are essential to the modern presidency (such as legislative affairs and media relations) and perform functions carried out nowhere else, other units cannot make this claim. The White House Office should be organized so that important areas of responsibility will be pushed off to lodge elsewhere, such as in the departments of government rather than in the White House itself.

While each President will have to structure the White House Office according to his own administrative proclivities, the attention of the paring knife might well be directed toward such areas as legal affairs (could not the Justice Department serve all or most of this function?), political affairs (could not the National Committee of the President's party serve all or most of this function?), and public liaison (does not the cabinet provide an opportunity for pressure-group contact with the executive branch?). Additional White House units whose functions are poorly defined or ambiguous (such as intergovernmental affairs) might also be cut back or eliminated.

The unfocused, poorly supervised, and poorly coordinated involvement that too broad a White House operation almost assures is, in the final analysis, damaging to presidents and injurious to their power. Stephen Hess warns:

By extending the chain of command, presidents have built additional delay and distortion into the system. Tensions between White House staff and cabinet officers become inevitable. In the game of "who saw the president last," the department heads are badly positioned, and their exclusion from the inner circle creates a vicious cycle—the loss of power generating the further loss of power. Morale declines in the departments; the careerists who ultimately must implement presidential policy no longer have as much stake in its success. They need only wait long enough and there will be another president.[35]

Downsizing the White House Office would have the desirable effect of bolstering the status of the departments of government. They should be, after all, primarily responsible for policy development and implementation, and these functions should be returned to them. Although a

President certainly will have to observe political niceties in constructing his cabinet (appointing women and minorities, persons from different geographical areas, and so on), he should also give attention to finding persons for both cabinet and subcabinet positions who share his general outlook on the issues central to his administration and who are willing to work with him in advancing and achieving his goals. If potential appointees are clearly incompatible with the President in any important respect, they should not be appointed. A cabinet of persons who share the basic philosophy of the President can assist him in establishing and implementing his own policy preferences in the departments of government.

At the same time, a smaller, more cohesive, more intimate White House staff can assist the President in the overall management of the executive branch. It can serve as his eyes and ears in working with the departments of government and strive to advance his interests with the federal bureaucracy.

The recommendation to downsize the White House Office is supported by those who have held key positions in that office over the years. In the mid-1980s, the University of California at San Diego brought together eight key White House staff members from six different administrations from Eisenhower to Carter to discuss their experiences and put their individual experiences into a broader context. The consensus that seemed to emerge from their discussions was that "when it comes to the size of the White House staff, small is beautiful," and that its range of activities should be narrow. Alexander Haig remarked that "the leaner and meaner you are, the more effective your White House will be." H. R. Haldeman, Nixon's chief of staff from 1969 to 1973, suggested that the White House staff "should be an operational unit, not a policy-making or policy-executing unit." And Donald Rumsfeld, staff coordinator for President Ford until 1975 when he became secretary of defense, recommended that the tendency for White House office growth "must be countered . . . by moving more issues out to the departments."[36] The men who have actually been there, then, believe that the White House Office should return to what it once was—a relatively small, personal staff for the President, rather than a large, poorly coordinated body of assistants who become the locus of policy making for the administration.

REINVENTING THE CHIEF OF STAFF

To further assist him in effectively coordinating the activities of his administration, the President should appoint a chief of staff, or at least someone to do those essential things a chief of staff normally does, at the outset of his administration. A strong but essentially anonymous chief of staff can run interference for the President and shield him from some of the debilitating pressures that can and should be avoided. In other words, he or she can help provide some semblance of order to the managerial presidency.

For almost three years, the Carter administration was an excellent example of the managerial presidency gone wild. Since President Carter wanted to be deeply involved in the activities of his administration and felt that a chief of staff would limit the extent of that involvement, he did not appoint someone to fill such a post until as late as the summer of 1979. As a result, he found himself overwhelmed by the details of the executive branch and at risk of losing the sense of perspective so valuable to high-level decision makers.

Carter himself complained of some of the problems that confronted him after he took office. First, there were the staggering "mountains of paperwork" that came to his desk:

[S]ixty or seventy documents arrived on my desk each day, some of them consisting of many pages of detailed analysis. There would be proposals from Cabinet officers that I had to approve; correspondence to sign; presidential appointments to major executive posts to be considered; reports from meetings in the Situation Room on foreign intelligence or defense subjects; facts about legislation before Congress, or proposals we were developing to send to Capitol Hill. Throughout the day, I would also receive copies of news bulletins and diplomatic reports that Jody [Press Secretary Jody Powell] or Zbig [National Security Advisor Zbigniew Brzezinski] thought I should see. [37]

Second, although he wanted to meet frequently with his cabinet, Carter was bothered by the "persistent problem" of how to exclude unnecessary people from cabinet meetings. So much prestige was involved in attending a cabinet session that White House staff members and the heads of minor agencies regularly struggled to be present. Carter's initial response to each of these problems is revealing: in order to deal with his mountainous paperwork, he took a speed-reading course and quadrupled his reading speed; as for the cabinet meeting "gate crashers," he "had to intervene personally" and use his "full authority to hold the group down to a reasonable size." [38]

No wonder that Carter aged so dramatically during his four years in the White House! Even he reveals that on the day that he left office in 1981, he looked at himself in the mirror and wondered "if I had aged so much as President or whether I was just exhausted."[39] While the hostage crisis and other problems clearly took their toll on this President, so did the years during which he tried to micromanage his administration.

At least some of the pressures he experienced might have been alleviated if President Carter had appointed a strong and effective chief of staff at the beginning of his administration. Such a person could have shielded Carter from some of the paperwork that poured onto his desk and, at the same time, made certain that only authorized personnel attended cabinet meetings. Speed-reading and personal intervention are useful techniques for presidents, but they are not substitutes for appropriate staff assistance.

Jack Watson, who became Carter's chief of staff in 1980, decries his administrative style during the first two and a half years of his presidency. He reported that the system used by Carter resulted

in a lack of cohesion, a lack of organization and cutting in on decision making before it reaches the Oval Office, the presidential level. . . . I think that many of our problems on the Hill, many of our Congressional relationships, difficulties, who's speaking for the President, would have been solved had we started from the very beginning with a strong chief of staff.[40]

Ronald Reagan, on the other hand, found himself saddled, during his second term, with a chief of staff who was *too* strong. Instead of being a faithful and faceless staff aide, Donald Regan seemed at times to view the administration as his own rather than as Reagan's. As we have seen, he even went so far as to boast to reporters that he had excluded the President from participating in decision making during his convalescence from colon surgery. A public boast of this sort reveals a mindset antithetical to that of an effective chief of staff. Guiding the President's involvement in the work of his administration must be the chief of staff's goal. Supplanting him directly must never be.

Within months of taking office as Reagan's chief of staff, Donald Regan saw the President become more and more deeply entangled in the arms-for-hostages scandal that would badly undermine his administration, and did nothing to rescue him. Regan seemed concerned more with preserving and enhancing his own prerogatives rather than ensuring that the President would get the advice and assistance he needed at a critical moment of his personal and political life.

Reagan's normal foreign policy apparatus included the Department of

State, the Department of Defense, and the National Security Council.[41] By allowing a sick and distracted President to circumvent this apparatus by consenting, on his own authority and without adequate consultation, to an arms-for-hostages "deal," Regan failed to serve him well, and both the President and the chief of staff suffered mightily from all that ensued. Ironically, if Reagan's first chief of staff, James Baker, had still held that office during the second term, the damaging Iran-Contra scandal might never have occurred, and Reagan's place in history would almost certainly have been higher.

These two recent administrations, therefore, illustrate the virtues and vices of the chief-of-staff system. In the contemporary presidency, a chief of staff is needed to act as a personal, faceless aide to the President, one who assists the President in using his time most prudently and directs the President to those situations where his personal intervention would be most appropriate. A skillful chief of staff must submerge his ego to that of the President. He cannot view himself as the President's equal or as his rival for executive leadership. He is in the White House solely to assist the President; the President is not there to assist him. As George Bush once said, "The country can have only one President at a time, and the Vice President is not the one."[42] Neither is it the chief of staff! A clear understanding of this fact is needed both by presidents and by those they would appoint to the position. Once that understanding is obtained, the chief of staff should be an extremely helpful feature of the White House Office. The roles of gatekeeper, mediator, and channel of communication are vital to the staff system of the modern presidency; and without them, the administrative pressures on the President are needlessly magnified.

The recommendations that the White House Office be downsized, and that a chief of staff (if not in name, at least in fact) be part of every presidential administration, are intended to make the presidential office more manageable. They are not recommendations that the presidency remove itself from its administrative role, or that a President cease trying to function as "chief administrator" of the United States. Presidential objectives can only be achieved, in fact, by successfully mobilizing and directing the "fourth branch" of government.

Political scientist Richard Waterman writes, "Presidents who can extend their influence over the bureaucracy have a good chance of successfully promoting their policy objectives; those who cannot, however, face frustration and failure."[43] As we have seen, frustration and failure contribute to both the pathology and the mortality of American presidents. In an effort to reduce the frustrations inherent in the burgeoning administrative responsibilities of the presidency, the size and range of activities of the White House Office should be reduced, and the policy function should be rechanneled to the departments of government. A downsized White House staff, led by a chief of staff who clearly understands his role, should operate as a personal staff to the President, one that helps him manage the executive branch and coordinate the policy-making activities of the departments of government. It should, in other words, take some of the administrative burdens off the President's shoulders, as it was intended to do, instead of adding to those burdens as has long since been its fate.

The steps proposed here are, of course, only of limited scope and will not "solve" the problem of the excessive demands and expectations that have come to surround the President. But there are limits to how far we can go in restructuring his office. Too much downsizing would inevitably damage the essential nature of the modern presidency. This, in turn, would even more seriously compound the pressures of the office and heighten, rather than diminish, its physical and mental dangers.

The Vice Presidency Upgraded

Since the presidency will remain a stressful, debilitating position, and since the Twenty-fifth Amendment does not—and cannot—resolve every problem associated with presidential disability, new attention should be focused on the vice presidency of the United States. This office has been described in negative terms, even by some of the men who have held it. Our first vice president, John Adams, complained that "my country has in its wisdom contrived for me the most insignificant office that ever the invention of man contrived or his imagination conceived." Thomas Marshall likened his experience as Woodrow Wilson's vice president to that of "a man in a cataleptic fit [who] is conscious of all that goes on but has no part in it."[44] Probably the most graphic and brutal description of the vice presidency came from John Nance Garner, who compared it to "a pitcher of warm spit."[45]

The salient point, however, is that while the vice presidency may be little in itself, it may become everything. The vice president becomes President upon the death, removal, or resignation of a President, and becomes acting president in cases of presidential disability, according to provisions of the Twenty-fifth Amendment. The incidence of presidential illness and death has been so high in the United States that the vice presidency should no longer be viewed as an unimportant appendage to the presidency. Instead, it should be filled with individuals who are of presidential stature, a practice that has not always been followed by either party during the past century or more.

It has become common to use the vice presidency for reasons that have nothing to do with competence or ability to succeed effectively to the highest office in the land. As political scientist Paul C. Light suggests, "the political Vice Presidency arrived *before* the policy Vice Presidency."[46] He means, of course, that vice-presidential nominations have generally been used to balance a ticket geographically, ideologically, or, generally speaking, for electoral advantage rather than for the future advisory role the vice president might play in the administration. Vice-presidential candidates have even been chosen to prevent the presidential nominee from feeling threatened or overshadowed by his running mate, probably the most demeaning of all reasons.

Prior to the 1950s, the selection of the vice-presidential candidate was generally left to convention delegates, with the presidential candidate often playing a guiding role from behind the scenes. Even as late as 1956, Adlai Stevenson threw the choice of his vice-presidential running mate to the convention delegates, who, after a fierce battle, chose Tennessee's Senator Estes Kefauver for second place on the Democratic ticket over John F. Kennedy. Since 1956, however, the conventions of both parties have simply ratified the vice-presidential choice of the presidential nominee. Some of those vice-presidential choices have been extremely controversial in that the ability of the candidate chosen to function effectively as President, should the occasion arise, has been highly doubtful.

A case in point is Spiro Agnew who, chosen by Richard Nixon to run with him in 1968, served as vice president of the United States until 1973, when he was forced to resign from office after pleading nolo contendere (no contest) to charges of income tax evasion. Another is Dan Quayle, chosen by George Bush to be his running mate in 1988 and widely perceived as being incompetent to succeed to the presidency, even after several years in the vice-presidential office. The explanation for the selection of both Agnew and Quayle is largely political. The Marylander Agnew provided geographical balance for a Nixon ticket and was at the same time acceptable to both liberals and conservatives in the Republican party. The Hoosier Quayle provided geographical balance to the ticket, was pleasing to right-wing Republicans who were distrustful of George Bush, and was certain not to overshadow the presidential nominee, who had been described by some segments of the media as a weakling or "a wimp."

In addition to Agnew and Quayle, some vice-presidential nominees have been chosen essentially to appeal to particular groups of the population viewed as key to the election victory of the party ticket. The New York Congresswoman Geraldine Ferraro's selection by Walter Mondale as his vice-presidential running mate in 1984 is illustrative of this practice. Ferraro, the first woman ever nominated to a major party ticket, clearly was chosen to appeal to female voters, thereby bolstering the election prospects of the Democratic ticket. Obviously the strategy had flaws, and the Mondale-Ferraro ticket went down to a resounding defeat, repudiated even by female voters, who gave a decisive majority of their votes to the Republicans.

In each of these cases, the vice-presidential candidate brought certain strengths to the ticket. In each instance, he or she was viewed as a political asset or possibly even as the lesser of evils available to the presidential nominee. But in none of these cases was competence prominent among the vice-presidential candidate's list of qualifications for office, and in none was the vice-presidential nominee viewed as the second most competent individual to occupy the presidency.

As long as vice-presidential candidates are chosen for essentially the wrong reasons, and as long as presidential death and illness are so common in the United States, the nation confronts a serious problem that is not being satisfactorily addressed. Since to expect presidential candidates to omit purely political considerations from their choice of a running mate would be expecting the impossible, victory being paramount in their strategic calculations, some commentators have suggested variations on that central theme. For example, the choice could be made by the voters themselves rather than by the presidential nominee of the party. A vice-presidential primary would vest the choice in party members throughout the country and remove it from the choice of one individual acting for personal and selfish reasons. It has also been suggested that we return to a bygone era and allow the party convention to fill the second place on the national ticket, acting according to its own devices and preferences.[47] Such proposals, however, are unwarranted and unwise.

To advocate a national primary for vice president ignores the fact that such a primary is not used to choose the presidential nominee. It also ignores the facts that primaries are expensive and participation in them is low (in a vice-presidential primary, it might well be minuscule), and that primary voters tend to be somewhat unrepresentative and atypical of their parties. Even more to the point, the suggestion ignores the fact that the presidential candidate *needs* to have a partner with whom he or she will be able to work, not only during the campaign but for the duration of the presidential administration as well. In other words, the presidential and vice-presidential candidates must be compatible. Otherwise, their working relationship will be strained, and the President will be unlikely to give the vice president the kinds of functions that will enhance the office or even the degree of access that will give the latter influence within the administration. Allowing either primary voters or convention delegates acting alone to choose the vice-presidential nominee would seem to jeopardize a useful role for the vice president in future administrations, except in those lucky—and probably rare—instances when the presidential candidate is fully pleased with what primary voters or convention delegates have done.

Suggestions that the runner-up in presidential-delegate votes at the convention should receive the vice-presidential nod encounter the same difficulty. To require the presidential nominee to share the same ticket with perhaps his most bitter rival seems foolhardy at best and dangerous at worst. It does not even assure that a vice-presidential figure acceptable to the party will emerge from this process. Indeed, such a suggestion might produce an unbalanced ticket doomed to defeat at the polls and/or a ticket composed of thoroughly incompatible candidates unlikely to work well together in the event of election-day victory.

In light of the difficulties inherent in the system of vice-presidential candidate selection now used as well as in the replacements for it I have outlined, it has even been suggested that the vice-presidential office be abolished; and that, in the event of the President's death, removal, or resignation, the secretary of state be allowed to serve as an interim successor, pending the outcome of a special election.[48] There are serious problems with this sweeping proposal as well. First, it would give great power to an unelected official, even if temporarily. Second, it would require that a special election be held, an expensive and difficult undertaking. If such an election were held only if the deceased President's term had two years or more to run, both parties would have to nominate candidates for President and vice president—with all the system's present defects still intact—and then organize and finance their campaigns (unless public funding be extended to such an election). If such an election were waived in cases where less than two years remained in the deceased President's term, the secretary of state would remain as acting President for a potentially long period. In short, elimination of the vice presidency would create disturbing problems in its own right and should not be seriously considered. Strengthening the vice presidency seems infinitely preferable to eliminating it, since the office provides the country with an elected stand-in who can move up to the presidency should the occasion for succession arise.

The best solution, of course, would be to expect our presidential nominees to consider overall competence as the irreducible minimum for any potential running mate. This might be achieved, according to one scholar, by requiring the President to designate specific responsibilities for the vice president. Political scientist Marie D. Natoli writes:

An informal understanding that a President will assign his Vice President major roles in either domestic or foreign affairs is both constitutionally feasible and a flexible enough mandate so as not to unduly harness a President. Any Vice President incapable either intellectually or politically of being given such assignments should not be in line of presidential succession. Such an understanding would force presidential candidates to give ever greater thought to the qualifications of the individual chosen as vice presidential running mate. [49]

The difficulty here is that presidential candidates always argue—publicly, at least—that their vice-presidential running mate is capable of handling any such assignments. Their private thoughts on the subject, however, remain highly "classified." Since their immediate goal is to win the election, and their inclination is to worry about governing later, presidential nominees are still likely to focus on the political attributes of their potential running mates and to defer until later consideration of the vice president's substantive role in the administration. So, while the suggestion that the President designate specific executive powers and responsibilities to the vice president is a good one, it is not likely, in and of itself, to produce excellent vice-presidential nominees.

Perhaps the most reasonable solution, then, would be to recommend that both parties institute a modest change in the way vice-presidential nominees are chosen. Under this proposed rule change, the presidential nominee would be permitted to offer to the convention the names of *three* acceptable running mates and then have the final choice made by majority vote of convention delegates themselves. The presidential candidate should know the identity of some, if not all, of these vice-presidential possibilities before the convention meets, so the time frame of the convention need not pose an insurmountable obstacle to this recommendation. In order to give the presidential nominee time to consult with party leaders from around the country, and party leaders the chance to weigh the choices offered them, it might be wise to schedule the presidential balloting for the first night of convention proceedings and the vice-presidential balloting for the third night. This would also allow public interest to build and might provide some moments of real drama and excitement to what has become of late a dreary and soporific experience. Ever since primaries and caucuses have given the presidential nomination to candidates *before* the convention even gathers to anoint the "people's choice," popular interest in convention proceedings has been on the wane. Having convention delegates exercise final—even if limited—choice over the vice-presidential selection might reverse the trend and revivify the convention system. Indeed, it might give the convention system a new lease on life, since it would provide delegates with something practical, important, interesting, and visible to do.

Also, allowing the presidential candidate to choose the three "finalists" for the vice-presidential nomination would give him the opportunity to limit that choice to compatible vice-presidential running mates, an extremely important objective. It would also give voters an opportunity to judge the caliber of the presidential candidate's vice-presidential choices on a much broader and more revealing scale than the present choice of one individual allows. If, for example, a presidential candidate should choose *three* obscure and/or controversial figures as potential running mates, the public might get a better reading of his or her inadequacies as an executive than now becomes evident from the choice of one running mate alone. Effective leaders do not typically surround themselves with weak associates. If a potential President is so insecure or so inept that he or she chooses three weak or seriously flawed potential running mates, voters would do well to know of this fact before rather than after the election. Indeed, just such an eventuality is likely to force a presidential candidate to upgrade his vice-presidential choices.

Finally, a modified vice-presidential selection process would give party leaders a greater role in national candidate selection than they have had for several decades. One reason for the decline and decay of American political parties can be linked to the changes that have been made in the way candidates are nominated for public office. Briefly put, primary voters rather than party leaders make the choices, and parties sometimes reel under the choices made. Allowing convention delegates—party leaders by definition—to make the final choice of the vice-presidential candidate, even if limited to the three names provided by the presidential nominee, will strengthen the party organization in both parties and might provide a welcome, if measured, reversal in party decline.

To be sure, the procedure recommended here might occasionally produce divisive convention battles that might damage the ticket's electability in November. But not only does this seem the only negative to a suggestion that has many positives, but also it would be an additional factor that would cause the presidential nominee to exercise great care in making his or her three selections. Also, let us not forget that the present system can also produce divisive unpleasantness at the convention, as the Democrats demonstrated in 1960 when liberals erupted over Kennedy's choice of Lyndon Johnson for second place on the ticket; and as Republicans demonstrated in 1980 when conservatives vented their unhappiness over Reagan's selection of George Bush for vice president. In fact, allowing convention delegates to choose from a list of three names might even *reduce* friction at some conventions, since the feeling of being arbitrarily dictated to would be avoided and a sense of participation and power engendered.

Most important, this recommendation might lead to an overall improvement in the status of the vice presidency and in the quality of vice-presidential candidates offered to and chosen by our party conventions. In light of the frequent illness and death of American presidents as examined here, this represents the primary and most pressing objective of the proposal. Simply put, a vice-presidential nomination is too important a post to be filled through the whim and wish of one person alone, acting for personal and/or selfish reasons. Adoption of this proposal by both parties should invigorate our convention system, strengthen party structures, heighten public interest, and upgrade the vice presidency in both importance and prestige—all notable achievements in their own right. It might well also reassure the nation that the person who stands a heartbeat away from the presidency has been chosen more carefully and more democratically for the post he or she occupies, and that factors of quality, as well as politics, were involved in the choice.

Conclusion

The pathology and mortality of American presidents remain sobering realities. Although as a nation we can continue to hope for the best, we must also be prepared for the worst, since the worst has frequently befallen us. Constitutionally, we have probably done as much as can be done to deal with the problem. Politically, however, more remains to be done.

Before becoming the nation's chief executive, Woodrow Wilson warned that "men of ordinary physique and discretion cannot be President and live, if the strain be not somehow relieved. We shall be obliged always to be picking our chief magistrates from among wise and prudent athletes—a small class."[50] Wilson, however, who was finally broken by the pressures of the presidency, seems to have overlooked the fact that even wise and prudent athletes can be disabled, if not destroyed, by mental anguish.

In the years since Wilson left the White House, the nation has witnessed again and again the realities of presidential illness, anguish, and death. Indeed, it has suffered—and occasionally wept—because of those realities. Even by themselves, the presidents examined here illustrate all too clearly the mental and physical dangers of the office and the political repercussions of those dangers. Although the American people want their presidents to be heroic and larger-then-life figures, those presidents remain all too mortal, and the stressful position they occupy makes them even more susceptible than other human beings to serious illness and to premature death.

Since 1967, the Constitution has acknowledged the problem of presidential disability and provided legal remedies to deal with it. It remains now for presidents and parties to show the will and determination to apply political remedies to a problem that, though essentially incurable, cannot be dismissed or wished away. Our mortal presidents may expect no more than this; our nation's health should demand no less.

Notes

INTRODUCTION   The President Collapses

1   Interviews with Dr. E. Connie Mariano, 11 September 1997, 16 September 1997, 2 October 1997, 8 October 1997.
2   *Newsweek,* March 31, 1997, p. 7.
3   *New York Times,* 5 May 1991, pp. A1, A38.
4   Dr. Isadore Rosenfeld, quoted in *Newsweek,* 13 May 1991, p. 29.
5   Dr. L. F. Panzir, National Institute of Health, quoted in the *New York Times,* 6 May 1991, p. B9.
6   *New York Times,* 5 May 1991, p. A38; *Newsweek,* 13 May 1991, p. 29.
7   George Bush, *Looking Forward* (New York: Doubleday, 1987), p. 12.
8   Ibid., p. 269.
9   *New York Times,* 6 May 1991, p. B8.
10   Interview with Dr. Lawrence C. Mohr, 21 October, 1997.
11   *New York Times,* 7 May 1991, p. A1.
12   *Newsweek,* 20 May 1991, p. 27.
13   Ibid.
14   Ibid.
15   *New York Times,* 9 January 1992, p. A8.
16   Ann McDaniel and Bill Powell, "A Case of Political Flu," *Newsweek,* 20 January 1992, p. 30.
17   Ibid.; see also the *New York Times,* 9 January 1992, p. A8.
18   *Washington Post,* 9 January 1992, p. 31.
19   *New York Times,* 9 January 1992, p. A8.
20   Ibid.
21   Ibid., p. A1.
22   Ibid., p. A8.
23   *Washington Post,* 9 January 1992, p. 1.
24   Ibid., p. 31.
25   Ibid., p. 29.
26   Ibid., p. 1.
27   *New York Times,* 9 January 1992, p. A8.
28   *Washington Post,* 9 January 1992, p. 29.

ONE   Presidential Pathology and Mortality

1   Dorothy Buckton James, *The Contemporary Presidency* (New York: Pegasus, 1969), p. 104.
2   Milton Plesur, "The Health of Presidents," in Rexford G. Tugwell and

Thomas E. Cronin, eds., *The Presidency Reappraised* (New York: Praeger, 1974), p. 189.

3   Richard M. Pious, *The American Presidency* (New York: Basic Books, 1979), p. 12.

4   Thomas E. Cronin, *The State of The Presidency* (Boston: Little, Brown, 1980), pp. 1, 379.

5   Frederick M. Kaiser, "Presidential Assassinations and Assaults: Characteristics and Impact on Protective Procedures," *Presidential Studies Quarterly* (Fall 1981): 545.

6   Paul H. Jacobson, "An Estimate of the Expectation of Life in the United States in 1850," *Millbank Memorial Fund Quarterly* (April 1957): 197.

7   Louis I. Dublin, Alfred J. Lotka, and Mortimer Spiegelman, *Length of Life* (New York: Ronald Press, 1948), pp. 66, 217, 222.

8   Theodore C. Sorenson, *Kennedy* (New York: Harper & Row, 1965), p. 376.

9   Lyndon B. Johnson, *The Vantage Point* (New York: Holt, Rinehart & Winston, 1971), p. 566.

10   Eric Goldman, *The Tragedy of Lyndon Johnson* (New York: Alfred A. Knopf, 1969), pp. 511–12.

11   Reagan is presently suffering from advanced Alzheimer's disease, which his doctors believe developed *after* he left office. See *New York Times,* 5 October 1997, p. 1.

12   James W. Davis, *The National Executive Branch* (New York: Free Press, 1970), pp. 1–2.

13   James, *Contemporary Presidency,* p. 101.

14   Rowland Evans, Jr. and Robert D. Novak, *Nixon in the White House: The Frustration of Power* (New York: Random House, 1971), p. 48.

15   Robert Graves's translation of a poem by Domingo Ortego, quoted in Sorenson, *Kennedy,* p. 336.

16   *Science Newsletter,* 13 February 1965, p. 102.

17   Patrick Anderson, *The President's Men* (New York: Anchor Books, 1969), p. 8.

18   Johnson, *Vantage Point,* p. ix.

19   See *Newsweek,* 8 July 1991, p. 47.

20   R. H. Rosenman, M. Friedman, R. Straus, M. Wurm, C. D. Jenkins, and H.B. Messinger, "Coronary Heart Disease in the Western Collaborative Group Study," *Journal of the American Medical Association* 195 (1966): 86–89.

21   Rufus P. Browning and Herbert Jacob, "Power Motivation and the Political Personality," *Public Opinion Quarterly* 28 (1964): 82.

22   Gary M. Maranell, "The Evaluation of Presidents: An Extension of the Schlesinger Polls," *Journal of American History* (June 1970): 104–13.

23   Ibid., p. 112.

24   Robert K. Murray, *The Politics of Normalcy* (New York: W. W. Norton, 1973), p. 21.

25   Francis Russell, *The Shadow of Blooming Grove* (New York: McGraw-Hill, 1968), p. 559.

26   Ibid., p. 588.

27   Richard A. Hansen, *The Year We Had No President* (Lincoln: University of Nebraska Press, 1962); p. 49; also Plesur, "Health of Presidents," p. 189.

28   Hugh L'Etang, *The Pathology of Leadership* (London: William Heinemann Medical Books, 1969), p. 55.

29   Ibid.
30   Holman Hamilton, *Zachary Taylor* (New York: Bobbs-Merrill, 1951), p. 352.
31   Ibid.
32   Brainerd Dyer, *Zachary Taylor* (New York: Barnes & Noble, 1946), p. 332.
33   Elbert B. Smith, *The Presidencies of Zachary Taylor and Millard Fillmore* (Lawrence: University Press of Kansas, 1988), p. 156.
34   K. Jack Bauer, *Zachary Taylor* (Baton Rouge: Louisiana State University Press, 1985), pp. 314–15.
35   Dyer, *Zachary Taylor*, p. 405.
36   Robert Karasek, Dean Baker, Frank Marxer, Anders Ahlbom, and Tores Theorell, "Job Decision Latitude, Job Demands, and Cardiovascular Disease: A Prospective Study of Swedish Men," *American Journal of Public Health* 71 (July 1981): 684.
37   Robert A. Karasek, "Job Demands, Job Decision Latitude, and Mental Strain: Implications for Job Redesign," *Administrative Science Quarterly* 24 (June 1979): 303.
38   Metropolitan Life Insurance Company, "Statistical Bulletin," December 1970, p. 3.
39   Ibid., October 1971, pp. 3–4.
40   Ibid.
41   See *Science News*, March 1978, p. 151; see also David C. Glass, "Stress, Competition and Heart Attacks," *Psychology Today*, December 1976, p. 57; and Stephen M. Sales and James House, "Job Dissatisfaction as a Possible Risk Factor in Coronary Heart Disease," *Journal of Chronic Disease* 231 (1971): 861–73.
42   Martin G. Lewis and Terence M. Phillips, "The Possible Effects of Emotional Stress on Cancer Mediated Through the Immune System," in Jean Tache, Hans Selye and Stacey B. Day, eds., *Cancer, Stress and Death*, (New York: Plenum Medical Books, 1979), p. 25.
43   *Science News*, March 1978, p. 151.
44   *Harper's Bazaar*, August 1976, p. 105.
45   *Scientific Digest* 90 (September 1982): 92.
46   Ibid.
47   Lawrence S. Sklar and Hymie Anisman, "Stress and Coping Factors Influence Tumor Growth," *Science*, 3 August 1979, p. 513.
48   *Science*, 2 July 1976, p. 74.
49   Hans Selye, "Stress, Cancer and The Mind," in Tache, Selye, and Day, eds., *Cancer, Stress and Death*, p. 17.
50   *New York Times*, 24 May 1983, p. C1.
51   Philip R. Moran, ed., *Ulysses S. Grant* (Dobbs Ferry, N.Y.: Oceana Publications, 1968), p. 17.
52   Paul Rosch, "Stress and Cancer: A Disease of *Adaptation?*" in Tache, Selye, and Day, eds., *Cancer, Stress and Death*, p. 191.
53   Arthur S. Link, *Wilson: The New Freedom* (Princeton, N.J.: Princeton University Press, 1956), p. 88.

TWO The Trauma of Death: Calvin Coolidge

1   See Robert K. Murray and Tim H. Blessing, *Greatness in the White House: Rating the Presidents, Washington through Carter* (University Park: Pennsylvania State University Press, 1988), pp. 16–17.

2   Sidney Warren, *The President as World Leader* (New York: McGraw-Hill 1964), p. 146.

3   Thomas Bailey, *Presidential Greatness* (New York: Appleton-Century-Crofts, 1966), p. 317.

4   Louis Koenig, *The Chief Executive* (New York: Harcourt Brace Jovanovich, 1975), p. 344.

5   Robert Murray, *The Politics of Normalcy* (New York: W. W. Norton, 1973), p. 143.

6   Milton Plesur, "The Health of Presidents," in Rexford G. Tugwell and Thomas E. Cronin, eds., *The Presidency Reappraised* (New York: Praeger, 1974), p. 188.

7   John C. Coolidge, Coolidge Collection, MS 1.1 (Forbes Library, Northampton, Massachusetts).

8   Ibid.

9   John Coolidge, *My Son Calvin Coolidge* (Northampton, Mass.: Forbes Library, 1923), p. 7.

10 Ibid., p. 10.

11 Ernest C. Carpenter, *The Boyhood Days of President Calvin Coolidge* (Rutland, Vt.: Marble City Press, 1925), pp. 115–25.

12 Donald McCoy, *Calvin Coolidge* (New York: Macmillan, 1967), p. 8.

13 Edward C. Lathem, *Your Son, Calvin Coolidge* (Montpelier: Vermont Historical Society, 1968), p. vii.

14 McCoy, *Calvin Coolidge*, p. 9.

15 Coolidge, *My Son Calvin Coolidge*, p. 11.

16 Carpenter, *Boyhood Days*, p. 78.

17 McCoy, *Calvin Coolidge*, p. 5.

18 Calvin Coolidge, *The Autobiography of Calvin Coolidge* (New York: Cosmopolitan Book Corporation, 1929), p. 13.

19 Edmund W. Starling, *Starling of the White House* (New York: Simon & Schuster, 1946), p. 211.

20 Ibid., p. 212.

21 Calvin Coolidge, *Autobiography*, p. 47.

22 Fuess Collection, MS 1.3 (Forbes Library, Northampton, Massachusetts).

23 Ibid.

24 Ibid.

25 Claude Fuess, *Calvin Coolidge* (Boston: Little, Brown, 1940), p. 123.

26 *Boston Traveler*, 2 January 1919, Scrapbook, vol. 8, p. 104 (Massachusetts State Library, Boston).

27 McCoy, *Calvin Coolidge*, pp. 79–80.

28 Ibid., p. 79.

29   *Boston Herald,* 30 June 1919, Scrapbook, vol. 9, p. 140 (Massachusetts State Library, Boston).
30   McCoy, *Calvin Coolidge,* p. 80.
31   *Springfield Republican,* 25 April 1919, Scrapbook, vol. 9, p. 67 (Massachusetts State Library, Boston).
32   *Boston Record,* 3 January 1919, Scrapbook, vol. 8, p. 100 (Massachusetts State Library, Boston).
33   Guy Fair Goodfellow, *Calvin Coolidge: A Study of Presidential Inaction* (Ann Arbor, Mich.: University Microfilms, 1969), p. 35.
34   *Western Massachusetts Labor Review,* 19 October 1919, Scrapbook, vol. 11, p. 43 (Massachusetts State Library, Boston).
35   McCoy, *Calvin Coolidge,* p. 79.
36   Calvin Coolidge, *Have Faith in Massachusetts* (Boston: Houghton Mifflin, 1919), pp. 191–94.
37   Fuess, *Calvin Coolidge,* p. 199.
38   McCoy, *Calvin Coolidge,* p. 84.
39   Calvin Coolidge, *Have Faith,* p. 221.
40   Ibid., pp. 222–23.
41   Calvin Coolidge, *Autobiography,* p. 141.
42   Fuess, *Calvin Coolidge,* p. 199.
43   McCoy, *Calvin Coolidge,* p. 82.
44   Ibid., p. 114.
45   Lathem, *Your Son, Calvin Coolidge,* p. 22.
46   Ibid., pp. 58, 106, 139, 150, 153.
47   McCoy, *Calvin Coolidge,* p. 121.
48   Calvin Coolidge, *Autobiography,* pp. 176–77.
49   Ibid., p. 177.
50   Theodore Roosevelt, Jr., "Diary," 3 August 1923, MSS, Library of Congress, Washington, D.C.
51   *Boston Sunday Post,* 27 March 1921, Scrapbook, vol. 14, p. 43 (Massachusetts State Library, Boston).
52   Thomas E. Cronin, *The State of the Presidency* (Boston: Little, Brown, 1975), p. 213.
53   Lathem, *Your Son, Calvin Coolidge,* p. 132.
54   Goodfellow, *Calvin Coolidge,* p. 115.
55   Philip R. Moran, ed., *Calvin Coolidge* (Dobbs Ferry, N. Y.: Oceana Publications, 1970), p. 10.
56   James MacGregor Burns, *Presidential Government* (Boston: Houghton Mifflin, 1965), p. 295.
57   Elmer E. Cornwell, *Presidential Leadership of Public Opinion* (Bloomington: Indiana University Press, 1965), p. 74.
58   Howard H. Quint and Robert H. Ferrell, *The Talkative President* (Amherst: University of Massachusetts Press, 1964), p. 20.
59   *Boston Globe,* 2 September 1923, Scrapbook, vol. 25, p. 37 (Massachusetts State Library, Boston).
60   Quint and Ferrell, *Talkative President,* p. 23.

61 McCoy, *Calvin Coolidge*, p. 151.
62 Goodfellow, *Calvin Coolidge*, p. 147.
63 McCoy, *Calvin Coolidge*, p. 197.
64 Robert Murray, *The Harding Era* (Minneapolis: University of Minnesota Press, 1969), p. 502.
65 McCoy, *Calvin Coolidge*, p. 197.
66 Goodfellow, *Calvin Coolidge*, pp. 208–37.
67 McCoy, *Calvin Coolidge*, pp. 178, 179.
68 Joseph E. Kallenbach, *The American Chief Executive* (New York: Harper & Row, 1966), p. 278.
69 Elmer E. Cornwell, "Coolidge and Presidential Leadership," *Public Opinion Quarterly* 21 (1957): 268; James David Barber, *The Pulse of Politics* (New York: W. W. Norton, 1980), p. 231; Goodfellow, *Calvin Coolidge*, p. 65.
70 Fred L. Israel, ed., *The State of the Union Messages of the Presidents, 1790–1966*, vol. 3 (New York: Chelsea House, 1967), pp. 2642, 2645, 2646, 2648, 2649, 2651.
71 Ibid., pp. 2642–43, 2654, 2649.
72 Goodfellow, *Calvin Coolidge*, p. 118.
73 Robert J. Maddox, "Keeping Cool with Coolidge," *Journal of American History*, 53 (1966–67): 774.
74 Barber, *Pulse of Politics*, p. 15.
75 William T. Hutchinson, *Lowden of Illinois* (Chicago: University of Chicago Press, 1957), p. 534.
76 *Boston Traveler*, 30 July 1924, vol. 35, p. 120 (Massachusetts State Library, Boston).
77 *Boston Herald*, 7 August 1923, Scrapbook, vol. 24, p. 114 (Massachusetts State Library, Boston).
78 Starling, *Starling of the White House*, p. 207.
79 Ibid., p. 221.
80 William Allen White, *A Puritan in Babylon* (New York: Macmillan, 1938), p. 308.
81 McCoy, *Calvin Coolidge*, p. 251.
82 White, *Puritan in Babylon*, p. 308.
83 Lathem, *Your Son, Calvin Coolidge*, pp. 190–91.
84 Dr. Joel Boone, Unpublished Autobiography, Box 67, Chapter XXI, p. 212 (Washington, D.C.: Library of Congress); Interview with John Coolidge, August 2, 1997; Edward D. Lathem, ed., *Meet Calvin Coolidge* (Brattleboro, Vt.: Stephen Green Press, 1960), p. 140.
85 Goodfellow, *Calvin Coolidge*, pp. 318–19.
86 Calvin Coolidge, *Autobiography*, p. 190.
87 McCoy, *Calvin Coolidge*, p. 251.
88 Ishbel Ross, *Grace Coolidge and Her Era* (New York: Dodd, Mead, 1962), p. 286.
89 Goodfellow, *Calvin Coolidge*, p. 322.
90 Fuess, *Calvin Coolidge*, p. 350.
91 Quint and Ferrell, *Talkative President*, p. 40.
92 Fuess, *Calvin Coolidge*, pp. 350–51.
93 Ross, *Grace Coolidge*, p. 123.
94 Lathem, *Your Son, Calvin Coolidge*, pp. 197, 198, 200, 204, 205.
95 Ibid., p. 216.
96 Starling, *Starling of the White House*, p. 224.

97 Grace Coolidge, Letters, Coolidge Collection (Forbes Library, Northampton, Massachusetts).
98 Ibid.
99 Marian G. Secundy, "Bereavement: The Role of the Family Physician," in James A. Fruehling, ed., *Sourcebook on Death and Dying* (Chicago: Marquis Professional Publications, 1982), p. 181.
100 McCoy, *Calvin Coolidge*, p. 267.
101 Murray, *Politics of Normalcy*, p. 142.
102 Wilfred E. Binkley, *President and Congress* (New York: Vintage Books, 1962), p. 277.
103 Arthur Schlesinger, "Annual Message of the Presidents: Major Themes of American History," in Fred L. Israel, ed., *The State of the Union Messages of the Presidents*, vol. 1 (New York: Chelsea House, 1965), p. xvii.
104 Israel, *State of the Union Messages*, vol. 3, pp. 2692, 2696, 2723, 2732.
105 Warren, *President as World Leader*, p. 147.
106 Fuess, *Calvin Coolidge*, p. 406.
107 Starling, *Starling of the White House*, p. 209.
108 Quint and Ferrell, *Talkative President*, p. 73.
109 James David Barber, "Classifying and Predicting Presidential Style: Two 'Weak' Presidents," *Journal of Social Issues* 24 (1968): 55.
110 *Boston Globe*, 19 November 1920, Scrapbook, vol. 14, p. 34 (Massachusetts State Library, Boston).
111 Calvin Coolidge, *Autobiography*, pp. 198–99.
112 Ibid. p. 190.
113 Erich Lindemann, "Symptomatology and Management of Acute Grief," *American Journal of Psychiatry* 101 (1944): 142.
114 Calvin Coolidge, *Autobiography*, p. 190.
115 White, *Puritan in Babylon*, p. 308.
116 Calvin Coolidge, *Autobiography*, p. 190.
117 Irwin Hood Hoover, *Forty-two Years in the White House* (Westport, Conn.: Greenwood Press, 1962), pp. 239, 235, 132.
118 Ibid., p. 232.
119 Karen Horney, *The Neurotic Personality of Our Time* (New York: W. W. Norton, 1937), pp. 248–49.
120 Karen Horney, *Our Inner Conflicts* (New York: W. W. Norton, 1945), p. 120.
121 Hoover, *Forty-two Years*, p. 132.
122 Goodfellow, *Calvin Coolidge*, p. 70.
123 Hoover, *Forty-two Years*, p. 233.
124 Lindemann, "Symptomatology," p. 142.
125 Horney, *Our Inner Conflicts*, pp. 121–22.
126 McCoy, *Calvin Coolidge*, p. 389.
127 Fuess, *Calvin Coolidge*, pp. 370, 430.
128 McCoy, *Calvin Coolidge*, p. 390.
129 Ibid.
130 Goodfellow, *Calvin Coolidge*, p. 69.
131 James David Barber, *The Presidential Character* (Englewood Cliffs, N. J.: Prentice-Hall, 1977), p. 147.

132 Horney, *Our Inner Conflicts,* p. 121.
133 Elmer Plischke, *Conduct of American Diplomacy* (Princeton, N. J.: Van Nostrand, 1967), p. 44.
134 American Psychiatric Association, *Diagnostic and Statistical Manual of Mental Disorders,* 3rd ed. (New York: Brunner/Mazel, 1981), pp. 213–14.
135 Erik H. Erikson, *Childhood and Society* (New York: W. W. Norton, 1963), p. 75.
136 Erik H. Erikson, *Identity and Life Cycle: Selected Papers* (New York: International Universities Press, 1959), p. 68.
137 Erik H. Erikson, "Life Cycle, The Human," *International Encyclopedia of the Social Sciences,* vol. 9 (New York: Macmillan, 1968), p. 289.
138 Erik H. Erikson, *Identity: Youth and Crisis* (New York: W. W. Norton, 1968), p. 138.
139 Erik H. Erikson, *Young Man Luther: A Study in Psychoanalysis and History* (New York: W. W. Norton, 1958), p. 225.
140 Erik H. Erikson, *Ghandi's Truth* (New York: W. W. Norton, 1969), p. 395.

THREE Functioning in Chains: Franklin D. Roosevelt

1 Rudolf Marx, *The Health of Presidents* (New York: G. P. Putnam, 1960), p. 353.
2 Noah D. Fabricant, *13 Famous Patients* (Philadelphia: Chilton Company, 1960), p. 3.
3 Ibid., p. 4.
4 John Gunther, *Roosevelt in Retrospect* (New York: Harper & Row, 1950), p. 219.
5 Eleanor Roosevelt, *The Autobiography of Eleanor Roosevelt* (New York: Harper & Row, 1961), p. 114.
6 Ibid., p. 115.
7 James Roosevelt and Sidney Shalett, *Affectionately FDR* (New York: Harcourt, Brace and Company, 1959), p. 142.
8 Gunther, *Roosevelt in Retrospect,* p. 222.
9 Hugh G. Gallagher, *FDR's Splendid Deception* (New York: Dodd, Mead, 1985), p. 13; Elliot Roosevelt and James Brough, *An Untold Story: The Roosevelts of Hyde Park* (New York: G. P. Putnam, 1973), pp. 143–45.
10 Gallagher, *FDR's Splendid Deception,* p. 17; Gunther, *Roosevelt in Retrospect,* p. 227.
11 Eleanor Roosevelt, *Autobiography,* p. 117.
12 Ibid., p. 119.
13 Robert D. Graff and Robert E. Ginna, *FDR* (New York: Harper & Row, 1963), p. 59; Kenneth S. Davis, *FDR: The New Deal Years* (New York: Random House, 1986), pp. 158–59.
14 Frank Freidel, *Franklin Roosevelt* (Boston: Little, Brown, 1952), p. 191.
15 Kenneth S. Davis, *FDR: The Beckoning of Destiny* (New York: G. P. Putnam, 1972), p. 655.
16 Eleanor Roosevelt, *Autobiography,* p. 117.

17 Alfred B. Rollins, *Roosevelt and Howe* (New York: Alfred A. Knopf, 1962), p. 192.

18 Arthur M. Schlesinger, *The Crisis of the Old Order* (New York: Houghton Mifflin, 1956), p. 372.

19 Gunther, *Roosevelt in Retrospect*, p. 233.

20 Gallagher, *FDR's Splendid Deception*, p. 60.

21 Ibid., p. 62.

22 Ibid., p. 65.

23 Bernard Bellush, *Franklin D. Roosevelt as Governor of New York* (New York: Columbia University Press, 1955), p. 8.

24 Theo Lippman, *The Squire of Warm Springs* (Chicago: Playboy Press, 1977), p. 66.

25 *New York Times*, 23 October 1928, p. 12.

26 Earland I. Carlson, "Franklin D. Roosevelt's Post-Mortem of the 1928 Election," *Midwest Journal of Political Science* 8 (1964): 300–301.

27 Elliot Roosevelt and James Brough, *A Rendezvous with Destiny* (New York: G. P. Putnam, 1975), p. 64.

28 Lippman, *Squire of Warm Springs*, p. 76.

29 Gunther, *Roosevelt in Retrospect*, p. 236.

30 Gallagher, *FDR's Splendid Deception*, p. 163.

31 Lippman, *Squire of Warm Springs*, p. 63.

32 Michael B. Grossman and Martha Joynt Kumar, *Portraying the President* (Baltimore: Johns Hopkins University Press, 1981), pp. 27–28.

33 Gallagher, *Roosevelt in Retrospect*, p. 94.

34 Lippman, *Squire of Warm Springs*, p. 184.

35 *Life*, 16 August 1937, p. 26.

36 Elmer Cornwell, *Presidential Leadership of Public Opinion* (Bloomington: Indiana University Press, 1965), pp. 255–64.

37 J. B. West, *Upstairs at the White House* (New York: Coward, McCann & Geoghegan, 1973), p. 17.

38 Ibid., p. 18.

39 John B. Moses and Wilbur Cross, *Presidential Courage* (New York: W. W. Norton, 1980), p. 137.

40 Fabricant, *13 Famous Patients*, p. 27.

41 Grace Tully, *FDR: My Boss* (New York: Charles Scribner, 1949), p. 273.

42 James Roosevelt, *My Parents: A Differing View* (Chicago: Playboy Press, 1976), p. 86.

43 Nathan Miller, *FDR: An Intimate History* (New York: Doubleday, 1983), p. 382.

44 *Public Papers and Addresses of Franklin D. Roosevelt* (New York: Random House, 1938), p. 235.

45 Joseph Alsop, *FDR: A Centenary Remembrance* (New York: Viking Press, 1982), p. 97.

46 Alonzo L. Hamby, "Sixty Million Jobs and the People's Revolution: The Liberals, the New Deal and World War II," *Historian*, 30 (1968): 578.

47 Miller, *FDR: An Intimate History*, p. 198.

48 Gallagher, *FDR's Splendid Deception*, p. 95.

49 *Public Papers and Addresses of Franklin D. Roosevelt,* 1938, p. 235.

50 Lippman, *Squire of Warm Springs,* p. 68.

51 President's Personal File, file 528, Franklin D. Roosevelt Library, Hyde Park, New York.

52 Tully, *FDR: My Boss,* p. 33.

53 Schlesinger, *Crisis of the Old Order,* p. 406.

54 Frances Perkins, *The Roosevelt I Knew* (New York: Harper & Row, 1946), p. 29.

55 A. McCormick, "Let's Try It! Says Roosevelt," *New York Times Magazine,* 26 March 1933, p. 19.

56 Herbert E. Bateman, "Observations on President Roosevelt's Health During World War II," *Mississippi Valley Historical Review* 43 (1956): 82.

57 Tully, *FDR: My Boss,* p. 273.

58 Moses and Cross, *Presidential Courage,* p. 200.

59 Ross T. McIntire, *White House Physician* (New York: G. P. Putnam, 1946), p. 14; Tully, *FDR: My Boss,* p. 273; J. A. Halstead, "FDR's 'Little Strokes': A Medical Myth," *Today's Health* 40 (1962): 74.

60 Emerson Letter, 1987 (Franklin D. Roosevelt Library, Hyde Park, New York).

61 Paul H. Appleby, "Roosevelt's Third Term Decision," *American Political Science Review* 46 (September 1952): 754–65.

62 Gallagher, *FDR's Splendid Deception,* p. 172.

63 Tully, *FDR: My Boss,* p. 273.

64 James MacGregor Burns, *Roosevelt: The Soldier of Freedom* (New York: Harcourt Brace Jovanovich, 1970), p. 143.

65 Bert E. Park, *The Impact of Illness on World Leaders* (Philadelphia: University of Pennsylvania Press, 1986), p. 227.

66 Emerson Letter, 1987.

67 McIntire, *White House Physician,* p. 19.

68 Roosevelt and Brough, *Rendezvous with Destiny,* p. 87.

69 Hugh L'Etang, *The Pathology of Leadership* (New York: Hawthorn Books, 1970), p. 92.

70 Rexford G. Tugwell, *The Democratic Roosevelt* (New York: Doubleday, 1957), p. 635.

71 Papers of Ross McIntire, press interview, 13 March 1951, box 8 (Franklin D. Roosevelt Library, Hyde Park, New York).

72 McIntire, *White House Physician,* p. 183.

73 Eleanor Roosevelt, *Autobiography,* p. 268.

74 President's Personal File, box 528.

75 Emerson Letter, 1987.

76 *New York Times,* 5 February 1944, p. 17.

77 Jim Bishop, *FDR's Last Year* (New York: William Morrow, 1974), p. 4; Burns, *Roosevelt,* p. 448.

78 Park, *Impact of Illness on World Leaders,* p. 223.

79 McIntire, *White House Physician,* p. 20.

80 Howard G. Bruenn, "Notes on the Illness and Death of President Franklin D. Roosevelt," *Annals of Internal Medicine* 72 (1970): 580–81.

81 Park, *Impact of Illness on World Leaders,* p. 227.

82 Bruenn, "Notes," p. 580.
83 Bishop, *FDR's Last Year*, p. 6.
84 Joseph P. Lash, *Eleanor and Franklin* (New York: W. W. Norton, 1971), p. 698.
85 Bruenn, "Notes," p. 583.
86 Bishop, *FDR's Last Year*, p. 202.
87 Ibid., p. 4.
88 Park, *Impact of Illness on World Leaders*, p. 227.
89 Bruenn, "Notes," p. 581.
90 Park, *Impact of Illness on World Leaders*, p. 229; see also Bruenn, "Notes," p. 581.
91 McIntire, *White House Physician*, pp. 183–84.
92 Tully, *FDR: My Boss*, p. 274.
93 Bishop, *FDR's Last Year*, p. 7.
94 Papers of Anna Roosevelt Halsted, box 66 (Franklin D. Roosevelt Library, Hyde Park, New York).
95 Bateman, "Observations on President Roosevelt's Health," p. 91.
96 Emerson Letter, 1987.
97 Merriman Smith, *Thank You, Mr. President* (New York: Harper, 1946), pp. 135, 25.
98 Gallagher, *FDR's Splendid Deception*, p. 193.
99 Lash, *Eleanor and Franklin*, p. 708.
100 Eleanor Roosevelt, *Autobiography*, p. 269.
101 McIntire, *White House Physician*, p. 193.
102 James Roosevelt, *My Parents: A Differing View*, p. 278.
103 James A. Farley, *Jim Farley's Story* (New York: McGraw-Hill, 1948), p. 365.
104 McIntire, *White House Physician*, pp. 194–95.
105 Robert E. Sherwood, *Roosevelt and Hopkins* (New York: Harper, 1948), p. 821.
106 Kenneth Crispell and Carlos Gomez, *Hidden Illness in the White House* (Durham, N. C.: Duke University Press, 1988), p. 108.
107 Farley, *Jim Farley's Story*, p. 359.
108 Lash, *Eleanor and Franklin*, p. 708.
109 Burns, *Roosevelt: The Soldier of Freedom*, pp. 505–6.
110 H. Goldsmith, "Unanswered Mysteries in the Death of Franklin D. Roosevelt," *Surgery, Gynecology and Obstetrics* 149 (December 1979): 902.
111 Park, *Impact of Illness on World Leaders*, p. 239; Burns, *Roosevelt*, p. 508.
112 Papers of Ross McIntire, Creel interview, 3 March 1945, box 5 (Franklin D. Roosevelt Library, Hyde Park, New York).
113 Sherwood, *Roosevelt and Hopkins*, p. 820.
114 Gallagher, *FDR's Splendid Deception*, p. 195.
115 Sherwood, *Roosevelt and Hopkins*, p. 825.
116 *The Public Papers and Addresses of Franklin D. Roosevelt* (New York: Russell & Russell, 1950), p. 290.
117 West, *Upstairs at the White House*, p. 46.
118 Smith, *Thank You, Mr. President*, pp. 158–59.
119 Goldsmith, "Unanswered Mysteries," pp. 902–3.

120   McIntire, *White House Physician*, p. 210.
121   Papers of Ross McIntire, press interview, 13 March 1951, box 8 (Franklin D. Roosevelt Library, Hyde Park, New York).
122   Perkins, *The Roosevelt I Knew*, p. 39.
123   Ibid., p. 393.
124   Eleanor Roosevelt, *Autobiography*, p. 273.
125   Perkins, *The Roosevelt I Knew*, p. 393.
126   Harry S Truman, *Memoirs: Year of Decision* (New York: Doubleday, 1955), p. 2.
127   Edward R. Stettinius, *Roosevelt and the Russians* (Garden City, N. Y.: Doubleday, 1949), p. 72.
128   James Roosevelt, *My Parents: A Differing View*, p. 281.
129   John T. Flynn, *The Roosevelt Myth* (New York: Devin-Adair, 1948), p. 394.
130   Moses and Cross, *Presidential Courage*, p. 209.
131   James F. Byrnes, *Speaking Frankly* (New York: Harper & Row, 1947), p. 22.
132   Charles E. Bohlen, *Witness to History* (New York: W. W. Norton, 1973), p. 171.
133   W. Averill Harriman and Elie Abel, *Special Envoy to Churchill and Stalin 1941–1946* (New York: Random House, 1975), pp. 388–89.
134   Bohlen, *Witness to History*, p. 171.
135   Bishop, *FDR's Last Year*, pp. 294–95.
136   Gunther, *Roosevelt in Retrospect*, p. 357.
137   Fabricant, *13 Famous Patients*, p. 29.
138   Winston Churchill, *Triumph and Tragedy* (Boston: Houghton Mifflin, 1953), p. 346.
139   John R. Boettiger, *A Love in Shadow* (New York: W. W. Norton, 1978), p. 260.
140   Gaddis Smith, *American Diplomacy During the Second World War 1941–1945* (New York: John Wiley, 1965), p. 131.
141   Tully, *FDR: My Boss*, p. 274.
142   Tugwell, *Democratic Roosevelt*, p. 635.
143   Park, *Impact of Illness on World Leaders*, p. 228.
144   Papers of Ross McIntire, press interview, 13 March 1951, box 8.
145   Fred Plum and Jerome B. Posner, *Diagnosis of Stupor and Coma* (Philadelphia: F. A. Davis, 1972), p. 170.
146   Park, *Impact of Illness on World Leaders*, p. 236.
147   W. G. Eliasberg and H. O. Teltscher, "How Long Was Roosevelt Ill Before His Death?" *Diseases of the Nervous System* 14 (1953): 5.
148   Ibid., p. 56.
149   Bohlen, *Witness to History*, p. 177.
150   *Foreign Relations of the United States: The Conferences at Malta and Yalta* (Washington, D.C.: Government Printing Office, 1955), p. 566.
151   *Foreign Relations of the United States* (Washington D.C.: Government Printing Office, 1950), p. 52.
152   Bohlen, *Witness to History*, p. 160.
153   Churchill, *Triumph and Tragedy*, p. 358.
154   Department of State Bulletin, 12, 8 April 1945, p. 600.

155 Byrnes, *Speaking Frankly*, p. 41.

156 *Foreign Relations of the United States, 1955*, pp. 48–49.

157 Elmer Plischke, Conduct of American Diplomacy (Princeton, N.J.: Van Nostrand, 1967), p. 566.

158 *Foreign Relations of the United States, 1955*, p. 64.

159 Ibid., p. 905.

160 Stettinius, *Roosevelt and the Russians*, p. 298.

161 Ted Morgan, *FDR: A Biography* (New York: Simon & Schuster, 1985), p. 746.

162 Bohlen, *Witness to History*, p. 196; Gunther, *Roosevelt in Retrospect*, p. 359.

163 *Foreign Relations of the United States, 1955*, p. 567.

164 Bohlen, *Witness to History*, p. 197.

165 Ibid.

166 Stettinius, *Roosevelt and the Russians*, p. 268.

167 John Morton Blum, *From the Morgenthau Diaries: Years of War* (Boston, Houghton Mifflin, 1967), p. 85.

168 Francis L. Loewenheim, Harold D. Langley, and Manfred Jonas, *Roosevelt and Churchill: Their Secret Wartime Correspondence* (New York: E. P. Dutton, 1975), p. 656.

169 Stettinius, *Roosevelt and the Russians*, p. 305.

170 Byrnes, *Speaking Frankly*, p. 43.

171 Stettinius, *Roosevelt and the Russians*, pp. 298, 300.

172 *Foreign Relations of the United States, 1955*, pp. 702, 971.

173 Churchill, *Triumph and Tragedy*, p. 365.

174 *Foreign Relations of the United States, 1955*, p. 617.

175 Harriman and Abel, *Special Envoy*, p. 405.

176 Gallager, *FDR's Splendid Deception*, p. 204; Burns, *Roosevelt*, p. 573.

177 Churchill, *Triumph and Tragedy*, p. 387.

178 *Foreign Relations of the United States, 1955*, p. 781.

179 Stettinius, *Roosevelt and the Russians*, p. 301.

180 *Foreign Relations of the United States, 1950*, p. 905.

181 Bohlen, *Witness to History*, p. 192.

182 *Public Papers and Addresses of Franklin D. Roosevelt, 1950*, p. 582.

183 Eleanor Roosevelt, *Autobiography*, p. 274; McIntire, *White House Physician*, p. 221; Bohlen, *Witness to History*, p. 200.

184 Churchill, *Triumph and Tragedy*, p. 401.

185 *Foreign Relations of the United States, 1955*, pp. 854, 905.

186 Stettinius, *Roosevelt and the Russians*, p. 270.

187 James MacGregor Burns, *Roosevelt: The Lion and the Fox* (New York: Harcourt, Brace & World, 1956), p. 469.

188 Burns, *Roosevelt*, p. 574.

189 Stettinius, *Roosevelt and the Russians*, p. 73.

190 Bohlen, *Witness to History*, p. 172.

191 Bruenn Letter, 1951, Papers of Ross McIntire, box 6 (Franklin D. Roosevelt Library, Hyde Park, New York).

192 Eleanor Roosevelt, *Autobiography*, p. 223.

193 Roosevelt and Brough, *Rendezvous with Destiny*, p. 404.

194 Sherwood, *Roosevelt and Hopkins*, p. 874.
195 Burns, *Roosevelt*, p. 579.
196 Samuel I. Rosenman, *Working with Roosevelt* (New York: Harper, 1952), p. 527.
197 *Public Papers and Addresses of Franklin D. Roosevelt*, 1950, p. 570.
198 Ibid., p. 571.
199 Stettinius, *Roosevelt and the Russians*, p. 281.
200 Roosevelt and Brough, *Rendezvous with Destiny*, p. 401.
201 *Public Papers and Addresses of Franklin D. Roosevelt*, 1950, p. 583.
202 Churchill, *Triumph and Tragedy*, p. 390.
203 Eleanor Roosevelt, *Autobiography*, p. 274.
204 Loewenheim, Langley, and Jonas, *Roosevelt and Churchill*, p. 668.
205 Ibid., pp. 689–90.
206 Joseph Stalin, *Correspondence with Roosevelt and Churchill* (Moscow: Foreign Languages Publishing House, 1957), p. 208.
207 Loewenheim, Langley, and Jonas, *Roosevelt and Churchill*, p. 70.
208 Stettinius, *Roosevelt and the Russians*, p. 309.
209 Francis L. Biddle, *In Brief Authority* (New York: Doubleday, 1962), p. 376.
210 Bishop, *FDR's Last Year*, p. 528.
211 Papers of Ross McIntire, Creel memorandum, 29 April 1946, box 6, p. 13 (Franklin D. Roosevelt Library, Hyde Park, New York).
212 J. Paullin Letter, Papers of Ross McIntire, box 6.
213 Bishop, *FDR's Last Year*, p. 620.
214 Bernard Asbell, *When FDR Died* (New York: Holt, Rinehart & Winston, 1961), p. 128.
215 Goldsmith, "Unanswered Mysteries," p. 899.
216 McIntire, *White House Physician*, p. 14.
217 L'Etang, *Pathology of Leadership*, p. 95.
218 *New York Times*, 19 February 1986, p. 8.
219 James Roosevelt, *My Parents: A Differing View*, p. 278.

FOUR Pain and Duty: Dwight D. Eisenhower

1 *Public Papers of the Presidents, Dwight D. Eisenhower, 1956* (Washington, D.C.: U.S. Government Printing Office, 1958), p. 229.
2 Dwight D. Eisenhower, *At Ease* (Garden City, N. Y.: Doubleday, 1967), p. 76.
3 Milton Eisenhower, Oral History (1967), p. 104 (Abilene, Kans.: Dwight D. Eisenhower Library).
4 Marquis Childs, *Eisenhower: Captive Hero* (New York: Harcourt, Brace & World, 1958), p. 18.
5 Bela Kornitzer, *The Great American Heritage* (New York: Farrar, Straus & Cudahy, 1955), p. 73.
6 Eisenhower, *At Ease*, p. 32.
7 Ibid., p. 31.
8 John Gunther, *Eisenhower* (New York: Harper, 1951), p. 49.

9   Eisenhower, *At Ease,* pp. 37, 32.

10 Merle Miller, *Ike The Soldier* (New York: G. P. Putnam, 1987), p. 51.

11 Robert F. Burk, *Dwight D. Eisenhower, Hero and Politician* (Boston: Twayne, 1986), p. 4.

12 David Eisenhower, *Eisenhower: At War* (New York: Random House, 1986), p. 201.

13 Kornitzer, *Great American Heritage,* p. 25.

14 Burk, *Dwight D. Eisenhower,* p. 4.

15 Eisenhower, *At Ease,* p. 76.

16 Ibid., p. 51.

17 Merriman Smith, *Meet Mister Eisenhower* (New York: Harper, 1954), p. 223.

18 Eisenhower, *At Ease,* p. 353.

19 Thomas Mattingly, A Compilation of the General Health Status of Dwight D. Eisenhower, box 1, "General Health," p. 10 (Abilene, Kans.: Dwight D. Eisenhower Library).

20 Kevin McCann, *Man from Abilene* (Garden City, N. Y.: Doubleday, 1952), p. 63.

21 Elmo Richardson, *The Presidency of Dwight D. Eisenhower* (Lawrence: Regents Press of Kansas, 1979), p. 3.

22 Eisenhower, *At Ease,* p. 12.

23 Miller, *Ike The Soldier,* p. 23.

24 McCann, *Man from Abilene,* p. 63.

25 Eisenhower, *At Ease,* p. 15.

26 Stephen E. Ambrose, *Eisenhower,* vol. 1 (New York: Simon & Schuster, 1983), p. 65.

27 Robert L. Branyan and Lawrence H. Larsen, *The Eisenhower Administration,* vol. 1 (New York: Random House, 1971), p. 4.

28 Ambrose, *Eisenhower,* pp. 119, 127.

29 Stephen E. Ambrose, *The Supreme Commander: The War Years of General Dwight D. Eisenhower* (Garden City, N. Y.: Doubleday, 1970), p. 320.

30 Steve Neal, *The Eisenhowers: Reluctant Dynasty* (New York: Doubleday, 1978), p. 228.

31 Eisenhower, *At Ease,* p. 354.

32 Kay Summersby, *Eisenhower Was My Boss* (New York: Prentice-Hall, 1948), p. 29.

33 Joseph Patrick Hobbes, *Dear General: Eisenhower's Wartime Letters to Marshall* (Baltimore: Johns Hopkins University Press, 1971), p. 228.

34 David Eisenhower, *Eisenhower: At War,* p. 356.

35 Blanche Wiesen Cook, *The Declassified Eisenhower* (New York: Doubleday, 1981), pp. 63–64.

36 Wilton Persons, Oral History (1970), p. 35 (Abilene, Kans.: Dwight D. Eisenhower Library).

37 Gunther, *Eisenhower,* p. 89.

38 Miller, *Ike The Soldier,* p. 204.

39 I. F. Stone, *The Haunted Fifties* (Boston: Little, Brown, 1963), p. 105.

40 Mattingly, box 1, "General Health," p. 19.

41 Eisenhower, *At Ease,* p. 353.

42 Mattingly, box 1, "General Health," p. 23.
43 Miller, *Ike The Soldier*, p. 257.
44 Mattingly, box 1, "General Health," p. 21.
45 David Eisenhower, *Eisenhower: At War*, p. 440.
46 Mattingly, box 1, "General Health," p. 53.
47 Piers Brendon, *Ike* (New York: Harper & Row, 1986), p. 179.
48 Mattingly, box 1, "General Health," p. 69.
49 Ambrose, *Eisenhower*, pp. 479, 483; Childs, *Eisenhower: Captive Hero*, p. 110.
50 Howard McCrum Snyder, Papers, box 11, "Draft on DDE 1949–50," p. 116 (Abilene, Kans.: Dwight D. Eisenhower Library).
51 Eisenhower, *At Ease*, p. 354.
52 Snyder, box 11, "Draft on DDE 1949–50," pp. 120, 123, 128.
53 Burk, *Dwight D. Eisenhower*, p. 105; Peter Lyon, *Eisenhower, Portrait of the Hero* (Boston: Little, Brown, 1974), p. 394.
54 Mattingly, box 1, "Cardiovascular System," part I, pp. 5, 40–41.
55 Ibid., p. 27.
56 Ibid., p. 29.
57 Miller, *Ike The Soldier*, p. 40.
58 Eisenhower, *At Ease*, p. 355.
59 Mattingly, box 1, "Cardiovascular System"—part I, addenda.
60 Snyder, box 11, "Draft on DDE 1951," p. 176.
61 Eisenhower, *At Ease*, p. 377.
62 Ambrose, *Eisenhower*, p. 551.
63 Smith, *Meet Mister Eisenhower*, p. 229.
64 Stephen E. Ambrose, *Eisenhower, The President*, vol. 2 (New York: Simon & Schuster, 1984), p. 95.
65 Lyon, *Portrait of the Hero*, p. 532.
66 Childs, *Eisenhower: Captive Hero*, p. 189.
67 Mattingly, box 1, "General Health," pp. 91, 92.
68 Ibid., p. 92.
69 Ibid., box 1, "Cardiovascular System," part I, pp. 4, 5, 7, 9.
70 Paul Dudley White, *My Life and Medicine* (Boston: Gambit Press, 1971), p. 183.
71 Snyder, box 11, "Draft on DDE's Heart Attack, September, 1955," p. 3.
72 Dwight D. Eisenhower, *Mandate for Change* (Garden City, N. Y.: Doubleday, 1963), p. 536.
73 Snyder, box 11, "Draft on DDE's Heart Attack," p. 4.
74 Mattingly, box 1, "Cardiovascular System"—part I, addenda, p. 18.
75 Richard M. Nixon, *Six Crises* (Garden City, N. Y.: Doubleday, 1962), p. 137.
76 Snyder, box 11, "Draft on DDE's Heart Attack," p. 6.
77 Ibid., p. 8.
78 Ibid., p. 10.
79 Ibid., p. 12.
80 Mattingly, box 1, "Cardiovascular System"—part I, addenda, p. 33.
81 Snyder, box 11, "Draft on DDE's Heart Attack," p. 14.
82 Ibid., p. 17.
83 William E. Robinson, Papers, 1932–69, box 3, "Eisenhower—October 1955" (Abilene, Kans.: Dwight D. Eisenhower Library).

84   James C. Hagerty, Papers, box 43, "James C. Hagerty's Press Conferences, 24 September through 8 October 1955, p. 1 (Abilene, Kans.: Dwight D. Eisenhower Library).

85   Mattingly, box 1, "Cardiovascular System," part I, p. 40.

86   Snyder, box 11, "Draft on DDE's Heart Attack," p. 19.

87   Hagerty, Box 43, "James C. Hagerty's Press Conferences," 24 September–8 October 1955, p. 1.

88   Piers Brendon, *Ike* (New York: Harper & Row, 1986), p. 313.

89   White, *My Life and Medicine*, pp. 178–79.

90   Snyder, box 11, "Draft on DDE's Heart Attack," p. 28.

91   Hagerty, box 43, "James C. Hagerty's Press Conferences," 24 September–8 October 1955, pp. 1, 3.

92   Mattingly, box 1, "Cardiovascular System"—part I, addenda, p. 20.

93   Snyder, box 11, "Draft on DDE's Heart Attack," p. 30.

94   Mattingly, box 1, "Cardiovascular System"—part I, addenda, p. 22.

95   Ibid., box 1, "Cardiovascular System"—part II, addenda 1–4.

96   Snyder, box 11, "Draft on DDE's Heart Attack," p. 32.

97   Mattingly, box 3, "Cardiovascular System," part VIII, p. 15.

98   Mattingly, box 1, "Cardiovascular System"—part I, addenda, p. 25.

99   James C. Hagerty, Oral History (1968), p. 296 (Abilene, Kans.: Dwight D. Eisenhower Library).

100 Ibid., p. 297.

101 Robert J. Donovan, *Eisenhower, The Inside Story* (New York: Harper, 1956), p. 367.

102 White, *My Life and Medicine*, p. 181.

103 Hagerty, Oral History, p. 300.

104 Eisenhower, *Mandate for Change*, p. 538.

105 C. D. Jackson, Papers, box 56, "Time, Inc. File—Log—1955" (Abilene, Kans.: Dwight D. Eisenhower Library).

106 Dwight D. Eisenhower, Papers as President of the United States, Ann Whitman File, Speech Series, box 14 (Abilene, Kans.: Dwight D. Eisenhower Library).

107 Snyder, box 7, "Medical Diary re DDE," 24 September–31 December 1955 (2).

108 Eisenhower, *Mandate for Change*, p. 544.

109 Dwight D. Eisenhower, Papers as President of the United States, Ann Whitman File, DDE Diary Series, box 11 (Abilene, Kans.: Dwight D. Eisenhower Library).

110 Richardson, *Presidency of Dwight D. Eisenhower*, p. 88.

111 Nixon, *Six Crises*, p. 154.

112 Richard M. Nixon, *RN* (New York: Grosset & Dunlap, 1978), p. 168.

113 Sherman Adams, *Firsthand Report* (New York: Harper, 1961), p. 191.

114 Dwight D. Eisenhower, Papers as President of the United States, Ann Whitman File, Cabinet Series, box 6, p. 5 (Abilene, Kans.: Dwight D. Eisenhower Library).

115 Nixon, *Six Crises*, p. 152.

116 Snyder, box 7, "Medical Diary re DDE," 24 September 1955 (2).

117 Donovan, *Eisenhower,* p. 397.
118 Snyder, box 7, "Medical Diary re DDE."
119 Eisenhower Papers, Cabinet Series, box 6.
120 Dwight D. Eisenhower, Papers as President of the United States, Ann Whitman Diary Series, box 8 (Abilene, Kans.: Dwight D. Eisenhower Library).
121 Eisenhower, *Mandate for Change,* p. 545.
122 John S. D. Eisenhower, *Strictly Personal* (New York: Doubleday, 1974), p. 184.
123 Emmet John Hughes, *The Ordeal of Power* (New York: Atheneum, 1963), pp. 193, 227.
124 Nixon, *Six Crises,* p. 147.
125 Ibid., p. 157.
126 Eisenhower Papers, Cabinet Series, box 6, Cabinet Meeting of 13 February 1956, p. 4.
127 Eisenhower, *Mandate for Change,* p. 567.
128 John Mason Brown, *Through These Men* (New York: Harper & Row, 1956), p. 88.
129 William Bragg Ewald, *Eisenhower The President* (Englewood Cliffs, N. J.: Prentice-Hall, 1981), p. 179.
130 Eisenhower, *Mandate for Change,* p. 571.
131 Clarence Randall, Journals, box 3, p. 2 (Abilene, Kans.: Dwight D. Eisenhower Library).
132 Dwight D. Eisenhower, Papers as President of the United States, Ann Whitman File, Name Series, box 12, "Eisenhower, Dr. Milton S.," 1955 (1) (Abilene, Kans.: Dwight D. Eisenhower Library).
133 John Foster Dulles, Papers, White House Memorandum Series, box 3, p. 4 (Abilene, Kans.: Dwight D. Eisenhower Library).
134 Ibid., p. 5.
135 Ewald, *Eisenhower The President,* p. 183.
136 Nixon, *Six Crises,* p. 162.
137 Childs, *Captive Hero,* p. 223.
138 Dwight D. Eisenhower, Papers as President of the United States, Ann Whitman File, Press Conference Series, box 4, "Press Conference 1/8/56" (Abilene, Kans.: Dwight D. Eisenhower Library).
139 Eisenhower, *Mandate for Change,* p. 571.
140 Eisenhower Papers, Press Conference Series, box 4, "Press Conference (Dr. White), 2/14/56."
141 Nixon, *Six Crises,* p. 154.
142 Mattingly, box 1, "General Health," p. 94.
143 Eisenhower Papers, Press Conference Series, box 4, p. 11.
144 Hughes, *Ordeal of Power,* p. 196.
145 Ambrose, *Eisenhower,* vol. 1, p. 281.
146 Robert H. Ferrell, *The Diary of James C. Hagerty* (Bloomington: Indiana University Press, 1983), p. 240.
147 Nixon, *Six Crises,* p. 163.
148 Eisenhower Papers, Name Series, box 12, "Eisenhower, Dr. Milton S.," 1955 (1).

149 Robert Keith Gray, *Eighteen Acres Under Glass* (Garden City, N. Y.: Doubleday, 1962), p. 204.
150 Public Papers, 1956, p. 191.
151 Hagerty, Oral History, p. 314.
152 Nixon, *Six Crises*, p. 152.
153 Eisenhower Papers, Press Conference Series, box 4.
154 Adams, *Firsthand Report*, p. 220.
155 Richardson, *Presidency of Dwight D. Eisenhower*, p. 17.
156 Gray, *Eighteen Acres Under Glass*, p. 111.
157 Snyder, box 11, "Draft on DDE's Ileitis Operation, June 1956," p. 1.
158 Mattingly, box 3, "Gastrointestinal System"—part II, addenda 1–11, pp. 8–10.
159 Andrew Goodpaster, Oral History (1980), p. 28 (Abilene, Kans.: Dwight D. Eisenhower Library).
160 Leonard Heaton, Oral History (1975), p. 40 (Abilene Kans.: Dwight D. Eisenhower Library).
161 Snyder, box 11, "Draft on DDE's Ileitis Operation, June 1956," p. 28.
162 John Eisenhower, *Strictly Personal*, p. 186.
163 Eisenhower Papers, Ann Whitman Diary Series, box 8.
164 Heaton, Oral History, pp. 27, 46.
165 Ibid., p. 56.
166 Hagerty Papers, box 45, "James C. Hagerty's Press Conferences," 8 June–15 July 1956 (1); see also Leonard D. Heaton, Isador S. Ravidin, Brian Blades, and Thomas J. Whelan, "President Eisenhower's Operation for Regional Enteritis," *Annals of Surgery* 159 (1964): 663.
167 Adams, *Firsthand Report*, p. 194.
168 E. Frederick Morrow, *Black Man in the White House* (New York: Coward-McCann, 1963), p. 77.
169 John Eisenhower, *Strictly Personal*, p. 186.
170 Nixon, *Six Crises*, p. 168.
171 Eisenhower Papers, Ann Whitman Diary Series, box 8, "June 1956 Diary."
172 Nixon, *Six Crises*, p. 168.
173 Hughes, *Ordeal of Power*, p. 176.
174 John Eisenhower, *Strictly Personal*, p. 187.
175 Nixon, *Six Crises*, p. 169.
176 Ibid.
177 Snyder, box 1, "Medical Diary re DDE," 1 January–30 September 1956 (1).
178 Ibid. (2).
179 Dwight D. Eisenhower, *Waging Peace* (Garden City, N. Y.: Doubleday, 1965), p. 14.
180 Hughes, *Ordeal of Power*, p. 198.
181 Ibid., p. 22.
182 Mattingly, box 1, "Cardiac System," part III, p. 10.
183 Snyder, box 1, "Medical Diary re DDE," 1 October–31 December 1956.
184 Mattingly, box 1, "General Health," p. 97.
185 Hughes, *Ordeal of Power*, pp. 228, 196.
186 *New York Times*, 6 November 1956, p. 1.

187   Mattingly, box 1, "Cardiovascular System," part III, p. 28.
188   Ibid., p. 25.
189   Ambrose, *Eisenhower The President*, p. 440.
190   Mattingly, box 3, "Nervous System," p. 5.
191   Mattingly, box 1, "General Health," p. 8.
192   Gray, *Eighteen Acres Under Glass*, p. 134.
193   Snyder, box 9, "Medical Diary re DDE," 1 October–31 December 1959 (2).
194   Snyder, box 8, "Medical Diary re DDE," 1 January–31 May 1959 (3).
195   Eisenhower, *Waging Peace*, pp. 227–28.
196   Gray, *Eighteen Acres Under Glass*, p. 197.
197   Snyder, box 1, "Medical Diary re DDE," 1 July–31 December 1957 (4).
198   Richardson, *Presidency of Dwight D. Eisenhower*, p. 132.
199   Nixon, *Six Crises*, p. 171.
200   Adams, *Firsthand Report*, p. 197.
201   John Eisenhower, *Strictly Personal*, p. 196.
202   Adams, *Firsthand Report*, p. 197.
203   White House Office, Office of the Staff Secretary, box 22, "President's Illness," November 1957 (1) (Abilene, Kans.: Dwight D. Eisenhower Library).
204   Mattingly, box 1, "General Health," pp. 99–100.
205   Ambrose, *Eisenhower*, p. 438.
206   Nixon, *Six Crises*, p. 174.
207   Neal, *Eisenhowers: Reluctant Dynasty*, p. 392.
208   Eisenhower Papers, Ann Whitman Diary Series, box 9.
209   Lyon, *Eisenhower: Portrait of the Hero*, p. 761.
210   Snyder, box 1, "Medical Diary re DDE," 1 July–31 December 1957 (3).
211   Ambrose, *Eisenhower The President*, pp. 438–39.
212   Snyder, box 1, "Medical Diary re DDE," 1 July–31 December 1957 (3).
213   Randall, Journals, box 4, "Diary, Monday, December 2, 1957, Executive Office," pp. 3–4.
214   Ambrose, *Eisenhower The President*, p. 439.
215   William Rogers, Papers, box 50, "Eyes Only Memo," p. 1 (Abilene, Kans.: Dwight D. Eisenhower Library).
216   Nixon, *Six Crises*, p. 176.
217   White House Office, Office of the Staff Secretary, box 22, "President's Illness," November 1957 (2), pp. 1–2.
218   Snyder, box 1, "Medical Diary," 1 July–31 December 1957, p. 5.
219   Mattingly, box 3, "Nervous System," p. 11.
220   Snyder, box 1, "Medical Diary," 1 July–31 December 1957 (5).
221   Herbert S. Parmet, *Eisenhower and the American Crusades* (New York: Macmillan, 1972), p. 516.
222   Arthur Larson, *Eisenhower, The President Nobody Knew* (New York: Charles Scribner, 1968), p. 176.
223   Nixon, *Six Crises*, p. 175.
224   Rogers, Papers, box 50, pp. 4–5.
225   Eisenhower, *Waging Peace*, p. 231.
226   Neal, *Eisenhowers: Reluctant Dynasty*, p. 393.
227   Mattingly, box 3, "Nervous System," p. 13.

228   Neal, *Eisenhowers: Reluctant Dynasty*, p. 393.

229   Randall, Journals, box 4, p. 7.

230   Eisenhower Papers, Ann Whitman Diary Series, box 9, "January 1958 (3)."

231   Larson, *Eisenhower, The President Nobody Knew*, p. 177.

232   Snyder, box 8, "Medical Diary re DDE," 1 January–30 June 1958 (2).

233   Mattingly, box 3, "Nervous System," p. 14.

234   Eisenhower, *Waging Peace*, p. 233.

235   Mattingly, box 1, "General Health," p. 98.

236   Snyder, box 8, "Medical Diary re DDE," 1 January–30 June 1958 (1), (4), (5).

237   Snyder, box 8, "Medical Diary re DDE," 1 July–31 December 1958 (2).

238   Snyder, box 8, "Medical Diary re DDE," 1 January–31 May 1959 (2).

239   Snyder, box 9, "Medical Diary re DDE," 1 June–30 September 1959 (1).

240   Hugh L'Etang, *The Pathology of Leadership* (New York: Hawthorn Books, 1970), p. 183.

241   Mattingly, box 1, "General Health," pp. 7, 104.

242   Theodore H. White, *The Making of the President 1960* (New York: Atheneum, 1961), p. 310.

243   Snyder, box 10, "Medical Diary re DDE," 1 September–31 December 1960 (3).

244   Ibid.

245   Snyder, box 10, "Medical Diary re DDE," 1 September–31 December 1960 (2).

246   Ibid. (3).

247   Mattingly, box 1, "General Health," p. 103.

248   Eisenhower, *Waging Peace*, p. 602.

249   Snyder, box 10, "Medical Diary re DDE," 1 September 1960–31 December 1960 (3).

250   Snyder, box 10, "Medical Diary re DDE," 1 January–30 September 1956 (2); Mattingly, box 1, "General Health," pp. 104–5.

251   Snyder, box 9, "Medical Diary re DDE," 1 January–30 April 1960 (5).

252   Mattingly, box 1, "General Health," p. 115.

253   Ibid., pp. 114, 120.

254   Carl W. Hughes, Joseph H. Baugh, Lewis A. Mologne, and Leonard D. Heaton, "A Review of the Late General Eisenhower's Operation: Epilog to a Footnote to History," *Annals of Surgery* 173 (5 [May 1971]): 793.

255   Ibid., p. 794.

256   Mattingly, box 3, "Nervous System," p. 15.

257   Eisenhower, *Strictly Personal*, p. 336.

258   Brendon, *Ike*, p. 353.

259   Larson, *Eisenhower, The President Nobody Knew*, p. 173.

260   Ibid., p. 161.

261   Nixon, *RN*, p. 173.

262   Elmer E. Cornwell, *Presidential Leadership of Public Opinion* (Bloomington: Indiana University Press, 1965), p. 182.

263   Larson, *Eisenhower, The President Nobody Knew*, p. 158.

264   Ibid., p. 161.

265   Eisenhower, *Strictly Personal*, p. 257.

266   Patrick Anderson, *The President's Men* (New York: Doubleday, 1968), p. 138.
267   Mattingly, box 1, "General Health," p. 5.
268   Adams, *Firsthand Report,* p. 50.
269   Stephen Hess, *Organizing the Presidency* (Washington, D.C.: Brookings, 1988), p. 61.
270   Charles C. Alexander, *Holding the Line: The Eisenhower Era* (Bloomington: Indiana University Press, 1975), p. 99.
271   Adams, *Firsthand Report,* p. 185.
272   Herbert Brownell, Oral History (1968), p. 241 (Abilene, Kan.: Dwight D. Eisenhower Library).
273   Nixon, *Six Crises,* p. 148.
274   Ibid., p. 145.
275   Ibid., p. 151.
276   Adams, *Firsthand Report,* p. 186.
277   Ibid.; Parmet, *Eisenhower and the American Crusades,* p. 416.
278   Nixon, *Six Crises,* p. 149.
279   Adams, *Firsthand Report,* p. 185.
280   Interview with Herbert Brownell, Austin, Texas, 5 November 1990.
281   Fred I. Greenstein, *The Hidden Hand Presidency* (New York: Basic Books, 1982), p. 124.
282   Eisenhower Papers, Name Series, box 13, "Eisenhower, Milton," 1956 (2).
283   Eisenhower Papers, Administration Series, box 28.
284   Dwight D. Eisenhower, Papers as President of the United States, NSC Series, box 7, p. 2 (Abilene, Kans.: Dwight D. Eisenhower Library).
285   Ibid., pp. 8–9.
286   Ibid., p. 3.
287   Ibid., pp. 5–6.
288   Eisenhower Papers, Cabinet Series, box 5, p. 1.
289   Ibid., p. 2.
290   Ibid., p. 3.
291   Ibid., p. 4.
292   Nixon, *Six Crises,* p. 150.
293   H. W. Brands, *Cold Warriors* (New York: Columbia University Press, 1988), p. 4.
294   Donovan, *Eisenhower: The Inside Story,* p. 378.
295   Eisenhower Papers, NSC Series, box 7, "260th Meeting of the NSC," 6 October 1955.
296   Nixon, *Six Crises,* p. 151.
297   Dulles, Papers, White House Memorandum Series, box 3, "Meetings with the President" 1955 (2), pp. 1–2.
298   Ambrose, *Eisenhower The President,* pp. 277–78.
299   Lyon, *Eisenhower: Portrait of the Hero,* p. 671.
300   Kenneth W. Thompson, "The Strengths and Weaknesses of Eisenhower's Leadership," in Richard A. Melanson and David Mayers, eds., *Reevaluating Eisenhower* (Urbana: University of Illinois Press, 1987), p. 18.
301   Ezra Taft Benson, *Cross Fire: The Eight Years with Eisenhower* (Garden City, N. Y.: Doubleday, 1962), p. 282.

302 Eisenhower Papers, DDE Diary Series, box 11, "DDE Diary."
303 Anderson, *President's Men*, p. 141.
304 Townsend Hoopes, *The Devil and John Foster Dulles* (Boston: Atlantic Monthly Press, 1973), p. 331.
305 Herman Finer, *Dulles Over Suez* (Chicago: Quadrangle Books, 1964), p. 46.
306 John Robinson Beal, *John Foster Dulles* (New York: Harper, 1957), pp. 258–59.
307 Michael A. Guhin, *John Foster Dulles* (New York: Columbia University Press, 1972), p. 271.
308 Finer, *Dulles Over Suez*, p. 481.
309 Ibid., p. 52.
310 Andrew H. Berding, *Dulles on Diplomacy* (Princeton, N. J.: D. Van Nostrand, 1965), p. 108.
311 Cook, *Declassified Eisenhower*, p. 151.
312 Eisenhower, *Strictly Personal*, p. 187.
313 Brownell, Oral History, p. 243.
314 Eisenhower Papers, Administration Series, box 8, "Herbert Brownell, Jr.," 1957 (3), pp. 3–4.
315 Eisenhower Papers, Name Series, box 7, "Disability of President Memo."
316 Dwight D. Eisenhower, Papers as President of the United States, Ann Whitman File, Legislative Meetings Series, box 2, "Legislative Leaders Meetings," 1957 (2), March–April (Abilene, Kans.: Dwight D. Eisenhower Library).
317 Nixon, *Six Crises*, p. 179.
318 Eisenhower Papers, Administration Series, box 32, "Rogers, William P.," 1958 (5).
319 Eisenhower, *At Ease*, p. 306.
320 Ibid., p. 52.
321 Ibid., p. 32.
322 Oliver Spurgeon English and Gerald H. J. Pearson, *Common Neuroses of Children and Adults* (New York: W. W. Norton, 1937), p. 271.
323 Greenstein, *Hidden Hand Presidency*, p. 45.
324 Michael Beschloss, *Eisenhower* (New York: Edward Burlingame, 1990), p. 28.
325 John Eisenhower, *Dwight D. Eisenhower: Letters to Mamie* (New York: Doubleday, 1978), p. 95.
326 English and Pearson, *Common Neuroses*, p. 189.
327 Eisenhower, *At Ease*, p. 181.
328 Lyon, *Eisenhower: Portrait of The Hero*, p. 57.
329 Eisenhower, *At Ease*, p. 181.
330 Beschloss, *Eisenhower*, p. 28.
331 Eisenhower, *Strictly Personal*, p. 329.
332 English and Pearson, *Common Neuroses*, p. 189.
333 Otto Fenichel, *The Psychoanalytic Theory of Neurosis* (New York: W. W. Norton, 1945), p. 143.
334 Greenstein, *Hidden Hand Presidency*, p. 38.
335 Cook, *The Declassified Eisenhower*, p. 60.
336 McCann, *Man from Abilene*, p. 234.
337 Ambrose, *Eisenhower*, p. 523.

338   Eisenhower Papers, Press Conference Series, box 4, "Press Conference 1/19/56," p. 3.
339   Greenstein, *Hidden Hand Presidency*, p. 45.
340   Eisenhower, *Mandate for Change*, p. 567.
341   Eisenhower Papers, Press Conference Series, box 4, "Press Conference 1/8/56," p. 3.
342   Nixon, *RN*, p. 169.
343   Public Papers, 1956, pp. 288, 291–92.
344   Morrow, *Black Man in the White House*, p. 190.
345   Neal, *Eisenhowers: Reluctant Dynasty*, p. 393.
346   Eisenhower Papers, Name Series, box 18, "Hazlett, Swede," January 1956–November 1958 (2), p. 5.
347   Eisenhower, *At Ease*, p. 316.
348   Ibid., p. 336.
349   Ambrose, *Eisenhower*, p. 479.
350   Eisenhower, *At Ease*, p. 361.
351   Robert H. Ferrell, *The Eisenhower Diaries* (New York: W. W. Norton, 1981), p. 372.
352   Smith, *Meet Mister Eisenhower*, p. ix.
353   Richardson, *Presidency of Dwight D. Eisenhower*, p. 15.
354   Branyan and Larsen, *Eisenhower Administration 1953–1961*, p. 20.
355   Eisenhower, *At Ease*, p. 371.
356   Ferrell, *Eisenhower Diaries*, p. 374.
357   Ibid., p. 375.
358   Eisenhower Papers, Name Series, box 18, "Hazlett, Swede," 1955 (1).
359   James David Barber, *The Presidential Character* (Englewood Cliffs, N. J.: Prentice-Hall, 1992), p. 193.
360   Erik Erikson, *Childhood and Society* (New York: W. W. Norton, 1950), p. 60.
361   Fenichel, *Psychoanalytic Theory of Neurosis*, p. 102.
362   Karen Horney, *Neurosis and Human Growth* (New York: W. W. Norton, 1950), p. 166.
363   Thompson, "Strengths and Weaknesses," p. 25.
364   Miller, *Ike The Soldier*, p. 217.
365   Eisenhower, *At Ease*, p. 323.
366   Brendon, *Ike*, p. 12.
367   Eisenhower, *At Ease*, p. 302.
368   Ibid., p. 356.
369   Ambrose, *Eisenhower The President*, p. 295.
370   Richardson, *Presidency of Dwight D. Eisenhower*, p. 12.
371   Eisenhower Papers, Press Conference Series, box 4, "Press Conference 1/8/56," p. 2.
372   Fenichel, *Psychoanalytic Theory of Neurosis*, p. 102.
373   Horney, *Neurosis and Human Growth*, pp. 102, 112, 144.
374   Ibid., pp. 148–49.
375   Nixon, *Six Crises*, p. 175.
376   Snyder, box 10, "Medical Diary re DDE," 1 September–31 December 1960 (3).

FIVE Illness at Camelot: John F. Kennedy

1 James MacGregor Burns, *John F. Kennedy: A Political Profile* (New York: Avon Books, 1959), p. 33.
2 David Burner, *John F. Kennedy* (Boston: Little, Brown, 1988), p. 8.
3 Gary Wills, *The Kennedy Imprisonment* (Boston: Little, Brown, 1982), p. 67.
4 Marcia Chellis, *Living with the Kennedys* (New York: Simon & Schuster, 1985), p. 38.
5 Burns, *John F. Kennedy*, p. 37; James David Barber, *Presidential Character* (Englewood Cliffs, N. J.: Prentice-Hall, 1977), p. 298.
6 Burner, *John F. Kennedy*, p. 9.
7 William Manchester, *Portrait of a President* (Boston: Little, Brown, 1967), p. 175.
8 Ralph G. Martin, *A Hero for Our Time* (New York: Macmillan, 1983), p. 33.
9 Barber, *Presidential Character*, p. 296.
10 Gail Cameron, *Rose* (New York: G. P. Putnam, 1971), p. 85.
11 Burner, *John F. Kennedy*, p. 10.
12 Henry Fairlie, *The Kennedy Promise* (New York: Doubleday, 1974), p. 185.
13 Barbara Gibson, *Life with Rose Kennedy* (New York: Warner Books, 1986), p. 43.
14 Burns, *John F. Kennedy*, pp. 37–38.
15 Ibid., p. 40.
16 Martin, *A Hero for Our Time*, pp. 31, 32.
17 Richard J. Whalen, *The Founding Father* (New York: New American Library, 1964), pp. 164–65.
18 Martin, *A Hero for Our Time*, p. 31.
19 Gibson, *Life with Rose Kennedy*, pp. 40–41.
20 Herbert Parmet, *Jack* (New York: Dial Press, 1980), p. 20.
21 Rose Kennedy, *Times to Remember* (New York: Doubleday, 1974), p. 93.
22 Kenneth Crispell and Carlos Gomez, *Hidden Illness in the White House* (Durham, N. C.: Duke University Press, 1988), p. 167.
23 Kennedy, *Times to Remember*, p. 84.
24 Ibid., p. 202.
25 Janet Travell, Oral History (1966), p. 19 (Boston: John F. Kennedy Library).
26 Kennedy, *Times to Remember*, p. 303.
27 Personal Papers of John F. Kennedy, box 1 (Boston: John F. Kennedy Library).
28 Ibid.
29 Leo Damore, *The Cape Cod Years of John Fitzgerald Kennedy* (Englewood Cliffs, N. J.: Prentice-Hall, 1967), p. 50.
30 Herbst Medical File, JFK Medical Records, accession 83–38 (Boston: John F. Kennedy Library).
31 Arthur Krock, Oral History (1964), p. 11 (Boston: John F. Kennedy Library).
32 Manchester, *Portrait of a President*, p. 151.
33 Kennedy, *Times to Remember*, p. 282.
34 Nancy Gager Clinch, *The Kennedy Neurosis* (New York: Grosset & Dunlop, 1973), p. 108.
35 Travell, Oral History, p. 1.

36 Kennedy, *Times to Remember*, p. 214.
37 Joan Blair and Clay Blair, *The Search for JFK* (New York: Berkley and G. P. Putnam, 1976), p. 23.
38 Travell, Oral History, p. 3.
39 Janet Travell, *Office Hours: Day and Night* (New York: World, 1968), p. 309.
40 Travell, Oral History, p. 10.
41 Kennedy, *Times to Remember*, p. 214.
42 Blair and Blair, *Search for JFK*, p. 585.
43 Bill Adler, "The Kennedy Wit," in Jay David, ed., *The Kennedy Reader* (New York: Bobbs-Merrill, 1967), p. 51.
44 Arthur Schlesinger, *A Thousand Days* (Cambridge: Houghton Mifflin, 1965), p. 95.
45 Manchester, *Portrait of a President*, p. 154.
46 Personal Papers of John F. Kennedy, box 11A, U.S. Naval Hospital, Chelsea, Massachusetts (Boston: John F. Kennedy Library).
47 Schlesinger, *A Thousand Days*, p. 95.
48 Personal Papers of John F. Kennedy, box 11A, U.S. Naval Hospital, Chelsea, Massachusetts.
49 Personal Papers of John F. Kennedy, box 11A, U.S. Naval Hospital, Charleston, South Carolina (Boston: John F. Kennedy Library).
50 Personal Papers of John F. Kennedy, box 11A, U.S. Naval Hospital, Chelsea, Massachusetts.
51 Ibid.
52 Blair and Blair, *Search for JFK*, p. 387.
53 Ibid., p. 511.
54 Burner, *John F. Kennedy*, p. 22.
55 Theodore Sorenson, *Kennedy* (New York: Harper & Row, 1965), p. 41.
56 William Leuchtenburg, "A Visit with LBJ," *American Heritage*, May/June 1990, p. 56.
57 Robert F. Kennedy, Oral History (1964), p. 645 (Boston: John F. Kennedy Library).
58 Kenneth P. O'Donnell and David F. Powers, *Johnny, We Hardly Knew Ye* (Boston: Little, Brown, 1970), p. 79.
59 Ibid., p. 96.
60 Evelyn Lincoln, *My Twelve Years with John F. Kennedy* (New York: David McKay, 1965), pp. 53–54.
61 Ibid., p. 53.
62 Robert Kennedy, Oral History, p. 648.
63 O'Donnell and Powers, *Johnny, We Hardly Knew Ye*, p. 96.
64 Travell, Oral History, p. 3.
65 Blair and Blair, *Search for JFK*, p. 569.
66 Schlesinger, *A Thousand Days*, p. 96.
67 Clinch, *Kennedy Neurosis*, p. 142.
68 Travell, Oral History, p. 3.
69 Ibid.
70 Judie Mills, *John F. Kennedy* (New York: Franklin Watts, 1988), p. 119.

71   Paul Fay, *The Pleasure of His Company* (New York: Harper & Row, 1963), p. 172.
72   Sorenson, *Kennedy*, p. 40.
73   Schlesinger, *A Thousand Days*, p. 96.
74   Peter Collier and David Horowitz, *The Kennedys* (New York: Warner Books, 1984), p. 253.
75   Krock, Oral History, p. 25.
76   John F. Kennedy, *Profiles in Courage* (New York: Harper & Row, 1955), p. 21.
77   Travell, Oral History, pp. 1, 9, 14.
78   Ibid., p. 2.
79   Ibid., p. 15.
80   Ibid., p. 5.
81   Ibid., p. 3.
82   Travell, *Office Hours: Day and Night*, p. 309.
83   Travell, Oral History, p. 5.
84   Ibid., p. 16.
85   Ibid., p. 17.
86   Travell, *Office Hours: Day and Night*, p. 322.
87   Schlesinger, *A Thousand Days*, p. 98.
88   Frank Saunders, *Torn Lace Curtain* (New York: Holt, Rinehart, 1982), p. 44.
89   Hugh Sidey, *John F. Kennedy, President* (New York: Atheneum, 1963), p. 209.
90   Travell, Oral History, p. 21.
91   Ibid.
92   Ibid., p. 24.
93   George Burkley, Oral History (1967), p. 5 (Boston: John F. Kennedy Library).
94   Sorenson, *Kennedy*, p. 369.
95   Papers of President Kennedy, President's Office Files, Staff Memoranda, box 67 (Boston: John F. Kennedy Library).
96   Blaine Taylor, "The Kennedys: A Partial Medical Case History," *Maryland State Medical Journal* 24 (December 1975): 64.
97   Sorenson, *Kennedy*, p. 368.
98   Benjamin C. Bradlee, *Conversations with Kennedy* (New York: W. W. Norton, 1975), p. 200.
99   Burkley, Oral History, p. 11.
100 Mary B. Gallagher, *My Life with Jacqueline Kennedy* (New York: David McKay, 1969), p. 273.
101 Kennedy, *Times to Remember*, p. 453.
102 Travell, Oral History, p. 18.
103 Burkley, Oral History, p. 8.
104 Ibid., p. 23.
105 Ibid., p. 13.
106 Edward B. MacMahon and Leonard Curry, *Medical Cover-ups in the White House* (Washington, D.C.: Farragut, 1987), p. 132.
107 Papers of President Kennedy, President's Office Files, box 67.
108 Bradlee, *Conversations with Kennedy*, p. 159.
109 Taylor, "The Kennedys," p. 65.

110 Bradlee, *Conversations with Kennedy*, p. 200.
111 O'Donnell and Powers, *Johnny, We Hardly Knew Ye*, p. 4.
112 *The Official Warren Commission Report on the Assassination of President John F. Kennedy* (Garden City, N. Y.: Doubleday, 1964), p. 105.
113 Martin, *A Hero for Our Time*, p. 97.
114 Blair and Blair, *Search for JFK*, p. 565.
115 Ibid., pp. 567, 561.
116 Krock, Oral History, p. 9.
117 Blair and Blair, *Search for JFK*, p. 585; MacMahon and Curry, *Medical Cover-ups*, p. 122.
118 Calvin Ezrin, John O. Godden, and Robert Volpe, *Systematic Endocrinology* (New York: Harper & Row, 1979), p. 213.
119 Schlesinger, *A Thousand Days*, p. 19; Sorenson, *Kennedy*, p. 39.
120 Joseph Kraft, Oral History (1967), p. 1 (Boston: John F. Kennedy Library).
121 Manchester, *Portrait of a President*, p. 168.
122 Schlesinger, *A Thousand Days*, p. 96.
123 Taylor, "The Kennedys," p. 56.
124 Sorenson, *Kennedy*, p. 39.
125 Karl E. Paschkis, Abraham E. Rackoff, Abraham Cantarow, and J. Rupp, *Clinical Endocrinology* (New York: Harper & Row, 1967), p. 363.
126 Schlesinger, *A Thousand Days*, p. 96.
127 MacMahon and Curry, *Medical Cover-ups*, p. 123.
128 Jean D. Wilson and Daniel W. Foster, *William's Textbook of Endocrinology* (Philadelphia: Saunders, 1985), p. 852.
129 Paschkis et al., *Clinical Endocrinology*, p. 365.
130 Wilson and Foster, *William's Textbook*, p. 851.
131 Ibid.
132 Travell, Oral History, p. 14.
133 Ibid., p. 11.
134 J. Nicolas, C. Burstein, C. Umberger, and P. Wilson, "Management of Adrenocortical Insufficiency During Surgery," *A.M.A. Archives of Surgery* 201 (1955): 739.
135 Blair and Blair, *Search for JFK*, p. 567.
136 Sorenson, *Kennedy*, p. 41.
137 Ezrin, Godden, and Volpe, *Systematic Endocrinology*, p. 213.
138 George W. Thorn, *The Diagnosis and Treatment of Adrenal Insufficiency* (Springfield, Ill.: Charles C. Thomas, 1949), pp. 130, 146.
139 Nicolas et al., "Management of Adrenocortical Insufficiency," p. 739.
140 Ibid., p. 740.
141 Travell, Oral History, p. 17.
142 Ibid., p. 12.
143 Travell, *Office Hours: Day and Night*, p. 330; J. Nicols, "President Kennedy's Adrenals," *Journal of the American Medical Association* 201 (1967): 116.
144 Janet Travell, Papers, box 1 (Boston: John F. Kennedy Library).
145 Bradlee, *Conversations with Kennedy*, p. 68.
146 Blair and Blair, *Search for JFK*, p. 575.

147 Kenneth P. O'Donnell, Oral History, (1969), p. 10 (Boston: John F. Kennedy Library).
148 Blair and Blair, *Search for JFK*, p. 575.
149 Travell, Oral History, p. 21.
150 Travell, Papers, box 1.
151 Theodore H. White, *The Making of the President 1964* (New York: Atheneum, 1965), p. 413.
152 Burkley, Oral History, p. 6.
153 Travell, Oral History, p. 21.
154 Taylor, "The Kennedys," p. 63.
155 Lincoln, *My Twelve Years*, p. 172.
156 Travell, Oral History, p. 17.
157 Sorenson, *Kennedy*, p. 59.
158 Blair and Blair, *Search for JFK*, p. 576.
159 Travell, Oral History, p. 14.
160 Thorn, *Diagnosis and Treatment*, p. 23.
161 Blair and Blair, *Search for JFK*, p. 578.
162 Travell, Oral History, p. 12.
163 John F. Kennedy Medical Records, accession 83–38, Vernon Dick Letter (Boston: John F. Kennedy Library).
164 Burns, *John F. Kennedy: A Political Profile*, p. 46.
165 William G. Carleton, "Kennedy in History: An Early Appraisal," *Antioch Review* 24 (1964): 282.
166 Pierre Salinger, *With Kennedy* (Garden City, N. Y.: Doubleday, 1966), p. 117.
167 Gallagher, *My Life with Jacqueline Kennedy*, p. 292.
168 Clinton Rossiter, *The American Presidency* (New York: Harcourt, Brace & World, 1960), p. 180.
169 Lucius Clay, Oral History (1964), p. 15 (Boston: John F. Kennedy Library).
170 Roger Hillsman, *To Move a Nation* (New York: Doubleday, 1967), p. 581.
171 Blair and Blair, *Search for JFK*, p. 582.
172 O'Donnell and Powers, *Johnny, We Hardly Knew Ye*, p. 111.
173 Burns, *John F. Kennedy*, p. 150.
174 Donald C. Lord, *John F. Kennedy: The Politics of Confrontation and Conciliation* (New York: Barron's, 1977), p. 56.
175 G. Robert Blakey and Richard N. Billings, *The Plot to Kill the President* (New York: Times Books, 1981), p. 6.
176 Bruce Mazlish, "Kennedy: Myth and History," in J. Richard Snyder, ed., *John F. Kennedy: Person, Policy, Presidency* (Wilmington, Del.: SR Books, 1988), p. 29.
177 Lincoln, *My Twelve Years*, p. 4.
178 *Public Papers of the Presidents: John F. Kennedy, 1962* (Washington, D.C.: U.S. Government Printing Office, 1963), p. 555.
179 Eunice Shriver, Oral History (1968), p. 28 (Boston: John F. Kennedy Library).
180 *Public Papers of the Presidents: John F. Kennedy, 1961* (Washington, D.C.: U.S. Government Printing Office, 1962), pp. 67, 183, 759.
181 *Public Papers: John F. Kennedy, 1962* p. 114.

182   *Public Papers of the Presidents: John F. Kennedy, 1963* (Washington, D.C.: U.S. Government Printing Office, 1964), pp. 191, 858.
183   U.S. Congress, Senate Subcommittee of the Committee on Communications, *The Joint Appearances of Senator John F. Kennedy and Vice President Richard M. Nixon, Presidential Campaign of 1960*, 87th Cong., 1st sess., 1961, p. 114.
184   Travell, Oral History, p. 20.
185   Kennedy, *Times to Remember*, p. 145.
186   Victor Lasky, *JFK: The Man and the Myth* (New York: Macmillan, 1963), p. 70.
187   Sorenson, *Kennedy*, p. 42.
188   Salinger, *With Kennedy*, p. 41.
189   *Public Papers: John F. Kennedy, 1961*, p. 259.
190   Richard Goodwin, *Remembering America* (Boston: Little, Brown, 1988), p. 180.
191   Graham Allison, *Essence of Decision* (Boston: Little, Brown, 1971), pp. 193, 214–15.
192   Robert F. Kennedy, *Thirteen Days* (New York: W. W. Norton, 1971), pp. 74–75.
193   Elie Abel, *The Missile Crisis* (Philadelphia: J. B. Lippincott, 1966), p. 215.
194   Raymond Garthoff, *Reflections on the Cuban Missile Crisis* (Washington, D.C.: Brookings Institution, 1987), pp. 57–58.
195   *Public Papers: John F. Kennedy, 1961*, p. 815.
196   Henry M. Pachter, *Collision Course* (New York: Praeger, 1964), p. 87.
197   Clay, Oral History, p. 3.
198   Carleton, "Kennedy in History," p. 299.
199   Nancy Dickerson, *Among Those Present* (New York: Random House, 1976), p. 238.
200   *Public Papers: John F. Kennedy, 1963*, pp. 238, 329, 894.
201   Travell, Oral History, p. 20.
202   Bradlee, *Conversations with Kennedy*, p. 51.
203   Herbert Parmet, *JFK* (New York: Dial Press, 1983), p. 18.
204   Paschkis et al., *Clinical Endocrinology*, p. 385.
205   Hugh L'Etang, *The Pathology of Leadership* (London: Heinemann, 1969), p. 187.
206   L. Soffer, "Addison's Disease and Adrenal Insufficiency," in E. Astwood, ed., *Clinical Endocrinology* (New York: Grune & Stratton, 1960), p. 337; William Jubiz, *Endocrinology* (New York: McGraw-Hill, 1985), p. 162.
207   Parmet, *JFK*, p. 18.
208   Bradlee, *Conversations with Kennedy*, p. 68.
209   Blair and Blair, *The Search for JFK*, p. 567; Lloyd Shearer, "Sick Men Who Ruled the World," *Parade*, 11 October 1970, p. 6.
210   Travell, Oral History, p. 20.
211   Hugh L'Etang, "The Effects of Drugs on Political Decisions," *Politics and the Life Sciences* 7 (August 1988): 15.
212   B. Rensberger, "Amphetamines Used by a Physician to Lift Moods of Famous Patients," *New York Times*, 4 December 1972, p. 34.
213   Ibid.
214   Ibid.

215 Ibid.
216 *Newsweek,* 18 December 1972, p. 73.
217 White House Central Files, John F. Kennedy, box 971, 3–4 June 1961 (Boston: John F. Kennedy Library).
218 Rensberger, "Amphetamines," p. 34.
219 L'Etang, "Effects of Drugs," p. 15.
220 MacMahon and Curry, *Medical Cover-ups,* p. 137.
221 Ibid.
222 Robert F. Kennedy, Oral History, p. 630.
223 Andrei Gromyko, *Through Russian Eyes* (Washington, D.C.: International Library, 1973), p. 139.
224 Hillsman, *To Move a Nation,* p. 136.
225 *Public Papers: John F. Kennedy, 1961,* p. 443.
226 Bruce Miroff, *Pragmatic Illusions* (New York: David McKay, 1976), p. 57.
227 Montague Kern, Patricia W. Levering, and Ralph B. Levering, *The Kennedy Crisis* (Chapel Hill: University of North Carolina Press, 1983), p. 79.
228 William C. Spragens, "John F. Kennedy," in William C. Spragens, ed., *Popular Images of American Presidents* (Westport, Conn.: Greenwood Press, 1988), p. 448.
229 Kennedy, *Times to Remember,* p. 202.
230 Blair and Blair, *Search for JFK,* p. 582.
231 P. Hoffer, "Kennedy and the Regeneration of America," in Snyder, ed., *John F. Kennedy,* p. 40; Wills, *Kennedy Imprisonment,* p. 32.
232 Personal Papers of John F. Kennedy, box 1.
233 Constantina Safilios-Rothschild, *The Sociology and Social Psychology of Disability and Rehabilitation* (New York: Random House, 1970), p. 97.
234 Karen Horney, *Neurosis and Human Growth* (New York: W. W. Norton, 1950), p. 21.
235 Ibid., p. 22.
236 Heinz Kohut, *The Restoration of the Self* (New York: International Universities Press, 1977), p. 5.
237 Ibid., pp. 5–6.
238 Dickerson, *Among Those Present,* p. 60.
239 Horney, *Neurosis and Human Growth,* p. 21.
240 Kennedy, *Times to Remember,* pp. 120, 116.
241 Sorenson, *Kennedy,* p. 38.
242 Travell, Oral History, pp. 9, 17.
243 Martin, *A Hero for Our Time,* pp. 528, 395.
244 Salinger, *With Kennedy,* p. 41.
245 Schlesinger, *A Thousand Days,* p. 19.
246 Travell, *Office Hours: Day and Night,* p. 330.
247 O'Donnell and Powers, *Johnny, We Hardly Knew Ye,* p. 7.
248 Horney, *Neurosis and Human Growth,* p. 24.
249 Karen Horney, *The Neurotic Personality of Our Time* (New York: W.W. Norton, 1937), p. 102.
250 Horney, *Neurosis and Human Growth,* pp. 24–28.
251 Bradlee, *Conversations with Kennedy,* p. 32.

252 *Public Papers: John F. Kennedy, 1961*, p. 1.
253 *Public Papers: John F. Kennedy, 1963*, pp. 889–90.
254 Burkley, Oral History, p. 8.
255 Ibid., pp. 13–14.
256 Travell, Oral History, pp. 19, 17.
257 See Robert Robins and Henry Rothschild, "Ethical Dilemmas of the President's Physician," *Politics and the Life Sciences*, 7 (August 1988): 6–10.
258 Jim Bishop, *A Day in the Life of President Kennedy* (New York: Random House, 1964), p. 25.

SIX Ambition and Torment: Lyndon B. Johnson

1 Hugh Sidey, *A Very Personal Presidency* (New York: Atheneum, 1968), p. 7.
2 Doris Kearns, *Lyndon Johnson and the American Dream* (New York: Harper & Row, 1976), p. 25.
3 Merle Miller, *Lyndon* (New York: G. P. Putnam, 1980), pp. 19–21.
4 Robert Dallek, *Lone Star Rising* (New York: Oxford University Press, 1991), p. 39.
5 Ibid., p. 38.
6 James David Barber, *The Presidential Character* (Englewood Cliffs, N. J.: Prentice-Hall, 1977), p. 129.
7 Ibid., p. 131.
8 Lyndon B. Johnson, *The Vantage Point* (New York: Holt, Rinehart, 1971), p. v.
9 Hyman L. Muslin and Thomas H. Jobe, *Lyndon Johnson: The Tragic Self* (New York: Insight Books, 1991), p. 65.
10 Mary Rather, Oral History (January 13, 1975), p. 19 (Austin, Tex.: Lyndon B. Johnson Library).
11 Ronnie Dugger, *The Politician* (New York: W. W. Norton, 1982), p. 198.
12 Robert A. Caro, *The Years of Lyndon Johnson: The Path to Power* (New York: Alfred A. Knopf, 1982), p. 436.
13 Ray E. Lee, Oral History (February 8, 1979), pp. 28–29 (Austin, Tex.: Lyndon B. Johnson Library).
14 Caro, *Path of Power*, p. 443.
15 Ibid., p. 494.
16 Ibid. p. 704.
17 Ibid.
18 White House Press Office Files, Working Files: "Bits and Pieces of Useful Information," Box 135 (Austin, Tex.: Lyndon B. Johnson Library).
19 Dallek, *Lone Star Rising*, p. 230.
20 Dugger, *Politician*, p. 249.
21 Vaughn Davis Bornet, *The Presidency of Lyndon B. Johnson* (Lawrence: University Press of Kansas, 1983), p. 220.
22 Dugger, *Politician*, p. 248.

23 Robert Caro, *The Years of Lyndon Johnson: Means of Ascent* (New York: Alfred A. Knopf, 1990), p. 140.

24 Warren Woodward, Oral History (June 3, 1960), p. 9 (Austin, Tex.: Lyndon B. Johnson Library).

25 Ibid., p. 12.

26 Ibid., p. 18.

27 Walter Jenkins, Oral History (August 14, 1970), p. 27 (Austin, Texas: Lyndon B. Johnson Library).

28 Woodward, Oral History, p. 25.

29 Ibid., pp. 26–27.

30 Jenkins, Oral History (July 22, 1983), p. 27.

31 Woodward, Oral History, p. 31.

32 Ibid., p. 35.

33 Alfred Steinberg, *Sam Johnson's Boy* (New York: Macmillan, 1968), p. 393.

34 Dr. James Cain, Oral History (February 22, 1970), p. 8 (Austin, Tex.: Lyndon B. Johnson Library).

35 Jenkins, Oral History (July 19, 1984), p. 2.

36 William S. White, *The Professional: Lyndon B. Johnson* (Boston: Houghton Mifflin, 1964), p. 204.

37 Sam Houston Johnson, *My Brother Lyndon* (New York: Cowles Book Co., 1969), p. 97.

38 Dallek, *Lone Star Rising*, p. 484.

39 Rowland Evans and Robert Novak, *Lyndon B. Johnson: The Exercise of Power* (New York: New American Library, 1966), p. 90.

40 George R. Brown, Oral History (April 6, 1968), p. 22 (Austin, Tex.: Lyndon B. Johnson Library).

41 Frank Oltorf, Oral History (August 3, 1971), p. 28 (Austin, Tex.: Lyndon B. Johnson Library).

42 Clinton P. Anderson, Oral History (May 20, 1969) p. 10. (Austin, Tex.: Lyndon B. Johnson Library).

43 Oltorf, Oral History, p. 28.

44 Anderson, Oral History, p. 10.

45 Oltorf, Oral History, p. 31.

46 Dallek, *Lone Star Rising*, p. 486.

47 Ibid.; Evans and Novak, *Exercise of Power*, p. 92; Robert A. Divine, *The Johnson Years*, vol. 2 (Lawrence: University Press of Kansas, 1987), p. 191.

48 Cain, Oral History, p. 15.

49 Dr. Willis Hurst, Letter to Author (August 6, 1993).

50 Evans and Novak, *Exercise of Power*, p. 92.

51 Booth Moody, *LBJ: An Irreverent Chronicle* (New York: T. Y. Crowell, 1976), p. 198.

52 Jenkins, Oral History (July 19, 1984), pp. 8–9.

53 Rather, Oral History (December 10, 1974), p. 2.

54 Kearns, *Lyndon Johnson*, p. 125.

55 Booth Moody, *The Lyndon Johnson Story* (New York: Farrar, Straus & Cudahy, 1956), p. 154.

56 Ibid.

57   Dallek, *Lone Star Rising*, p. 487.

58   Jenkins, Oral History (July 19, 1984), p. 9.

59   George Reedy, *Lyndon B. Johnson* (New York: Andrews & McMeel, 1982), p. 52.

60   Marie Smith, *The President's Lady* (New York: Random House, 1964), p. 52.

61   Bornet, *Presidency of Lyndon B. Johnson*, p. 290.

62   Cain, Oral History, p. 13.

63   See Jerrold M. Post and Robert S. Robins, *When Illness Strikes the Leader* (New Haven, Conn.: Yale University Press, 1993), p. 92.

64   Johnson, *Vantage Point*, pp. 89–90.

65   Doris Kearns Goodwin, *The Fitzgeralds and the Kennedys* (New York: Simon & Schuster, 1987), p. 780.

66   Sidey, *Very Personal Presidency*, p. 169.

67   Dallek, *Lone Star Rising*, p. 571.

68   Kenneth P. O'Donnell, Oral History (July 23, 1969), p. 10 (Boston: John F. Kennedy Library).

69   Brown, Oral History, p.18.

70   Woodward, Oral History (May 26,1969), p. 30.

71   Theodore H. White, *The Making of the President 1960* (New York: Atheneum, 1961), p. 174.

72   Marie D. Natoli, *American Prince, American Pauper* (Westport, Conn.: Greenwood Press, 1985), p. 33.

73   Irving Bernstein, *Guns or Butter* (New York: Oxford University Press, 1996), p. 6.

74   Even apart from rumors about Kennedy's poor health, Lyndon Johnson surely was aware that, as of 1960, seven vice presidents had succeeded to the presidency upon the death of the sitting president. This may have been a persuasive factor in itself.

75   Lawrence F. O'Brien, Oral History (September 18, 1985), p. 11 (Austin, Tex.: Lyndon B. Johnson Library).

76   Smith, *President's Lady*, p. 129.

77   Reedy, *Lyndon B. Johnson*, p. 54.

78   Dallek, *Lone Star Rising*, p. 587.

79   Harry McPherson, *A Political Education* (Boston: Little, Brown, 1972), p. 184.

80   Evans and Novak, *Exercise of Power*, p. 349.

81   Kearns, *Lyndon Johnson*, p. 164.

82   Liz Carpenter, *Ruffles and Flourishes* (Garden City, N. Y.: Doubleday, 1970), p. 325.

83   Bruce J. Schulman, *Lyndon B. Johnson and American Liberalism* (New York: Bedford Books, 1995), p. 58.

84   Johnson, *Vantage Point*, p. 93.

85   Lady Bird Johnson, *A White House Diary* (New York: Holt, Rinehart & Winston, 1970), p. 138.

86   Ibid., pp. 176, 192, 139.

87   Johnson, *Vantage Point*, p. 96.

88   White House Press Office Files, Press Secretary's News Conference, Box 8, #562, p. 4 (Austin, Tex.: Lyndon B. Johnson Library).

89 Hubert H. Humphrey, *The Education of a Public Man* (Garden City, N. Y.: Doubleday, 1976), p. 314.
90 *New York Times*, January 24, 1965, p. 46.
91 White House Press Office Files, Press Secretary's News Conference, Box 5, #560, January 23, 1965, p. 1; Box 8, #561, p. 1.
92 Lady Bird Johnson, *White House Diary*, p. 231.
93 White House Press Office Files, Box 8, #561, p. 2; #562, p. 2.
94 Lady Bird Johnson, *White House Diary*, p. 231.
95 Robert Sherrill, *The Accidental President* (New York: Grossman, 1967), p. 18.
96 Lady Bird Johnson, *White House Diary*, p. 232.
97 George Christian, *The President Steps Down* (New York: Macmillan, 1970), p. 9.
98 Michael Davie, *LBJ: A Foreign Observer's Viewpoint*, (New York: Duell, Sloan and Pearce, 1966), pp. 13–14; Joseph Kraft, *Profiles in Power* (New York: New American Library, 1966), p. 9.
99 O'Brien, Oral History (February 11, 1986), p. 7.
100 Lady Bird Johnson, *White House Diary*, p. 27.
101 Theodore H. White, *The Making of the President 1964* (New York: Atheneum, 1965), p. 370.
102 Lady Bird Johnson, *White House Diary*, p. 317.
103 Dr. James M. Young, Letter to Author, February 22, 1997.
104 Cain, Oral History, p. 9.
105 White House Press Office Files, Press Secretary's News Conference, Box 8, October 5, 1965, p. 1.
106 White House Press Office Files, Background Briefings, News Conference, Box 81, #133A, October 5, 1965, pp. 2, 3.
107 *New York Times*, October 6, 1965, p. 1.
108 Lady Bird Johnson, *White House Diary*, p. 326.
109 White House Press Office Files, Press Secretary's News Conference, Box 8, #133A, p. 3, #137A, p. 2.
110 Cain, Oral History, p. 11.
111 White House Press Office Files, Press Secretary's News Conference, Box 8, #139A.
112 White House Press Office Files, Press Secretary's News Conference, Box 8, #141A, p. 3; #142A, p. 1.
113 White House Press Office Files, Press Secretary's News Conference, Box 8, #145A, October 10, 1965.
114 White House Press Office Files, Press Secretary's News Conference, Box 8, #149A, #150A.
115 White House Press Office Files, Press Secretary's News Conference, Box 8, #144A, Box 26, p. 5.
116 White House Press Office Files, Press Secretary's News Conference, Box 8, #153A.
117 White House Press Office Files, Press Secretary's News Conference, Box 8, #159A.
118 White House Press Office Files, Press Secretary's News Conference, Box 26; News Briefing, October 22, 1965, 1:20 p.m., p. 3.

119   Interview with Dr. James M. Young, August 16, 1997.
120   Evans and Novak, *Exercise of Power*, p. 561.
121   White House Press Office Files, Press Secretary's News Conference, Box 9, #219A, p. 4.
122   Carpenter, *Ruffles and Flourishes*, p. 325.
123   Joseph A. Califano, *The Triumph and Tragedy of Lyndon Johnson* (New York: Simon & Schuster, 1991), p. 98.
124   White House Press Office Files, Press Secretary's News Conference, Box 9, #238A, December 11, 1965; #262A, December 29, 1965.
125   White House Press Office Files, Press Secretary's News Conference, Box 12, #640A, November 16, 1966.
126   White House Central Files, Name File, Dr. J. C. Cain, March 13, 1966.
127   White House Press Office Files, Press Secretary's News Conference, Box 12, #643A, November 16, 1966.
128   Cain, Oral History, p. 18.
129   White House Press Office Files, Press Secretary's News Conference, Box 12, #653A, November 19, 1966.
130   Steinberg, *Sam Johnson's Boy*, p. 798.
131   Bornet, *Presidency of Lyndon B. Johnson*, p. 293.
132   Lady Bird Johnson, *White House Diary*, p. 637.
133   White House Central Files, Name File, Dr. J. C. Cain, January 10, 1967.
134   Bornet, *Presidency of Lyndon B. Johnson*, p. 293.
135   White House Central Files, Papers of Lyndon Baines Johnson, Ex PP. 13–8, Box 114.
136   Bornet, *Presidency of Lyndon B. Johnson*, p. 294.
137   Lady Bird Johnson, *White House Diary*, p. 593.
138   Bornet, *Presidency of Lyndon Johnson*, p. 297.
139   Lady Bird Johnson, *White House Diary*, p. 362.
140   George C. Herring, "The Reluctant Warrior: Lyndon B. Johnson as Commander in Chief," in David L. Anderson, ed., *Shadow of the White House* (Lawrence: University Press of Kansas, 1993), p. 91.
141   Sam Houston Johnson, *My Brother Lyndon*, p. 4.
142   Richard N. Goodwin, *Remembering America* (Boston: Little Brown, 1988), pp. 393–403.
143   Eric F. Goldman, *The Tragedy of Lyndon Johnson* (New York: Alfred A. Knopf, 1968), p. 511; Goodwin, *Remembering America*, p. 522.
144   Lady Bird Johnson, *White House Diary*, p. 642.
145   Clark Clifford, *Counsel to the President* (New York: Random House, 1991), p. 523.
146   Dr. George G. Burkley, Oral History (December 3, 1968), p. 22 (Austin, Tex.: Lyndon B. Johnson Library).
147   Humphrey, *Education of a Public Man*, p. 358.
148   Johnson, *Vantage Point*, p. 425.
149   Lady Bird Johnson, *White House Diary*, p. 644.
150   Ibid., p. 701.
151   White House Press Office Files, Press Secretary's News Conference, Box 14, #1329A, August 8, 1968; #1330A, August 8, 1968.

152 Lady Bird Johnson, *White House Diary*, p. 729.

153 Lewis L. Gould, *Lady Bird Johnson and the Environment* (Lawrence: University Press of Kansas, 1988), p. 225.

154 Richard Harwood and Haynes Johnson, *Lyndon* (New York: Praeger, 1973), p. 160.

155 Paul Conklin, *Big Daddy from the Pedernales* (Boston: Twayne, 1986), p. 294.

156 Harwood and Johnson, *Lyndon*, p. 160.

157 Kearns, *Lyndon Johnson*, p. 16.

158 Harwood and Johnson, *Lyndon*, p. 169.

159 Miller, *Lyndon*, p. 552.

160 Harwood and Johnson, *Lyndon*, p. 169.

161 Kearns, *Lyndon Johnson*, p. 16.

162 Jack Valenti, *A Very Human President* (New York: W. W. Norton, 1975), p. 377.

163 Philip Reed Rulon, *The Compassionate Samaritan: The Life of Lyndon Baines Johnson* (Chicago: Nelson-Hall, 1981), p. 311.

164 *New York Times*, January 23, 1973, p. 25.

165 George Reedy, Oral History (August 16, 1983), p. 90 (Austin, Tex.: Lyndon B. Johnson Library).

166 Clifford, *Counsel to the President*, p. 388.

167 Reedy, *Lyndon B. Johnson*, p. 157.

168 O'Brien, Oral History (September 11, 1986), p. 34.

169 Evans and Novak, *Lyndon B. Johnson*, pp. 500, 561.

170 O'Brien, Oral History (February 11, 1986), p. 10.

171 Birch Bayh, *One Heartbeat Away* (Indianapolis: Bobbs-Merrill, 1968), p. 94.

172 John W. McCormack, Oral History, September 23, 1968, p. 33 (Boston: John F. Kennedy Library).

173 Bayh, *One Heartbeat Away*, p. 164.

174 *Public Papers of the Presidents, Lyndon B. Johnson, 1965* (Washington, D.C.: Government Printing Office, 1966), p. 8.

175 Ibid., pp. 101–102.

176 *Public Papers of the Presidents, Lyndon B. Johnson, 1963–64* (Washington, D.C.: Government Printing Office, 1965), p. 279.

177 Divine, *Johnson Years*, p. 191.

178 *Public Papers of the Presidents, 1963–64*, p. 478.

179 Dr. Michael E. De Bakey, Oral History (June 29 1969), p. 7 (Austin, Tex.: Lyndon B. Johnson Library).

180 *Public Papers of the Presidents, Lyndon B. Johnson, 1965* (Washington, D.C.: 1966), pp. 1090–91.

181 Sheri I. David, "Medicare: Hallmark of the Great Society," in Bernard J. Firestone and Robert C. Vogt, eds., *Lyndon Baines Johnson and the Uses of Power* (Westport, Conn.: Greenwood Press, 1988), p. 44.

182 O'Brien, Oral History (September 11, 1986), p. 7.

183 Johnson, *Vantage Point*, p. 220.

184 Leon J. Saul, *The Childhood Emotional Pattern* (New York: Van Nostrand Reinhold, 1977), p. 14.

185 Kearns, *Lyndon Johnson*. p. 361.

186 Dallek, *Lone Star Rising*, p. 49.
187 Steinberg, *Sam Johnson's Boy*, p. 27.
188 Miller, *Lyndon*, p. 22.
189 Ibid., pp. 20–22.
190 Caro, *Path to Power*. p. 76.
191 Schulman, *Lyndon B. Johnson and American Liberalism*, p. 8.
192 Caro, *Path to Power*, p. 98.
193 Sam Houston Johnson, *My Brother Lyndon*, pp. 265–66.
194 Dallek, *Lone Star Rising*, p. 45.
195 Dugger, *The Politician*, p. 66.
196 Steinberg, *Sam Johnson's Boy*, p. 28.
197 Rulon, *Compassionate Samaritan*, p. 18.
198 Kearns, *Lyndon Johnson*. p. 370.
199 Dallek, *Lone Star Rising*, p. 589.
200 Otto Fenichel, *The Psychoanalytic Theory of Neurosis* (New York: W. W. Norton, 1945), p. 102.
201 Dallek, *Lone Star Rising*, p. 45.
202 Johnson, *Vantage Point*, p. 569.
203 Portions of this chapter appeared in my articles "The Political Effects of Presidential Illness: The Case of Lyndon B. Johnson," *Political Psychology*, 16, No. 4 (December 1995), 761–76, and "Lyndon B. Johnson's Physical and Psychological Pain: The Years of Ascent," *Presidential Studies Quarterly*, 26, No. 3 (Summer 1996), 694–707.

SEVEN Scars in the Teflon: Ronald Reagan

1 William A. Niskanen, *Reaganomics* (New York: Oxford University Press, 1988), p. 288.
2 Ronald Reagan, *An American Life* (New York: Simon & Schuster, 1990), p. 21.
3 Ibid.
4 Anne Edwards, *Early Reagan* (New York: William Morrow, 1987), p. 58.
5 Reagan, *An American Life*, p. 28.
6 Ibid., p. 9.
7 Maureen Reagan, *First Father, First Daughter* (Boston: Little, Brown, 1989), pp. 59, 62.
8 Paul D. Erickson, *Reagan Speaks* (New York: New York University Press, 1985), p. 54.
9 Haynes Johnson, *Sleepwalking Through History* (New York: W. W. Norton, 1991), p. 43.
10 Garry Wills, *Reagan's America* (New York: Doubleday, 1987), p. 17.
11 Reagan, *An American Life*, p. 35.
12 Johnson, *Sleepwalking Through History*, p. 44.
13 Edwards, *Early Reagan*, p. 477.
14 Maureen Reagan, *First Father, First Daughter*, p. 59.

15 Lou Cannon, *President Reagan: The Role of a Lifetime* (New York: Simon & Schuster, 1991), p. 213.
16 Reagan, *An American Life*, p. 28.
17 Ibid., p. 29.
18 Ronald Reagan and Richard G. Hubler, *Where's the Rest of Me?* (New York: Karz, 1981), p. 7.
19 Reagan, *An American Life*, p. 33.
20 Ibid.
21 Sidney Blumenthal, *The Rise of the Counter Establishment* (New York: Times Books, 1986), p. 245.
22 Reagan, *An American Life*, p. 25.
23 Ibid., p. 34.
24 Reagan and Hubler, *Where's the Rest of Me?*, p. 18.
25 Reagan, *An American Life*, p. 89.
26 Lou Cannon, *Reagan* (New York: G. P. Putnam, 1982), p. 28.
27 Ibid., pp. 27–28.
28 Reagan and Hubler, *Where's the Rest of Me?*, p. 28.
29 Reagan, *An American Life*, p. 48.
30 Ibid., p. 20.
31 Ibid., p. 61.
32 Erickson, *Reagan Speaks*, p. 15.
33 Ibid.
34 Reagan, *An American Life*, p. 89.
35 Ronnie Dugger, *On Reagan* (New York: McGraw-Hill, 1983), p. 3.
36 Reagan, *An American Life*, p. 111.
37 Reagan and Hubler, *Where's the Rest of Me?*, p. 195.
38 Ibid., p. 214.
39 Ibid.
40 Reagan, *An American Life*, p. 128.
41 Ibid., p. 143.
42 Edwards, *Early Reagan*, p. 488.
43 Gary Hamilton and Nicole Woolsey Biggart, *Governor Reagan, Governor Brown: A Sociology of Executive Power* (New York: Columbia University Press, 1984), p. 198.
44 Bob Schieffer and Gary Paul Gates, *The Acting President* (New York: E. P. Dutton, 1989), p. 44.
45 Bill Boyarsky, *Ronald Reagan* (New York: Random House, 1981), p. 106.
46 Reagan, *An American Life*, p. 167.
47 Ibid., p. 168.
48 Ibid., p. 195.
49 Schieffer and Gates, *Acting President*, p. 55.
50 Reagan, *An American Life*, pp. 206–7.
51 Jack W. Germond and Jules Witcover, *Blue Smoke and Mirrors* (New York: Viking Press, 1981), p. 94.
52 Schieffer and Gates, *Acting President*, pp. 55, 90.
53 Martin Anderson, *Revolution* (New York: Harcourt Brace Jovanovich, 1988), p. 279.

54 Jack Hinckley and Jo Ann Hinckley, *Breaking Points* (Grand Rapids, Mich.: Chosen Books, 1985), p. 46.

55 Reagan, *An American Life,* p. 259.

56 Ibid.

57 Ibid., p. 260.

58 Interview with Dr. Benjamin Aaron, 20 June 1991.

59 John Pekkanen, "The Saving of the President," *Washingtonian,* August 1981, p. 109.

60 Interview with Dr. Daniel Ruge, 25 June 1991.

61 Pekkanen, "Saving of the President," pp. 109–11.

62 Interview with Dr. Aaron.

63 Interview with Dr. Eric Louie, assistant White House physician, 1981–1983, 2 July 1991.

64 Interview with Dr. Joseph Giordano, 18 July 1991.

65 Pekkanen, "Saving of the President," p. 113.

66 Bill Adler, *Ronnie and Nancy* (New York: Crown, 1985), p. 168.

67 Interview with Dr. S. David Rockoff, 30 October 1991.

68 Interview with Dr. Giordano.

69 Interview with Dr. Aaron.

70 Pekkanen, "Saving of the President," p. 118.

71 Lawrence Leamer, *Make-Believe* (New York: Harper & Row, 1983), p. 319.

72 Reagan, *An American Life,* p. 262.

73 Interview with Dr. Giordano.

74 Interview with Dr. Ruge.

75 William A. Henry III, *Visions of America* (Boston: Atlantic Monthly Press, 1985), p. 27.

76 Michael Reagan, *On the Outside Looking In* (New York: Kensington Publishing, 1988), p. 194.

77 Nancy Reagan, *My Turn* (New York: Random House, 1989), p. 10.

78 Donald T. Regan, *For the Record* (New York: Harcourt Brace Jovanovich, 1988), p. 165.

79 Alexander Haig, *Caveat* (New York: Macmillan, 1984), p. 157.

80 Interview with Dr. Aaron.

81 Interview with Dr. Giordano.

82 Interview with Dr. Ruge.

83 Michael K. Deaver, *Behind the Scenes* (New York: William Morrow, 1987), p. 22.

84 Thomas P. O'Neill, *Man of the House* (New York: Random House, 1987), p. 336.

85 Helene Van Damm, *At Reagan's Side* (New York: Doubleday, 1989), p. 194.

86 Casper W. Weinberger, *Fighting for Peace* (New York: Warner Books, 1990), p. 97.

87 Lawrence I. Barrett, *Gambling with History* (Garden City, N.Y.: Doubleday, 1983), p. 116.

88 George Bush, *Looking Forward* (New York: Doubleday, 1987), p. 223.

89 Ibid.

90 Larry Speakes, *Speaking Out* (New York: Charles Scribner, 1988), p. 10.

91 Terrell H. Bell, *The Thirteenth Man* (New York: Free Press, 1988), p. 66.
92 Interview with Dr. Samuel Spagnolo, 17 October 1991.
93 Pekkanen, "Saving of the President," pp. 121–22.
94 Interview with Dr. Spagnolo.
95 Ibid.
96 Nancy Reagan, *My Turn*, p. 11.
97 Interview with Dr. Rockoff.
98 Interview with Dr. Aaron.
99 Interview with Dr. Ruge.
100 Interviews with Dr. Giordano and Dr. Rockoff.
101 Interview with Dr. Aaron.
102 Interview with Dr. Spagnolo.
103 Ibid.
104 Maureen Reagan, *First Father, First Daughter*, p. 275.
105 Interview with Dr. Aaron.
106 Reagan, *An American Life*, p. 263.
107 Interviews with Dr. Ruge and Dr. Aaron.
108 Jane Mayer and Doyle McManus, *Landslide* (Boston: Houghton Mifflin, 1988), p. 26.
109 Cannon, *President Reagan*, p. 145.
110 Ibid., p. 467.
111 Bob Woodward, *Veil: The Secret Wars of the CIA, 1981–1987* (New York: Simon & Schuster, 1987), p. 122.
112 *Public Papers of the Presidents of the United States: Ronald Reagan, 1985* (Wshington, D.C.: U.S. Government Printing Office, 1988), p. 950.
113 Reagan, *An American Life*, p. 325.
114 William Schneider, "The November 6 Vote for President: What Did It Mean?" in Austin Ranney, ed., *The American Elections of 1984* (Durham, N.C.: Duke University Press, 1985), p. 224.
115 Elizabeth Drew, *Campaign Journal* (New York: Macmillan, 1985), pp. 573, 702.
116 Henry, *Visions of America*, p. 248.
117 Jack Germond and Jules Witcover, *Wake Us When It's Over* (New York: Macmillan, 1985), p. 524.
118 Albert Hunt, "The Campaign and the Issues," in Ranney, ed., *American Elections of 1984*, p. 153.
119 Germond and Witcover, *Wake Us When It's Over*, p. 510.
120 O'Neill, *Man of the House*, p. 360.
121 Mark Hertsgaard, *On Bended Knee* (New York: Farrar, Straus & Giroux, 1988), p. 247.
122 *Wall Street Journal*, 9 October 1984, pp. 1, 64.
123 Hunt, "The Campaign and the Issues," p. 153.
124 Germond and Witcover, *Wake Us When It's Over*, p. 510.
125 Hunt, "The Campaign and the Issues," p. 153.
126 Henry, *Visions of America*, p. 250.
127 Hunt, "The Campaign and the Issues," p. 158.
128 *Wall Street Journal*, 23 October 1984, p. 64

129   Schieffer and Gates, *Acting President*, p. 189.
130   Interview with Dr. Ruge.
131   Dennis L. Breo, "Experts Support Reagan's Care," *American Medical News*, 2 August 1985, p. 62.
132   *New York Times*, 15 July 1985, p. A10.
133   Nancy Reagan, *My Turn*, p. 272.
134   Speakes, *Speaking Out*, p. 186.
135   Joan Quigley, *What Does Joan Say?* (New York: Carol Publishing, 1990), p. 12.
136   Nancy Reagan, *My Turn*, p. 275.
137   Speakes, *Speaking Out*, p. 190.
138   *Public Papers of the Presidents, 1985*, p. 919.
139   Nancy Reagan, *My Turn*, p. 274.
140   *New York Times*, 14 July 1985, p. A20.
141   Ibid.
142   Ibid., p. A1.
143   Reagan, *An American Life*, p. 500.
144   Regan, *For the Record*, p. 9.
145   Speakes, *Speaking Out*, p. 191.
146   Mayer and McManus, *Landslide*, p. 112.
147   *Public Papers of the Presidents, 1985*, p. 919.
148   Reagan, *An American Life*, p. 501.
149   Breo, "Experts Support Reagan's Care," p. 1.
150   Interview with Dr. Kevan Hartshorn, Boston University School of Medicine, 9 October 1991.
151   *New York Times*, 16 July 1985, p. 10.
152   Maureen Reagan, *First Father, First Daughter*, p. 344.
153   Reagan, *An American Life*, p. 502.
154   Nancy Reagan, *My Turn*, p. 278.
155   Speakes, *Speaking Out*, p. 193.
156   Reagan, *An American Life*, p. 502.
157   Breo, "Experts Support Reagan's Care," p. 62.
158   Speakes, *Speaking Out*, pp. 193–94.
159   *New York Times*, 15 July 1985, p. A1.
160   Nancy Reagan, *My Turn*, p. 279.
161   Breo, "Experts Support Reagan's Care," p. 63.
162   Ibid., p. 64.
163   Ibid.
164   Ibid., p. 62.
165   Speakes, *Speaking Out*, p. 196.
166   Ibid., p. 198.
167   Sam Donaldson, *Hold On, Mr. President!* (New York: Random House, 1987), p. 138.
168   Speakes, *Speaking Out*, p. 199.
169   Nancy Reagan, *My Turn*, p. 282.
170   Geoffrey Cowley and Doris Sarovici, "Rethinking Prostate Surgery," *Newsweek*, 5 August 1991, p. 48.

171   Letter, Dr. Eric K. Louie, 25 September 1991.

172   Cannon, *President Reagan*, p. 726.

173   Bell, *Thirteenth Man*, p. 30.

174   Interview with Dr. Ruge.

175   Barrett, *Gambling with History*, p. 117.

176   Haig, *Caveat*, p. 159.

177   Ibid., 160.

178   Reagan, *An American Life*, p. 271.

179   Barrett, *Gambling with History*, p. 117.

180   Deaver, *Behind the Scenes*, p. 31.

181   Haig, *Caveat*, pp. 163–64.

182   Weinberger, *Fighting for Peace*, p. 89.

183   Barrett, *Gambling with History*, p. 119.

184   Weinberger, *Fighting for Peace*.

185   Bell, *Thirteenth Man*, p. 66.

186   *Gallup Report*, no. 188, May 181 (Princeton, N.J.), p. 13.

187   David Mervin, *Ronald Reagan and the American Presidency* (London: Longman, 1990), p. 113.

188   Clark Clifford, *Counsel to the President* (New York: Random House, 1991), p. 644.

189   *Gallup Report*, p. 13.

190   Sidney Blumenthal, *Our Long National Daydream* (New York: Harper & Row, 1988), p. 308.

191   Mayer and McManus, *Landslide*, p. 13.

192   Rowland Evans and Robert Novak, *The Reagan Revolution* (New York: E. P. Putnam, 1981), p. 240.

193   Barrett, *Gambling with History*, p. 125.

194   Daniel Patrick Moynihan, *Came the Revolution* (New York: Harcourt Brace Jovanovich, 1988), p. 10.

195   Hertsgaard, *On Bended Knee*, p. 116.

196   John Orman, *Comparing Presidential Behavior* (Westport, Conn.: Greenwood Press, 1987), pp. 158–59.

197   Cannon, *President Reagan*, p. 115.

198   Leamer, *Make-Believe*, p. 328.

199   Lester M. Salaman and Alan J. Abramson, "Governance: The Politics of Retrenchment," in John L. Palmer and Isabel V. Sawhill, eds., *The Reagan Record* (Cambridge, Mass.: Ballinger Publishing, 1984), p. 50.

200   David Stockman, *The Triumph of Politics* (New York: Harper & Row, 1986), p. 173.

201   Ibid., p. 174.

202   O'Neill, *Man of the House, p. 349.*

203   Salaman and Abramson, "Governance," p. 56.

204   Mary E. Stuckey, *Playing the Game* (New York: Praeger, 1990), p. 30.

205   Fred I. Greenstein, "Reagan and the Modern Presidency: Parallels and Departures," in Fred I. Greenstein, ed., *The Reagan Presidency* (Baltimore: Johns Hopkins University Press, 1983), p. 175.

206   Colin Campbell, *Managing the Presidency* (Pittsburgh: University of Pittsburgh Press, 1986), p. 94.

207   Ibid.
208   Van Damm, *At Reagan's Side*, p. 196.
209   Mayer and McManus, *Landslide*, p. 113.
210   Deaver, *Behind the Scenes*, p. 28.
211   Reagan, *For the Record*, p. 142.
212   Clifford, *Counsel to the President*, p. 645.
213   Jerry Hagstrom, *Beyond Reagan* (New York: W. W. Norton, 1988), p. 31.
214   Van Damm, *At Reagan's Side*, p. 197.
215   Regan, *For the Record*, p. 229.
216   Ibid., p. 137.
217   Ibid., pp. 229–30.
218   *The Tower Commission Report* (New York: Bantam Books, 1987), p. 129.
219   William S. Cohen and George T. Mitchell, *Men of Zeal* (New YOrk: Viking Press, 1988), p. 79.
220   *Tower Commission Report*, pp. 31, 142.
221   Schieffer and Gates, *Acting President*, p. 233.
222   Cohen and Mitchell, *Men of Zeal*, pp. 11–12.
223   Regan, *For the Record*, p. 83.
224   *Tower Commission Report*, p. 138.
225   *Report of the Congressional Committees Investigating the Iran-Contra Affair*, 100th Cong., 1st sess. (Washington, D.C.: U.S. Government Printing Office, 1987), p. 168.
226   Speakes, *Speaking Out*, p. 279.
227   Reagan, *An American Life*, p. 50.
228   Interview with Dr. Daniel Ruge, 27 June 1991.
229   Kenneth R. Crispell and Carlos F. Gomez, *Hidden Illness in the White House* (Durham, N.C.: Duke University Press, 1988), p. 236.
230   Norman J. Knorr, M.D., and Daniel Harrington, M.D., "Psychological Considerations," in Kenneth W. Thompson, ed., *Papers on Presidential Disability and the Twenty-fifth Amendment* (New York: University Press of America, 1988), p. 101.
231   Michael A. Ledeen, *Perilous Statecraft* (New York: Charles Scribner, 1988), p. 277.
232   Anderson, *Revolution*, p. 220.
233   Weinberger, *Fighting for Peace*, p. 367.
234   Walter Karp, *Liberty Under Siege* (New York: Henry Holt, 1988), p. 243.
235   Coral Bell, *The Reagan Paradox* (New Brunswick, N.J.: Rutgers University Press, 1989), p. 146; see also John Kenneth White, *The New Politics of Old Values* (Hanover, N.H.: University Press of New England, 1988), p. 19.
236   Hertsgaard, *On Bended Knee*, p. 334.
237   Mayer and McManus, *Landslide*, p. 387.
238   Regan, *For the Record*, p. 71.
239   Reagan, *An American Life*, p. 535.
240   Regan, *For the Record*, pp. 68, 70.
241   Mayer and McManus, *Landslide*, p. 115.
242   Ibid., p. 42.
243   Reagan, *An American Life*, pp. 72–73.

244 *Tower Commission Report,* p. 81.

245 Ibid., pp. 79–80.

246 Niskanen, *Reaganomics,* p. 288.

247 Reagan and Hubler, *Where's the Rest of Me?,* pp. 97–98.

248 Reagan, *An American Life,* p. 119.

249 Robert Dallek, *Ronald Reagan: The Politics of Symbolism* (Cambridge, Mass.: Harvard University Press, 1984), p. 18.

250 Ibid., p. 104.

251 Reagan, *An American Life,* p. 167.

252 Ibid., p. 502.

253 Nancy Reagan, *My Turn,* p. 273.

254 Ruth Ann Seilhamer and Theodore Jacob, "Family Factors and Adjustment of Children of Alcoholics," in Michael Windle and John S. Searles, eds., *Children of Alcoholics* (New York: Guilford Press, 1990), p. 169.

255 Charles Deutsch, *Broken Bottles, Broken Dreams* (New York: Teachers College Press, 1982), p. 5.

256 Janet G. Woititz, "Common Characteristics of Adult Children from Alcoholic Families," in Robert J. Ackerman, ed., *Growing in the Shadow* (Pompano Beach, Fla.: Heath Communications, 1986), pp. 183, 178.

257 Janet G. Woititz, *Adult Children of Alcoholics* (Pompano Beach, Fla.: Heath Communications, 1983), p. 77.

258 Schieffer and Gates, *Acting President,* p. 90.

259 Peggy Noonan, *What I Saw at the Revolution* (New York: Random House, 1990), p. 154.

260 Michael Reagan, *On the Outside Looking In,* pp. 122, 244.

261 Nancy Reagan, *My Turn,* p. 106.

262 Cannon, *President Reagan,* pp. 228–29.

263 Timmen L. Cermak, *Evaluating and Treating Adult Children of Alcoholics* (Minneapolis: Johnson Institute Books, 1990), vol. 1, p. 43.

264 Regan, *For the Record,* p. 144.

265 Woititz, "Common Characteristics," p. 183.

266 Regan, *For the Record,* p. 290.

267 Deaver, *Behind the Scenes,* p. 40.,

268 Noonan, *What I Saw at the Revolution,* p. 168.

269 Stockman, *Triumph of Politics,* p. 3.

270 Haig, *Caveat,* p. 311.

271 Woititz, "Common Characteristics," p. 183.

272 Mayer and McManus, *Landslide,* p. 30.

273 Hertsgaard, *On Bended Knee,* p. 149.

274 Speakes, *Speaking Out,* p. 192.

275 Maureen Reagan, *First Father, First Daughter,* p. 61.

276 Cannon, *Reagan,* p. 65.

277 Patricia Ann O'Connor, *The Iran-Contra Puzzle* (Washington, D.C.: Congressional Quarterly, 1987), p. 11.

278 Reagan, *An American Life,* p. 541.

279 Woititz, "Common Characteristics," p. 178.

280 Johnson, *Sleepwalking through History,* p. 44.

281 James David Barber, *Presidential Character* (Englewood Cliffs, N.J.: Prentice-Hall, 1977), p. 174.
282 Barrett, *Gambling with History,* p. 124.
283 Robert J. Ackerman, "Alcoholism and the Family," in Ackerman, *Growing in the Shadow,* p. 1.

EIGHT Prescriptions

1 Ruth Silva, *Presidential Succession* (New York: Greenwood Press, 1968), p. 8.
2 Marie D. Natoli, *American Prince, American Pauper* (Westport, Conn.: Greenwood Press, 1985), p. 16.
3 John D. Feerick, *From Failing Hands* (New York: Fordham University Press, 1965), p. 316.
4 Michael Turner, *The Vice President as Policy Maker* (Westport, Conn.: Greenwood Press, 1982), p. 26.
5 Birch Bayh, *Presidential Disability and Succession* (New York: Bobbs-Merrill, 1968), p. 278.
6 Paul B. Stephan III, "History, Background and Outstanding Problems of the Twenty-fifth Amendment," in Kenneth W. Thompson, ed., *Papers on Presidential Disability and the Twenty-fifth Amendment* (New York: University Press of America, 1988), pp. 67–68.
7 Irving G. Williams, *The Rise of the Vice Presidency* (Washington, D.C.: Public Affairs Press, 1956), p. 7.
8 Richard F. Fenno, *The President's Cabinet* (Cambridge: Harvard University Press, 1959), p. 5.
9 "Report of the Miller Center Commission on Presidential Disability and the Twenty-fifth Amendment" (Lanham, Md.: University Press of America, 1988), p. 18.
10 Ibid., p. 17.
11 Ibid., p. 26.
12 American Medical Association, Council on Ethical and Judicial Affairs, "Current Opinions," Chicago 1989, section 5.05; see also AMA, Council on Ethical and Judicial Affairs, "Fundamental Elements of the Patient-Physician Relationship, June 1990, p. 2.
13 "Report of the Miller Center Commission," p. 27.
14 Interview with Dr. C. Knight Aldrich, professor emeritus of psychiatry, University of Virginia Medical Center, 5 November 1990.
15 Interview with Michael S. Dukakis, 12 June 1991.
16 Norman J. Knorr, M.D., and Daniel Harrington, M.D., "Psychological Considerations," in Thompson, *Papers,* p. 120.
17 Interview with Dr. Jerrold S. Levine, Boston University School of Medicine, 25 November 1991.
18 Louis S. Goodman and Alfred Gilman, *The Pharmacological Basis of Therapeutics* (New York: Macmillan, 1975), p. 247.

19 Geoffrey Cowley, et al., "Sweet Dreams or Nightmare," *Newsweek,* 19 August 1991, p. 45.

20 Ibid.,; see also, *Washington Post,* 9 January 1992, p. 30.

21 *New York Times,* 18 February 1992, p. C3.

22 Bayh, *Presidential Disability and Succession,* p. 316.

23 Richard P. Nathan, *The Administrative Presidency* (New York: John Wiley, 1983), p. 5.

24 Alfred Dick Sander, *A Staff for the President* (Westport, Conn.: Greenwood Press, 1989), p. 372.

25 Charles B. Brownson and Anna L. Brownson, eds., *1988 CSD Federal Civilian Update* (Mount Vernon, Va.: Congressional Staff Directory, Ltd., 1988).

26 See U.S. House of Representatives, Committee on Appropriations, 103rd Congress, 1st sess., *Treasury, Postal Service and General Government Appropriations for Fiscal Year 1994,* Part 3 (Washington, D.C.: Government Printing Office, 1993), p. 482.

27 John Hart, *The Presidential Branch* (New York: Pergamon Press, 1987), p. 214.

28 Ibid., p. 3.

29 Nathan, *Administrative Presidency,* p. 29.

30 Thomas E. Cronin, *The State of the Presidency* (Boston: Little, Brown, 1975), p. 123.

31 Anna L. Brownson, ed., *1991/2 Federal Staff Directory* (Mount Vernon, Va.: Staff Directories, Ltd., 1991).

32 Samuel Kernell and Samuel L. Popkin, eds., *Chief of Staff* (Berkeley: University of California Press, 1986), p. 199.

33 Peri E. Arnold, *Making the Managerial Presidency* (Princeton, N.J.: Princeton University Press, 1986), pp. 361–62.

34 Stephen Hess, *Organizing the Presidency* (Washington, D.C.: Brookings Institution, 1988), p. 226.

35 Ibid., p. 231.

36 Kernell and Popkin, *Chief of Staff,* pp. 195, 199.

37 Jimmy Carter, *Keeping Faith* (New York: Bantam Books, 1982), p. 57.

38 Ibid., p. 59.

39 Ibid., p. 13.

40 Kernell and Popkin, *Chief of Staff,* p. 72.

41 Ryan J. Barilleaux, *The Post-Modern Presidency* (New York: Praeger, 1988), p. 115.

42 George Bush, *Looking Forward* (New York: Doubleday, 1987), p. 223.

43 Richard Waterman, *Presidential Influence and the Administrative State* (Knoxville: University of Tennessee Press, 1989), pp. 192–93.

44 Feerick, *From Failing Hands,* pp. 67, 164.

45 Natoli, *American Prince, American Pauper,* p. 133.

46 Paul C. Light, *Vice Presidential Power* (Baltimore: Johns Hopkins University Press, 1984), p. 60.

47 Joel Goldstein, *The Modern Vice Presidency* (Princeton, N.J.: Princeton University Press, 1984), p. 60.

48 Ibid., p. 294.

49 Natoli, *American Prince, American Pauper,* p. 183.

50 Woodrow Wilson, *Constitutional Government in the United States* (New York: Columbia University Press, 1908), pp. 79–80.

Index